SCENARIO-DRIVEN PLANNING

SCENARIO-DRIVEN PLANNING

Learning to Manage Strategic Uncertainty

Nicholas C. Georgantzas and William Acar

Quorum Books
Westport, Connecticut • London

HD30.28
.G46
1995

Library of Congress Cataloging-in-Publication Data

Georgantzas, Nicholas C.
　　Scenario-driven planning : learning to manage strategic
uncertainty / Nicholas C. Georgantzas and William Acar.
　　　　p.　　cm.
　　Includes bibliographical references and index.
　　ISBN 0–89930–825–2 (alk. paper)
　　1. Strategic planning.　2. Risk management.　　I. Acar, William,
1940–.　　II. Title.
　　HD30.28.G46　1995
　　658.4′012—dc20　　　　94–8540

British Library Cataloguing in Publication Data is available.

Library of Congress Catalog Card Number: 94–8540
ISBN: 0–89930–825–2

First published in 1995

Quorum Books, 88 Post Road West, Westport, CT 06881
An imprint of Greenwood Publishing Group, Inc.

Printed in the United States of America

∞™

The paper used in this book complies with the
Permanent Paper Standard issued by the National
Information Standards Organization (Z39.48–1984).

10 9 8 7 6 5 4 3 2

In memory of
Peter N. Georgantzas
and
Wadie and Eva Acar

Dedicated to
Arlene, Constantine, and Jackie Marie-Nicole
and to
Frances, Michael and Joseph
with gratitude for their
patience, support and love

Contents

Illustrations

FIGURES

TABLES

Preface

Scenarios are about the multiple perspectives that strategic thinkers use to defeat the tyranny of dogmatism that has assailed American business for the past two decades.[1] This book introduces the scope, methods, and uses of scenario-driven planning. Its extensive literature review, numerous examples, practical guidelines, and real-life cases show how scenarios help firms manage uncertainty, that necessary disciple of our free enterprise system.

Scenario-driven planning is a new management technology. Often, it is the technology behind the superior performance of world-class firms. Their managers use scenarios to articulate their mental models about the future and thereby make better decisions. Their outstanding performance is the result of their continuous effort to improve their strategy design, which scenario-driven planning enhances through a tireless renewal of organizational mind-sets. Computing scenarios can help a management team produce insights much richer than those expected from a single-point forecast.

In writing this book, we gathered our *clues* from a variety of sources—from the literature and from many colleagues and friends. We drew on talks, published works, presentations and personal communications. It is hoped that we have put them together in a way that will help our readers get more than a glimpse of the emerging management technology of scenario-driven planning.

Sincere thanks to our mentors, friends, early draft readers, and families.

NICHOLAS C. GEORGANTZAS
WILLIAM ACAR

---

1   For example, see the Special Issue of *Business Week* on business fads (January 20, 1986).

Introduction

In the last decade, Western economies have felt the pinch of foreign competition, particularly from the Pacific Rim nations. A recent *Business Week* article reports that Edith Cresson, the French prime minister, has been marshaling European countries into organized resistance. Political barriers to business may become one of Europe's answers to the Japanese onslaught. From a practical perspective, erecting political barriers to business and trade is much like taking arms against a sea of trouble. Trade barriers are not part of the United States' mercantile tradition.

US firms have made an implementation-oriented response to the Japanese challenge, shifting from the overcautious *just in case* approach to the exhilarating dare of *just in time* (JIT), rediscovering of statistical quality control (SQC), and placing a strong emphasis on total quality management (TQM). JIT, SQC and TQM stem from the wisdom and experience of Western Europe and the United States before World War II. While the West later abandoned these techniques, Japan both perpetuated their use and enhanced them.

Not only was the Western line of defense against foreign competition ineffective, but it was not even sustainable. Hard times require new organizational mindsets. Confusion still reigns in the West about the perspective from which to approach long-term strategic thinking and strategy design. In stark contrast to the multidisciplinary approach to management originating from the European tradition, the US consulting tradition has been primarily monothematic. Consequently, most US firms are designed to function according to a single scenario, the one representing"the official corporate future" (Schoemaker, 1993, p. 199).

Our more prominent learned societies, such as the Academy of Management and the MS/OR group, operate in near-isolation. Quantitative management scientists have devised problem-solving methods which have met with success in the military and business spheres, but have not sat well with generalists. When asked, the Japanese insist that ours is not a worker but a management problem.

Firms around the globe use scenarios to enhance institutional learning, to reengineer their systems, and to bolster productivity. In the US, however, debate is lively between those who feel that Americans do not plan enough for the long term and those who see us reach paralysis by analysis. Thus far, the 'quick fixers' have dominated the business press while purists have tied up the academic literature. This state of affairs has been more favorable to strategic implementation theory than to design. We hope that this book will redress this imbalance by appealing to both the academic and the consulting publics.

Learning about the subtleties of scenario methods and their variations can produce the best of both worlds in the 1990s. One is better management of strategic uncertainty through sharpened intuition, whereas the other is conducive to a deeper understanding of the principles underlying existing scenario methods and their range of variations. In order to disseminate this information to academics as well as managers and strategy consultants, this book undertakes the following tasks.

1. Charting the principal weakness of disconnected forecasts or wishes, including their lack of compatibility both in substance and in terms of their implicit assumptions.
2. Explaining the advantage of using internally coherent scenarios or scenario bundles.
3. Explaining the advantage of using computed decision scenarios. These allow an examination of the joint consequences of changes in the environment and in a firm's strategy, and not mistaking mere environmental hypothesizing for scenario-driven planning.

This important information should be disseminated to business managers, consultants, and academics. We try to do this here gradually, with increasingly focused chapters, and then we give illustrative examples. Our real-world examples emphasize how the value of scenario-driven planning lies in its ability to determine what changes in strategy can make its design more robust if a firm's desirable future shows signs of not happening.

INTENDED AUDIENCE

Planning with scenarios is exciting. It permits firms to transform themselves and their environment by managing strategic uncertainty and interdependence. At a modest price, planning with scenarios can make the work of managers and planners easier, yet more productive and rewarding.

Instructors of business policy and strategic management will find this book a useful companion to cases, for environmental and strategic scenarios bring creativity to the classroom. In addition, they complement the conventional approach to cases, that is, by argumentation alone. By computing scenarios, both student and instructor can learn much more from the strategic situations described in the cases. Action recommendations derived from computed scenarios give a whole new meaning to case analysis. Scenario-driven planning enables strategy students to move up toward higher learning and to build confidence and intuition beyond their instructor's initial insight.

Executive trainers will find the ideas underlying scenario-driven planning readily applicable to real-life strategic situations. The book will provide their course participants with a good introduction to this exciting and rapidly evolving management technology. It invites open communication and participation in a process of new information creation. Because scenario-driven planning does not solicit single-point forecasts from participants, it eliminates the need for any face-saving strategies.

Corporate planners will find in this book a critical evaluation of modern scenario techniques as well as procedures for tailoring these techniques to a firm's particular needs. Scenario-driven planning will help them revive and extend their field of competence beyond strategy design to the larger context of governing strategic uncertainty and interdependence. Those with expertise in scenarios will find the book valuable for sharing their knowledge with co-workers.

General managers concerned with creating a promising future will find a useful framework in this book. It can help them implant the systems view into their organizations and reengineer the process of strategy design so that strategic uncertainty can be transformed into opportunities for competitive advantage. The book may even help them stem the tide of offshore competitors. It is through institutional learning that world-class firms design their future.

Rather than being simply a gift, intuition is often the result of accumulated knowledge that comes from hard analytical thinking. Because computed scenarios sharpen intuition, they speed up organizational learning and better process reengineering efforts (Davenport, 1993; Tobias, 1991). A firm's capability of learning faster than its competitors may be the only sustainable competitive advantage (de Geus, 1988).

DRIVING PRINCIPLE

Looking beyond the quick fix, Ralph Kilmann (1989) urges managers to stop seeking single-track answers to business problems. Similarly, proponents of total quality management (TQM) dismiss the United States' fixation on worker motivation, which is often viewed as the sole task of managerial work (Zeleny, 1991). The progression from Fig. 1a to Fig. 1b illustrates the positive effect of management technology on productivity. This is the technology to which the Japanese attribute their worldwide business success. To these two factors, strategy researchers add the crucial role of the business environment.

Figure 1   (a) Cause-&-Effect View of Early Human Relations School
               (b) Japanese View of Management as Main Coproducer
               (c) View Advocated in This Book
                    (Adapted from Melcher, Acar, DuMont & Khouja, 1990)

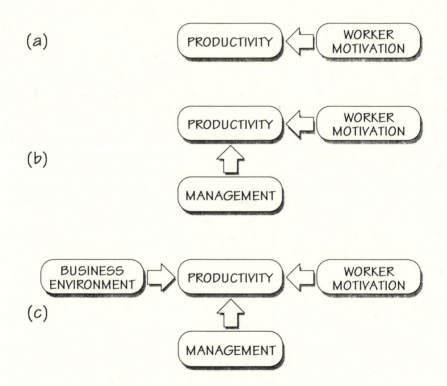

This book subscribes to the expanded view of Fig. 1c. It examines how firms account for environmental changes in their business strategies through scenario-driven planning, which blends hard and soft components of strategy design. The book addresses basic questions about what the future may hold for this new management technology.

Part I creates the context required for answering these questions, while providing a comprehensive glossary. This is necessary because, outside our teaching in the Management Systems Area at Fordham University and in the Administrative Science Department at Kent State University, business courses rarely cover the material treated in this book. Assuredly, MBA and undergraduate business policy and strategy courses cover some of our topics occasionally, but then only cursorily and without the benefit of a text. Nowhere else is scenario-driven planning treated in a unified and systematic way along with other important aspects of strategic intelligence.

We bring to the consulting and upper-level management audiences a better way to deal with strategic uncertainty. We do not talk about environmental scenarios alone because these are merely inputs to strategy design. Neither is our message about the usual sense of hypothesizing about a future. That may be the state of current practice, but it makes feeble use of scenarios. We promote scenarios with an analytical twist, putting forth scenario-driven planning as a multirational inquiry process for strategy design. Specifically, we introduce the notion of computed mixed or strategic scenarios, the outcomes of modeling strategic situations.

Conceptual confusion can lead to language games at best and to operational confusion at worst (Donaldson, 1992). Using the most recent technologies available, we can avert both types of confusion. Instead of shifting their focus away from actuality and rationality, our managers can improve their understanding of the fundamental assumptions underlying changes in strategy. The mind-set of scenario-driven planning and the ideas related to it make it specific enough to give practical guidance to those managing in the real world, both now and in the future.

ORGANIZATION OF THE TEXT

Part I

We have organized the text into seven parts. The first seeks to reduce the anxiety that linguistic ambiguity often causes. Chapter 1 is an introductory chapter that presents scenario-driven planning as a new proactive approach to strategy design for increased productivity. Bandied about so frequently, the word *productivity* often assumes the role of many-a-splendor curator's egg, an elixir of sorts. Yanking it back into strategic perspective is no easy feat.

Realizing how important productivity improvements are to managers, workers, consumers, and to national prosperity generally, helps to recognize the relationship of productivity to economic competition and strategy making. The Japanese and other observers see productivity as a strategic, not merely a labor, issue. Yet, can experience guide us adequately to renew our already rich management technology more productively?

Chapter 2 builds further on the proactivity perspective. In a reactive society only a few decision makers prepare for the future. The short-term year-to-year fluctuations are just about the proper horizon for most economists and politicians. Yet, confronted by contemporary high-velocity environments, corporate executives are becoming increasingly more interested in understanding environmental forces.

After listing potential areas of application, Chapter 2 illustrates the use of scenarios with three examples. Each example is self-contained and does not assume the reader's familiarity with scenarios. This may constitute a useful review of scenario-driven planning ideas, even for more advanced readers.

Insight and content diversity are the criteria we used in selecting these examples. The first example is Drucker's (1986) global predicament that the world economy has changed in its foundations and structure. Second is General Electric's approach to forecasting through scenario writing. The third example presents scenario generation at Shell, a unique contribution in scenario-driven planning.

Part II

Part II examines the components of scenario-driven planning. In doing so, it deals with three important facets of strategy design and implementation. The first facet involves understanding the business environment and the forces be hind its texture (Chapter 3). The second entails unearthing one's unstated assumptions about changes in the environment and their effects on a firm's performance (Chapter 4).

The third facet concerns the combined, or mixed, effects on performance of changes in both the environment and strategy. Even in mature economies, no matter how and how often restated, decision makers sometimes forget how the same action can yield a whole range of different outcomes, depending on environmental variables beyond a firm's control. Often, the result is disastrous.

Conversely, the tight coupling between mixed scenarios and strategic out comes can create new information in the process of strategic problem framing. The association of a mixed environmental and decision scenario in a one-to-one correspondence with a strategic outcome suits the normative inclination of strategic management theory, placing rationalistic inquiry at a par with the purely descriptive approaches in strategy research.

Part III

In Parts III and V, our unified treatment of the strategic scenario content and the strategy-making process grants a practical bonus, accounting for the book's peculiar nature. It is not only a conceptual or idea contribution, but also an application-oriented professional book that may very well serve as a textbook.

Parts III through V present examples, related ideas, and real-life cases of scenario-driven planning applications. Written with both the concrete and the abstract thinker in mind, these six chapters show how firms can build scenarios with a modest investment. Scenario-driven planning provides an effective management technology that serves well those who adopt it. It saves them both time and energy.

In Part III, Chapter 5 describes the process of implanting scenario-driven planning to Infoplus, the intrapreneurship project of GCB, a large public organization. Formulating this unique strategic situation incorporates market penetration as well as growth and survival issues. The purpose of our intervention detailed in Chapter 6 is to challenge the strategic foundations of Combank, a small, highly profitable commercial bank.

Both Combank (A) and Infoplus (A) comprise introductory applications, gradually painting the overture of scenario-driven planning through its rough-cut mapping and modeling stages. In itself, causal mapping is a learning experience, forcing participants to think not only about their business, but also about the way they think about their business. This is the foundation of strategic management systems reengineering (Davenport, 1993; Tobias, 1991).

Business systems reengineering is fun in the context and ambiance that scenario-driven planning initiates; otherwise, it can be a painful process. Scenario-driven planning does away with the "no pain, no gain" attitude of the dark ages. Both in our consulting and in our teaching experience, "no fun, no learning" has been the creed of scenario-driven planning, regardless of whether individual or organizational learning is involved.

The causal diagrams of Part III serve as an advance organizer for Part V. That is, they prepare the reader for the more sophisticated formal treatment of some of the central methods used for computing scenarios. The diagrams of Chapters 5 and 6 support the necessity of computing multiple scenarios to preserve the plural rationality evolving in a management team. These causal models also permit a careful, yet informal, treatment of MICMAC (*Matrice d'Impacts Croisés Multiplication Appliquée à un Classement*: cross-impact matrix multiplication applied to classification), a favorite among Godet's (1987) compendium of techniques.

Though computationally simple, MICMAC represents a particular way of approaching strategic planning theory and practice. The irreducible fact of the plurality of possibilities in strategy design makes MICMAC the simplest available technique required to explore the intricate mesh of interacting relationships among the variables pertinent to a strategic situation. MICMAC's square matrix multiplication allows the user to estimate the direct or first-order effect of a given action as well as its higher-order effects.

Part IV

The examples and notions of Part IV interrupt the continuity of the Combank and Infoplus case studies to create a mental pause. It may seem awkward that we interrupt the presentation of scenario-driven applications, postponing the computation of scenarios until Part V. Frequently, however, both our project and our course participants ask for a "mental pause" between rough-cut mapping and scenario computation. So, we give them a break.

1. To allow them to reflect on and internalize the diversity of world-views involved in causal mapping,
2. To prevent them from losing sight of the "big picture."

Underneath the gradual progression of scenes that reveal the situation-specific elements of Combank and Infoplus are major developments both in causal mapping and in behavioral decision theory. These allow us to transform the knowledge of our strategy-minded management teams into computed scenarios.

Part IV then provides the required and pedagogically correct mental pause between the causal mapping of Part III and the computed scenarios of Part V. In part, the merit of Chapter 7 rests on shifting attention from the intricacies of rough-cut causal mapping and modeling to managing strategic uncertainty through scenario-driven competitive intelligence.

Chapter 7 elaborates on the specific techniques used for scenario construction and analysis. It presents alternative scenario methods, such as data-driven versus worldview-driven, while considering environmental issues simultaneously with organizational learning. Although is difficult to keep a book for ever current on commercial scenario methods, we do provide enough information to give an idea of what will become available in the 1990s.

In Chapter 8, the introduction of the basic prerequisites and conceptual underpinnings pertaining to the design considerations of a proposed scenario-planning system is an intentionally destructive interjection. It allows the reader to reflect on and internalize the worldview diversity involved in the causal mapping and modeling introduced gradually in Chapters 5 and 6.

Battelle's real-life intervention in Chapter 7, as well as the basic prerequisites and design matters of the proposed planning system in Chapter 8, further support the necessity of computing scenarios to expand the thinking of those involved in strategy making. The framework in Chapter 8 builds on existing scenario construction methods and environmental scanning techniques. The integrative perspective of this framework delineates processes that enhance institutional learning, bolster productivity, and improve performance. It explains why business interest in scenarios is growing.

The framework links scenario-driven planning to the organizational domains it supports, combining qualitative and quantitative aspects of strategy design into a unified spectrum of problem-finding and problem-framing tools. These tools allow the firm-environment interaction to be viewed in a manner fit for scenario- driven support—fit for turning strategic uncertainty into sustain able advantage.

Although convenient for analysis, the square matrices of MICMAC and their mechanical multiplication, described in Sections 5.4 and 6.4 and detailed in Appendix C.3, are not self-explanatory. In practical applications, structural modelers who use square matrices often find it necessary to convert them to diagrams in or der to sketch out the complexity of the system studied. To this end, structural modelers combine matrix analysis with small and transparent causal diagrams to summarize the proximity among the variables pertinent to a decision situation, "bearing in mind the complexity of mutual influences" (Gérardin, 1979, p. 307).

Following the method developed for the benefit of the VII French National Plan (Gérardin, 1975), we juxtapose and contrast causal mapping and computed scenarios with MICMAC for the benefit of the Combank and Infoplus case studies. Although this does not entail any advanced integrative scheme, it does aim at obtaining a better understanding of the complexity of the interrelated problems facing Combank and Infoplus. Throughout the book, the methods we apply remain rather general and simple.

Part V

The title of Part V, Standard Applications, marks an emerging trend toward computed scenarios. Recent improvements in causal mapping and system dynamics simulation modeling contribute to this trend. New ideas, adopted from behavioral decision theory and cognitive science, allow the knowledge of managers to be translated into computer models. The emphasis is on small, transparent models of strategic situations and on dialogue between the manager's mental models and computed scenarios (Morecroft, 1988).

Part V presents environmental and decision scenarios computed on the causal map (Chapter 9) and on the computer through simulation models, both stochastic (Chapter 9) and deterministic (Chapter 10). Assuming our average reader has not previously computed scenarios either in shorthand form or on the computer, we begin Chapter 9 with very basic arithmetic calculations and a verbally lucid illustrative scenario propagated on the causal diagram of Infoplus (B). Both Infoplus (B) and Combank (B) end with the implementation of the Battelle BASICS approach, which is quite useful in computing probabilistic scenarios while accounting for the interdependence among the variables pertinent to a strategic situation.

Chapter 9 focuses on uncomplicated computational techniques and on comprehensive situation mapping (CSM) (Acar, 1983; Acar, Chaganti & Joglekar, 1985; Acar & Howard, 1987; Georgantzas & Acar, 1989, 1993; Heintz & Acar, 1992; Offodile & Acar, 1993). CSM is a useful strategic problem-framing tool that can serve as a transition between strategic situation analysis and full-fledged system dynamics simulation modeling. Strategic situation analysis should precede traditional system dynamics simulation modeling in order to provide a powerful and flexible strategy design (Morecroft, 1985a).

The idea of policy analysis and strategy design without simulation modeling repels most system dynamicists. Simulation often produces intriguing results and sometimes surprises because the behavior of social systems, such as business systems, often is counterintuitive (Forrester, 1975). Mohapatra & Sharma (1985) and Morecroft (1982) argue that, though widely popular, simple causal-loop diagrams do not provide a reliable guide to system behavior, for these diagrams indicate direction of causation but do not show the strength of the impact. Without simulation modeling support, they tug causal-loop analysis through "vague hand-waving arguments about loop polarity and dynamic behavior" (Morecroft, 1985a, p. 5).

Chapter 10 provides a brief nontechnical introduction to system dynamics simulation modeling. It includes a detailed biographical sketch of Jay W. Forrester, the architect of the field of system dynamics (Forrester, 1958, 1961, 1969). Section 10.3 presents the case of Datacom (unabridged). This is another real-life intervention, showing how a description of the premises of decision-making functions followed by computed scenarios enhance the interpretation of a system dynamics behavioral simulation model (Morecroft, 1985b).

The combined use of alternative scenario methods sets this book apart from other scenario works. In spite of our quest for the ideal scenario method, we still present different approaches to framing strategic situations. Each approach brings forth a new perspective to strategic problem framing. Together, the scenario methods presented provide a unique understanding both of the strategic situation at hand and of the value that scenario-driven planning adds to strategic management.

Part VI

Part VI tells what the future might hold for scenario-driven planning. Chapter 11 explores our increasingly transnational world economy, where the interdependent business environments of country economies determine its structural evolution. Nowhere else are the effects of this interdependence clearer than in the opening up of the former USSR. Its failing economy simply made it impossible for the country and its satellites in Eastern Europe to afford a rigid closed-market system any longer. Our Eastern European colleagues in Moscow and other universities in the newly formed Commonwealth of Independent States have solicited our help with scenario-driven planning.

Although the process of building macroenvironmental scenarios may seem to bear an indirect relation to our main topic of computing strategic decision scenarios, it would have been a glaring omission had we ignored the subject completely. In this context, the macroenvironmental scenario examples of Drucker (1986) in Chapter 2, the plot composition procedure of Schwartz (1991) in Appendix B, and the topical scenarios supervening the Soviet breakup in Chapter 11 should grant the subject adequate attention. Specifically profiled in five dimensions pertinent to the new Russia's alternative futures, five scenarios reinforce the importance of using internally consistent motifs to build macroenvironmental scenarios.

In international business, the eagerness of world-class firms to break free from the integration-responsiveness tradeoff of internationalization also deserves some scrutiny. The transnational strategy archetype has emerged from the strategy designs of world-class firms. Other firms, however, should not expect to drift into transnationalism either from a traditional or from a multi focal archetype. Their managers must design the transformation, for the longer a firm continues trading off global integration for local responsiveness, and vice versa, the more it might be alienating itself from transnationalism.

In Chapter 12, the transnational transformation requirements amount to a scenario of scenarios and to a transcendental attempt to bridge the gap between a focal strategic situation and its potential solutions. Because the new management technology of scenario-driven planning is useful, firms are gradually adopting it. And because firms are accepting it, personnel and financial resources are be coming available to expand it.

Refined taste, mature wisdom, and compelling visceral experiences are on the side of current technologies that allow stunning animation sequences, synthesized speech, and full-motion videos to be incorporated in computer simulations of strategic situations. The alliance of these innovations with simulation modeling software creates virtual realities that are healthy enough to be entrusted with training the younger generation of general managers and strategy students.

Assuredly, scenario experts will soon identify the new capabilities of existing scenario methods and will develop powerful extensions to these methods. These extensions might bring the institutional learning of more firms up to speed with world-class decision quality and performance.

Part VII

The appendixes of Part VII are for readers who wish to delve into the mechanics that lie behind a user-friendly interface. Appendix A reviews the theoretical and metatheoretical contributions leading to scenario-driven planning. Particularly emphasized are the works of the book's direct predecessors. Similarly, Appendix B steps into the arts of modeling strategic situations and scenario writing, whereas Appendix C reviews the modeling tools used in the book.

The purpose of these reviews is to assist the thoughtful reader who wishes to explore scenarios and related tools beyond a quick initial perusal. These are not comprehensive research reviews in a strict academic sense. Inadvertently, however, both the language and the mode of treatment become more rigorous there than in the rest of the text, despite our efforts to shy away from becoming too esoteric.

It is the delicate balancing act between the verbal and formal modes of presentation, i.e., graphics or mathematics, commanding that we introduce the theory gradually throughout the text. First prefaced by sufficient prose, the text is then interspersed with examples. It contains many diagrams and graphs, with short introductions to and summaries of its chapters. The book has more to offer than its direct predecessors (Amara & Lipinski, 1983; Godet, 1987) on each of the following counts.

- Presenting an up-to-date survey of the entire field of scenarios.
- Leading the reader through the benefits of uncertainty management.
- Presenting the material gradually and incrementally.
- Bridging the gap between the qualitative and quantitative domains.
- Organizing the material in a way that facilitates a quick initial scan.
- Presenting the content in a way that entices second readings.
- Including supportive material and references for thoughtful readers.

Part I

WHY SCENARIO-DRIVEN PLANNING?

Chapter 1

Productivity and Strategy

The real voyage of discovery consists,
not in seeking new landscapes,
but in having new eyes.
—Marcel Proust

American productivity has been declining. The Japanese and other observers see it as a strategic, not merely a labor, issue. Can experience guide us adequately? Can the usual interpretation of experience possibly deceive us? How can we make better use of our rich management technology? This chapter creates a context that is suitable to addressing these paradoxes. It presents scenario-driven planning as a new productivity source for strategy design and implementation.

1.1   THE PRODUCTIVITY DILEMMA

They are back. Productivity, unemployment, and corporate restructuring are again preoccupying our industrialized society, causing anxiety to firms unprepared to deal with these problems. Once again, our business press will be ready to echo the wailing of these firms. What *is* our problem? "Productivity is not quantity" laments Taiichi Ono—Japan's Henry Ford (Wright, 1990, p. 98). Productivity mirrors an entire network of relationships among socioeconomic variables affecting our quality of life. Declining productivity causes reductions in gross national product (GNP) and, ultimately, a decline in our standard of living. A successful economy is one that generates a rising standard of living for its citizens. To do so, it must have a healthy rate of productivity growth. Ours does not.

Over the past ten tears, the growth of US productivity has averaged only 0.8 percent per year. In our economy, private business firms are responsible for productivity. If our productivity growth is stagnant, perhaps US firms are no longer doing a great job. Looking at the situation more broadly, however, shows that this malaise is not specifically American but is shared by nearly all industrialized economies. Since Ono retired, even Japan's economy has been showing signs of slowing down.

The reality of management history has been that mistakes have been made and continue to be made. Many books and articles have been written on this subject. Particularly illuminating are the two books on management and marketing mistakes by R.F. Hartley which recount historic flops, such as the Edsel story (Hartley, 1976, 1983).

In today's transformation from the industrial to the postindustrial era, managers devote much energy and time on each firm's strategic posture. Taking advantage of new opportunities and deflating threats may be the essence of strategy, but changes in strategy do not just happen automatically. Strategy depends on a firm's ability to identify emerging patterns in the business environmentand to act accordingly on time. Strategy design depends on learning or, more precisely, on institutional learning (Barr, Stimpert, & Huff, 1992; de Geus, 1988; Senge, 1990). It is a commonplace belief that experience is the best teacher; indeed, it is usually easy to learn from experience. Those who try to teach experience share such beliefs.

The refusal to face environmental mutation has ample precedent in history. Prehistoric people resorted to magic after a defeat by enemies who brought novel warfare to the battlefield. In the same vein, modern corporations organize ritual pep rallies when they have been caught off guard by high-quality German and Japanese imports.

There is small comfort in historical analogies too. Societal mutations have either destroyed, bootstrapped or replaced the focal institutions of prior eras with new ones. In *The March of Folly* (1984), Barbara Tushman shows how major nations and cities destroyed themselves by refusing to learn from the past, even their own past. History documents how little we benefit from our much vaunted experience. The question that the mind-set of scenario-driven planning poses is whether we should continue making mistakes. Can we learn from experience alone?

The answer of Peters & Waterman's best-seller, *In Search of Excellence* (1982), is that too much analysis begets managerial paralysis. Their return to basics has become a "knee-jerk" response whenever profits drop or firms face novel challenge. The empirically deduced model that appears to legitimize sticking to the knitting is *logical incrementalism* or the art of muddling through as practiced in the 1950s. This way of thinking is quite popular in Britain and, to some extent, in the United States.

Concerned about the ability of firms to implement strategic change in the midst of organizational inertia or politics, H. Mintzberg (1993) of McGill and J.B. Quinn (1980) of Dartmouth have become eminent proponents of incrementalism. They see it as the key to success in the marketplace during major mutations. Changes in strategy are not deliberate, they state, but emerge from a pattern of consistent decisions. What generates the consistency remains somewhat of a puzzle. Yet, incrementalism and adherence to time-tested psychological basics often strike a responsive chord in the hearts of traditional consultants. Who could deny that change is almost always uncomfortable and usually takes a bit of getting used to?

In addition, managers who believe that their firms are immune to the turbulent forces of global change do use incrementalism, especially at the implementation stage. Often, however, the use of incautious incrementalism in strategy formulation or design generates failure archetypes (Miller & Friesen, 1978; Miller & Friesen, 1983).

Upon close analysis, the rationale underlying incautious (i.e., piecemeal) incrementalism may turn out to be as undiscriminating and impractical as a halfway compromise between contradictory opposites. As an example, just think about the council in some fabled country that had decided to change the side of the road on which traffic drove from the left to the right but was concerned about making too radical and rapid a switch. So, as an experiment, only the trucks changed sides for the first year!

A more cautious approach leads to *logical incrementalism*, with the changes in strategy derived from the combined state vector of a firm's current strategy and industry environment. The principle for change is the proximity or fit between a firm's current strategy and the environment. Logical incrementalism works best in fairly stable or gradually changing environments. It assumes that performance depends only on current affairs or on the most recent past. Usually, of course, this is more of a dearly held assumption than a cold fact (Bellman, 1961) because when the environment becomes challenging, success archetypes engage in competitive intelligence efforts (Ghoshal & Westney, 1991).

Rudyard Istvan (1992) of the Boston Consulting Group (BCG) concludes that neither traditional productivity notions nor conventional strategic analysis can account for the large differences in the performance of firms. Collected for a whole decade, BCG's productivity data show how differences among firms stem from a new productivity source, namely, system dynamics (Forrester, 1958; Lyneis, 1980; Morecroft, 1988; Mosekilde, Aracil, & Allen, 1988; Rasmussen, Mosekilde, & Sterman, 1985; Sterman, 1985).

The data also show that *saving time may be more critical than saving lines* because of the increased throughput. Adding full-time workers to a fully loaded operation for the sake of maintaining breaks and regular hours may violate all the productivity principles of our Western micro-specialist paradigm. Yet, excess capacity can reduce errors caused by fatigue and save a firm a bundle. By adding two full-time workers to a data processing unit in Missouri, Dow Jones saved one of its production facilities in another state "$1.2 million annually in direct labor costs alone!" (Istvan, 1992, p. 535). This could have important implications for current employment or, more accurately, unemployment policies in the United States.

Recognition of planning as a political process is essential for the successful implementation of strategic decisions (Benveniste, 1989; Dyson, 1990). Yet, strategic considerations grounded exclusively on the psychology of participation or on office politics may falter for two reasons. The first—as discussed in the following section—has to do with problem recognition and problem solving; the second has to do with haste.

Sometimes firms fall in the trap of rushing through the strategy process, leaving out some time-consuming minutiae, such as strategy design. Ironically, then, they end up wasting the very resource they are trying to save—time.

World markets have come to expect comparatively high variety both in goods (e.g., cars and computers) and in services (e.g., checking accounts, global custody and nursing homes). This means that dedicated production lines with long changeover times and long queues of dedicated customers are no longer appropriate because there is too much downtime and unproductive customer contact, respectively.

World-class firms have recognized the necessity of change, but the required modifications of the processes involved are so many and interdependent that piecemeal improvements are not only inadequate but also dangerous. At the production management level, process reengineering helps to analyze *what* is made or served and how (Davenport, 1993; Tobias, 1991). At the strategic management level, scenario-driven planning helps to improve both the content (what) and the process (how) of strategy design.

Strategic management is a process geared at detecting environmental threats and turning them into opportunities. The cones of resolution in Fig. 1.1.1 show exactly where in this complicated process scenario-driven planning can make a direct contribution. Schoderbek, Schoderbek, & Kefalas (1990) also use nested cones of

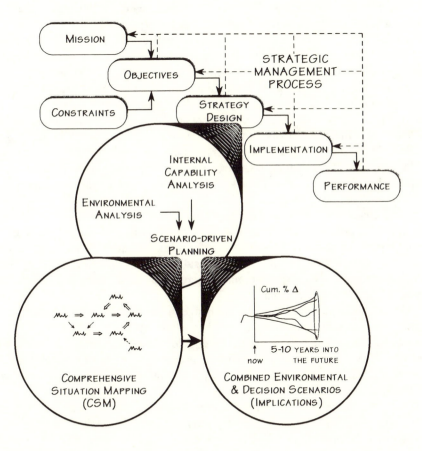

resolution to describe the steps in the process of modeling firm-environment inter-action systems. Similarly, Stafford Beer (1968) and Jay W. Forrester (1987, 1992) use cones of resolution to describe the hierarchy of systems and the conceptualiza-tion $\rightarrow$ quantification $\rightarrow$ computerization process of system dynamics simula-tion modeling.

Strategy design begins by identifying variables relevant to a firm's strategic sit-uation, along with their causal interrelationships. Changes in these variables can have potentially profound effects on performance.

Some of the variables belong to a firm's external environment. Examples are the intensity of competition, emergence of new products and processes, govern-ment regulation, and international interest and currency rates. Changes in these and other variables determine a firm's performance over time.

It is a manager's job to develop a good understanding of the causal linkages un-derlying a strategic situation. Scenario-driven planning can help managers antici-pate the effects of future changes triggered in the external environment.

Environmental analysis aims at gauging environmental trends leading to threats and opportunities. Internal capability analysis examines a firm's past policies and internal policy levers which can both propel and limit action, resources, skills, and weaknesses. Often, they cause difficulties with implementation. Chapter 8 deals with the internal forces and policy levers that can increase the vibrancy of organi-zational resistance to changes in strategy. Chapter 10 presents and extends a classic intervention (Morecroft, 1983, 1984, 1985b, 1990), showing the consequences of inertia in extant policy levers.

Some changes in variables are within a firm's control, a consequence of prevail-ing operating policies and managerial decisions. Pulling and pushing on these in-ternal levers can also affect the firm's performance. To evaluate a change in strat-egy, its results must be anticipated and considered, along with changes in the busi-ness environment, with respect to matching resource capabilities, stakeholder con-cerns, and organizational goals.

Most of these variables interact. A change in an internal lever can cause a dy-namic chain reaction, involving a whole sequence of events. Sometimes it helps managers to distinguish between *market* and *nonmarket* variables within environ-mental and decision variables, particularly in institutions whose strategy formula-tion entails aspects of political economy and administrative legislation (Baron, 1993, especially Chapter 7).

Often, the entire set of possible outcomes is obscure and difficult to determine. Moreover, if managers oversimplify the interrelationships involved, then they end up ignoring the combined effects of such chain reactions altogether. Conversely, combining environmental and decision scenarios computed along the interrelation-ship paths connecting the internal and external variables, that is, the $\mathcal{MV}$ icons of Fig. 1.1.1, can reveal unwarranted simplification. Oversimplification frequently results from well-intended rationality. Yet, cognitive simplification processes cause cognitive biases (CBs) that very often mislead decision makers (Eilon, 1984; Schwenk, 1984; Simon, 1957, 1979).

With the presence of scale economies, for example, prevailing prices alone cannot determine a firm's efficient production scale. In strategy, the scale of production itself is a design variable because it meets the two conditions that Stanford economists Milgrom and Roberts delineate:

1. It has predictable implications for various organization functions.
2. The mistakes associated with incorrect perceptions of it can be serious.

Depending on the sales volume that a firm anticipates, it will adjust its sales force, supplies and distribution, equipment, and facilities to match the scale of its production. Coherent and consistent actions taken by its production, marketing, personnel, distribution, and procurement managers demand a shared vision of the intended production scale. Sharing common perceptions about a firm's strategy is an important step toward coordinating implementation plans and managerial behavior (Milgrom & Roberts, 1992, p. 107). Devising scenarios will be of great help in this regard.

The anticipated scale of a firm's production affects more than just the scale of each management function. In the cases of GM and Toyota, the degree of "outsourcing" shows how production scale also determines the specialization of firms (Damanpour, 1991; Mintzberg, 1979; Robey, 1982). Smaller firms, operating without specialized equipment, typically rely on suppliers for even more components when the suppliers enjoy economies of scale of their own by serving many firms.

The use of specialized capital equipment makes vertical integration more profitable for large firms than for small competitors. Economies of scale permit reduced production cost, which is an important element in determining price. Low marginal cost, other things being equal, allows lower prices, which increase potential demand, which in turn supports increased production.

Firms can enjoy economies of scale even when they are producing at too small a scale in a market that is too small for them. A firm can make product components for multiple product markets. GE enjoys economies of scale in small electric motors, for example, when it uses the same motors in food processors, hair dryers, fans, and vacuum cleaners. CASIO enjoys economies of scale in liquid crystal displays (LCDs), which it uses in electronic address books, calculators, and music keyboards. The falling cost of LCDs led to penetration of multiple segments of the market for digital and analog wristwatches that use LCDs.

Under these circumstances, firms enjoy *economies of scope* by producing several products together at less cost than single-product firms. Economies of scope posit the same strategy design and decision coordination that economies of scale do (Milgrom & Roberts, 1992, p. 107).

The same limitations also apply. For example, meandering into a multitude of sidelines that share unique material or manufacturing techniques with Yamaha's core business has brought the firm into unfamiliar markets, with multiple environmental forces. Blithely obscured by the high rivalry of the television, VCR, and audio equipment industries, the cumulative effect of these forces has been a 30 percent decrease in Yamaha's profits from 1990 to 1992 (Schlender, 1993).

Scenario-driven planning can help a firm integrate its competitive intelligence efforts with strategy design, not as a narrow specialty, but as an admission of limitations and environmental complexity. The analysis of strategic situations requires a comprehensive inquiry into the environmental causalities and equivocalities that result from competitive actions. Scenarios probe the combined consequences of environmental trends, changes in the firm's own strategy, as well as the moves of its current and future competitors.

Computed scenarios help managers understand what they do not know, enabling strategy design and implementation through the coalignment of the "right" tactics to improve long-term performance. Through its judicious use of corporate resources, scenario-driven planning makes the tactics required for implementation clear. Also, it can reveal the required coalignment of tactics over time, so a firm can become both flexible and efficient, and save time!

The conventional perspective of copycat strategy shows linear thinking at best and clumsy benchmarking—also known as *shadow marketing*—at worst (Hatten & Hatten, 1987). Its proponents assume that they can improve long-term performance incrementally, with disconnected tactical moves alone, when improvements in strategy design should be their primary concern.

Piecemeal tactics can undermine strategy, but they are secondary. It may be possible to improve performance through efficient tactics, but it is better to design an efficient strategy that will expel counterproductive tactics. Examples of counterproductive tactics are those coercive moves that increase rivalry among competitors, without a real payoff, either direct or indirect, for the industry incumbent who initiates such moves. It is atypical of an industry or market leader to initiate such moves.

In strategy, superior implementation demands superior design.

According to the design school led by Ansoff, Channon, Hofer, McMillan, Porter, Schendel, Thomas, and others, logical incrementalism may help implementation, but it becomes a prescription for failure when the environment is shifting. Examples of such failures and reversals are abundantly documented in the business press. Rapid changes in information technology, global competition, family structure, and other facets of our global society's culture systems are foisting metamorphoses on the business environment.

To some, changes in the environment resemble tornado like forces, cutting a swath of destruction through corporate landscapes. They are forces that leave a litter of torn organizational charts and broken traditions in their wake. To others, environmental change represents a more beneficent maelstrom, a dynamic force that animates vibrant opportunities and infuses new life into tired organizational structures. But no matter how it is perceived, environmental change is a force that managers must deal with.

Global firms such as 3M, Apple, American Airlines, Campbell Soup, General Electric, Intel, Merck, and Philip Morris have a striking capability of institutionalizing change; they never stand still. Yet, even these masters of innovation sometimes refrain from taking a bold step toward complete renewal when a major change, for which they have not analytically or at least conceptually prepared, occurs in the environment (Sherman, 1984).

This is what Frederick W. Gluck, a director at McKinsey & Company, describes as the "unspoken problem." When industry forces change or new market opportunities open up, only a few corporations are able to rethink from ground zero the way they do business. The challenge is learning to recognize the permanence of change and to act proactively.

1.2 LEARNING FROM EXPERIENCE?

We have to break the vicious circle caused by the lack of productivity feeding onto and being fed by the lack of strategic vision. Unless sensitized with scenarios, it is hard to see the strategic coalignment of tactics, which is the very art of transforming environmental threats into opportunities. Moreover, vicious circles are hard to break.

To break free, let's begin with a question. Is it difficult because our elders have made mistakes and we can only learn from our own mistakes? Assuredly, we learn better from our own mistakes than from those of our predecessors. Yet, can our institutions really afford to learn on the job? Because a little institutional learning takes place when times are good, we have to look for another reason.

Is it true that one only learns by doing? Is there no way to shorten the cycle? Philosophers and educators have studied the general issue of learning from experience, and they have come up with a counterintuitive position. To learn from experience, they agree, we must already have some idea or expectations about how something works. Only when we have a mental model of how something operates can we properly interpret the outcomes of observation.

"So I decided to retire the multi-based blocks," writes John Holt on p. 219 of the revised edition of his book *How Children Fail*. These are those pale-looking, notched hardwood blocks that both the British and our own elementary schools have been using to help our children learn the meaning of base and place in the numeral system. After using the multibased blocks in his class for some time, Holt discovered that, in their new experience, children

> who already understood base and place, even if only intuitively, could see the
> connections between written numerals and operations with numerals and
> these blocks. Children who could convert 101 in base 2... to the equivalent
> number in base 10, without using blocks, could use the blocks to do the same
> thing, or to verify their answer. But children who could not do these prob-
> lems without the blocks didn't have a clue about how to do them with the
> blocks (Holt, 1982, pp. 218-219).

C. West Churchman (1968, 1969, 1971), who reintroduced great methodological works of the past into modern management, recounts a lively debate that
emerged between the seventeenth- and eighteenth-century Anglo-Irish empirical
philosophers Berkeley, Hume, and Locke, and the continental rationalists, such as
Descartes and Leibniz. The argument centered on whether learning starts with observation or with an idea. Whereas the empirical philosophers valued experience,
the rationalists emphasized analysis. In today's practical terms, the issue is
whether experience accumulated in a specific work setting is fully portable to another.

Kant and, more recently, Piaget show that learning calls for both analysis and
experience (Piaget, 1973). Both activities have to take place in an iterative manner.
In essence, rational thinking has to precede and guide observation in order for observation to become what we call experience. Contrary to popular belief, to see one
has to know what to look for; as well as where to look. How many of us have
watched apples and other objects fall without deducing any general principle?

Arie de Geus, executive in residence at the London Business School and formerly Group Planning coordinator for the Royal Dutch-Shell Group of Companies,
has been a pioneer in organizational learning. He is fond of telling the story of a
newly discovered tribe, isolated in the pristine wilderness of Southeast Asia.

> Two experimental neurobiologists call on this tribe, which has not even dis-
> covered the wheel yet. After some time, they manage to establish communi-
> cation with the tribe's chief, a man of wisdom who scores very high on their
> IQ test. So, they arrange to transport the chief to a large city, presumably
> Singapore.
>
> Naturally, both neurobiologists accompany the chief throughout his new
> experience, recording all his reactions to everything he sees and everything
> he does in great detail. Upon their return, the tribe prepares a feast to wel-
> come its chief back home. All was well again!
>
> After a superb meal around the fire, one neurobiologist casually asks
> whether anything in particular has impressed the chief about Western civi-
> lization. Without the slightest hesitation, the chief replies that our civilization
> is great because we can carry more bananas than even the strongest man in

his tribe could.

What he saw was somebody using a wheelbarrow to carry more bananas than he had ever thought possible. Yet, there was no wheelbarrow and nothing about bananas in neither of the two neurobiologists detailed notes. Only the chief spotted the bananas!

He was the only one prepared to see them too. This is how historian Barbara Tuchman might have interpreted this story: "Men will not believe what does not fit in with their plans or suit their prearrangements" (Tushman, 1981, p. 35).

Arie de Geus explains how scenarios enable new perceptions to enter the heads of decision makers, obliging them to recognize and revise their inner models of reality, their microcosms. Pierre Wack uses the term *microcosm* to distinguish between a manager's mental model of reality and the *macrocosm*, that is, reality itself (Wack, 1985a, 1985b). A few persons carry mental models of reality in their heads; the rest of us humans settle for microcosms of our contact with reality, not reality itself. It must be this human deficiency that makes problem framing, scenarios, and life sparkle. In that way, managers get ready to spot the bananas on the wheelbarrow of environmental change, even in the bedlam of large Western cities.

David Ingvar (1985) describes research being done at the University of Lund into the problem of how the human brain deals with the future. A part of the brain, it has been found, is constantly busy making not only one, but several time-action plans under different anticipated futures. In well-balanced people, usually a little more than half are favorable futures. The Lund studies show how our brain not only makes alternative time-action plans, but also stores them. We humans, it seems, have "memories of the future."

Peter Schwartz (1991) points out that individuals and even organizations have little control over environmental forces that cause change. Most of us get our leverage for dealing with them from recognizing them and their effects. Yet, our own actions also contribute to the driving forces that keep changing the business environment.

De Geus strongly opposes sending managers into positions of responsibility to learn from experience:

> The work of many managers has human consequences with potential for disaster equal to malfunctioning aeroplanes, chemical plants or dykes and dams. Nevertheless, we find it perfectly normal to send managers into positions of responsibility to learn by experience—by trial and error. We ask them to learn 'by experimenting with reality.' Being intelligent people, they will recognize and fear the consequences—and learn a lot less and slower than they would have done otherwise (de Geus, 1992, p. 4).

There is an increasing recognition that strategy design entails problem framing (Ackoff, 1978; Bower, 1982; Checkland, 1975; Kepner & Tregoe, 1965). A business problem may be defined as the gap between a firm's present situation and a desired future. This allows defining strategic problems according to their intrinsic characteristics. Strategy makers can describe a strategic situation using their knowledge about its nature and structure. Similarly, they can describe a desired situation using their knowledge of a firm's long-term goals. The present and desired situations are easy to characterize in most implementation problems. For example, efficiency calls for reduced work-in-process (WIP) inventory. In strategic situations, however, decision makers may know little about either the present or the desired state of affairs. They may just feel that something is wrong.

Many works describe the application of systems theory to production planning (Acar, 1984; Ackoff & Sasieni, 1968; Nadler, Hackman, & Lawler, 1979; Riggs, 1987; Rivett, 1980; van Gigch, 1978; Zeleny, 1986). Based on these works, Fig. 1.2.1 groups organizational problems into four kinds (Acar, 1984). Its principle is that an organizational problem may result from having erroneously specified either one of or many among the output of the system, the input to the system, the production process itself, or even the entire system. Within a firm, problems can occur singly or in combination as well as within specific organizational tasks, such as quality control (Acar, 1984; Acar & Booth, 1987; Nadler, 1970). This grouping scheme can help managers and planners characterize most business problems.

At any decision-making level, the less a firm's managers know about the causal structure of a problem, the more difficult it is to solve it. Managers need tools to transform ill-defined problems into better defined problems. Initially, we communicate strategy-design problems in fuzzy terms. To solve such problems, we need techniques to help us move up from problems of the fourth kind, out of the fuzzy-specification corridor of Fig. 1.2.1.

Systems theorists have developed methods for detecting problems of the first, second, and third kind even in problem-ridden systems (Acar, 1983; Ackoff, 1970, 1981; Neave & Petersen, 1980). In addition, managers can tackle any properly diagnosed problem, no matter how difficult it may be. The important point is to switch from the reactive to the proactive posture vis-à-vis strategic issue diagnosis (SID). This requires environmental scanning and scenario analysis which, coupled together, can bring a firm's learning up to speed with its pursuit of world-class performance and managerial decision quality.

This conviction may appear irreverent to some and excessively cautious to others. Yet, Pascale & Athos (1982), in documenting Honda USA's ascent to fame, posed some important questions. For example, they asked, why do the Japanese learn better from experience than we do? Is it because they stress *company wide* continuous improvement? For example, Japanese executives worry less about whether overhead allocation reflects the precise demands that each product makes on corporate resources than about how it affects the cost reduction priorities of middle managers and shopfloor workers. American executives often dismiss Japanese management accounting techniques as misguided, or even simplistic

Figure 1.2.1 Grouping Managerial Problems

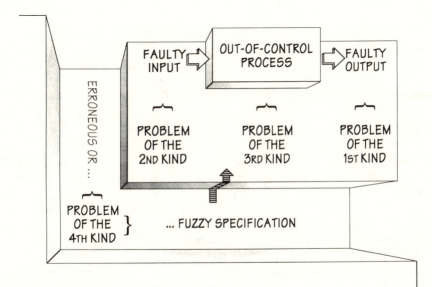

Source: Acar, 1984; Acar & Booth, 1987

(Hiromoto, 1988). Could it also be that the long-term orientation serves them well?

Business Week devoted its special issue of 6 June 1988 to the productivity paradox, citing the development of new methods for judging long-term business projects and programs. Kate Balden made the same point in her 13 March 1989 *Fortune* article. Accounting tools yielding the internal rate of return (IRR) or net presentvalue (NPV) may be hopeless for this purpose. Productivity improvements result from sound management technology. We need new control tools for the US enterprise management system.

To give a hint of what is to follow, the required shift is one from the calculus of short-term accounting transactions to one of computing long-term strategic implications. These implications are the consequences not of isolated events, but of the system structure underlying the cause-effect relationships among both environmental and strategic decision or policy variables (Clark, 1988; Istvan, 1992; Lyneis, 1980).

Managers have some idea of what's hooked up to what among the variables pertinent to a firm's strategic situation. This knowledge constitutes their mental models of the connections among variables as well as among variables and their consequences. Yet, the dynamic consequences or implications produced by a system's causal relationships are virtually impossible to predict through simple observation (Senge & Sterman, 1992). Managers need tools to help them gauge the assumptions that underlie their mental models about the future.

To improve their decision quality, they should become more aware of their assumptions, including assumptions about the way strategic variables are affected by and cause changes in other variables over time. The resulting confrontation between devil's advocates and proponents of a particular system structure that causes a dynamic behavior pattern becomes a learning experience. Institutional learning opportunities abound when rational confrontation becomes lively in a team because of an analytical approach (Cosier, 1981a, 1981b; Mason & Mitroff, 1981; Schwenk, 1984).

To encourage and to make learning an integral part of management technology, we must lift our sights from the short term. To design strategy, we must learn to search for and to identify patterns of change over time. To practice strategy design and to act proactively, we should replace our transaction-driven calculus with scenario analysis. Learning is not a luxury; it is how firms create their own future (Ackoff, 1981). Creating the organizational capability of and ambiance for learning will lead to a truly sustainable advantage.

Both the mind-set of scenario-driven planning and the emerging understanding in the strategic management literature contend that, to speed up institutional learning, we must articulate our mental models through formal analysis. A recent article argues that formal analysis of managers' cognitive maps will help them to overcome personal assumptions and to assess possible ramifications (Anthony et al., 1993). This is precisely the thrust of our book.

Some of this may sound like going back to basics. Basics they are, but going back we're not. We join the ranks of contemporary business planners and doers who advocate and use scenarios to explore the future.

Improving the mental models of those who propel changes in strategy is not easy. The transition required can change the rules that managers live by. To learn from experience, we must first learn how to filter the product of observation and to extract coherent information from it.

1.3   A WAY OUT?

In the 1950s through the 1970s, people who designed strategy were far removed from operations. Authority was in the hands of staff people who sifted data from other staff. The iron law of oligarchy did not allow constituents at the lower levels of the corporate hierarchy to read change signals in the environment. Their job was simply to execute orders pushed down from change agents at the top.

Those were the times when it was prudent to stick around the conference room or the plant with your back covered. Managers spent little time trying to understand the effect of environmental change on the business and its resource dependency. Seldom did they envision environmental and strategic scenarios, let alone computed ones.

How quickly that changed! In today's manufacturing renaissance, well-known corporations strive to recover, to revive, and to renew themselves. Besides the board, CEO and staff, strategy involves everyone in a firm—every manager, senior or junior, top-level and middle. Wharton's professor emeritus Russell L. Ackoff illustrates this shift in his pathbreaking texts *A Concept of Corporate Planning* (1970) and *Creating the Corporate Future* (1981). He shows that managers at all levels, and not just people at the top, can formulate and implement changes in strategy.

To enable implementation, managers can add value through better design for quality, speed of delivery, and jobs; labor relations, training, and staff support; in- and outsourcing, supplier and customer relations; service, plant, and office organization; equipment selection and maintenance; scheduling, inventory, transport, and handling; the accounting system; office and manufacturing automation; and so on. Every little bit helps. Yet, to design strategy, a firm's top managers must coordinate the way the firm *senses* its environment and in a way that *makes sense* to all involved.

Firms around the globe have been copying US business practices. To make further improvements, we must recognize that the insight needed to effect changes in strategy can come from every level in a firm. Planning for implementation should include possible market responses and should anticipate the reactions of the people affected by the proposed action.

Constituents at the lower levels of the corporate hierarchy are now free to read the organizational environment. Their job is to capture, filter, and interpret environmental change signals. This is how they create new information necessary for strategy design and implementation. In so doing, they generate knowledge and a new long-lasting capability of dealing with change, both internal and external. Managers at every level can now contribute to this *sense-making* function (Daft & Weick, 1984).

Scenario-driven planning is emerging from this context. It has an overriding goal and an underlying mind-set to meet that goal. The overriding goal is to improve the way managers think, learn, and reason about strategy design. This may sound too ambitious. The transformation is most difficult when attention is fixed on the next quarter instead of the next decade. Yet, changes in the global business environment call for a major change in the way managers think about it.

Scenario-driven planning can help managers view change as an opportunity instead of a threat. In this way, they can realize their full potential, their power to create a firm's future. With this mind-set, the improvement journey follows a surprisingly well-defined path, allowing the clearing away of obstacles so that strategy implementation becomes simple, efficient, and powerful.

This book guides the reader gradually through the ideas of scenario-driven planning and its new way of thinking about strategy making. The assumptions underlying one's mental model may be correct, but the human mind both individually or in the form of group consensus often draws the wrong conclusions. Managing is no longer a purely intuitive art; it now includes the science of strategic planning. Analysts such as Peter Drucker and Michael Porter have stressed the contributions of environmental scanning and analytical thinking to institutional learning and strategy design.

Specifically, Forrester's work on system dynamics in the 1950s and 1960s propagated the awareness that decision makers misjudge the dynamic behavior of social systems. Following his lead, Roger Hall (1976) studied the demise of the old *Saturday Evening Post*. His system dynamics model shows that when faced with complex and highly interactive systems, human judgment and intuition often lead to wrong decisions. More recently, MIT's John Sterman (1989) experimentally verified Hall's empirical observations.

That same year, (1976), Nobel Prize winner Herbert A. Simon delineated two related ways in which analytical models and computer simulation can provide knowledge—the one obvious and the other more subtle. Obviously, decision makers must painstakingly tease out the consequences of their assumptions even when they sense the correct premises.

The subtle way emerges when the decision makers have not had time to reflect much about the changing laws governing the behavior of their system. This is the essence of "assumptional analysis" (Mitroff & Emshoff, 1979).

Analytical systems allow us to explore and gain a deep understanding of the premises behind a firm's strategy and its environment (Merten, 1991; Sterman, 1989). We need a subtle form of understanding to produce and to trade profitably. Despite today's future-focused culture, often there is a reluctance to confront the new global economic realities (Drucker, 1989). This denial is destructive for business firms. Their survival depends on their managers' ability to anticipate, prepare for, and create their future.

SUMMARY

Despite repeated productivity and strategic losses at the hands of the Asian juggernauts, we continue deluding ourselves about having only a labor problem. The Japanese and other observers believe that we have a management problem. We rely exclusively on experience, but do not appear capable of learning readily from it in proportion to our potential.

Experience is a hard and costly school. If underexploited, it can be overrated. Experience is an exacting teacher, always calling for prior reflection. We have to think ahead and to design our long-term strategy carefully. Only then can we compete in our trade with Mexico, Japan, the Four Tigers of Southeast Asia (Taiwan, South Korea, Hong Kong, and Singapore) and other Little Dragons. Paradoxically, this proactivity may improve our ability to learn from experience and to capitalize on it. This is how the emerging approach of scenario-driven planning can help our firms create and sustain competitive advantage.

Scenario-driven planning generates three distinct advantages.

1. *Learning to better cope with strategic uncertainty through a better understanding of existing scenario methods and their variations.*
2. *Gaining a better understanding of the principles underlying the subtleties of these variations.*
3. *As a result, charting the principal weakness of disconnected single-point forecasts, which lack the useful synergy between judgmental and quantitative analyses. Scenario-driven planning offers one more advantage here. It allows computing coherent environmental and decision scenarios, which probe the joint consequences of*

   a. *changes in the environment,*
   b. *changes in a firm's own strategy, and*
   c. *changes triggered by its current and future competitors.*

Chapter 2

Environmental Triggers and Scenarios

Confronted by contemporary high-velocity environments, corporate executives are becoming more interested in understanding environmental forces. These enable or disable successful changes in strategy. This chapter examines the forces that influence the occurrence of change in organizational environments and, as a consequence, in corporate strategies. The chapter first introduces the notion of scenario. After listing the potential areas of application, it moves on to illustrate the use of scenarios through three examples: Drucker's spate of scenarios for the global economy; General Electric's approach to forecasting through scenario writing; and the classic experience of Shell with scenarios.

2.1   THE CONCEPT OF SCENARIO

History of the Concept

Literally, "scenario" means a script of a play or story, a projected sequence of events. Herman Kahn introduced the term to planning while at RAND Corporation in the 1950s. Scenarios were first used in the military strategy studies conducted by RAND for the US government. In the 1960s, H. Ozbekhan of the Wharton School used scenarios in an urban planning project for Paris, France. Organization theorists and even novelists were quick to latch on. The meaning of scenarios became primarily literary. Common sense and imagination produced flickering apocalyptic predictions of a strikingly optimistic or pessimistic future. Political, organizational, and marketing experts use scenarios today to conjure up visions of alternative favorable and unfavorable business environments.

Pierre Wack (1985a, 1985b) asserts that it was a group of strategic planners at Royal Dutch Shell that came up with the idea of scenario analysis. In the early 1970s, his team developed scenarios for strategic planning. In his book, Godet (1987) points to the French OTAM team as the first to use scenarios in a study of geographical futures undertaken by DATAR in 1971. Brauers & Weber (1988) proclaim that Battelle's method of scenario building and analysis was originally a German approach. Yet, most authors acclaim the formal scenario approach as typically American in its connection with planning.

US researchers Olaf Helmer and Norman Dalkey developed several formal methods of scenario construction at the RAND Corporation during the 1970s (see Amara & Lipinski, 1983). These methods incorporate techniques for eliciting and aggregating group judgments, namely, Delphi and cross-impact matrices. Helmer and Dalkey extended the analysis of cross impact within statistical decision theory. A synthesis of scenario methods began in the 1970s. It draws together in a single framework a variety of perspectives, including those of professional planners, analysts and line managers.

Many managerial changes have occurred during the last decade. Ansoff (1985) and other strategy theorists state that the 1970s witnessed the transformation of product markets into a global perspective. Changes in the external sociopolitical environment became pivotal in strategy making. Environmental challenges, many of them novel, also became progressively numerous. Combined with the geographical expansion of markets, they increased the complexity of managerial work. They rendered the managerial capability developed during the 1960s inadequate. Today, environmental challenges are developing progressively faster. Their novelty, complexity, and speed have increased the likelihood of strategic surprises.

In the 1970s scenario-driven planning spread. Strategic thinkers realized that effective changes in strategy require a clear perception of the prospects in the business environment. Some used scenarios and competitive analysis to capture the nonlinearity, complexity, and unpredictability of turbulent environments. Examples are Hax & Majluf (1984), and more clearly so Michael Porter (1985). Both texts consider scenarios to be instrumental in understanding and anticipating environmental trends. They recommend the construction of alternative scenarios as a form of sensitivity analysis performed on the most likely scenario. This scenario incorporates preferred strategic action and trends in the external environment.

Numerous researchers and practitioners are now flocking to put the label scenario on their work. Huss & Honton (1987) note that scenario analysis is emerging as a distinct field of study. They see scenario-driven planning as a hybrid of many disciplines. Unlike extrapolation techniques, scenarios encourage planners and managers to think more broadly about the future. This book provides a guided tour through the fascinating but possibly intimidating jungle of scenario definitions. One of its thrusts is to disconnect the scenario idea from unproductive guesswork and to anchor it to sound practices for strategic management.

Huss & Honton identify a variety of approaches to scenario-driven planning and provide a brief introduction to these methods and the ideas behind them. They fall under three major categories:

1. Intuitive logics, described by Wack (1985) and now practiced by SRI International.
2. Trend-impact analysis, practiced by the Futures Group.
3. Cross-impact analysis, practiced by the Center for Futures Research using INTERAX (Interactive Cross-Impact Simulation) and by Battelle using BASICS (Battelle Scenario Inputs to Corporate Strategies).

Benefits of Scenario-Driven Planning

We might as well state now where the bias of this book lies. Earlier than this mainstream sanction of using reference scenarios in planning, Ackoff joined his colleague Ozbekhan in advocating reference scenarios. Both contributed to the development of the scenario idea. Ackoff (1981) distinguishes between:

1. reference projections, that is, piecemeal extrapolations of past trends, and
2. the overall reference scenario resulting from putting them together.

Our work will further explore these useful distinctions for a practical managerial technology. This technology uses scenarios as the means toward achieving a well-structured process of managing ill-structured strategic situations.

Scenario-driven planning is a systematic approach to an increasingly important responsibility of general management: positioning today's business firm in a rapidly changing and complex global environment. To do so successfully, corporate leaders should install organizational processes that can help them understand how the environment might be changing and what the effect of likely consequences will be. Otherwise, despite their current strengths, business firms are unlikely to be able to meet the challenges of the emerging high-technology and deregulated global economy. Predicting a world in which technology and collective and competitive patterns change at an unprecedented rate is hard enough. Moving ahead of it is simply larger than the extended talents and resources that are now available in any of the world's leading firms.

Scenario-driven planning has evolved from humble beginnings and specific disciplines, such as strategic management and operational research, into a bandwagon that is attracting numerous researchers and practitioners. The demand for scenario-driven planning in business has been increasing for two reasons: first, there is abundant evidence that the strength of the US economy is declining or at least stagnating. Second, using scenarios as a strategic tool provides a handsome return on the investment it requires. The demand for strategic planning with scenarios is beginning to outstrip the supply of scenario analysts. To continue the introduction of scenario-driven strategies into the increasingly turbulent business environment, firms need more people capable of generating strategic change scenarios.

The technology of scenario-driven planning constitutes a superior approach to designing corporate and business strategies. Firms can use it in formulating and analyzing strategic situations productively. Scenario-driven planning is not a panacea but can be very successful in a variety of business settings. Because of its multidisciplinary nature, it can help professionals and managers in a variety of applications, namely, capital budgeting, career planning, competitive analysis, crisis management, decision support systems (DSS), macroeconomic analysis, marketing, portfolio management, and product development. Although scenarios have been used mostly to forecast future corporate environments, scenario-driven planning is increasingly of interest to functional managers in diverse business areas.

2.2   AREAS OF APPLICATION AND SCENARIO SCOPE

Because of their proprietary nature and for reasons of confidentiality, only a few corporate planning scenarios get published. Yet, prominent international firms have used scenarios to formulate, to analyze and to act on strategic situations.

Linneman & Klein (1983) surveyed the gradual emergence of scenario-driven planning among the *Fortune* 1,000 Industrials and found that only a handful of firms used scenarios in 1974. In the next two years their number doubled. Forty-seven firms used multiple scenarios in 1977. In Linneman & Klein's 1981 survey, 50 percent (108) of their respondents reported using scenarios. They also found that the use of scenario-driven planning was not uniform across industries. Among the industries in which scenario analysis and construction are fashionable (Table 2.2.1), the greatest concentration is in the aerospace and process industries.

Table 2.2.1   Industries That Benefit from Scenario-Driven Planning

Industry	Sample Source(s)
Aerospace & telecommunications	Millett & Randles (1986)
Agriculture	Helgason, T. & Wallace (1991); Waissbluth & De Gortari (1990)
Banking	Imundo (1986); Prebble & Reichel (1988)
Chemicals	Zentner (1987)
Data processing	Schultz (1986)
Petroleum	Gross (1984); Jones (1985); Wack (1985a & b); Wright & Hill (1986)
Public utilities	Lootsma, Boonekamp, Cooke & van Oostvoorn (1990); Potts (1985)

Two recent books on scenarios should be on the reference list of every proactive manager and planner. One is *Business Planning for an Uncertain Future*, by Amara & Lipinski (1983) and the other is a French book, *Scenarios and Strategic Management* (Godet, 1987). According to these sources, forecasting future corporate environments through scenarios has received most of the attention in the literature, but the derived benefits will be much higher if the emphasis shifts from forecasting to organizational problem learning and situation description. System dynamicists, such as Jay Forrester (1992) and his collaborators and disciples have made this point clear (Dangerfield, 1992; de Geus, 1992; Diehl, 1992b; Eberlein & Peterson, 1992; Morecroft & van der Heijden, 1992; Peterson, 1992).

A variety of business areas can benefit by combining macroenvironmental and strategic scenarios when dealing with problem framing and situation formulation. Documented applications and derived benefits exist for three successive planning levels: macroeconomic and environmental (industry), strategic (competitive) and marketing, and operational (Table 2.2.2). These success stories indicate that managers should learn to construct their own scenarios; only then will they use them in strategy design. Both internal consultants and external scenario experts can facilitate the process of installing scenario-driven planning. Consulting firms with scenario expertise include the Battelle Memorial Institute in Columbus, Ohio, the Futures Group in Glastonbury, Connecticut, and the Institute for the Future and Stanford Research Institute (SRI) in Menlo Park, California.

Yet, the consultants and scenario experts should not impose their own models and scenarios on managers. A firm should enable its managers through flexibility, initiative, and power to make scenario explorations genuine and their own. Papert recalls how "The 'right way' was not imposed on Keith... gave him enough flexibility and power so that his exploration could be genuine and his own" (1980, p. 104). The human mind is too valuable a thing to force.

Table 2.2.2   Business Areas That Benefit from Scenario-Driven Planning

Planning Level	*Sample Source(s)*
Macroeconomic & *environmental* (industry)	Galer & Kasper (1982)
Strategic (competitive) & marketing	De Carlo & Irwin (1981); Lahr (1983); Godiwalla, Meinhart & Warde (1981); Leavy (1986)
• Competitive analysis	Porter (1985); Prescott & Grant (1988)
• Crisis management	Leavy (1986)
• Corporate or portfolio analysis	Gammon & Labuszeski (1986); Kennedy & Sudgen (1986)
Operational	
• Decision Support Systems (DSS)	Remus & Kottemann (1986)
• New Product Development	Morris (1982); Stacey (1984)
• Career Planning	Hopwood & Stuart (1987); Page & Hopwood (1986); Prebble & Rau (1986)

Naturally, top management support is needed to build a companywide capability of modeling and scenario construction. As we will see, Shell's top executives first invited Pierre Wack and then provided him with the resources he needed. They also paid him the compliment of listening to him, and they listened well.

An exceptionally capable team surrounded Wack. Ted Newland and Napier Collyns were among its members. This team became critical to the success of scenario-driven planning at the Royal Dutch-Shell Group of Companies.

These two modes of approaching scenario-driven planning—companywide capability and top management support—are pervasive. They act like a pair of switches that can turn a firm's managers and executives into partners in taking the long view. If both switches are on, then a firm will benefit from scenario-driven planning. The benefit is not more accurate forecasts but *"better decisions about the future"* (Schwartz, 1991, p. 9).

During the 1972 energy crisis, only Shell was ready for the change among oil firms. The firm's executives and managers responded together and responded fast, proactively. So it was that Shell's strategic posture changed. Formerly one of the weaker of the "Seven Sisters," the seven largest oil firms, it now became second only to Exxon in size and, by the same token, the first in profits. Shell's senior planners were no longer concerned about forecasting. Their main concern became the mind-set of Shell's managers.

According to independent consultant Schwartz, it was not an accident that Wack's articles (1985a, 1985b) were about reperceiving rather than predicting the future. Scenarios are valuable as long as they cause a new form of interaction among those who must decide and act. Wack had no interest in predicting the future. While at Shell, he aimed at liberating management insight, at inspiring the long-term view. Scenario-driven planning enables managers to reperceive a strategic situation, to discern their assumptions about the situation so that they can improve their decision quality.

A point glossed over in the literature of scenarios is that the upper level environmental scenarios resulting from macroeconomic analysis and the strategic scenarios differ. Environmental scenarios become inputs to the computation of strategic change scenarios. In turn, strategic or competitive scenarios can serve as inputs for devising specific or special-purpose operational scenarios.

This theoretical consideration allows us to penetrate the jungle of scenario theories. For example, Chapter 13 of Porter's *Competitive Advantage* (1985) refers to all three levels of scenario analysis, linking several different approaches with each level. Yet, "Scenario thinking is an art, not a science," writes Peter Schwartz (1991, p. 29). He is talking about macroenvironmental scenarios, the inputs to scenario-driven planning that allows a whole array of possible futures to be addressed before a firm's managers rehearse their responses to each one of them (see Section B.2 in Appendix B).

Methodological problems and difficulties still abound, but research is progressing rapidly in scenario-driven planning. Chandler & Cockle (1982) and Godet (1985; translation, 1987) are both useful reviews for the planning theorist. They provide reasonably comprehensive discussions of differences among methods for generating scenarios. Unfortunately, neither of them focuses on the scenario construction process nor on related problems. A state-of-the-art methodological review and critique focusing specifically on this process is needed.

The following sections of this chapter provide three scenario examples. The two criteria used in their selection were insight and content diversity. The first example is Drucker's (1986) global predicament that the world economy has changed in its foundations and structure. In all probability, Drucker argues, the change is irreversible. The supportive environmental scenarios were built in 1985 by S. Marris. This example gives the clearest and most persuasive illustration of how externally built scenarios can be used to support an internal theme.

To a large extent, the popularity of scenarios is attributed to the work performed at the Royal Dutch-Shell Group of Companies. Shell's use of scenarios as a strategic tool has been described by numerous authors (Chandler & Cockle, 1982; de Geus, 1988; Page & Hopwood, 1986; Porter, 1985). Shell made a unique contribution in scenario-driven planning. Its scenario experience produced both promising results and methodological innovations. Since the oil crisis of 1973, numerous studies have either duplicated or built on Shell's scenario work.

The second example presents GE's (General Electric's) classic experience with the scenario approach, and the third example recounts scenario generation at Shell, drawing primarily on Wack's well-known work (1985).

Klein & Linneman found scenario writing to be the most widely used forecasting technique after trend extrapolation. Again, among corporations in the top *Fortune* 1,000 Industrials, the use of scenarios increased from 22 percent in 1977 to 57 percent in 1981. Klein & Linneman anticipate that the use of scenarios will increase. Yet, they point out that most companies use a "very informal scenario writing approach, with little reliance on rigorous methodologies" (1984, p. 72). In contrast to this rather pessimistic assessment, the three following examples present a more upbeat picture of a gradually emerging operational technology for the managerial practice.

2.3   EXAMPLE 1: DRUCKER'S MACROENVIRONMENTAL SCENARIOS

This book's focus is on computed strategic scenarios. Environmental scenarios serve as input to the computation of strategic scenarios. Historically speaking, environmental scenarios were the first to appear on the scene. They represent one of the few ways strategic managers can account for the overriding, pervasive issues of business and the economy.

The world economy is composed of the "real" economy of goods and services and the "symbolic" economy of money. In the world economy, credit and capital are no longer tightly bound to each other. They are, indeed, moving further and further apart. Economists expect the real economy and the symbolic economy to come together again. They do, however, disagree on whether they will do so in a soft landing or in a head-on collision.

Drucker (1986) contemplates a total of five environmental scenarios: two hard-landing scenarios and three involving a softer landing.

Under the first hard-landing scenario, with every deficit year the indebtedness of the US government increases, as do the interest charges on the US budget. This in turn raises the deficit even further. Sooner or later, foreign confidence in the United States and the US dollar will be undermined. Foreigners will stop lending money to the United States and try to convert their dollars into other currencies. That will bring the dollar's exchange rates crashing down and also create an extreme credit crunch, if not a liquidity crisis in the US. The question is whether the result for the US would be a deflationary depression, a renewed outbreak of severe inflation or, the most dreaded affliction, stagflation—a deflationary stagnant economy combined with an inflationary currency.

Under the second hard-landing scenario, it is Japan, not the United States, which will have to face an economic crisis. The Japanese hold about half the dollars the US owes to foreigners. In addition, practically all their other claims on the outside world are in dollars. The Japanese have resisted all attempts to make the yen an international trading currency, lest their government lose control over it. This is the first time in peacetime history that the major debtor nation owes its foreign debt in its own currency. To get out of this debt, the US needs neither to repudiate it, nor declare a moratorium, nor negotiate a rollover. All it has to do in this scenario is devalue its currency and the foreign creditor has effectively been expropriated. The repercussions for Japan extend deep into its trade and domestic economy. By far the largest part of Japan's exports go to the United States. If a hard landing were to come about, the US might well turn protectionist almost overnight. It is unlikely that Americans would let in large volumes of imported goods were the domestic unemployment rate to soar. This would immediately cause severe unemployment in Tokyo, Nagoya, and Hiroshima, and might indeed set off a true depression in Japan.

The third scenario envisaged is no longer the hard-landing kind. Under this rather soft-landing scenario, neither the United States, nor Japan, nor even the industrial economies altogether experience the hard landing. Hit instead are the already depressed producers of primary products—food, forest products, metals, and minerals. Practically all these items are traded in dollars. Their prices might not go up at all should the dollar be devalued. Actually, they went down when the dollar plunged by 30 percent between the summer of 1985 and the winter of 1986. Thus, Japan may be practically unaffected by a dollar devaluation. Japan needs dollar balances only to pay for primary product imports, for it buys little else from the outside world and has no foreign debt. The United States may not suffer either and may even benefit as its industrial exports become more competitive. Although the primary producers sell mainly in dollars, they have to pay in the currencies of other developed nations for a large part of their industrial imports. The world's leading exporter of industrial goods, the United States, after all still accounts for only one-fifth of the total. Moreover, the dollar prices of the industrial goods furnished by others—the Germans, Japanese, French, British, and so on—are likely to go up. This might bring about a further drop in trade for the already depressed primary producers. Some estimates of the possible deterioration go as high as 10 percent. That would entail considerable hardship, not only for metal mines in South America and Zimbabwe, but also for farmers in Canada, Kansas and Brazil.

Under the fourth scenario, there is no landing to speak of, either hard or soft. The scenario method indicates that, after all, it is possible that the economists are wrong. Both the US budget and trade deficits could continue growing, albeit at lower levels than in recent years. This could happen if other countries were willing to put money into the United States based on other than purely economic considerations, on their own internal domestic politics, for example, or simply on the desire to escape risks at home far worse than a US devaluation. Although this fourth scenario is so far more supported by facts than macroeconomic theory, it is already playing. The US government talked the dollar down by almost one-third, from a rate of 250 yen to 180 yen to a dollar, between the summer of 1985 and the winter of 1986. This was one of the most massive devaluations ever of a major currency, even though it was simply called a readjustment.

The United States' creditors unanimously supported this devaluation and indeed demanded it. More amazing still, they responded by increasing their loans to the United States and substantially so. International bankers agree that, paradoxically, the more lenders stand to lose by lending to it, the more credit-worthy the US becomes! Again, a major reason for this attitude is that the biggest US creditors, the Japanese, clearly prefer even heavy losses on their dollar holdings to domestic unemployment. Without exports to the United States, Japan might have unemployment close to that of Western Europe. A 9 to 11 percent unemployment rate is already concentrated in politically sensitive smokestack industries in which Japan is becoming increasingly vulnerable to competition from newcomers such as South Korea.

Lastly, the fifth is a clear soft-landing scenario. Both the US government deficit and the US trade deficit are expected to decrease together until both attain surplus or at least balance, sometime in the early 1990s. Presumably both capital flows and exchange rates will then stabilize, with production and employment increasing and inflation decreasing in major developed countries. This is the global, that is, macroenvironmental, scenario to which the Clinton administration appears committed, as are the governments of most other developed countries.

This section presented an example of classical environmentally driven scenarios. We introduced Peter Drucker's scenarios first because he is an influential author. His work is widely available in libraries and bookstores worldwide. Yet, the thrust of this book is not toward the fairly unstructured forecasts of the future. That is the domain of the emerging field of 'futurology.' Our work duplicates neither in its objectives nor methodologically that of Olaf Helmer and Norman Dalkey.

The thrust of this book is to show how firms not only can anticipate their future, but also actively engage in creating it. A first, most important step is to analyze those mechanisms that might bring it about. For this purpose, the prevalent practice of guesstimating environmental scenarios is methodologically flawed. Far sounder and more productive for strategy design is the new concept of computed scenario. Throughout this book, we point out that the first-generation environmental scenarios should serve as input to computing a second generation of scenarios. Computed second-generation scenarios become a direct instrument for decision making. This should explain the name *decision* or *strategic* scenarios for these computed scenarios.

2.4 EXAMPLE 2: GE'S FORECASTING WITH SCENARIOS

To control for the deficiencies in guesstimating environmental scenarios, General Electric (GE) drew together into a single framework a variety of forecasting tools. GE's approach to scenario construction is based on a Delphi expert panel and on trend-impact and cross-impact analyses. The output of these techniques is used to develop probable future scenarios.

Figure 2.4.1 details the sequence of steps of the procedure used by GE from the 1960s until the early 1980s, and no longer in use, as recounted in the business policy textbook series of Jauch & Glueck as well as in other authors. The Jauch & Glueck textbooks are published by McGraw-Hill, but the GE framework has been well disseminated and there are numerous references to it. An in-depth assessment of its components emerges gradually throughout this book. The principal ones noted here are the use of the Delphi technique to detect critical variables and indicators, and that of the trend-impact analysis and the cross-impact analysis to assess the implications of the interactions among critical variables and indicators.

Much ink and effort are expended annually on the Delphi technique in the US. Because its name is reminiscent of the ancient oracle of Delphi in Greece, people ascribe to it the quasimythological quality of being at once scientific and visionary. It's in fashion. Essentially, the Delphi technique involves asking an anonymous panel of experts to estimate individually the probability that certain events will occur in the future.

The panel members have several opportunities to revise their initial estimates. They look at the anonymous responses from other experts on the panel to gauge how much their individual estimates deviate from other estimates. Accordingly, Delphi forecasting can be described as constrained guesswork. Yet, its probability estimates are trusted because the panelists selected are experts in their respective fields. GE's procedure entails an initial determination of the key trends by the planning analysts, followed by constrained expert guesswork by one or several panels of outside experts.

Cross-impact analysis (CIA) is a complex technique typically performed by computer. Its output is a matrix showing the favorable or unfavorable interaction of likely developments generated earlier by the Delphi panel. In the southeast corner of Fig. 2.4.1, for example, the CIA matrix predicts that nuclear energy by fusion—instead of fission—will reduce the oil price agreed upon by OPEC members. It may also lead to more safety and environmental laws regarding the mining and burning of coal.

In the procedure pioneered by GE, the cross-impact effects among likely developments are dealt with qualitatively, with + or − signs. Yet, the cross-impact technique has quantitative derivatives. One such method is the Battelle BASICS technique presented in Section 5.3.

Trend-impact analysis (TIA) begins with an outside expert's assessment of the

Figure 2.4.1 **GE's Environmental Analysis Procedure Used from 1960 Until the Early 1980s**
Initial Source: **General Electric Company**

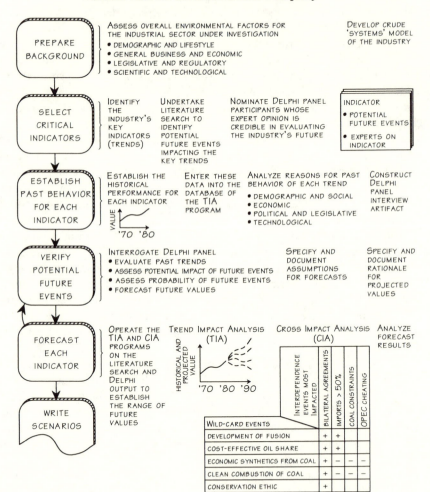

Delphi panel's forecast of an environmental trend. For example, those interested in measures that curb greenhouse gases might use extrapolation to forecast a continuing downward trend in the use of ozone-gobbling chlorofluorocarbons (CFCs). Possible influential factors, such as the way people trade off a life saved today against one saved tomorrow, could then be added to the forecast to generate alternative future trends.

Finally, the output from the Delphi panel, cross-impact analysis and trend-impact analysis would then be used to develop a series of probable future scenarios.

As a historical introduction, the following section will present an example of the type of business-level scenario that an individual SBU (strategic business unit) might undertake. In fact, throughout the book we will be making the point that the first-generation environmental scenarios should serve as input to the computation of second-generation scenarios. These second-generation scenarios are computed to become direct instruments of decision making—hence the name decision scenarios for these computed scenarios. We will also call the final scenarios strategic scenarios. Appendix A provides more information on the underlying theory.

2.5   EXAMPLE 3: SHELL'S CLASSIC SCENARIO EXPERIENCE

Scenario-driven planning was introduced at Shell on an experimental basis in 1970. One of the first efforts of Pierre Wack's corporate planning team was a major project called Year 2000 (1985). Wack's team presented a grim outlook for the world economy. Its scope convinced many executives at headquarters that the existing systems of planning and forecasting were no longer adequate and that something new was needed. By 1972, scenario-driven planning had gained support among members of the Committee of Managing Directors, the top corporate policymaking group at Shell.

Next, Wack's corporate planning group focused on the development of a first tier of six different scenarios about the global environment, with a fifteen-year planning horizon. Many of these scenarios indicated a probable major disruption of the traditional energy supply situation. They suggested that an energy crisis might not be far away. Many managers were skeptical of these warnings, but the energy crisis of 1973 gave Shell's planners new credibility throughout the firm.

In addition to Wack's efforts, his insightful prediction of the 1973 crisis, together with a couple of costly investment failures under the traditional forecasting approach, further aided scenario-driven planning. One mistake was Shell's joint venture with Gulf Oil into high-temperature reactors; it turned into a $750 million loss. Another was the questionable investment of $63 million in a polyethylene plant at Carrington in Britain. Such events helped to secure a major role for scenario-driven planning at Shell. Its development continued throughout the 1970s. Gradually, it evolved from the management of pure industry or environmental scenarios to the computation of fairly specific short-term event sequences.

The long-run global scenarios developed by Wack's corporate planning team were disseminated to the planning departments of Shell's operating companies. These strategic business units (SBUs) were encouraged to use the corporate environmental scenarios in their own strategic planning. Yet, the scope of the corporate scenarios was often too broad for use in a specific SBU's strategic situation. They did not directly help, for example, an SBU manager decide on the expansion of a service station network in a particular district. As a result, Wack's team distributed scenarios more selectively and encouraged the operating companies to prepare some of their own.

A second tier of short-term scenarios for near-term planning was also developed at Shell. Wack's team introduced this tier in 1975 to aid the short-term planning process. These scenarios were different not only in their time horizon, but also in content. Shell's operational corporate scenarios focused more on short-term economic and business cycle developments. It was hoped that these would be directly usable by the SBUs. The second-tier scenarios turned out to be one more step in the company's learning process.

The third level of scenario-driven planning at Shell consisted of environmental change scenarios developed by individual SBUs. The global scenarios coming from Wack's planning team did not focus on the factors critical to SBU managers. SBUs were encouraged to develop their own competitive scenarios. Yet, the managers of any particular SBU, say Shell UK, were unlikely to limit themselves to developing purely local scenarios. Although they might not agree with the corporate scenario, they would want some idea of the international variables that could affect their operations.

So, Shell's SBU managers developed global scenarios of their own. At Shell, such differences in scenarios were welcome because they stimulated thought and were creative rather than destructive. Yet, Shell feared that two related SBUs, that is, chemical and refining, might develop conflicting scenarios and plans.

As Shell gained experience with scenario-driven planning, the techniques evolved and became more systematic. Participation spread from corporate planning to the individual SBUs. The time frame expanded to incorporate both long-term and short-term scenarios. Coverage included economic, political, social, and technological factors. Scenario-driven planning came to be accepted as a helpful alternative to traditional forecasting. Where possible, variables such as GNP, inflation, and oil prices were quantified. However, its long-run scenarios remained qualitative in nature.

Another change came in the number of scenarios prepared. The 1972 effort had no fewer than six global scenarios with a fifteen-year horizon. The number was later reduced to three. Dissatisfaction was also expressed with this approach because many managers took a middle course when confronted with several alternatives. They planned without seriously considering the outlying scenarios. As a result, Shell corporate planners eventually reduced the number of scenarios to two.

Typically, these were strongly opposing pairs generating a semblance of devil's advocacy, a concept much valued by Cosier and Schwenk (Cosier, 1981a, 1981b; Schwenk, 1984). Wack's planning team based this approach on the argument that it is impossible to predict the future exactly and dangerous to try. "The idea is that neither scenario is right, but that if you're prepared for both, you'll be ready to cope with the real world. The important thing is to *think*, to break through the manager's conventional views."

Shell's experience with scenarios rightly reveals their importance for strategic planning. The information published by Shell and Wack reveals more about the overall environmental scenarios and trends than about specific changes in strategy. Shell UK regularly avails its planning blue book to the public and thereby excludes its own responses to environmental signals and pressures. There are indications, however, that Shell undertakes strategic-scenario analysis.

Changes in strategy should be capable of modification in case of rapid response from rivals firms. Managerial plans and strategies are supposed to be resilient about all possible combinations of global developments. As will be stressed in the course of our narrative, mid-level strategic scenarios eminently deserve to be undertaken. Consequently, we will dwell at great length on the techniques appropriate to the generation and analysis of midlevel strategic scenarios rather than on the extreme cases of global or local scenarios.

2.6   WHY ARE FORECASTS ALWAYS WRONG?

Forecasting with Delphi

We have been talking about scenario generation, not forecasting. Both in the United States and abroad, business and government policymakers endorse environmental forecasting enthusiastically. Yet, despite the popularity, growth, and enthusiastic reception of environmental forecasting, the usefulness of straightforward mathematical extrapolations is severely constrained in practice. The reason is that predictions of the effects of changes in the environment are much more difficult than foreseeing the primary changes themselves. Integrating environmental scenario implications into the strategic plans of a strategic business unit (SBU) is even more problematic. Yet, in the organizational context of limited resources, established programs and political interests, potential changes and combined effects must be linked to strategy design.

Forecasting is an indispensable management tool but for the short term only. Forecasts of future trends are seldom value free. Often, they are meant to be self-fulfilling prophecies, to marshal resources and efforts toward stated goals and objectives. Alternatively, they are self-defeating prophecies that create action to avoid the negative consequences of the status quo. (Utterback, 1979).

In 1963, a stunning analysis of cotton prices questioned both the assumption of normal distribution of log-returns and the absence of long-term trends and cycles from the capital asset pricing model (Mandelbrot, 1963).The tails were four times as fat as one would expect if the log-returns followed a Gaussian or normal distribution. The Brownian motion assumptions underlying financial time series undermine the CAPM (capital asset pricing model) and the efficient market theory (Korsan, 1992). Economists have finally agreed that relying on straight forecasts, even sophisticated ones, may not work.

Futures research sometimes ignores the intellectual roots of systematic conjecture, concentrating instead on specific techniques, albeit sophisticated, and on specific forecasts. To be effective, the planner's mathematical sophistication has to be commensurate with his or her conceptual sophistication. Application of the principles of value-free science to forecasting may at best be a self-deception. At worst, it is a limitation imposed on the range of human possibility.

Several methods have been developed in attempts to forecast the direction of changes in the business environment and their effects on the firm. They include various means for the aggregation of expert opinion, constrained extrapolation of past trends, and scanning or monitoring the environment. The aggregation of expert opinion or Delphi method was introduced in Section 2.4. Usually, it entails scoring or weighing the experts' estimates of the probability that a future event will occur, or the time by which the experts feel it will occur.

In the Delphi technique, such questions are asked of an anonymous panel of experts. The panel members are given several opportunities to revise their estimates, and are given feedback on the distribution of the panel's estimates and, sometimes, the reasons for extreme positions. Versions using a computer to increase interaction and feedback among panelists have been developed. Delphi has been used widely to forecast demographic, political and social changes that affect the business environment.

The use of the Delphi technique, which originated at RAND, has been sharply criticized from the same source. According to Sackman (1975), the popularity of this approach to forecasting changes in the business environment has resulted in poorly designed studies. These were rendered inappropriate by the peer pressure on each participant for converging toward the average group response. Delphi-style consensus-seeking methods do not provide for a dialectical debate among decision-making participants (Acar, 1983; Linstone & Turoff, 1975; Mason & Mitroff, 1981).

The Linstone & Turoff text gives a comprehensive treatment of Delphi and finds most of the existing forecasting techniques unsatisfactory on grounds both of substance and method. Ackoff (1981) concurs and goes on to describe three sets of conditions under which perfectly accurate forecasts could be obtained. First, if a system and its environment did not and could not change, and we knew its state at any one moment of time, then, of course, we would know its state at any other moment of time, including the future. Clearly, these conditions do not exist, but even if they did, preparation would not be possible because it requires change. Second, perfectly accurate forecasts would be possible if a system and its environment were, or were part of, a deterministic system. If the future of a system that could be so predicted were determined, it would not be subject to change. Preparation presupposes choice but determinism presupposes a lack of it. Third, we would be able to predict the future perfectly if we were omnipotent (Ackoff, 1981, pp. 59-60).

Indirectly, this quote also illustrates the reasons why we consider the most popular Delphi method to be more of a consensus-building rather than a direct forecasting technique. Hax & Majluf (1984) oppose bounding strategic situations by making a pseudoscience out of the art of consensus building

The simplest and by far most common forecasting method is *trend extrapolation*. Extrapolation of trends in technological parameters and capabilities has been one of the earliest methods used to forecast changes in technology. According to empiricists, current rates of substitution are used to project the future substitution of one product for another (MacNulty, 1977).

Originally, extrapolations of past trends were simpleminded and amounted to little more than graphically extrapolating a curve. With the developments in quantitative methods, the discipline known as operational research or management science (OR/MS) has become quite sophisticated in carrying out those extrapolations. The art of monitoring and scanning environmental signals today relates to statistical decision theory. Prior probabilities assigned to competing hypotheses about the future are revised as more tangible evidence of changes in the business environment becomes available.

Forecasts of general trends, structural changes, and performance of the economy can be quite accurate. Yet, changes in political and legal constraints are most difficult to anticipate and may strongly affect accuracy in other areas. Even if economic trends are clear, their effects on a specific firm's choices are not. Neither is the effect of foreseen technological change in the environment obvious.

Farmer (1973) emphasizes the shortcomings of forecasting changes in the environment. After examining forecasts published in *Fortune* from 1933 to 1950, Farmer concludes that even the most radical forecasts were too conservative when compared with actual trends. Single-point forecasts have not fared well during the past two decades either (Schnaars, 1989; Schnaars & Topol, 1987).

Environmental scanning or monitoring involves searching the environment for signals of change. Identifying possible consequences and choosing events to observe can help verify the speed and time of the anticipated change. This approach is predicated on the idea that changes in the environment will be visible in increasingly tangible forms before they assume economic, political, social, or strategic importance.

A most interesting environmental monitoring application is Utterback's trend analysis program developed for the Institute of Life Insurance. Members of the institute monitor different areas of change and contribute occasional reports on trends that might affect their industry. Yet, firms in other industries can benefit from these reports.

The most serious flaw of straight forecasts is their inconsistency and inability to fathom the impact of several changes taken together. Many forecasting and scenario construction techniques attempt to simplify significant interactions among important variables. When a simple structure exists, with a few interactions among variables, then a simple network or tree structure is often adequate in practice.

Shell's Scenarios Were *NOT* Forecasts

When the interactions among many variables are complex or unknown, then computerized matrix methods such as cross-impact analysis or analysis of system structure are used. Here critics will point out the switch from pure forecasting models to some form of structural equation modeling and simulation.

Simulation models that forecast changes in the business environment have been largely exploratory. Measurement problems and a lack of understanding of the interrelationships among variables do not help either. Often, such models capture the interaction between environmental variables and constraints, but very little substantive or content-oriented theory is ever applied.

In 1983 Peter Schwartz surprised his superiors at Shell with a proposal to study the future of the Soviet Union. An end to the Cold War was unimaginable at the time. With Mikhail Gorbachev still unknown in the West, the mere utterance of terms like 'glasnost' (openness) and 'perestroika' (restructuring) could have made Margaret Thatcher, Yuri Andropov and Ronald Reagan shudder.

Yet, the scenario *discipline* that had already evolved at Shell let its managers and planners reexamine their mind-sets. It enabled them to bring forth prior prejudices and to rethink carefully whether ancestral assumptions kept their hidden fears vivid although repressed. They felt uncomfortable with the Troll's large shadow approaching.

The Troll project involved a large deposit of natural gas under water in the North Sea. The necessary platform and satellite wells bear a cost estimate of 6 billion dollars. Yet, if available, Soviet gas would have been much cheaper than the gas from Troll. Articulating whether to go ahead with the Troll gas field required suppressing the enthusiasm that still makes Shell's top executives innately optimistic about new projects, especially when the prices of oil and gas are high.

Collaborating with a tough-minded, creative Dutchman, the research team of

Schwartz presented a plausible future in which the prices of oil and gas could fall. OPEC's solidarity could collapse. Also, demand for oil could decline easily in an era of ecological frugality and energy efficiency. That could cause a collapse in the prices of both oil and gas.

Probing further, the research team asked what could change the Soviet Union. In 1983, the team presented Shell's top executive directors with two scenarios: *Incrementalism* was the first, and the *Greening of Russia* the second.

> The answer was clear: a failing economy might simply make it impossible for the Soviet Union to afford its rigid system. We saw that the Soviet economy was facing a major crisis: its productivity was declining, and its birthrate had declined twenty years before its standard of living, the Soviet Union had only two alternatives: either muddle through, or open up (Schwartz, 1991, pp. 57-58).

Where Information Technology and Scenarios Come Together

It is not surprising that good scenarios sometimes resemble predictions. In the 1950s, Forrester developed the system dynamics simulation modeling approach to study the effects of feedback loops on highly interconnected industrial management systems. System dynamics is a field of inquiry that offers a new way to think about organizational problems. Using basic concepts of system structure, especially interconnectedness through feedback loops, it can explain how structure determines behavior (Forrester, 1968b). System dynamics simulation models can provide strategy support (Hall, 1976; Merten, 1991; Morecroft, 1984 & 1990; Morecroft & van der Heijden, 1992; Senge, 1990; Senge & Sterman, 1992), and a tool for companywide continuous improvement (Richmond & Peterson, 1992a).

This method comes complete with a simulation language called DYNAMO©— DYNAmic MOdels (Pugh & Carrasco, 1983), with both mainframe and microcomputer versions. New system dynamics simulation languages, running exclusively on machines with the Intel i386 or better microprocessor, include DYSMAP2 (Dangerfield, 1992) and Vensim™ (Eberlein & Peterson, 1992), while *iThink*™ (Peterson, 1992; Richmond, Peterson, & Charyk, 1992), Microworld Creator™ (Diehl, 1992a; Diehl, 1992b) and STELLA®—Systems Thinking Experiential Learning Laboratory with Animation (Peterson, 1992; Richmond & Peterson, 1992b) have been available to Macintosh users for years. Since 1994, these simulation languages have also been available to Microsoft® Windows™ users.

An exemplary application of system dynamics as a forecasting tool is Forrester's attempt to model the United States' economy. This effort followed his seminal studies of *Industrial Dynamics* (Forrester, 1961) and *Urban Dynamics*

(Forrester, 1969). With relationships and data reasonably well known and available, Forrester's team showed that the US economy was less responsive to monetary and fiscal policies than was usually assumed. It also showed that the underlying structure of its production system has greater long-term effects on the economy's dynamic behavior than is generally expected.

Despite severe criticisms and a great deal of talk these days about the deindustrialization of the United States, Forrester's results were fairly accurate. It is not the US economy that is being deindustrialized but its labor force. Since 1973, manufacturing production has been uncoupled from manufacturing employment. During the last seventeen years, manufacturing production in the US rose by almost 40 percent in constant dollars. Yet, manufacturing employment went down steadily.

On 19 July 1990, the 16 participants of a system dynamics course at Fordham University's graduate business school were experimenting with an early version of Morecroft & van der Heijden's model of the oil producers (1992). One participant asked:

> Professor, if the oil swing producer country is unhappy about its market
> share and floods the market with oil, that will bring both the spot and the fu-
> tures price per barrel down. Will the rest of OPEC just sit and watch?

On 3 August 1990, the cover page of the *International Herald Tribune* rumbled something about a *surprised* Bush administration caught off-guard by Iraq's invasion of Kuwait on 2 August 1990. Iraq's rationale for invading Kuwait's oil fields was that Kuwait was forcing down oil prices by flooding the oil market through overproduction (Farris, 1990).

Critics of system dynamics point out that it involves some creative structural equation modeling and should not be construed as an instance of straightforward forecasting. They see its success as a greater proof of the power of modeling and simulation than of straight forecasting.

They are right! Scenarios are not about predicting *the* future, but about perceiving and reperceiving possible *alternative* futures. Good scenarios tempt managers to examine carefully what might have been sacred premises before and say: "Yes. I can see how that might come about. And what I might do about it." Scenarios help managers and firms learn and anticipate.

Does this sound familiar or have we not been to this neck of the woods before? Organizational learning makes it necessity to develop a gut-level feeling about the relationships underlying a firm's strategic situation. Then, the implications of foreseen changes may be understood. Only the managers know the important actors and variables affecting their business, for they live with them on a daily basis. More than anyone, they understand how the search for cause-effect relationships to explain system behavior sometimes gives way to a belief in irrationally random events. Managers deal with the important actors and variables affecting their system daily, trying to deflect environmental threats or, better still, to turn them into business opportunities. The way a firm can and should deal with changes in its environment must be factored by means of scenario-driven planning into the strategy process to attain strategic productivity.

Managers should incorporate both in their mental models and in their plans, the same way that their competitors might move or respond to tactical moves. Their analysts should sit with them, encouraging them to articulate and to analyze the relationships among these important issues. In sessions with managers, analysts need to become good sparring partners. Attaining greater specificity will empower the managers for better insights. Then, the meaning of combined changes in the environment and in strategy will be understood. At implementation time, this will result in better communication and in a more analytically bent leadership style.

SUMMARY

In the face of today's societal shift from the industrial to the postindustrial era, the business environment is dynamically complex, discontinuous, and turbulent. No matter how perceived, this shift is a force that business clearly must deal with. Scenario-driven planning *has an overriding goal and an underlying mind-set to help companies confront looming challenges and render themselves efficiently adaptive. Its overriding goal is to enrich the way managers and their consultants think, learn, and feel about strategic situations in the turbulent global environment.*

In times of rapid and unexpected change, strategic incrementalism guided by mental models alone becomes insufficient. It is in such situations that scenario-driven planning has leverage and can make the difference between good and poor decisions. Because they are alternative ways of seeing the world, scenarios afford us a systematic method of breaking out of the decision maker's single worldview. Scenario-driven planning offers a fresh perspective and provides the ability to reperceive reality.

Parts I, II, and IV of this book survey the use of scenario-driven planning for strategic management. Parts III and V provide a primer on its applications. The Appendix introduces the theoretical foundations of existing scenario methods and reviews the planning tools used in the book.

Part II

THE ROLE OF THE ENVIRONMENT

Chapter 3

Environmental Turbulence and Uncertainty

An important facet of strategy design is to gain an informed yet optimistic under-standing of a firm's environment, both business and sociopolitical. This chapter provides a primer on the way the strategic management literature has dealt with the environment and the various kinds of environmental uncertainty. Is there un-certainty about the shape of the playing field itself?

3.1   ENVIRONMENTAL TURBULENCE

The Industry Environment

Environmental Signals. In 1989, Lockheed ran a series of advertisements in *Business Week* to remind its readers of the invaluable role that the Texas Rangers played during the 1846-1848 war with Mexico. This was a spirited way of showing the invaluable contribution of competitive intelligence to strategy design. Lockheed's point was that all natural systems, organizations included, are embedded in a network of relationships involving other systems. A business firm depends on its environment for resources and support. In turn, the environment depends on business firms for output and jobs.

Systems theorists apply the second law of thermodynamics to business and government. They note that maintaining permeable boundaries to absorb inputs can prevent a system's degeneration into unstructured random states (Ashby, 1963; Beer, 1981; Deutsch, 1963; Wiener, 1948). This is the good news. The bad news is the implication that the environment is fast paced in its changes and fluctuations. Managers have to navigate rough seas that are not always of their own making.

The considerable contribution of economics to strategic management highlights the importance of environmental analysis for today's managers. Changes in the environment originate either in a firm's macro environment or in its task environment. The *macro environment* is outside the industry or industries within which a firm is competing, whereas the *task environment* includes clients and customers, suppliers, regulatory agencies, competitors, labor markets, the scientific community, and other relevant stakeholder groups. The task environment, also called the transactional environment, is often the focus of analysis aiming at uncovering an industry's structure.

The economists' implicit assumption has been that market imperfections arise from the collective behavior of firms within an industry or strategic business area (SBA). Yet, the strategy field holds that collections of firms cannot produce any material asymmetries, and it is good that they do not. Instead, competitive asymmetries arise from the unique capabilities of individual firms or strategic business units (SBUs). A recent empirical study shows that industry effects account for only 8 percent of the variability in returns of SBUs contained entirely within a single industry (Rumelt, 1991).

Whether change signals originate in the firm's macro or task environment, their propagation proceeds mechanistically through the network of cause-effect relationships in which every organization is embedded. These signals might be as much a matter of decisions made by change agents (i.e., other firms or governments) as they might be the result of fortuitous environmental influences. In either case, the propagation of change signals cannot be halted. Signals about changes triggered in the environment initiate a process of strategic response, which determines the magnitude and timing of control levers that a firm's managers might attempt to manipulate. Anticipating changes in the environment while creating a firm's own future is, in our view, the best response to environmental uncertainty.

A costly investigation leading to the negligence liability ruling by a court may concretely signal a firm's failure to anticipate changes in its task environment. An equally loud but early and easily detectable signal entails punishment in the form of shopping elsewhere, the natural modus operandi of customers caught in a low-quality delivery situation. Even if they cannot observe quality directly, often customers will infer product and service quality from the behavior of sellers (Davis & Holt, 1993).

Customers know, for example, that it is less expensive to attach directly observable extra features, such as warranties, to high-quality products and services than to low-quality products and services. Firms that sell high quality frequently signal the value of their products and services by including such features. Competing firms that fail to detect such informational asymmetries promptly develop a reputation. Assuredly, they deserve the direct regulation of their future.

Strategic Threats and Opportunities

A threat or opportunity in the environment may be disregarded by some firms and eagerly anticipated by others. Danger arises when a firm behaves as though it could dominate and predict all changes in its environment. Danger also arises when attempts to dismiss uncertainty reduce a firm's sensitivity to changes in the environment and its flexibility to deal with them.

Timing changes in strategy rests on a firm's strategic readiness for response, which in turn depends on

- its environmental surveillance system,
- the techniques applied to environmental scanning and analysis, and
- the mentality and alertness of its managers to .i.environmental change signals (Georgantzas, 1992).

Aguilar (1967) describes environmental scanning as the process that seeks information about events and relationships in a firm's environment, the knowledge of which can help top management chart the firm's future. Environmental scanning entails partitioning the external environment into sectors, namely, cultural, economic, political, technological, and so on. This helps to establish a firm's information needs within those sectors. Data are usually collected by monitoring and forecasting changes in important variables identified in each sector. The data are then transformed into consolidated information, which is integrated into the firm's strategic planning process.

Several studies explore the effects of practicing environmental scanning on corporate performance. Glueck & Jauch (1984) examine several business cases to determine whether environmental analysis is indeed useful, and they identify a positive link between environmental assessment and corporate performance. Similarly, the data of Newgren, Rasher, & LaRue (1984) show that firms that practiced environmental assessment between 1975 and 1980 outperformed significantly those that did not.

Recognition of the environment's importance can be traced to economic theory, where competing firms affect the strategic choices of each other. The competitive structure of an industry's environment has long been recognized for its effects on strategy making. Economists have shown that pricing decisions, profits and investments vary depending on the degree of rivalry among competing firms. Markets for capital goods, finished goods, and services are essential for production. Barriers to perfect competition emerge when a few firms control the factors of production. In turn, these barriers create conditions of monopolistic competition, oligopoly, or monopoly.

Porter (1980, 1985), perhaps more than anyone else, has drawn management's attention to the necessity of analyzing business mobility barriers, particularly competitive entry barriers. Harrigan (1985) and MacMillan & McCaffery (1982) discuss exit and inertia barriers in more detail.

Table 3.1.1 shows entry barriers that prevent or seriously inhibit the movement of competitors into a product/market position. Entry and exit barriers inhibit or prevent the movement of competitors from industry to industry. Inertia barriers seriously slow down a firm's response to changes in its environment. It is challenging but useful to identify barriers unique to an industry.

Managers who choose to secure and to maintain control of strategic resources within an industry know and understand these barriers intimately. Mature firms do not usually lack resources but sometimes lack control over their resources. The challenge lies in a firm's capacity to anticipate the emergence of future barriers. Texas Instruments has consistently used experience curve effects to create barriers for other entrants, even in the Japanese market.

When entry barriers are low, emerging inertial barriers can help an aggressor improve judgments as to what is the most appropriate timing for a contemplated tactical move. In addition, the aggressor can estimate the lag required before defenders start responding in sufficient numbers. This has been the characteristic of many of Citibank's new products introductions in the 1960s and 1970s.

It has become axiomatic that strategic planning starts with some form of environmental analysis of managerial economics. Increased rivalry among firms in an industry and Porter's emphasis on the bargaining power of buyers and suppliers, as well as on the threats of new entrants and substitutes, strongly support this axiom. In effect, environmental analysis is often reduced in practice to industry analysis. Yet, changes in the environment beyond an industry's boundaries almost always significantly affect, and sometimes largely determine, what happens within the industry and its entry, exit and inertia barriers.

Table 3.1.1   Common Response Barriers [a]

Entry Barriers (Adapted from Porter, 1980 & 1985)

Capital requirements: to lease equipment and to build credit and image.
Components and raw material: access to supplies is blocked.
Differentiated product: customers are loyal to a specific product or brand.
Distribution channels: access to distribution channels is blocked.
Economies of scale: high investment is needed to be cost competitive.
Experience curve: know-how is kept from competition.
High expected retaliation: competitors will retaliate violently.
Specialized skills: access to critical skills is blocked.
Switching costs: customers would have to pay a lot to switch brands.

Exit Barriers (Adapted from Harrigan, 1985, and Porter, 1980 & 1985)

Customers, distributors, suppliers prevent exit.
Effect of large investment writeoffs.
Government proscription: government prevents exit.
Large cleanup cost: to leave sites in original condition.
Shared cost: which would have to be borne by other products/markets.
Union agreements: prevent exit.

Inertia Barriers (Adapted from MacMillan & McCaffery, 1982)

Bureaucratic politics: response creates shifts in power structure.
Portfolio position: affected division has low priority in corporation.
Procedures: response calls for policy or costly revision of procedures.
Strategic challenge: the move of an aggressor is nonthreatening.
Distraction: all competitors are busy fighting the last war.

---

a   Macroenvironmental and industry analyses are necessary for understanding strategic barriers.

Similarly, it is the environment beyond a country's boundaries that often determines what happens within the country. Prevailing economic theory, whether Keynesian, monetarist, or supply-side, considers the national economy, especially that of large developed countries, to be autonomous. It is the unit of both economic analysis and economic policy. According to Drucker (1986), this macroeconomic axiom of the modern economist has become increasingly shaky. Neither Britain nor the United States, the two major subscribers to this axiom, has done very well in the last thirty years. By all accounts, Britain has fared poorly among the group of leading EEC nations. Conversely, Germany and Japan have based their economic policies on the global economy. Both have systematically tried to anticipate its trends and exploit its changes as opportunities. Over the last thirty years, these two countries have fared better, both economically and socially, than Britain and the United States. Their focus on the global economy and the priority they give it may be the secret of their success. In the language of systems theory, both countries maintain permeable boundaries to prevent degeneration into unstructured random states.

Successful cosmopolitan firms, such as the Japanese and German car makers Honda, Toyota, Mercedes, and BMW, and the Swedish-Swiss conglomerate ABB (Asea Brown Boveri) anticipate changes in the global environment as opportunities. So do Citibank and Shell. Competitive dynamics has decisively shifted from the local industry environment to the global environment, as it has decisively shifted from the national economy to the world economy.

Firms that want to prosper must accept the idea that strategy design at the local industry level will succeed if and only if it strengthens, or at least does not impair, global strategic posture. They also have to accept the necessity of selecting the relevant milieu of important variables and relationships to be mapped on a case-by-case basis. These may not be best captured by simply going down the categories of a preestablished checklist. Environmental scanning, mapping, and modeling are worthwhile, value-adding, but demanding business activities.

Levels of Environmental Turbulence

The 1980s brought momentous changes to the world's sociopolitical systems and business scenes (Lorange, Scott-Morton, & Ghoshal, 1986). Increasingly, strategic management theory reflects this focus on the environmental and corporate changes. Yet, many approaches to strategy design still rely on processing industry information primarily at the national level.

Empirical researchers appear to be preoccupied with cross-sectional studies that examine the static rather than the dynamic aspects of strategy making. (Bourgeois & Eisenhardt, 1988). When the rate of change is extremely high, that information is often of questionable accuracy and quickly obsolete. Bourgeois & Eisenhardt term such conditions *high-velocity environments*, as exemplified by the airlines, banking, and microcomputers. The *dynamism* of these environments, as termed by Dess & Beard (1984), *turbulence*, in the language of Ansoff (1985), or *volatility*, in the terminology of Bourgeois (1985), is characterized by sharp and discontinuous changes.

A few researchers offer ideas about the actual processes by which changes in the environment occur in product markets, industries, and societies. From the manager's standpoint, the question is: Are these changes linked and systematic or fortuitous and arbitrary? As Glover (1966a, 1966b) argues, the effects of forces and events that may otherwise cause rapid change, that is, innovations, are dampened by the rate at which interconnected environmental components can absorb and accommodate such change, that is, acceptances.

Birnbaum & Ottensmeyer (1984) make the same point in a study of organizational adaptation to regulatory change. They note that organizational environments are partly institutionalized infrastructures associated with individual industries. If an industry is disturbed, it requires a long time to develop new structural dependencies for facilitating physical systems and transactions with other organizations. According to this optimistic view, the process of mutual adjustment mitigates and dampens the rate at which changes in the environment can occur.

Systematic research on this topic is limited. The conceptual foundations of environmental analysis cover an entire spectrum of theoretical assumptions. These are assumptions about the scope, structure, and organizational behavior that potential changes in the environment may cause. On one hand, organization theorists view the environment as being primarily unknowable and, for all practical purposes, a result of people's perceptual and cognitive mechanisms. On the other hand, some theorists agree with Michael Porter that industry structure is an objective economic reality. In the middle are some strategy theorists who visualize the environment as being a network of relationships, with changes stemming sometimes from the environment and sometimes from the organization itself (Lenz & Engledow, 1986). With a twist, this is the strategic management analogue of the rape-victim-calls-for-it syndrome. Yet, in this case, neither managers who lost their shirt because of a poor forecast nor their tax collectors are amused.

There is uncertainty about the structure of environmental uncertainty. This is a kind of *meta-uncertainty* that empirical studies of environmental analysis have attempted to dispel. Unfortunately, these studies have been too general in scope and unsuccessful with researchers. Typically, they lack clearly defined and differentiated environmental dimensions to facilitate the operationalization and measurement of theoretical constructs. So far, this line of theoretical research has not been of great assistance to practitioners either.

Several business commentators agree with our views. Magnet (1985) hints that cognitive and evolutionary-era models can always be enacted to spot megatrends in times of uncertainty. Also, the academic codification of environmental dimensions guided by the resource-dependence theory may still not meet the practical needs of strategic planners. They require precise referents for directing environmental scanning and analysis.

The state of the art in strategy is the same as that in organization theory, where the environment is described with the help of typologies. Such classification schemes provide an initial rough-cut theorization, allowing only a vague sense of the specific environment encountered. Among the numerous conceptual schemes that have evolved to describe the environment, one in particular has been quite influential in guiding strategic thinkers. It is the classification initially proposed by Emery & Trist (1965) and simplified by Duncan (1972). It captures four sets of environmental conditions, each more complex and troublesome for the firm than the preceding one (Fig. 3.1.1).

- *Placid environment.* External changes are not interrelated and are randomly distributed in the environment. Surprises are rare, but there are no major opportunities to exploit either. Duncan calls this the *simple-static environment* (cell 1).
- *Placid-clustered environment.* Changes are more patterned, and fore-casting them becomes crucial. Comparable to the economist's idea of imperfect competition, this type of environment allows firms to develop distinctive competencies to fit limited opportunities leading to growth and bureaucracy. Duncan terms this the *complex-static environment* (cell 2).
- *Disturbed-reactive environment.* Changes are patterned but subject to influence by firms. Comparable to oligopoly in economic theory, this type of environment makes changes difficult to predict, leading companies to increase their operational flexibility through decentralization. In Duncan's terminology, this is the *simple-dynamic environment* (cell 3).
- *Turbulent field.* Changes are more dynamic and complex, originating not only from autonomous shifts in the environment itself, but also from interdependence between firms and conglomerates. Organizational response is guided by social values that have been accepted by all members of the field. Turbulent environments are both *complex and dynamic* (cell 4).

Such classifications represent embryonic theories about the environment but lack specificity in describing a particular firm's strategic situation. Hiromitsu Kojima observes that

> conventional contingency theory concentrated on typifying the relationships between task environment and organizational characteristics. It gives only fragmentary answers to the question of why the effectiveness of the organization increases when there is a certain relationship between these factors (Kojima, 1989, p. 476).

Assuredly, 2×2 typologies are significant from the viewpoint of the clarity of exposition. They are more frequent in the organization theory and strategic manag-

Figure 3.1.1 Environmental Dimensions and Perceived Uncertainty
(Reproduced from Duncan, 1972)

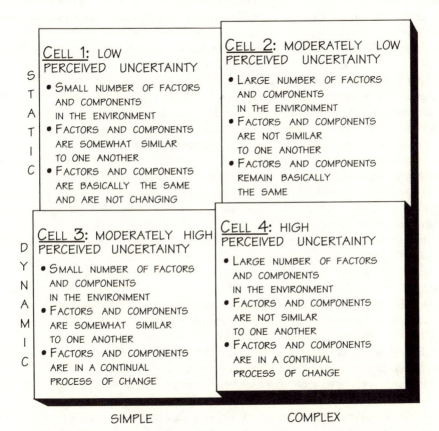

ement literatures than any other classification scheme. The mystical significance of dichotomous classifications affected even Leibniz, who associated 1 with God and 0 with nothingness in the binary system. Yet, the general class solutions that dichotomies provide leave out the specifics that decision makers need. Managers cannot wait until a better theory of the business environment comes along; they have to act now.

Their actions are more likely to succeed if they are able to anticipate the effect that changes in the global environment may have on their firms. Anticipating the severity and timing of impact depends on understanding the nature and structure ofa firm's strategic situation in relation to the environment. In turn, this requires understanding the causalities involved in the firm-environment interface. Both evolve over time according to case-specific patterns.

When environmental uncertainty increases, so does the need *not* for more, but for more pertinent information (Ackoff, 1967; Rappaport, 1968). It is the quality of information that counts, not the quantity. It is precisely at this point that the information processing perspectives on strategy and organizational design often err. Their conventional control-driven prescriptions require firms to increase their information processing capacity, assuming that more information will reduce and thereby control environmental uncertainty (Kojima, 1989, p. 476).

Unfocused information will not by itself do the trick. To produce innovative changes in strategy, managers must consciously ascertain the cause-effect relationships implicit in their thinking.

For innovation is not so much a process of gradually reducing uncertainty (processing information) in moving toward a prescribed goal. Rather, it is a process through which uncertainty is intentionally *increased* when circumstances demand the generation of chaos from which new meaning can be created. This process is full of discovery, surprise, and redundancy. Senior managers at Honda, in forcing the project members to challenge their most deeply held assumptions, forced them not to process information but to create it (Nonaka, 1988, p. 12).

To enhance their creativity, managers must explicitly ascertain deeply held assumptions in their mental models through causal models.

Bland generalities concerning broad classifications of turbulence will not do. In his text on strategy implementation, Ansoff (1984) extends the common dichotomous perceptions of environmental uncertainty. Essentially, he breaks down turbulent environments into *discontinuous* and *surpriseful*. This is a step in the right direction. Yet, it is not as helpful as a causal model might be, specific to the system structure of a firm's strategic situation.

The present volume marks a departure from mere classifications and advocates causal thinking. Initially relying on folk wisdom, a simple cause-effect explanation may take the form of a crudely visualized proportion between two variables. Yet, our strategy students quickly realize that explaining why a firm has performed well is more involved than merely observing that revenues have exceeded expenses for some time.

To fully gauge a strategic situation, seasoned managers probe the dynamic behavioral patterns caused by changes in the environment and in strategy. The new reality emerging in the economic and corporate scenes has to be somehow captured and incorporated into strategic management. In matters of strategy, the effective manager looks forward to managing uncertainty through new information creation, no matter how turbulent the environment.

3.2 ENVIRONMENTAL UNCERTAINTY

Managers at once incorporate at least two dimensions in their mental models about the future. One dimension is *time*. It keeps a manager busy asking: "How far into the future should I think about the implications of my decisions?"

Yet, systems theorists attribute most causes of strategic uncertainty to changes in a firm's external environment. Their argument rests on the second dimension, that of *uncertainty* about these implications, often located in the external environment. This uncertainty can stir a manager's mind constantly. Here are some examples of mind-spinning questions:

- Will there be significant differences between these implications, which we estimated at the start of our planning process (ex ante), and the actual measurable consequences at the end of the planning period (ex post)?
- What variables will determine the type and size of these differences?
- Will they originate inside my firm or will they result from independent changes in the external environment? (Schoderbek, Schoderbek, & Kefalas, 1990, p. 280).

The role of the environment is crucial in strategy making. The environment cannot be brushed aside; it must be used in taking stock of a firm's strategic situation. The increasing turbulence, complexity, and rate of changes in our global environment contribute to our lack of productivity and competitiveness. They render managerial decisions more and more difficult.

Linked to the systems approach (which Section 10.2 introduces briefly), organization theorist James D. Thompson (1967) considers dealing with uncertainty as *the essence of the administrative process*. The increasing uncertainty facing managers today not only impedes their primary task but, as discussed in Chapter 1, also slows down their capacity to learn from experience.

Research on changes in the firm-environment interface has not yet evolved into a coherent body of knowledge because of such conceptual and methodological issues. Early writers bemoaned uncertainty but seldom discussed it in detail. A pioneering study by Friend & Jessop (1969) advocated distinguishing between the environment, the strategic choices available, and the values held as potential sources of uncertainty.

Yet, the study did not clarify in what way perceptions of the environment partly relate to and partly complicate strategic choices in practice. March & Simon (1958) observe that, to cope with uncertainty, managers competing in a dynamic industry are likely to segment only the homogeneous aspects of the environment.

Much of the uncertainty literature tries to capture the notion of environmental stability. This stability dogma appears to be a reasonable aspiration, but even the simplistic structure of very simple systems often denies it (Beltrami, 1987, p. 51). Miles & Cameron (1982) try to distinguish between the rate and unpredictability of changes in the environment. Global firms use tactics such as buffering, collusion, long-term contracts, vertical integration moves and, more recently, the design and management of strategic networks to create a more predictable environment (Jarillo, 1988).

Environmental uncertainty also affects structure because more information must be processed among decision makers to achieve a given level of performance. Both Jay Galbraith and Oliver Williamson have made this point clear. Galbraith (1973) advocates the divisionalization of organizations, that is, the M-form, and Williamson (1991) restructuring, with an eye toward facilitating internal information flows.

Empirical environmental analyses have not clearly identified whether objective or subjective indicators should be used to assess environmental uncertainty (Bourgeois, McAllister, & Mitchell, 1978; Downey, Hellriegel, & Slocum, 1975; Mintzberg, 1979; Tinker, 1976). Wherever both objective and subjective measures are used, very low correlations between the two types are reported. Studies using subjective measures usually show stronger support for contingency propositions than studies using objective measures.

In contrast to subjective assessments of environmental turbulence, objective indicators are obtained independently of managers' perceptions of the environment. Their use reduces the bias and error inherent in perceptual measures obtained through structured questionnaires. Objective environmental indicators used include actual sales fluctuations in the recent past, price-cost margin fluctuations, frequency of product changes for the firm, instability in total employment, and census data for the locale of the organization. Most of these indicators are part of the transactional exchange of a firm's goods or services for money. They represent competitive or operating activities, which consist of purchasing, fabricating, distributing, pricing, promoting, advertising, and selling.

In addition, a business firm interacts with its environment through an adaptation activity. It is the activity that changes the markets the firm serves, the technology it offers, the products or services it sells, and the way it sells, promotes and advertises. This is the strategic activity that develops the firm's future growth and profitability potential. Operating activity only converts the potential of yesteryear's strategic activity into next year's profits. The two activities are closely coupled, but the nature of organizational work that conducts them is very different, as is clearly emphasized in the literature (Ansoff, 1985; Burgelman, 1983). This distinction may explain the low correlations between objective and subjective indicators of environmental uncertainty.

Another possible explanation for the inconsistencies within and across investigations of environmental uncertainty can be found within behavioral decision theory, particularly in research emanating from Carnegie-Mellon University and its disciples. Behavioral decision theorists conclude, with ample empirical support, that managers make choices using only a few sources of information processed with simple rules of thumb (Hogarth, 1980; Tversky & Kahneman, 1974).

Frances Milliken (1987) cautions managers about their lack of knowledge of environmental uncertainty in three crucial areas. Managers, she states, may be uncertain of

- Variables or states in the environment.
- The effect of environmental states or variables on organizational performance.
- Their organization's capability to take appropriate action.

This newer classification is easier to work with than the categories devised by Friend & Jessop cited earlier in this chapter. This is not to say that Milliken's typology cannot be improved. Its merit rests in redirecting the attention of managers and strategy researchers away from obvious categories toward a new way of thinking, in line with the harder sciences. Building on this foundation, we propose the uncertainty typology of Fig. 3.2.1.

It is possible to distinguish among four major sources of uncertainty. The rationale is that each source of uncertainty generates its own concerns, which have to be dealt with in a strategic inquiry. These sources are as follows:

U_1 = uncertainty about environmental events and trends
U_2 = uncertainty regarding competitors' moves and signaling tactics
U_3 = uncertainty about a firm's decision and action capability
U_4 = uncertainty regarding the coalignment of implementation tactics

Assuredly, strategic management cannot ignore the last type of uncertainty, U_4. Computed scenarios can and should be used to assess the feasibility of tactics for implementation. Yet, because of the direct effects of U_1, U_2, and U_3 on strategy design, this book focuses primarily on the first three uncertainty bundles.

Specifically, we propose a method that can serve as a transition between strategic problem framing and full-fledged system dynamics simulation modeling of strategic decision situations. Full-fledged system dynamics models are implemented on computers to simulate the dynamic behavior patterns produced by the system feedback-loop structure that underlies the relationships among variables pertinent to a strategic situation.

A good model of a firm's strategic situation should incorporate both hard and soft variables that contribute either directly or indirectly to the strategic uncertainties specific to the situation under consideration. Chapter 10 gives a brief introduction to the fire-rapid evolution of the system dynamics field, along with an illustration showing the potential insight provided by a system dynamics model.

The method we propose is neither purely computational nor purely conceptual; rather, it combines qualitative and quantitative analysis into an integrative strategic tool. It can deal with U_1 through the causal mapping we propose, namely comprehensive situation mapping (CSM). Then, the scenario generation phase of CSM handles U_2. Lastly, the scenario analysis and sensitivity phase allows U_3 to be re-duced. The same sequence would hold if the firm and its analysts were to go all the way down this road, and eventually to trade off causal mapping for full-fledged modeling and computer simulation of interacting environmental and strategic decision variables.

Chapters 5, 6, and 9 describe CSM gradually and illustrate its use through real-life business applications. Appendix C.2 gives a comprehensive summary of its features, whereas Part V illustrates the sensitivity analysis of various decision situations to multiple mixed and pure scenarios.

According to researchers who look at the way ideas are formed from perceptual experience, managers may perceive their environment incorrectly. For example, Daft & Weick (1984) and Dutton, Fahey & Narayanan (1983) reinforce Weick's view that firms read into the environment different attributes, with a complex interplay of perceptual, psychological, and political dynamics. The disquieting message emanating from this line of research is that firms might not actually have a real environment that could be objectively described.

To recall a point made in the previous section, Weick (1979) has advanced the intriguing thesis that managers actually manufacture their organizational environments. He describes this act of imagination as *enacting* one's environment. If Weick's vision is correct, there might well be no real environment out there to govern the destiny of business firms. Rather, organizations enact or invent their environment. In this case, however, why bother studying the environment if it is mainly an organizational myth or managerial fiction?

To sum up, several categories of environmental uncertainty beset the business enterprise. Weick's thesis adds a twist of the knife. We do not even know the extent of our uncertainty either about the firm or its environment. To paraphrase Peters & Waterman's cautioning words, Is this the case of paralysis by analysis?

Figure 3.2.1 Uncertainties Besetting Strategic Management

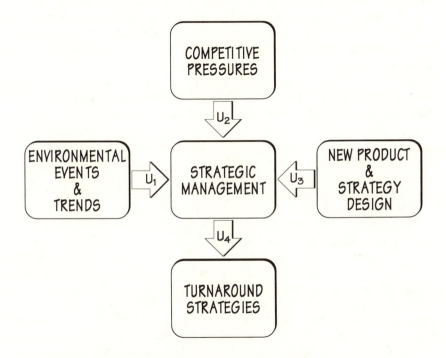

U_1 = uncertainty about environmental events and trends
U_2 = uncertainty regarding competitors' moves and signaling tactics
U_3 = uncertainty about a firm's decision and action capability
U_4 = uncertainty regarding the coalignment of implementation tactics

Not quite. For it is not our reflection on this particular managerial predicament that is creating it. We could adopt the incrementalist policy of blaming the stakeholder or the messenger for the bad news and having him or her beheaded. This ostrichlike policy, tantamount to burying one's head in the sand, is as old as humankind. The message of modern planners is to cast off past defeatism. Despite the difficulties, something can be done about environmental uncertainty and strategic interdependence.

Simple but dynamic environments are more difficult to gauge and to model than complex but static ones. Yet, most intractable are those fields that are both complex and dynamic; they are rightly termed discontinuous or turbulent environments. The usual information systems may fail to keep apace because of the turbulence. As discussed, the predicament of tomorrow's manager is further compounded if we acknowledge that it is at best tainted with uncertainty and at worst enacted by, or is a figment of, perceptions and imagination.

Something has to give, and something has to be done. Uncertainty should be neither denied nor worshiped; rather, it should be managed. It can and will be increasingly dealt with by scenario-driven planning.

SUMMARY

The art of strategy design begins with the recognition of environmental threats and their transformation into opportunities. The first pillar of wisdom is an awareness of the firm's dependency on its environment. Firms must learn to act on Porter's five forces, namely, competitors, buyers, suppliers, substitute producers, and potential new entrants. A second wise move would be to engage actively in environmental scanning, building competitive intelligence systems beyond internal management information systems.

In their responses to environmental challenges, firms are hampered by a variety of response barriers, such as entry, exit, and inertia barriers. These require keeping track of competitors' moves, resource requirements, and environmental opportunities. The strategic designers of the twenty-first century will be far more outward-bound than the organizational designers of the twentieth. They will have to scan the transnational business scene and to see well past the narrow task environment of a specific product line or line of business. They will have to devise ways to keep track of and to model environmental changes through triggering events and trends.

This must be done carefully, to ensure that the various changes considered are compatible. Because there is no guarantee that scenario components are compatible, managers and planners must screen both their basic assumptions and the compatibility of their scenarios. The following chapter deals with this challenge.

Chapter 4

Assumption Analysis for Strategic Turnaround

*Can this uncertainty be captured adequately for effective strategy design? There is
no need for pessimism here. We could at least look into the reasons for uncertainty
by pausing to consider what we are assuming about everything, and the likelihood
of all these assumptions turning out for the better. This chapter investigates the
crucial role of assumption analysis.*

4.1   THE ROLE OF ASSUMPTIONS

On page 55 of his 1992 book *Long-Range Planning of Japanese Corporations*, Toyohiro Kono, a leading Japanese authority on corporate planning, presents a model describing the multiplicity of processes and feedback loops involved in the strategy design process of successful Japanese firms. The feedback loops alone of our Fig. 1.1.1 give a rough idea of how complicated the strategic management process is. The actual process does not proceed in only one direction. Regardless of content, each round of decisions follows another round of decisions and earlier decisions become the underlying assumptions or premises of later decisions.

Yet, according to Kono, there is a starting point that could be used to sort out the potential mess, where "A plan of the plan is worked out.... The system of the plan, the process of planning and the assignment of responsibility for planning are all decided on" (Kono, 1992, p 54). In his model, Kono calls that starting point *Phase 1: Establishing Premises.*

Perceptive approaches to strategy support the necessity of problem framing. Some of these provide an indication of how to frame organizational problems in practice, often through a process of uncertainty dilution. Such is the process used in strategic assumption surfacing and testing (SAST), a noteworthy approach to strategy making (Mason & Mitroff, 1981; Mitroff & Emshoff, 1979; Mitroff, Emshoff, & Kilmann, 1979). This provocative approach opens up some interesting avenues worth exploring.

The premise underlying SAST is that modern managers face constantly changing conditions and environmental turbulence. Under the condition of environmental turbulence, problem framing becomes at least as important as problem solving. Conventional problem-solving techniques address well structured problems. Strategic planning methodology proceeds from stakeholder assumptions to data to strategy design. To gain a depth of perspective, SAST proposes to work initially backward from the strategy to the data to the underlying assumptions.

Like other systems-inspired methods, SAST views corporate performance as a complex joint product of a firm's environment and of its strategy. Figure 4.1.1a illustrates this through a complex web of causal relations connecting strategy and its effects on performance. In this context, analyzing or estimating a firm's performance becomes predicated on understanding the relationships among decision and environmental variables.

Assumption analysis attempts to uncover the real relationships depicted in Fig. 4.1.1a. It tries to unearth the assumptions made in the mental models of the managers crafting a strategy and in the formal models they use. An example of a formal model is the small causal map of Fig. 4.1.1b. This map shows a simplification of reality based on some stringent assumptions.

Figure 4.1.1 Examples of (a) a Corporate Model and
(b) a CSM Causal Map

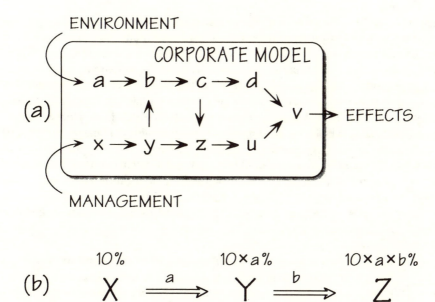

The first step is to proceed from the strategic direction already contemplated to uncover the basic assumptions embedded in the manager's choice of a strategy. Selecting the best strategy rests on identifying an acceptable set of assumptions. Once negotiated among strategy-team participants, and between at least two dialoguing teams, this composite set of assumptions becomes the explicit foundation of strategy design. It enables strategy options to be appraised in classical decision theory terms (Ackoff & Sasieni, 1968; Bellman, 1961; Drenick, 1986; Marschak & Randers, 1972).

The second step is to discover new strategies for consideration as potential solutions and to do so creatively. The authors of SAST recommend that this phase be a dialectic in which counterassumptions are generated and examined. Implausible assumptions and counterassumptions should be dropped. The management team now has a consolidated pool of plausible assumptions and can move deductively to identify new strategies.

These are the main lines of strategic assumption surfacing and testing. The basic idea is rich and inspiring. In practice, extreme care should be exercised in forming the management team that will uncover hidden assumptions. Mason & Mitroff (1981) recommend maximizing the differences in perspective among groups, so that each group's assumptions are indeed challenged by others. Ackoff goes so far as to argue that, even if there are only two people on the team, they should have different backgrounds. Ackoff's seminal text (1981) and the Mason & Mitroff book (1981) should be on the reading list of every thoughtful manager and planner.

The idea is that background differences would bring to bear quite distinct insight, and the resulting synergy could be very fruitful. Such a view is obviously attractive. Mason & Mitroff also recommend minimizing the differences within each group in order to reduce the possibility of internal conflict.

Once the team is formed, its members are asked to list important stakeholder groups. Later, they are asked:

- What is it that you assumed about the stakeholder groups so that, starting from these assumptions, you were able to derive your policy?
- What basic hypotheses have been traditionally held and why?
- Is the current set of assumptions internally consistent with other assumptions?
- What is the effect of making other assumptions?
- Can the particular policy under consideration stand up to other assumptions? Is it compatible with them? (Mitroff, Emshoff & Kilmann, 1979, pp. 586-587).

Stakeholder groups constitute a firm's transactional environment. The entire field of transaction cost economics vies to clarify the symmetrical contractual arrangements between each stakeholder group or constituency and the firm (Milgrom

& Roberts, 1992; Williamson, 1985, 1991). Walking the team through this list of questions is bound to be helpful. SAST assumes that, once unimportant and implausible assumptions have been dropped, the generation of counterassumptions will pose no problems. Yet, how are counterassumptions generated?

Some assumptions may be negated by a single opposite; others may possess several alternatives. The resulting set of assumptions to examine may be very large. The SAST authors acknowledge a difficulty in this regard. They recommend that each group list the one or two key assumptions associated with a proposed strategy. The underlying hypothesis is that each strategy rests on a unique set of assumptions to which it is best matched.

If a synthesis cannot be achieved, an assessment of the real cost (RC) and visible cost (VC) of all combinations of assumptions and strategies is in order. The visible cost VC is an interesting concept, but is all too often forgotten. It refers to observing the cost of a strategy when some other strategy is in fact correct. Indeed, information has a price. With the exception of Bayesian decision-making applications, this is all too often forgotten in organizational problem solving (Drenick, 1986; Marschak & Randers, 1972).

A real-cost RC is incurred if another set of assumptions turns out to be true. RC is defined as the estimated real loss in profit. Assumption analysis approaches such as SAST serve the useful purpose of considering the cost of lost opportunities. SAST brings up the issue; once it has surfaced, this method prods the managerial team into realizing that foregone strategic opportunities represent a real cost to the firm.

Mason & Mitroff (1981) give numerous examples of consulting interventions using the SAST. Their text should be on the reading list of every planning analyst or executive, together with the works by Ackoff (1970) and Ansoff (1965).

Mason & Mitroff emphasize the importance of assumption analysis to situation analysis, thereby raising some interesting questions. SAST proposes an innovative idea that we retain in our approach to scenario-driven planning. The idea is to design a method for uncovering present assumptions and strategies that may lead to the discovery of new assumptions and strategies.

SAST can be used in situations highlighted by the *culture* and *coalition* metaphors—two groups pulling in different directions—and when it seems sensible to apply an intervention technique that views all situations as simple-pluralist. It is designed to address pluralism, while its lack of concern about complexity has its advantages in simple situations. In such contexts, SAST can help explore different worldviews and bring about a synthesis, or at least an accommodation, as quickly as possible, so that participants can take some sort of action together (Flood & Jackson, 1991).

Yet, being an assortment of incompatible methodological elements, by itself SAST does not provide the comprehensive tool that managers need to benefit from its dialectical component. A conceptual foundation is missing, and computed scenarios are needed to assess the implications of strategic planning assumptions.

Our approach to scenario-driven planning has comprehensive situation mapping (CSM) at its core. CSM is a desktop tool that managers can use individually or in teams to make the system structure of a strategic situation visible, explicit, and comprehensible. Figure 4.1.1b presents an example of the CSM-type causal map.

Extending the work pioneered by the SAST authors, Acar's CSM intermeshes an analytic technique with a dialectical debate component. Chapters 5, 6, and 9 describe CSM gradually and illustrate its use through examples. Appendix C.2 gives a comprehensive summary of its features.

Briefly, however, CSM combines the alternative of a single-perspective analytic with pluralistic or multiperspective dialectics. This amounts to a simultaneous divergence-convergence scheme that is isomorphic or parallel to the proposition advanced by Alan Singer (1991, 1992). Singer has taken a radical step on behalf of the collective rational agency, drawing a sharp distinction between the single and the plural rationality in individuals, teams, and firms.

If Singer is right, then, are the goals that a firm's management team sets for the firm or of the firm? With both individuals and teams being multi- or plurally rational, Milan Zeleny rightfully and in a timely fashion asks: "Is Tom Peters right in insisting that markets do not buy anything, only individuals do?" (1992, p. 5).

In the first or divergence part of CSM's dialectical mapping, the view of each team is explored singly by building a separate causal map and computing change scenarios. In the second or convergence phase of dialectical mapping, the views of different teams come together through a dialectical debate. This debate consists of round-robin presentations, minor and major assumption analyses, and a possible consolidation of the participants' comprehensive situation maps.

This book describes CSM gradually, with detailed illustrative examples in the chapter ahead. Its convergence-divergence scheme owes an intellectual debt to the authors of SAST. Yet, by virtue of its use of CSM, assumption analysis is methodologically anchored in and supported by causal mapping (Acar, 1983; Acar, Chaganti, & Joglekar, 1985).

CSM integrates causal diagramming, dialectical mapping, and assumption surfacing and testing into an inquiry system of highly interactive, fully compatible components. This renders it at once methodologically sound and easy to use, in practice as well as in the classroom, for strategic situation formulation and for case analysis, respectively. Both managers and strategy students can use CSM, either individually or in teams, to explore ill-structured strategic situations and to create new knowledge out of their own questions, ideas, and experiences. CSM enables a smooth transition from the conventional case approach, by argumentation alone, to full-scale formal modeling for "learning all the time" (Holt, 1991).

Georgantzas (1990) supports the argument that modeling can transform strategy design into a systematic and purposeful-learning experience (Senge, 1990). The argument then goes from the process of real-world corporate planning and strategy design to the way it is simulated in our business school classrooms. The contribution of CSM and formal modeling to strategic management is rationality, the synthesis of perception and analysis (Star, 1990). We submit that business policy and strategy teachers should combine modeling with case studies to prepare their students for work in the real world.

The present situation is one of overreliance on the Harvard-style case method. A case study provides information that initiates debate and dialogue leading to action recommendations (Christensen et al., 1987). What the conventional approach to cases provides is a context of drama and realism, where the interplay between observation and debate may produce consensus. Yet, observations alone increase the likelihood of substantial misinterpretation (Copeland, 1958). The risk is even greater if the conventional case method remains the moot point in a complex, heterogeneous and rapidly-shifting global environment, for "it may well have done them [managers] and their organizations a terrible disservice, encouraging superficial strategies that violate the distinctive competencies of their organizations" (Mintzberg, 1990, p. 188).

4.2   CHANGES IN STRATEGY AND ORGANIZATIONAL LEARNING

Need for and Resistance to Change

In discussing changes in strategy regarding content, strategy researchers focus on shifts in business strategy as well as in corporate strategy. Those focusing on changes in corporate strategy define strategic change as the realignment in a firm's selection of market domains and in the resource allocation among them (Andrews, 1987; Ansoff, 1965; Gluck, Kaufman, & Walleck, 1980; Henderson, 1979). Those researchers focusing on changes in business strategy define strategic changes as the alterations in competitive decisions within particular market domains (Porter, 1980, 1985, 1991; Rumelt, 1974, 1991; Rumelt, Schendel, & Teece, 1991). But whatever their focus, strategy theorists propose formal mechanisms both for environmental monitoring and for managing changes in strategy.

According to Ansoff, existing mechanisms are not industry specific but relate to the velocity or rate of environmental change. Ansoff, one of the founders of strategic thinking, points out that such diverse industries as aerospace, banking, and semiconductors have developed and used essentially the same strategic management systems. Each system is responsive to a particular velocity, which a firm, no matter in what industry, must confront. To choose the system a firm needs, first, the velocity of its environment is diagnosed. Second, its managers select the system appropriate for this velocity. Hence the prevalent emphasis is on the notion of environmental turbulence and its levels.

An alternative route exists. In discussing changes in strategy regarding the process of strategic change, researchers also focus on shifts in formal management systems and structure as well as transformations of organizational culture (Barr, Stimpert, & Huff, 1992; Mackenzie, 1989; Tushman & Romanelli, 1985). In the process approach, it helps to think of an organization as a set of processes put in motion to change or turn it around for the better. This approach contrasts sharply with the more static view of an organization as a fixed entity and unit of analysis.

Modern organizations are incredibly complex and continually try to adapt to changes in their environment. The technology of scenario construction allows discovering possible implications of a problematic structure. Through computed scenarios firms can define and analyze changes in strategy as concrete and observable phenomena rather than as metaphor.

Covering the issue globally, Meyer, Brooks, & Goes (1990) and Drucker (1989) remind us that industry changes can be evolutionary or revolutionary. In the same vein, changes in strategy can be smoothly adaptive or creatively abrupt. The capability of managing abrupt changes cannot emerge from flimsy evidence and unplanned implementation. On the contrary, modern technology now provides us with ways to deal both with uncertainty and with change. Those who keep predicting the death of planning should recognize that, instead of simply saying "our organization is undergoing change," it has become possible with modern technology to define and to track down the changes. Instead of being satisfied saying "there is a need for a lot of change," one can now state how much, where, who, and what is involved. Visualizing a firm in the causal network of relationships with its environment (Fig. 4.1.1) allows one to approach strategy design with the right questions and mood.

The question of how often firms should or do undergo changes in strategy is a central debate in organizational theory regarding the effects of internal inertia, external, that is, environmental control of the firm (by stakeholder groups), and strategic choices over time (Romanelli & Tushman, 1986). According to one view, unless a firm modifies its orientation to the environment by altering its strategy-making process drastically, it adjusts its strategy incrementally rather than through a fundamental change.

The principal proponents of incrementalism are Quinn and Mintzberg. Quinn (1980) explains that strategy making is actually an incremental political process. Mintzberg (1987) points out that strategy might not always be consciously formulated, but gradually emerges from a pattern of incremental or small-scale decisions, that is, tactics. Ginsberg bypasses this subtlety by introducing the term *changes in strategy* to replace the term *strategic change*. On the other hand, Ginsberg (1988) dismisses strict incrementalism as unnecessarily restrictive. His dismissal of incrementalism is supported by the market and technology leaders' fundamental shifts or strategic reorientation, typically perceived as incremental (Pondy & Huff, 1985; Porter, 1985).

Mintzberg & McHugh (1985) are quick to point out that whether or not an organizational change is defined as strategic depends not only on "*where* you sit, but *when* you sit: what seems tactical today could prove strategic tomorrow." Because they often result from the ordinary workings of day-to-day processes, such shifts are often not discovered to be fundamental until after the fact. Yet, for the greater part, changes have to be deliberate to be sustainable (Hayes, Wheelwright, & Clark, 1988; Nord & Tucker, 1987).

Shifts in strategy occur when pressure for change overcomes resistance to change (Ansoff, 1984; Bigelow, 1982; Lundberg, 1984). Changes in strategy reflect the decisions of managers as they respond to future environmental threats and opportunities. These decisions can result from intentional rationality and learning (Bourgeois & Eisenhardt, 1988), assumptions about both the environment and the intrusiveness of organizations, or impulses (Daft & Weick, 1984; Singh, House, & Tucker, 1986).

Friesen & Miller have examined the relationship between pressure for and resistance to changes in strategy. It is a function of corporate executives' continuous effort to minimize two kinds of cost. The first kind of cost is a consequence of being mismatched with the economic and sociopolitical environment. Discretionary in nature, the second is the cost of changes in strategy to avoid the mismatch (Friesen & Miller, 1986; Miller & Friesen, 1984).

Both external and internal conditions specific to a firm's strategic situation can dictate the nature and timing of changes in strategy. Whether these conditions encourage or block changes, a central research question arises from an adaptation theory perspective. It concerns identifying and explaining how external and internal variables characterize the forces that signal disequilibrium in corporate behavior.

The primary implementation question concerns how changes in environmental and decision variables interact to stimulate movement toward continuous performance improvements. In the same vein, Mintzberg examines why periods of changes in magnitude are interspersed with periods of discontinuous changes in pattern. Mintzberg & Waters (1982) attribute these changes to the predominance of inertial forces in organizations. The frequency and duration of changes can vary across different external and internal conditions or environmental changes.

Mintzberg & McHugh observe that cycles of incremental and revolutionary changes in strategy are shorter in some organizations and more balanced between change in magnitude and change in configuration. Longer cycles are interrupted by occasional, brief, and disruptive spurts (Mintzberg & McHugh, 1985).

Cognitive Filters and Resistance to Change

Daft & Weick (1984) maintain that the interpretation of changes in the environment and in strategy depends on shared beliefs among a firm's managers. These are beliefs about the environment, whether analyzable or unanalyzable, and about the firm's intrusiveness, whether active or passive.

The notion of "ecological intrusiveness" (Witt, 1986, p. 41) is best understood in the context of what Sarason refers to as "behavioral regularities" (1982, p. 97). A *behavioral regularity* is the regular occurrence or nonoccurrence of a behavior or a series of behaviors—for example, our culture's behavioral regularity of not having chicken for breakfast. Behavioral regularities are often observed among children at school (Wahler, 1975), where their behaviors co-vary in orderly ways according to the behavioral repertoires of individual children (Martens & Witt, 1984; Voeltz & Evans, 1982).

While using these notions to describe the behavioral repertoires of business organizations, Daft & Weick (1984) suggest that when environmental uncertainty cannot be minimized by organizational action, managers may alter their perceptions of the environment so that it appears to be more certain. This happens because the psychological state of uncertainty regarding important decisions is very painful. As a result, decision makers may repress awareness of the uncertainty and act on a simplified interpretation of reality.

Behavioral decision theorists believe that five information filters surrounding the strategic decision-making process promote this phenomenon. The following filters encircle decision-making units (Hogarth, 1980; Morecroft, 1988; Tversky & Kahneman, 1974).

1. People's cognitive limits and Simon's notion of bounded rationality.
2. The influence of operating goals, rewards, and incentives to control information flows.
3. The effects of information, measurement and communication systems on decision making.
4. The effects of organizational and geographical arrangements.
5. The effects of tradition, culture, folklore, and leadership on information about changes in the firm's environment.

The concentric circles surrounding the strategic decision process of Fig. 4.2.1 represent these organizational and cognitive filters, which can both propel and limit the information made available to a firm's managers. Cognitive filter 1 prevents managers from processing all the information that a business or social system may present to them in the form of potential or desirable changes. The outer filters, 2, 3, 4, and 5, represent the ways in which the firm conditions the information available to its strategy makers.

The point of this theory of cognitive filters is that changes in a firm's external or internal environment can increase both pressures for and resistance to change. Changes in the external and internal environments reflect shifts in the values and

Figure 4.2.1 **Changes in Strategy Framework Extending the One Presented by Ginsberg (1988)**

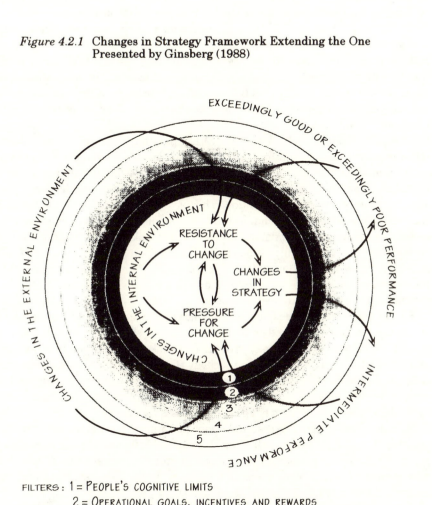

FILTERS: 1 = PEOPLE'S COGNITIVE LIMITS
2 = OPERATIONAL GOALS, INCENTIVES AND REWARDS
3 = INFORMATION, COMMUNICATION AND MEASUREMENT SYSTEMS
4 = GEOGRAPHICAL AND ORGANIZATIONAL STRUCTURE
5 = CULTURE, FOLKLORE, LEADERSHIP AND TRADITION

expectations of key stakeholder groups. Such changes can impair the firm's alignment with its institutional context. This, in turn, decreases the legitimacy of continuing with the previous strategy and encourages behaviors consistent with changes in strategy (Abrahamson, 1991).

Changes in the external environment indicate shifts in consumer values or competitive dynamics, whereas changes in the internal environment indicate shifts in organizational structure or managerial capability. Both external and internal changes lead to pressures for change by providing feedback that a firm is misaligned with its economic and sociopolitical environments. The realization of this misalignment decreases the effectiveness of continuing with the current strategy and increases the effectiveness of changes in strategy (Friesen & Miller, 1986; Leontiades, 1980).

This part of the framework in Fig. 4.2.1 culls some basic principles of human and organizational decision making. It explains how firms can display effective decision making despite members' cognitive limits and the overabundance of information. Managers make their judgments and decisions in a psychological environment provided by the organization. This psychological environment limits the range of changes considered and, in principle, supplies only the relevant information, a tiny subset of the available information, for making the correct choices at a given center of responsibility (Ackoff, 1967; Rappaport, 1968; Simon, 1957). The five filters show the components of the psychological environment and provide a convenient basis for obtaining strategic decision makers' perceptual measures of external and internal environmental changes.

Figure 4.2.1 also indicates that performance outcomes can influence changes by providing feedback on whether or not the current strategy is effective or just efficient. Alternatively, they may provide feedback on the corporation's willingness for, or capability of, changes in strategy (Ginsberg, 1988). Oddly enough, by either highlighting the effectiveness of current strategy or by revealing slack resources, exceedingly good performance can increase resistance to change. Typically, slack resources negatively affect willingness for change.

Similarly, the effect of exceedingly poor performance can be either positive or negative. This depends on whether it reflects the effectiveness of the current strategy or the capability of changes in strategy. In providing negative feedback on the current strategy, it can create pressure for change. In providing feedback regarding resource scarcity, it can create resistance to change.

In summary, performance outcomes increase resistance to change if they are exceedingly good or exceedingly poor. Conversely, they create pressure for change when they are at intermediate levels (Fombrun & Ginsberg, 1986).

Breaking out of the Impasse: Visualizing the Propagation of Change

The above arguments suggest that strategy implementation may have to be soft pedaled (Quinn, 1980). Yet, it cannot be soft. Our contention is that nothing is better for smooth strategy implementation than a superior design.

Despite these arguments and their empirical support, many organization theorists persist in modeling changes in strategy and structure as one-dimensional fixed entities. Damanpour (1991) urges these researchers to stop treating organizational innovation and change as unidimensional concepts. This analytical anachronism is the source of confused thinking about the nature and structure of strategic situations. It seriously impairs designing organizations that can efficiently adapt to changes in the environment (Georgantzas & Shapiro, 1993).

Figure 4.1.1 gives a brief overview of our approach to scenario-driven planning which leads to an alternative view of the firm-environment interface. It allows us to trace the cascading effects and sources of change both within the organization and within its global environment. Our treatment of scenario-driven planning captures the deterministic consequences of highly connected strategic situations.

We speak of the propagation of change signals rather than that of changes themselves. In some cases, a signal of change reaching a firm in a particular industry may not become operative. Heise (1975) used the idea of change signals to analyze dynamic causal networks. We call signals input at and propagated by a source of change *triggers* because the term is so descriptive of the transfer of change in a firm's economic and sociopolitical environment.

The idea of change signals can help firms chart the control levers that various actors or stakeholder groups might attempt to manipulate. We treat sources of change in the external environment as external change *triggers*. Sources of change in the internal environment are called internal change *levers* in the scenarios method we advocate.

Once initiated, the propagation of environmental changes and accompanying signals cannot be halted. Their start and propagation may be the result of some actors' decision or of some fortuitous environmental influence. In all cases, scenario-driven planning should allow identifying, at least temporarily, all change stimuli originating in various sources and purposeful actors, that is, persons or groups controlling those sources. When a change signal at one source triggers a chain reaction of change transfer, the initial change stimulus being propagated can be called the *triggering change*.

This approach to strategy design is fairly rich. It does not require us to assume that a particular firm or set of environmental forces remain in control of the same sources of change over time (Acar, 1983).

Part III, which serves as an advance organizer for Part V, introduces the case studies of Combank and Infoplus. These real-life applications as well as the Battelle case study of Chapter 7 and the basic prerequisites and design matters of the proposed planning system in Chapter 8, support the necessity of computing scenarios to enhance the plural rationality typically evolving in a management team.

Part IV provides a mental pause between the causal mapping of Part III and the computed scenarios of Part V. In part, the merit of Chapter 7 rests in shifting attention from the intricacies of rough-cut causal mapping and modeling, to managing strategic uncertainty through scenario-driven competitive intelligence.

Chapter 8 offers a devil's advocate interjection or counterpoint. Its basic prerequisites and conceptual underpinnings pertaining to the design of a scenario-planning system should let you reflect on and internalize the worldview diversity involved in the causal mapping and modeling of strategic decision situations.

SUMMARY

Environmental uncertainty can be crippling. Managers have to battle with two kinds of uncertainty. One affects the causalities involved in the transmission of change among environmental decision variables, and the second kind has its locus of control within their own value systems. Researchers who look at the way ideas are formed from perceptual experience conclude that managers may perceive their environment incorrectly, often reading into it different attributes according to a very complex interplay of perceptual, psychological, and political dynamics.

The increasing turbulence, complexity, and speed of change in the global environment contribute to the lack of productivity and competitiveness. They render managerial decision making more and more difficult. Not only does the increasing uncertainty facing managers today impede their primary task, but it also slows down their capacity to learn from experience.

The role of the environment is crucial in strategy making. The environment should not be brushed aside but should be used in formulating strategic situations. An effort to anticipate changes in the environment is one response to uncertainty. Changes in the environment originate either in a firm's macroenvironment, outside the industry or industries within which it competes, or in its task environment.

A triggering event in the environment is what starts the process of strategic response. It determines the magnitude and timing of control levers that a firm's management team might attempt to manipulate.

Several methods have been developed to forecast the direction of changes in the environment and their effects on the firm. They include various means for quantification of expert opinion, constrained extrapolation of past trends, and scanning or monitoring the environment. The most serious flaw of existing forecasting techniques, however, is their inconsistency and inability to fathom the impact of several changes taken together.

Despite empirically supported arguments, many organization theorists persist in modeling changes in strategy and structure as unidimensional static entities. This analytical anachronism is the source of confusion about the nature of strategic situations, which seriously impairs designing organizations to become more efficiently adaptable and creative. Our approach to scenario-driven planning leads to an alternative view of the firm-environment interface. It will allow the cascading effects and sources of change to be traced both from within the firm, through internal levers, and across its global environment, through external triggers.

Part III

INTRODUCTORY APPLICATIONS

Chapter 5

Infoplus (A)

This example relates one of our research projects undertaken in the newly formed division of a large nonprofit institution in New York City. Our intervention aimed at helping a team of public servants and government contractors design the strategy and organizational structure of an intrapreneurship *project. The unique situation of Infoplus provides an interesting case study that incorporates market penetration as well as growth and survival issues. We have changed the real names of both the parent and the startup organization to GCB and Infoplus in this writeup. In addition, we mention no project participant by name. Simplified for illustrative purposes, the present chapter excludes some details from our original report to the GCB and Infoplus constituents.*

5.1   INTRODUCTION TO INFOPLUS

Executive Summary

Infoplus is a nonprofit service of the General Consortium for Business (GCB) in New York City. Designed to help local business and industry retool through information technology (IT), this newly formed division of GCB contributes to the economic development of the local business community. Infoplus represents a unique form of partnership between local business and government.

GCB's IT strategy has given Infoplus access to hundreds of government databases within the Bureau of the Census, the Bureau of Labor Statistics, and the Bureau of Economic Analysis. It also has direct access to GCB's internal consultants, specializing in business and industry, government, social sciences, and demography. Besides having distinguished researchers among them, these experts can help Infoplus' partner firms interpret and use consolidated information in the context of business applications.

The director of Infoplus and two GCB internal consultants were the primary participants in our project. Infoplus had originally been their idea, so they were the natural choice for identifying variables pertinent to its strategic situation. The variables identified include

- Initial support and funding by federal, state and city foundations.
- Partial autonomy from GCB.
- Development of human, financial, and physical resources.

An intriguing question arose during our intervention. It was whether Infoplus would be able to stand on its own within three years from its inception, without any further support from its parent company other than using the services of GCB's internal consultants. Whatever the effects and interconnections among its pertinent variables, Infoplus' future is not predetermined. It remains open to several possible scenarios. The actors in the system possess multiple degrees of freedom which they will be able to exercise through action to attain their professional and organizational objectives. We computed a number of scenarios to help management explore whether Infoplus would "pass the acid test."

To answer this question, we helped our participant crew at Infoplus frame its strategic situation from several different perspectives. To enable the participants reperceive Infoplus' future through a multiperspective dialectic, our scenario-driven planning approach combined the following modeling methods.

- The causal diagramming method of CSM: Comprehensive Situation Mapping (Acar, 1983).
- The variable classification approach of MICMAC: Matrice d'Impacts Croisés Multiplication Appliquée à un Classement (Godet, 1987): cross-impact matrix multiplication applied to classification.
- The computational method of BASICS: BAttelle Scenario Inputs to Corporate Strategy (Honton, Stacey, & Millett, 1985).

Our scenario-driven planning intervention unearthed Infoplus' sensitivity to external funding for financial resources as well as to GCB's initial support for human and physical resources. Infoplus had been using both resource bundles since its inception. We showed that, if the allocation of these resources were to continue as planned, then their synergistic effects would enable Infoplus to increase its capacity and service capability. In turn, this might generate more demand for Infoplus' services and bring long-term revenues to ensure its survival.

Conversely, the worst-case scenario embodies possible budget cuts at GCB that may result in low initial support and resources for Infoplus. If stringent, these cuts could bind Infoplus' capacity and capability. A reduction in GCB's internal consultants would certainly downcast Infoplus' visibility in the local business community and thereby reduce revenues. If this scenario plays, then Infoplus may not pass its three-year acid test.

Budget cuts can reduce the availability of research consultants. Yet, the overhead that GCB will no doubt charge may alone suffice to enact the low-revenue scenario. If high enough, the overhead charges will deflect revenue from Infoplus and thereby restrict its resource-allocation decision autonomy, again binding its capacity and service capability . Then, again, Infoplus will not be able to stand on its own within three years from its inception.

Our scenario-driven analysis of GCB's partnership with business sought to gain insight into the dynamic behavior caused by the system structure underlying this strategic situation. The results show exactly how Infoplus' future performance depends on the moves of multiple actors, such as the federal, state and city foundations, as well as GCB's managers, internal consultants, and spokespersons.

Information Technology Trends

First, let us examine the context within which Infoplus operates. Highly competitive world markets force managers into a desperate search for business solutions. Those motivated by an overriding desire to survive do everything they can to increase profit margins. Firms and their governments adopt no-smoking policies to lower insurance premiums; unions agree to wage cuts. Top managers fly coach and fire their middle managers.

Gone are the days when good management and hard work invariably led to success. The work ethic has now become a mere prerequisite to business survival. Ironically, only recently have US firms realized that information technology (IT) can give them a competitive edge. Assuredly, we read about new and innovative uses of information systems every day. Yet, our business community may have been unhurried in designing IT strategies for competitive advantage.

The 14 June 1993 *Business Week* Special Report on "The Technology Payoff" concludes that more than a country's macroeconomic policy, "international trade agreements, and even access to natural resources, the ability to harness extraordinary technological change will define economic winners and losers in the foreseeable future" (Gleckman et al., 1993, p. 68). The report is talking neither of hardware nor of software alone, but of "the new industrial revolution" driven by technology as a form of social transformation (Zeleny, 1986). Along with its brainware and support net components, firms and their governments can use information technology *not* to control but to find order in the chaotic world of today's global economy. If both the Japanese and the Germans use information and other forms of high technology to upset competitive positions (Georgantzas, 1991), why can't we?

To give but one example, Germany has built an export infrastructure to support the performance of its Mittelstand or midranking, that is, small and medium-size, firms. Aside from its banking and trading system situated in the nineteenth century, other aspects of this support net formed after the end of World War II. Bankers, diplomats, and trade association officials are part of it.

In dozens of countries, Germany's embassies, banks, and chambers of commerce funnel the details of potential export deals through newsletters and electronic databases. Most Mittelstand respond quickly—so fast, in fact, that they may not even bother to patent their ideas before taking them to the market. For example, Geers moved its tiny microchip-based hearing aid from the drawing board to retailers in nine months. Former US President Ronald Reagan was pleased to wear one (Schares et al., 1991).

The results of a Peat Marwick survey of 150 British firms show that 60 percent of them do not use information about competitors or markets when designing their strategies (Peat Marwick Management Consultants, 1990). Historically, tradition-minded managers would introduce or accept changes in strategy only when they had to; now, they may have to.

The stark reality of the business world is that IT strategies provide firms with opportunities to create a competitive advantage or to negate the advantage of a leading competitor. Firms whose managers confine themselves to the electronic data processing (EDP) view of information technology lose ground, eventually reverting to survival or *crisis* management.

Information technology is gradually becoming the common thread of every strategic concern in business. It can both drive and enable the financial imperative that profit should be a top management consideration. Those who must look ahead increasingly realize that IT is now crucial to the success of nearly every business, and thereby support the necessity of information technology. IT has thus become the responsibility not only of line managers but also of information executives. It is thought that IT-based research pays off: firms with high return on investment (ROI) spend twice as much on computers and information systems as do firms with low ROI (Long, 1989).

Yet, if IT-based research is the most effective means for searching for a competitive advantage, then why hasn't every firm and country undertaken one?

Designing an IT strategy requires human, financial, and energy resources. It is also time consuming. The implementation of information systems to achieve a competitive advantage is a perfect example of a situation in which firms and governments find themselves investing a lot to enjoy a marginal ROI.

If achieving a competitive advantage were easy, then a firm's competitive advantage would be no advantage. There are also risk and uncertainty in the implementation of information systems. Traditionally, managers prefer to maintain the status quo rather than subject their firms to the downside risk of failure, even at the expense of losing market share. Gaining market share is the upside potential of investing heavily in IT.

New information technology results resolutely from changes in strategy. Reducing resistance to change again requires investing in human, financial, and time resources (Ansoff, 1984). Fortunately, the global business environment and fierce overseas competitors now focus managers' attention on computer and information resources. Firms and governments that challenge their managers to tap the potential of these resources are gaining a competitive advantage. These successes press status quo champions to change their attitude.

Such traditionalists may be reluctant to share information because they equate information with power. Indeed, most information technology solutions make more information available to more people, including subordinates and customers. To achieve an IT-driven competitive advantage, managers must be willing to dispel the prevailing introcentric attitude toward strategy design. Cavaleri & Obloj associate this attitude with the exclusive use of "internal financial data and previous track record" (1993, p. 206).

The mind-set of the new realities of the 1990s is that if information is to be beneficial to a firm, then it should be shared. Therefore, in theory at least, Infoplus should become very busy and its IT-based research services highly sought after. Infoplus could give its future partners a competitive edge by letting them share consolidated information pertinent to their market and business environment.

James A.F. Stoner states that strategy design serves the systemic function of reaching out to the business environment. Then, firms internalize the interests and concerns of customers into an integrated process management (IPM) through information sharing (Stoner, 1989; Stoner, Taylor, & Wankel, 1988). The objective is not simply to inform, but to *in-form* the customer into the product life cycle through IPM (Zeleny, 1991).

Deming (1986) supports the necessity of IPM, with a product in the customer's hands still viewed as part of the production cycle. According to other IPM and TQM (total quality management) proponents at Fordham, the "customer is the purpose and driving force of the enterprise, and must be integrated into the process of production or service delivery. Improving the quality of such customer integrated process becomes the tool to assure customer satisfaction, and to amplify the customer's role as a driving force for the enterprise" (Hessel, Mooney, & Zeleny, 1988, p. 142).

We live in the age of information; this *is* the computer revolution era. Yet, progress in information technology management is much slower than what television advertisements would have us believe. The social transformation of IT management entails a certain mind-set that is to be nurtured. The transformation cannot just happen.

Leading firms in the United States have adopted the mind-set required for designing new business IT-enabled strategies. To add value to each customer transaction, they treat information technology as a new resource of innovation. They use it neither to control nor to replace them, but to support the quality-improvement effort of front-line service employees. In these fortunate firms, top managers take every available opportunity to encourage their subordinates and peers to use IT automation and job enrichment (Long, 1989; Schlesinger & Heskett, 1991).

Yet, how do they know that their firm is using effective IT tactics? Where and how do information technology decisions affect potential business opportunities? What are the requirements for strategy to guide IT planning?

These are some of the questions that information technologist Peter Keen tackles in his book *Shaping the Future* (1991). Keen believes that the ideal objective of an information technology strategy is to transform an organization into a fully open system. Accordingly, he delineates the business functionality of the IT *platform*, a construct that incorporates the reach and range dimensions of information technology. In his ideal IT platform, any computer-generated transaction, document, message, or telephone call should be used in any other system, regardless of the hardware and software configuration of its source.

Following the direction of Keen's line of reasoning, what might be the *ideal* management technology that can transform organizational mind-sets?

So, we get to the process of modeling strategic decision situations, the management technology platform from which a management team can frame questions, study, look at, adjust, test, change, and discover how things work and why things happen in strategic situations. The rough-cut mapping and modeling process introduced here and in the following chapter can create other models and thereby generate both questions and answers—the essence of creative learning.

Modeling is a fundamental process by which individuals and organizations learn and discover. It has nearly the same meaning as discovering too. When we think of models, we picture the physical type we can perceive with our senses. Yet, there are also models within the wondering perplexity of human minds. There, they exist mentally as well as physically.

5.2   ORGANIZATIONAL SETTING

The Infoplus institute attempts to increase both the reach and the range of the IT platform beyond the level that small local firms could afford on their own. If it survives, this unique partnership between business and government will contribute to the economic development of the local business community.

GCB created Infoplus to help the American *Mittelstand* of New York City discard any prevalent introcentric mind-set toward strategy design. The mission of Infoplus is to provide its business partners (i.e., firms with a limited IT platform and no research facilities of their own) with the most recent and comprehensive information on, and expert analysis of

- Global business and industry trends
- Competitive and environmental intelligence
- Foreign and local market studies
- Worldwide patent and trademark searches
- Legal precedents
- Foreign and local government regulations
- Foreign country risk

Infoplus seeks to build and maintain a procurement assistance service for its business partners, a current awareness service on import and export possibilities, business transfers, and expansion plans. At the request of a customer or partner, Infoplus can also undertake original research in the areas of accounting, banking and finance, management, surveys, and market studies under the supervision of GCB's internal consultants. Original data searches are carried out by experienced information specialists or by subject experts of GCB's worldwide information centers, under contract.

To become useful information, data must be interpreted by experts. GCB's internal consultants give Infoplus the expertise needed to interpret and use information in the context of business applications. Infoplus can release no information without GCB's approval.

Infoplus may be a division of GCB, but it was really the intrapreneurial pet project of a GCB account executive, now Infoplus' director, and two of GCB's internal consultants. On the very first day of our intervention, all three of them confronted us with their need to clarify Infoplus' organizational structure. They were in the process of drafting a grant proposal for external funding for Infoplus. One of the potential granting agencies had requested a description of Infoplus' organizational structure. Naturally, this immediate concern was voiced within five minutes into our first meeting.

We could have dismissed the organizational design problem as extraneous to our scenario-driven planning project. Yet, ruling it out might have meant foregoing an opportunity to build a model and to compute scenarios motivated by a real problem. Besides, our client group felt strongly about this problem.

Our decision to collaborate with Infoplus' director and the two GCB consultants gave credibility to our intervention. It transformed a potentially short intensive project into an extensive working relationship. Moreover, this decision was consistent with the modeling recommendations of Edward B. Roberts of Pugh-Roberts Associates in Boston. He notes: "If you want to achieve changes in an organization as a result of your corporate modeling work, the problem or opportunity that you select must be important to the client. Otherwise, that client will neither pay much attention to the modeling effort, nor bother with its resulting recommendations" (Roberts, 1978, p. 79).

The purpose of our intervention was to build a deeper understanding of the dynamic interactions between Infoplus and GCB as well as between Infoplus and its potential customers. Our participation in the design of Infoplus' organizational structure helped us understand exactly how it planned to transform each initial sales call and customer transaction into a service relationship through partnership.

Figure 5.2.1 depicts a segment of our design work for Infoplus. The figure shows the adopted organizational structure, which incorporates the flows of author ity, work, and resources, as well as the projected transformation of each initial sales call and customer transaction into a long-term partnership.

Infoplus' director commands a small regiment of online database searchers, full-time clerical staff, and research fellows. A small salesforce 'sells' Infoplus' services to new customers. As business grows, this force will help Infoplus maintain an ongoing service relationship with those customers who choose to become partners.

Portrayed in Fig. 5.2.1 are GCB's liaison and the external, mostly IT, consultants who periodically confer with the director and the partners of Infoplus. Along with this advisory role, the GCB liaison also coordinates the assignment of internal consultants to research projects that either new customers or partner firms initiate.

By adopting the *matrix* organization of Fig. 5.2.1, Infoplus has abandoned a fundamental management tenet of each subordinate reporting to one and only one superior officer (Fayol, 1972). Instead, Infoplus has chosen to implement its strategy and to coordinate business transactions through an unconventional, multiple command system (Davis & Lawrence, 1977). The following section describes how the decision to adopt the matrix structure was reached.

Figure 5.2.1 INFOPLUS' Organization

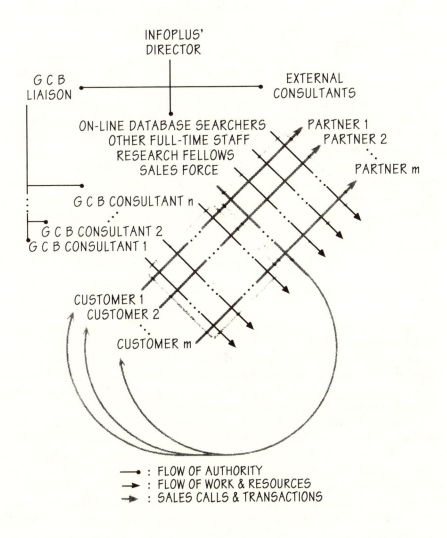

The director of Infoplus and GCB's internal consultants serve as input managers, while new customers and partners specify the desired output of research and computer searches. Infoplus employees and GCB's internal consultants meet with new customers or established partners on a daily basis. They work with them in small adhoc client-worker teams to diagnose the research needs of each client and to plan detailed computer searches.

Adopted as a result of our intervention, the matrix structure of Infoplus allows managing environmental uncertainty, which concerns both new market and new IT developments, to maintain a high operational efficiency and to implement its growth-through-partnership strategy. Assuredly, the matrix structure creates administrative tension. Yet, it provides the flexibility required to make changes in strategy at every level. New market opportunities and the development of new information technology frequently require such changes.

The GCB liaison and Infoplus' director also work together as a team. They coordinate business transactions, including new capacity additions. These additions allow strengthening Infoplus' capability and thereby managing the tension that the matrix organization creates.

Yet, new capacity additions require personnel and capital investment. One of the questions that arose during our intervention was whether Infoplus could build a customer-partner base large enough to stand on its own within three years from its inception. This translates into whether Infoplus could accumulate demand for its services and thereby enough revenue to operate without further support from GCB, other than using internal research consultants.

5.3   TRANSFORMING INFLUENCE DIAGRAMS INTO CAUSAL MAPS

To address the issue of expanding Infoplus' customer base, we helped the two GCB consultants and Infoplus' director reperceive its future by framing and reframing its strategic situation from different perspectives. Our approach to scenario-driven planning combined introductory elements of CSM, MICMAC, and BASICS to help our clients consider different points of view and perceive how their articulated strategy could determine Infoplus' future.

Nearly all our work sessions were in the director's new corner office, overlooking Park Avenue with a side view of the MetLife building. We used the round table in the director's office, with a legal size note pad and a pen in one hand and a freshly brewed mug of coffee in the other. The freshly painted walls of the new office, the newly installed carpet, a sizzling zillion-byte RAM, 50 megahertz workstation, with its optical drive to enhance multimedia presentations, and, of course, a percolating coffee machine created the right ambiance for our late-Friday-afternoon meetings.

In the process of articulating Infoplus' matrix structure and strategy, Infoplus' director and the two GCB internal consultants identified many variables pertinent to its strategic situation. The entire Infoplus crew is familiar and felt comfortable with influence diagramming (ID). So, we used our recycled paper pads not only to list variables and actors pertinent to the situation, but also to map the relationships among variables.

Throughout the intervention, each participant took turns translating the verbal arguments and comments that the rest of us made about variables and relationships into simple causal maps. This hands-on involvement of the Infoplus crew in causal mapping produced high ownership of the constructed models on the part of each participant.

ID is a desktop tool that business managers and researchers can use individually or in teams. It allows capturing the web of relationships among variables pertinent to a business situation, and its purpose is to clarify the relationships among such variables. In the specific version of ID we have adopted, short names describe the variables, each a source of change in itself or for other variables. The connecting arrows are not vague conceptual relationships, but show the channels for propagating the effects of change over time (Maruyama, 1963; Weick, 1979).

Most practitioners and researchers do not distinguish between cognitive mapping and influence diagramming; yet, there is a difference. Cognitive mapping can take many different forms (Bannister & Fransella, 1971; Eden, 1978, 1988; Eden et al., 1979; Kelly, 1955). ID is a well-defined modeling technique (Diffenbach, 1982; Hall, 1984; Ramaprasad & Poon, 1985; Richardson & Pugh, 1981) ideal for the simple representation and communication of the system structure underlying a strategic situation. Appendix C gives a brief summary of influence diagramming, a scenario-driven planning tool.

Four weeks into our intervention, with our organizational design work for Infoplus complete, we tried pulling together all of our ID sketches into one cohesive influence diagram. We did this by splitting our small group into two teams. Each team used an Ackoff-Ozbekhan reference scenario—the time development of system behavior Infoplus would have had if there were no significant changes in its strategy and environment (Ackoff, 1981; Ozbekhan, 1977). In each team this scenario served as a tangible manifestation of system behavior portrayed by the smallest possible set of cause and effect relationships among the variables pertinent to Infoplus' strategic situation.

In week five, we started our session early. Each team had to present its work to the other, without any discussion permitted during these round-robin arguments. It was interesting to observe how each team had rearranged and even renamed most of the variables and relationships it had identified in the first four meetings. One team presented an influence diagram with twenty-seven variables, while the second had reduced its map to twenty variables.

Our approach to scenario-driven planning incorporates the divergence-convergence cycle of information creation suggested by Rappaport (1960). This cycle is a material ingredient for a dialectical inquiry (DI) interchange aimed at unearthing critical assumptions and prominent cognitive biases (CBs). We let this divergence-convergence cycle continue until all participants had acknowledged and understood opposing worldviews. The process helped us direct their attention away from CBs. With cognitive and mental blocks removed, our participants could move toward a shared understanding of the underlying system structure, starting to anticipate its dynamic implications. The consensus or dialectical inquiry process necessary for constructing these maps is discussed extensively in Acar (1983).

Following its opening presentation, each team presented the other's ID to the satisfaction of its designers. Next, each team was directed to specify conditions that render its causal diagram invalid. This is an extension of SAST (strategic assumption surfacing and testing) which accommodates multiple strategic options; forces of continuity, tradition, and cognitive inertia; and in-depth analyses; thus, decision teams become less vulnerable to nonpenetrating thinking, nor do they fall victim to implicit critical assumptions (Mason & Mitroff, 1981).

In the convergence phase, the two teams were racing each other, trying to simplify their IDs, so that they could easily integrate their converging insight of Infoplus' underlying system structure into a single map. They already recognized that, though inseparable, strategic and tactical models are different. Tactical and operational models are large, detailed, and most specific in the quantification of relationships among variables. Conversely, strategic models are small, synoptic, and less concerned with numerical precision.

Hatten & Hatten (1987, pp. 149-150) point out that many sophisticated strategy models, such as Porter's generic strategies (1980) and Utterback & Abernathy's optimization strategies (1975), are at once *dirt* simple and correct. Simple and correct strategy models are easy to use but difficult to build.

At the end of the day we had a much smaller model, with nine variables only (Table 5.3.1). One GCB consultant noted that, despite its small size, the new influence diagram had somehow preserved the richness of the structure underlying Infoplus' system. We agreed. Our GCB-Infoplus participants found the structure of their consolidated ID both persuasive and plausible.

During one of the subsequent meetings, we asked our participants to quantify the relationships among the variables of Infoplus' influence diagram. In the process, we helped them transform their ID into a comprehensive situation map (CSM). The "map swap" as they called it helped them develop even deeper insights, not only into the system structure underlying Infoplus' situation, but also into the dynamic implications of that structure.

Figure 5.3.1 shows the ID and a streamlined CSM of Infoplus' strategic situation. Usually, the arrows of an influence diagram bear + and − signs to specify the positive and negative relationships among variables. Yet, omitting the + sign helps to lighten the diagrams of Fig. 5.3.1.

A word of caution here. These relationships are neither positive nor negative in the sense of being either favorable or unfavorable. A positive link is one that channels from an upstream to a downstream node or variable without changing it from, say, an increase to a decrease or a decrease to an increase. Conversely, a negative link is one that, while transmitting a change from an upstream to a downstream variable, changes the direction of the change from, say, a decrease to an increase or an increase to a decrease.

In our CSM system of causal mapping, the arrows specify both the direction and, when not directly proportional, even the magnitude of the percentage change that a change in a sender variable will transmit to its receiver. In addition, if change is to be transmitted with a time lag, then a caption indicating the amount of lag is written next to the appropriate time lag.

We start our example with an influence diagram (ID) because influence diagramming is the first step toward transforming cognitive mapping into a standard systematic model. For instance, in Fig. 5.3.1a, an increase in actual service would trigger an increase in revenue that would in turn increase Infoplus' resources. In our ID, the influences are not undefined conceptual relationships, but each is interpreted as the effect of the change in a variable over the change in a subsequent variable.

Still, influence diagramming remains a simple procedure using only one kind of linkage. Though popular, influence and causal-loop diagrams do not provide a reliable guide to system behavior. They indicate the direction of causation but do not show the strength of effects among variables (Mohapatra & Sharma, 1985; Morecroft, 1982, 1985a).

To capture more information, we now turn to the CSM causal mapping mode to which we have been making repeated references. CSM, a more refined system, uses three kinds of linking relationships, time lags, and change transmittance coefficients that determine the magnitude of transmitted change. The CSM of Fig. 5.3.1b shows that, under a pure scenario of change transfer, for example, a 10 percent increase in actual service would cause a relative 10 percent increase in revenue, with a one-month time lag. This one change would then instantaneously cause a relative one-tenth rise in Infoplus' resources, independently from external funding.

Comparing methods (a) and (b), the ID of Fig. 5.3.1a merely indicates that a rising actual service would result in some increase in revenue. The CSM of Fig. 5.3.1b provides much more specific information. Back to our example, we can now also tell that, with a four-month time lag, the 10 percent increase in actual service would show up as a 10 percent increase in Infoplus' capacity and capability and, with a one-month time lag, as a 7.5 percent increase in Infoplus' visibility (10% × 0.75). Both changes would be expressed in terms of the previous levels of these variables.

To insert a small "flash forward," let us state immediately that a basic premise of planning is the generation of scenarios (Amara & Lipinski, 1983; Godet, 1987);

a basic premise of the generation of scenarios is modeling and simulation (Watson, 1981); and a basic premise of modeling and computer simulation is an understanding of causal effects (Roberts et al., 1983). The triggering effects that Infoplus' managers had to understand to lever chains of events that might evoke possible alternative futures are those describing the transmission of change through an interplay of triggering events and causal effects (Tushman & Anderson, 1986).

Table 5.3.1   Variables Pertinent to Infoplus' Strategic Situation

Variable Name		Meaning
Actual service	:	actual services delivered to Infoplus customers and partners
Capacity & capability	:	capacity for service and online search and research capability
Demand for service	:	requests by new customers and established partners
External funding	:	institutional, excluding city, state and federal funding
Infoplus' resources	:	capital, human, and physical, excluding GCB consultants
Initial support	:	by GCB, including city, state, and federal funding
Partial autonomy	:	from GCB, particularly in resource allocation decisions
Revenue	:	fees charged for rendered services
Visibility	:	in the local business community, attributed to actual service

CSM embodies all these features. In addition, it allows qualitative conditions to be expressed by capturing qualitative restrictions. For example, in Fig. 5.3.1b, the broken-line arrow connecting the initial support variable with the diagram node representing Infoplus' resources indicates that a drastic change in GCB's initial support policy, a qualitative restriction, may prevent Infoplus' resources from changing, even in the presence of external funding. The 10 percent increase in revenue would immediately cause a relative one-tenth rise in Infoplus' resources, if and only if there is no drastic change in GCB's initial support policy for Infoplus.

Similarly, in Fig. 5.3.1b again, the broken-line arrow connecting Infoplus' partial autonomy variable to its capacity and capability node indicates another qualitative restriction. It shows that a drastic change in Infoplus' partial autonomy from GCB may prevent Infoplus' capacity and capability from changing. The agreed-upon CSM expresses the participants' belief that a one-tenth rise in Infoplus' resources would turn up as a 10 percent increase in Infoplus' capacity and capability, with a three-month time lag if and only if there is no drastic change in Infoplus' partial autonomy from its parent organization.

As mentioned earlier, there was no way of differentiating such conjunctive effects from qualitative restrictions in a causal map of the classic ID variety, such as

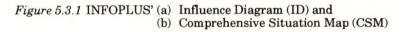

Figure 5.3.1 INFOPLUS' (a) Influence Diagram (ID) and
(b) Comprehensive Situation Map (CSM)

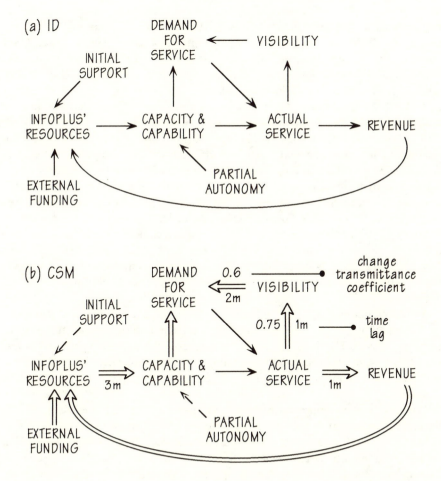

the one in Fig. 5.3.1a (Diffenbach, 1982; Maruyama, 1963; Ramaprasad & Poon, 1985; Weick, 1979). We find Acar's CSM useful for causal mapping because it is amenable to formal analysis; it can become part of an institution's memory; and it assists in the monitoring of organizational learning.

CSM allows the causalities involved in the transmission of change to be captured and presented to higher authorities (Acar, 1983; Acar, Chaganti, & Joglekar, 1985). CSM can help firms capture and retain "the space and time memories that systems display and which increase the risk of bringing about unanticipated consequences far away and a long time after the change agents have been applied and removed" (Holling & Goldberg, 1971, p. 225).

Proponents of dialectical inquiry (DI) have repeatedly suggested that a manager's understanding of decision scenarios may depend on the process entailed in diagramming a strategic situation (Ackoff, 1981; Chanin & Shapiro, 1985; Georgantzas, 1990; Mason & Mitroff, 1981; Shapiro & Chanin, 1987). In the CSM construction process, individually advocated or "owned" maps become the grounded data for the construction of an aggregate or group map, a device for facilitating group decision making or negotiation.

To facilitate negotiation, CSM creates a dialectic by enabling decision makers to formulate a decision situation and to envision reference scenarios (Ackoff, 1981; Godet, 1987; Ozbekhan, 1977). This helps them uncover implicit assumptions about the situation and let them surface (Georgantzas, 1990; Mason & Mitroff, 1981). A "natural dialectic" may then occur because team members contribute their own views about a situation (Eden, 1988). Grounded to the team itself, in a way that does not require any face-saving strategies, this dialectic increases the possibility of individual "ownership"—a behavioral synonym for commitment, creativity, and interest in the implementation of recommended actions. It can also help build computer simulation models that force counterintuitive outcomes (Roberts et al., 1983; Watson, 1981). Part V presents examples of full-scale computer simulation models, both stochastic (Chapter 9) and deterministic (Chapter 10).

As shown in Fig. 5.3.1a, the influence diagram failed to resolve whether capacity and capability or visibility will be more decisive in determining Infoplus' demand for service. There was no way of telling from the ID which path will dominate. This lack of guidance could mislead managers and planners into a naive and incorrect determination of the critical role that some variables play in a decision scenario.

Conversely, the comprehensive situation map of Fig. 5.3.1b possesses simulationlike capabilities that can assess the complex effects of changes both in "hard" and "soft" as well as in external and internal variables. Comprehensive situation mapping is a good first step toward effective computer modeling and simulation. Starting from the CSM of Fig. 5.3.1b, specific scenarios can be tested to explore possible alternative futures.

Part V presents environmental and decision scenarios computed both on the CSM (Chapter 9) and on computers through full-scale simulation models, both stochastic (Chapter 9) and deterministic (Chapter 10). The following section applies a sociometric approach called MICMAC to the case of Infoplus. Derived from the sociometric authors of the 1950s and 1960s, and advanced by J. C. Duperrin and M. Godet between 1972 and 1974 (Godet, 1987, p. 38), MICMAC allows linking causal diagrams to their affiliated "adjacency" matrices.

Combining the use of MICMAC with CSM shows how some of the severe limitations of the human mind can be stretched out in future planning by use of the proper planning technology. Appendix C.3 presents the somewhat abstract notions and mathematical formalism associated with MICMAC.

5.4   EXPOSURE AND INFLUENCE AT INFOPLUS

MICMAC allows the assessment of second-, third-, and higher-order interaction effects among the variables on a causal map pertinent to a firm's strategy design (Godet, 1987, p. 38). This section illustrates how this simple analytical approach can enhance the mind's limited capability to assess the multiple and sometimes long-linked interdependencies among the variables on a causal map.

The entire section is an application of the somewhat abstract notions and mathematical formalism presented in Appendix C.3, such as Infoplus' square adjacency matrix. The matrix lists the direct or first-order relationships among the variables that Infoplus' planning team found pertinent to its strategic situation. Appendix C.3 also provides the formal definitions of the terms we use here, whereas this illustrative example of combining CSM with MICMAC helps transform the abstract into concrete.

The direct or first-order relationships among seven of Infoplus' strategic variables allowed the formulation of Infoplus' relationship or adjacency matrix **M**. Associated with this matrix is an *influence vector* embodying the sums of the first-order paths originating at various elements of the matrix and an *exposure vector* embodying the sums of the first-order paths ending at various elements of the matrix.

Only seven of the nine variables listed in Table 5.3.1 were included in Infoplus' relationship matrix because its scenario-driven planning team chose not to quantify the effects of the initial support and partial autonomy variables, but to treat them as qualitative restrictions. The broken-line arrows on the CSM of Fig. 5.3.1b clarify the qualitative restrictions that these two variables impose on Infoplus' resources and on its capacity and capability, respectively.

In Appendix C.3, Infoplus' adjacency matrix shows the first-order effects among the strategic variables pertinent to Infoplus' strategic situation. These relationships can be established by merely inspecting the comprehensive situation map of Fig. 5.3.1b. Sender nodes enter the matrix as row variables and receiver nodes as column variables.

A straightforward examination of the CSM should reveal the first-order effects directly. Yet, the mere inspection of the map may not immediately uncover all the indirect relationships among the variables pertinent to Infoplus' strategic situation, which the consecutive powers of Infoplus' adjacency matrix can capture.

Although the entries of **M** are the direct first-order links between pairs of variables or diagram nodes, the entries of M^2 are the second-order linkages among the nodes. In the 1950s and 1960s sociometrists showed that these could be computed directly from a diagram's adjacency matrix.

When Infoplus' adjacency matrix is raised to the matrix power of $N=2$, then its entries denote the second-order paths of change transmission. One could still verify some of these change transmission paths by tracing them in Fig. 5.3.1b. For example, it should be easy to see the second-order paths of

- actual service $\rightarrow$ revenue $\rightarrow$ Infoplus' resources, and
- actual service $\rightarrow$ visibility $\rightarrow$ demand for service

When Infoplus' adjacency matrix is raised to the matrix power of $N=14$, however, tracing or at once keeping track of all eighty-three fourteenth-order paths of change transmission ending at actual service may not be easy. The human brain was designed neither for conceiving nor for dealing with the information overload that the sheer magnitude of these effects entails (Miller, 1956).

This is one way in which MICMAC can be useful. It allows us to assess the role that strategic variables play in the network of feedback loops underlying the causal structure of a strategic situation. The identification of indirect effects through the mere inspection of a CSM can be laborious. Yet, the computationally efficient powers of Infoplus' adjacency matrix in Appendix C.3 can easily capture all indirect effects throughout its causal map. In addition, if we think of the variables pertinent to a strategic situation as means and ends, or, alternatively, as driver and dependent variables (Godet, 1987, p. 44), then MICMAC allows grouping these variables according to their overall influence and exposure. Figure 5.4.1 shows exactly what the outcome of this efficient procedure might look like.

Again, Appendix C.3 formally defines the four quadrants of Fig. 5.4.1. Briefly, *singular variables* include isolated variables that both affect and are exposed only to a few strategic variables. *Dispersing variables* affect many but are exposed to a few, influencing other variables directly or indirectly. *Absorbing strategic variables* affect a few but are exposed to many. They depict both explicit and implied performance objectives, met through multiple means, but their high exposure makes them vulnerable even to small changes on a causal map. Lastly, *linking variables* are both highly exposed and highly influential.

The successive powers $N=1$ through $N=15$ of the relationship matrix, and the exposure and influence vectors along **M** through M^{15}, provide useful information

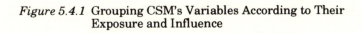

Figure 5.4.1 Grouping CSM's Variables According to Their Exposure and Influence

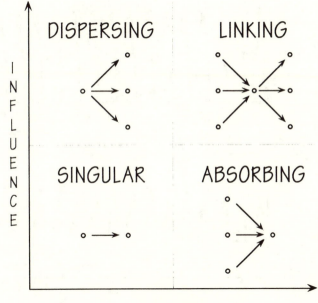

Figure 5.4.2 Overall (a) Exposure & (b) Influence at INFOPLUS

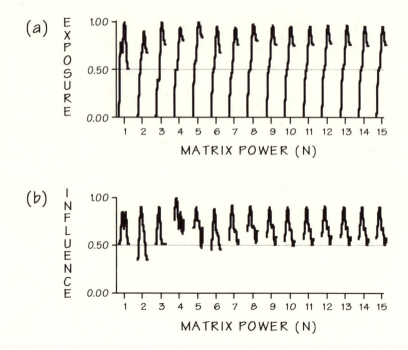

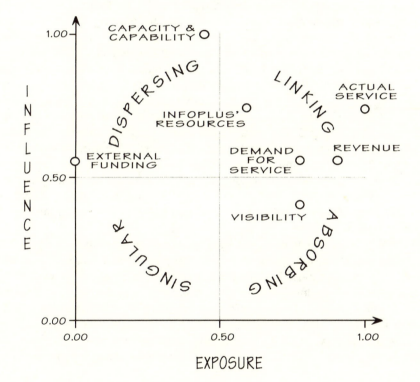

Figure 5.4.3 Grouping INFOPLUS' Variables into Dispersing,
Linking and Absorbing According to Their
Exposure and Influence (Matrix Power = 14)

about the structural role that each strategic variable plays in a comprehensive situation map. Specifically, the overall effects among the variables of the CSM in Fig. 5.3.1b yield a hierarchy of strategic variables, depending on their direct and indirect, that is, feedback, effects on each other.

The consecutive line plots along matrix powers $N=1$ through $N=15$ of Fig. 5.4.2 show the behavioral patterns of change in the overall (a) exposure and (b) influence of Infoplus' strategic variables. Both the *overall* exposure and the *overall* influence values have been "normalized" to allow us to compare directly the powers of Infoplus' adjacency matrix. These normalized values show how the overall exposure and influence vectors of Fig. 5.4.2 become stable after matrix power $N=8$.

The normalized vectors for $N=14$ captured the overall influence and exposure of Infoplus' strategic variables in the CSM of Fig. 5.3.1b. Plotting these values along the overall exposure and overall influence dimensions helped to improve understanding at Infoplus about the crucial role some of its strategic variables could play in creating its future. Assessing their structural role helped the Infoplus planning team reperceive the hierarchy of external and internal variables according to their direct and indirect effects as well as their sensitivity to changes in other variables.

Most of the MICMAC results confirmed the team's initial expectations, captured in the CSM of Fig. 5.3.1b. Yet, the grouping of strategic variables according to their overall exposure and overall influence in Fig. 5.4.3 helped to enliven the discussion. It was interesting to observe how Infoplus' capacity and capability, which moved up the hierarchy considerably, captured the project participants' attention. They had originally thought that the most influential variable would be external funding. Similarly, actual service became the most exposed variable, with revenue ranking second.

Many alternative explanations can be advanced to interpret these changes, but one or two should suffice. When we joined Infoplus, its management team was busy drafting grant proposals for external funding. Combining CSM with MICMAC showed that Infoplus *should carefully manage the transformation of external funds and other resources into capacity and capability*. The variable classification of Fig. 5.4.3 reinforced the importance of actual service as well as the necessity of new capacity additions to strengthen Infoplus' capacity and capability. These additions would allow the firm to manage the tension that its matrix organization creates.

These preliminary results conclude the case study of Infoplus for now. They serve as an advance organizer for Part V, supporting the necessity of computation required to assess a planning team's mental models. In Part V, environmental and decision scenarios are computed on the CSM (Chapter 9) and on the computer through full-scale simulation models, both stochastic (Chapter 9) and deterministic (Chapter 10).

SUMMARY

This is the first introductory application, gradually showing how to implant scenario-driven planning to enhance strategy design toward accomplishing favorable outcomes consistent with long-term goals. Our intervention at Infoplus helped its planning team refine and jointly formulate Infoplus' strategic decision situation. Infoplus' director and two GCB internal consultants shared their divergent but complementary views of their situation. The case narrates the strategic situation through a description that combines the evolving views of Infoplus' planning team.

In the process of implanting scenario-driven planning with Acar's CSM, we seek to bring out assumptions about the relationships among strategic variables and thereby create new information in the process. Our project participants analyzed these relationships for accuracy of perception through a dialectical *form of group dynamics. The consecutive use of three computational methods allows the propagation of three generations of change scenarios, analyzing the same relationships for possible future implications on a what if basis.*

Section 9.1 will detail Infoplus' computed scenarios. The insight gained from the scenario-driven planning process leads to the strategic recommendations listed in the executive summary at the beginning of this chapter.

Chapter 6

Combank (A)

Plan or be planned for.
—Russell L. Ackoff

Our second case study was undertaken in the field of commercial banking. It relates one of our research projects at a commercial bank's Wall Street location in New York City. Our intervention aimed at helping a team of top managers refine and jointly formulate their firm's strategic decision situation—its problématique. The case deals with the process conducive to the strategy design from long-term goals to attain a more favorable market position or an enhanced strategic posture. We have changed the bank's real name to Combank, and we mention none of the project participants by name. We have also organized the illustrative material beyond the quick summary presented to the bank's strategic planning group.

6.1   INTRODUCTION TO COMBANK

Executive Summary

Ackoff's exhortation, "Plan or be planned for," reflects today's mood. The systems age has brought all businesses an increased environmental turbulence. Deregulation compounds the turbulence even more for financial institutions. In this time of acquisitions, mergers, and divestment, US banks are facing mounting pressures to meet the global challenge.

Peters & Waterman's (1982) phrase "bias for action" was the byproduct of the overplanning and underdoing in the 1970s. A bias for action does not mean the absence of planning. Planning is necessary for companies that choose to become actively engaged in creating their own future. Scenario-driven planning is a novel approach to fixing a firm's strategy process, even "if it ain't broke."

Despite the lack of tangible expectations of an upbeat turn in the US economy, opportunities still exist, especially for those connected with the inflow of foreign funds from overseas. Neither overseas nor domestic corporations should give in to environmental business conditions triggered blindly by industry and market forces. Some choose to engage in creating their own future. Prudent ones invest in small US firms.

One such institution is Combank, which is poised to take advantage of the inflow of overseas investment in the US market. Its parent firm has given Combank freedom of choice. Now it has a strategy to design for itself and later to negotiate with its overseas headquarters.

Combank's senior vice-president of strategic planning assumed responsibility for our intervention. Under his aegis the vice-presidents of finance, marketing, operations and planning shared their divergent but complementary views of the firm. This chapter recounts Combank's strategic situation through a description that combines the bank's marketing- and technology-centered views.

At the heart of our scenario approach is comprehensive situation mapping (CSM). Acar (1983) developed CSM during his doctoral work at the Wharton School of the University of Pennsylvania with Ackoff's program there, and he tested the method in a case study with the Volunteer Action Council (VAC) of Philadelphia. In combining scenario-driven planning with CSM, we seek to bring out assumptions about the relationships among the variables that opposing schools of thought in a business firm find essential. We analyze these through CSM for accuracy of perception as well as for their future scenario implications.

In addition, we have used the MICMAC variable classification approach and the BASICS computational method as detailed in the Appendix. The consecutive use of these methods enables the propagation of three generations of change scenarios. The causal maps of the marketing- and technology-centered views of Combank led to the first generation of scenarios. The combined view condensed the strategic situation's description and became the basis for computing a second and a third generation of scenarios. Section 9.2 describes Combank's second and third generation of scenarios, with examples of computing a second generation of scenarios in the divergence phase of scenario-driven planning. Section 6.4 shows how mechanistic matrix methods could still be used to complement the more dialectical CSM if one were seeking (weighted) macroenvironmental scenarios. The insight gained from the scenario-driven planning process leads to the strategic recommendations below.

- Combank should refine its tactics to manage the influx of foreign funds to its advantage. This depends on its ability to develop advisory services and new market portfolio investments. The development of such services will take time and resources. Yet, Combank will learn a lot about its clients in the process. Knowing its clients will enable it to remain *their* commercial bank in a transnational or at least *tripolar*—EEC, Japan, and USA—economy.
- Combank should expect growth in profit even with a medium tug toward developing capable people, consolidating support services, and attracting foreign funds. Its competitive posture in the low-volume, high-margin end of commercial banking augurs profit growth. Partly a result of Combank's operations flexibility, this favorable position gives its clients a highly personalized service. This is a realistic expectation, assuming the absence of a drastic change in Combank's size.
- Combank should continue to stay close to its clients with a global presence. This is one of the bank's strategic thrusts. Another is the ability to project a strong quality image, with a state-of-the-art IS technology infrastructure to support it. This ability is in turn contingent on the bank's continued dedication to developing and retaining top-notch people and to improving the efficiency of support services. These two powerful *internal levers* are both complementary and at Combank's disposal. Combank should explore them further.

Combank's competitive advantage stems from an already established position in the low-volume, high-margin end of commercial banking. Other commercial banks envy this preemptive posture. They have to decide what sort of special banks they want to be in the long term. As they do, however, Combank can expect them to try entering its path. To fend them off and to manage strategic uncertainty both for itself and for its clients, Combank may have to do things differently as well as do new things.

We deeply appreciate the encouragement and time of the senior and other vice-presidents who became team participants in our study. A very special word of thanks should go to the senior vice-president of planning for his help and guidance throughout the process. We are also grateful to Combank's CEO and to Fordham's Dean for presenting us with this intervention opportunity.

The computed scenarios helped clarify the bank's range of alternative futures. The dialectic that began during this short study will most likely endure and develop, reinforcing and strengthening Combank's strategic planning and reorganization.

Trends in Commercial Banking

Fund managers and individual investors need someone to coordinate their assets. Commercial banks sell custody services precisely to fulfill that need. In the United States fund managers are required by law to use an independent custodian to hold their stocks. Although European fund managers have the option of generating a steady-fee income from in-house custodian services, they often pass the business to affiliated commercial banks.

Fund managers and investors looking for opportunities not only locally but also worldwide must coordinate their stock and cash holdings away from home. This is exactly what a *global*-custody service does, and it is a rapidly growing business. Commercial banks that sell global custody look after their clients' stocks and cash worldwide. Specifically, they provide clients with

- physical custody of share certificates in markets that still use paper,
- efficient movement of stock issues to settle transactions,
- prompt response to rights issues and other corporate restructuring,
- tax breaks and reclaims where and when possible,
- punctually claimed dividends and, most importantly,
- swift and accurate reports.

The market for global custody is currently growing at 25 to 30 percent, or $1 billion each year. Investment managers in continental Europe, who traditionally have had firm links to domestic banks, are now discovering their wide choice of custodians in foreign markets, many of which offer services that are not available at home. The United Kingdom is the biggest market for global custody. More than 18 percent of British investments are held in foreign stock, compared to 6 to 7 percent in the US and 5 percent in Japan. At 1.9m, the number of overseas equity bargains executed in London in 1990 was up 52 percent on 1989, with sales totaling £294 billion ($525 billion).

A recent study by Business International, a member of the Economist Group, found that one-fifth of British fund managers were interested in using the services of global custodians. Especially attractive are the small funds that lack a critical mass in overseas markets. Leading merchant banks, which traditionally have managed large foreign investments and cross-border flows of capital on their own, also consider adopting one or two commercial banks as global custodians to replace their subcustodian networks. They are happy to unload the custody of foreign stocks, which they see as a peripheral, often profitless, activity (Anon., 1991).

The price of custody often varies widely. In big European markets, commercial banks might reasonably charge five basis points, or 0.05 percent, on the value of a transaction, plus five for custody. In a smaller and more difficult market, that is, one without an automated transaction-tracking system, the total charge might be 50 to 75 basis points, or 0.50 to 0.75 percent.

Commercial banks often roll their transaction cost into a single fee, with domestic custody cross-subsidizing custody abroad. Also, different customers pay differently. A big industrial or institutional account, for example, with an active portfolio of stock and cash holdings may get custody almost free, while the client of a private bank may be charged one percent a year for custody alone.

Yet, with the world's financial markets in the throes of reconstruction, the global banking system is also changing to channel cheap capital to industry. Competitive pressure is mounting, while clients on both sides of the Atlantic insist on an unbundled fee, preferring to pay charges on a service-by-service basis. This recent trend has already cut profit margins, with custody fees falling by 5 percent a year in the United States.

Competitive strategy principles may not readily apply to commercial banking. Technological innovations, for example, typically can drive whole industries to fast growth and consolidation. In commercial banking, however, advances in information technology may become the very cause of fragmentation. Although profit margins are growing thin, they remain attractive because the demand for global custody is growing. It is possible that the twenty or so biggest global custodians will squeeze margins hard enough to force small banks out of anything other than the basic service. Yet, the big providers will then have to differentiate their service all over again, with extra features and better quality.

A related trend in global banking is persistent compartmentalizing, which sets off a chain reaction. Various sorts of banks, such as short- and long-term lending and funding, trust, mutual and regional, compartmentalize. Compartmentalizing also persists between banking and the securities industry. The bankers' effort to fend off others trying to enter their patch knows no boundaries. The net effect is an increasingly turbulent, high-velocity global environment, where the distinctions between different sorts of financial businesses begin to blur.

Surface segmentation may permit the world's financial system to survive for some time. To prosper, however, banks have to make both tactical and strategic moves. In the short term, they can boost their earnings through internal reforms. For example, investments in automation reforms provide high-quality services, while improving asset-liability management. They are good tactics.

Yet, these tactics will work only if banks hold down their growth in lending. A particular bank needs to use these tactics anyway to become more competitive, namely, more profitable. In the long term, however, it has to decide what sort of special bank it wants to be.

Traditional nontrust banking business may include long-term corporate lending, letters of credit and collections, as well as securities investment and trading. These provide commercial banks with a smaller base than their competitors from which to develop new services and sources of cash. Poorly positioned to compete, many commercial banks lack the city and regional banks' deep roots in retail banking. Similarly, the securities companies in capital markets are tough competitors.

Most commercial banks concentrate on what they see as their strength, namely, the management of assets. This outlook complements traditional commercial loans with reliable commission income from investment and pension trusts. It also makes investing trust assets in equities easier and encourages industrial and institutional clients to put spare money into stocks.

All that has been easy in the bull market. The October 1987 stock market crash and the credit exposure to Latin America left their negative mark on commercial banks. Banks wrote off billions of bad loans in 1991, and many posted huge losses. Citibank, for example, went $500 million into the red that year. Some sold off their Latin American loans to secondary markets. Others took a further step by completely removing such nonperforming assets from their balance sheet. They may have missed an opportunity to include them in their primary capital in the form of loan loss reserves. Locally, as the US economy has started to perk up, some nonperforming assets, including real estate loans, have begun to perform again.

In 1934, the Glass-Steagall Act prohibited commercial banks, which accept deposits and make loans, from underwriting securities as they had done previously. Investment banks arose to take over the underwriting function, and investment banking emerged as an industry in the United States. Modern investment banks, such as Salomon Brothers, are involved in two main financial activities: corporate finance, and securities sales and trading. Corporate finance includes underwriting new securities issued by business firms, government institutions, and other not-for-profit organizations.

Commercial banks in North America have become dependent on the US Federal Reserve. They depend on its policy for cushioning the economic exchange of real goods and services from negative externalities, such as the October 1987 market crash.

Despite the bad news and the flow of red ink, US commercial banks are already involved in investment banking. They know how to give the next nudge to the securities industry's back door. Growth opportunities have emerged from the influx of foreign funds, primarily from the EEC and Japan. Some have direct access to the London and Tokyo markets through partially or wholly owned subsidiaries.

Our commercial banks have widespread contacts with corporate customers that transcend big industrial groups. They have good relations with regional banks, which gives them a large distribution network, and bigger capital bases than all but the biggest city banks. Last, but not least, they have top-notch personnel.

6.2   THE INTERVENTION PROCESS

Such was the staff we worked with at Combank's Wall Street location in New York City. We began by studying the firm's most recent annual reports. An internal memo on corporate strategy, addressed to all officers, gave us a concrete starting point. That document clarified the bank's mission in normative terms: achieving balance sheet strength while remaining a service business highly responsive to client requests. These two strategic thrusts have propelled Combank into the securities business.

With no Glass-Steagall Act hurdles to clear on securities underwriting, Combank is heavily into acquisitions. This is a strategy of building on businesses already in place. This thrust portrays its goal of offering a broad range of financial services to overseas investors.

Yet, the bank stays close enough to its clients to lend them money and to provide advice for their long-term global business plans. The internal memo proposed building on the bank's reputation and history of serving foreign corporations and institutions in the US market. Combank continues to expand its role as the financial gateway for foreign investors in the United States. It also provides a range of high-quality financial services to the US subsidiaries of its customers worldwide.

With a strong money management unit, Combank's historical strength has been in Europe, but it is now looking toward the Pacific Basin as well. Combank is trying to position itself as an institution that handles, in a high-quality fashion, for eign investments into the United States.

Under the aegis of Combank's senior vice-president of strategic planning, the vice-presidents of finance, marketing, operations, and planning volunteered to participate in the project. Our participants thought it was critical to the success of the bank's strategy that its senior managers jointly reach a better understanding of the potential synergy among its products, and to explore the relationships among profit, volume capacity, and the importance of staying close to the customer. They wanted to refine and jointly formulate Combank's strategic situation. Their aspiration was to make profit or profit potential—not just revenue generation—the basis for future identification, measurement, and performance evaluation.

Our project participants' professional complementarities, as well as their time schedules and constraints, determined their voluntary assignment to two teams. The vice-president of finance and the vice-president of operations formed one team, while the marketing and planning vice-presidents formed another.

We first worked with each team separately to ease the development of two alternative formulations of Combank's strategic situation. In our first meeting, the finance and operations team built a CSM causal map that we termed *Combank's Technology-Centered View*. In a second divergent session, we worked with the marketing and planning team. We called the CSM that this team contributed *Combank's Marketing-Centered View*.

The Ackoff-Ozbekhan reference scenario idea (i.e., the time development of system behavior a firm would have had if there were no significant changes in its strategy and environment; see Ackoff, 1981; Ozbekhan, 1977) helped to focus the modeling effort of Combank's planning teams. Each team's reference scenario or *reference behavior pattern* (Randers, 1980) served as a tangible manifestation of system behavior portrayed by the smallest possible set of cause and effect relationships among the variables pertinent to Combank's strategic situation. The two alternative formulations contained several common variables, but the relationships among the variables were different. The two diagrams looked more complementary than similar.

Each view of Combank's situation focused on one of the two basic determinants of profit growth. The market-centered perspective involved primarily environmental variables associated with increasing revenues. The technology-centered view looked more closely at internal managerial variables that were conducive to streamlining the bank's operations.

The third and final meeting was our *convergent* session, in which we worked with both teams together. Also present at this meeting was Combank's senior vice-president of strategic planning. During this six-hour long session, each team first presented its causal map to the other. We did not encourage much dialogue during that part of the meeting other than, of course, clarification questions and answers.

Combank's senior planner, who had not participated in the divergence phase of modeling, asked most of the questions. It was encouraging and extremely helpful to watch him repeat or rephrase answers to his questions, ensuring that he and everyone else in the room shared the meaning of each variable and each arrow on each comprehensive situation map.

Once the initial presentations were over, Combank's senior vice-president of strategic planning interjected his own reflections, according to the causal links expressed in each team's causal map of the firm's situation. These reflections reinforced, and thereby helped to preserve the divergence or *plural rationality* in interpreting various elements on each map.

Alan E. Singer tackles the vexing question of plural rationality in individuals, groups, and organizations (Singer, 1991, 1992). His work justifies the use of a divergence-convergence scheme in scenario-driven planning by contrasting monothematic conventional *uni*verses of traditional rationality with the *multi*verse-directed view of modern plural rationality. In counterpoint, Section 10.3 of Morecroft's (1985b) system dynamics model of a sales organization traces the dysfunctional interactions among sales objectives, overtime, and salesforce motivation to the intended singular rationality that permeated thinking at Datacom.

Next, we walked the entire group through a series of pure and mixed reference scenarios computed on each team's CSM causal map. This first generation of computed scenarios gave Combank's planning group a better sense of the long-term implications of each alternative view. This first set of scenarios captured the behavioral patterns of profit growth, showing the potential synergy among Combank's services, volume capacity, and the importance of staying close to the customer. Combank's planning teams started to anticipate the dynamic implications of their divergent causal models.

We reaped the benefits of nurturing plural rationality at Combank when we engaged all participants in a dialectical form of group dynamics. We asked the members of the marketing and planning team to interpret the CSM of the finance and operations team to the satisfaction of the finance and operations team, and vice versa.

This dialectical-inquiry (DI) interchange sought to unearth critical assumptions and prominent cognitive biases (CBs). It enabled our project participants to shift their attention from individual CBs and to reperceive the structure and implications of Combank's strategic situation. The DI interchange moved participants closer to a shared understanding of the system structure underlying the situation of Combank. Acar (1983) gives an extensive treatment of the consensus or DI interchange process.

Combank's managers exchanged creative thoughts and used many examples to clarify their perceptions of the bank's strategic situation. For example, there was a sharing of an intriguing thought that had developed in one of the earlier divergent sessions. The members of the finance and operations team visualized some internal operations as the information systems (IS) analogue of a workshop's tool-train. This train would circulate among other workstations to collect transaction slips and to serve them.

This visual analogy—or visual model, as a management scientist would say—gave a better sense of which operations to consolidate and which to pair with client services. Programming the operations paired with client services into an IS-level consolidation could be inconsistent with Combank's highly customized and personalized service.

The underlying dynamic within the combined team and the natural dialectic between Combank's two alternative views led to a synthesis. An aggregate CSM map captured the convergent view of Combank's personnel. This we termed *Combank's Integrated View.*

Our intervention project at Combank aimed at two birds with a single stone throw. It helped translate, refine, and jointly formulate Combank's strategic situation from the bank's mission statement. It also provided a form of training in strategic situation formulation for everyone involved. This training was not in abstract ideas but was tied to every participant's job.

6.3   CAUSAL MODELING WITH CSM

Several variable descriptors along with their relationships were specified during our case intervention at Combank. Among the variables that persisted until the synthesis or convergence phases are:

1. Foreign funds
2. Development of advisory services and new market portfolio investments
3. Operations flexibility
4. Cost
5. Profit
6. Functional efficiency of support services
7. Quality image
8. Use of state-of-the-art is (information systems) technology
9. Effective delivery of customized services
10. Development of capable people

The four participants specified the relationships among these variables with the help of comprehensive situation mapping (Acar, 1983). In CSM, a short name represents each variable that changes itself and may cause change in other variables. The method *also* makes provision for those variables which, if they were to change radically, may *prevent* the transmission of change. An example is Combank's size in Fig. 6.3.1.

Three types of arrows connect variables in CSM.

1. A *double-line arrow* (i.e., $\Longrightarrow$) connects a sender and a receiver of change, if a change in the sender variable is sufficient by itself to transmit a change to the receiver of the arrow. In Fig. 6.3.1, for example, a change in either the cost or the quality image is by itself capable of inducing a change in profit.
2. A *single-line arrow* (i.e., $\longrightarrow$) links each sender to a receiver of change if two or more senders must vary to coproduce a change in the receiver. In Fig. 6.3.1, both the development of capable people and the use of state-of-the-art IS technology must change to generate jointly a change in the effective delivery of customized support services. Combank's managers felt that the efficient delivery of support

Figure 6.3.1 CSM of COMBANK's Integrated View

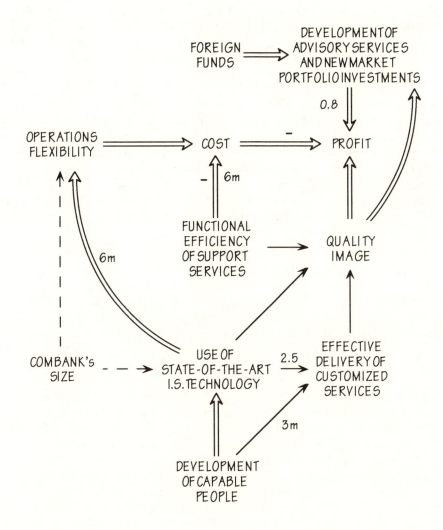

services would have an indirect beneficial effect on profit through a quality image.

In CSM, both time lags and change coefficients accompany each double-line and single-line arrow to quantify the transmission of change throughout the causal network over time. Every single- and double-line arrow bears a *change transmittance coefficient* written either above or next to it. This coefficient quantifies the relationship between two variables connected with an arrow. If the change induced in the receiver of the arrow is not comparable either in sign or in proportion to the change in its sender, then the change transmittance coefficient expresses the ratio of the induced percentage change to the one generating it.

For example, the $X \underset{3m}{\overset{-2}{\Rightarrow}} Y$ notation signifies that a *relative* change of 10 percent, 15 percent, or 20 percent originating in variable X, and counted from its base level, is transferred to variable Y with a three-month time lag. There, it causes a relative change of -20 percent, -30 percent or -40 percent in the value of Y. When downstream-transferred changes are proportional to the upstream changes causing them, and of the same sign, then the multipliers may be omitted from the map.

Similarly, every single- and double-line arrow bears a time lag. Written either below or to the right of each arrow, along with explicit time units, the time lag coefficient clearly specifies changes transmitted with a time lag (Acar, 1983).

3. Lastly, a *broken-line arrow* (i.e., - - ➤) connects a sender and a receiver of change if the sender is a variable that can prevent the receiver from changing, regardless of all other effects. It helps to think of a broken-line arrow as a binary on/off switch. As long as the sender variable remains relatively stable, then the switch is on, enabling other full or partial channels to transmit change to the receiver variable. However, when the sender variable changes significantly, that is, it departs from the status quo—or the statistician's most familiar six-sigma range—then the switch is off, blocking all other channels from transmitting changes to the receiver variable. In Fig. 6.3.1, Combank's size qualifies the transmission of change from the development of capable people to the use of state-of-the-art IS technology. Similarly, it qualifies the subsequent transmission of change to operations flexibility. A radical change in Combank's size would stop the transmission of change along these paths, and thereby render some relationships of Fig. 6.3.1 invalid.

Throughout the project, our job required arranging and rearranging 3M Post-it™ note pads on the white sheets of a flip-chart. Combank's executives offered their opinions on how their firm's strategic situation formulation would look. Adding, moving, or taking away yellow note pads followed every chunk of input.

At each meeting, the discussion revolved around many uncertainties, including what variables to include in the CSM and whether these should be connected with double-line, single-line, or broken-line arrows. Once a rough-cut map took shape, the magnitude and sign of the change transmittance coefficients and the time lags seized the planning team's attention.

Everyone had to be satisfied that Combank's CSM causal diagramming used was sound.

The marketing and planning team stuck to its guns until the synthesis or convergence phase, with a strong preference toward nonrecursive models. That is why there are no feedback loops in the comprehensive situation map of Fig. 6.3.1.

The composite causal network of Fig. 6.3.1 sums up the most salient features of Combank's two basic maps, representing the two basic views of it. It shows that, under a *pure* scenario of change transfer, for example, a 10 percent increase in the functional efficiency of support services would cause a relative 10 percent decrease in cost, with a six-month time lag. This one change would immediately cause a proportional relative to a one-tenth rise in Combank's profit, independently of the quality image effect and the development of advisory services and new market portfolio investments.

As mentioned above, comprehensive situation mapping also allows qualitative conditions to be expressed along with capturing qualitative restrictions. In Fig. 6.3.1, for example, the broken-line arrow connecting Combank's size with its operations flexibility and with the use of state-of-the-art IS technology shows that a drastic change in Combank's size may prevent an increase in the development of capable people from elevating the use of state-of-the-art IS technology. The same restriction, Combank's size, may also obscure the positive effect of the use of state-of-the-art IS technology on operations flexibility.

6.4   EXPOSURE AND INFLUENCE AT COMBANK

The specification of the first-order effects by Combank's project participants led to the construction of the causal map in Fig. 6.3.1. A mere inspection of the map leads to the identification of second- and third-order effects. We used the MIC-MAC variable classification approach (Godet, 1987, p. 38) to verify higher-order effects and to check the stability of the CSM diagram in Fig. 6.3.1.

Appendix C.3 presents the somewhat abstract notions and mathematical formalism behind MICMAC, providing the formal definitions of the terms used in this section. Briefly, MICMAC depends on the classical properties of *adjacency* matrices. If, for example, variable i directly affects variable k, and k directly affects variable j, then a change in variable i will affect variable j indirectly.

Figure 6.4.1 Overall (a) Exposure & (b) Influence at COMBANK

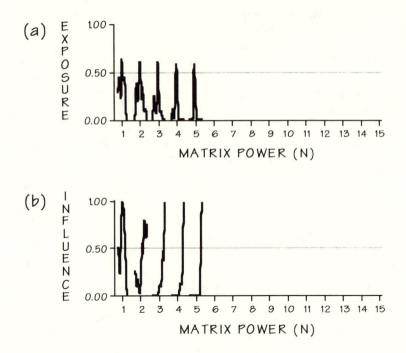

(a)

EXPOSURE

1.00

0.50

0.00

MATRIX POWER (N)

(b)

INFLUENCE

1.00

0.50

0.00

MATRIX POWER (N)

Combank's Boolean adjacency matrix in Appendix C.3 shows the first-order effects specified by the team members in Combank's aggregate CSM of Fig. 6.3.1. One could verify these relationships by merely inspecting the CSM of Fig. 6.3.1. A straightforward examination of the causal map should reveal the first-order effects directly.

Only ten of the eleven variables in Fig. 6.3.1 are in Combank's adjacency matrix because its planning group chose not to quantify the effects of, but to treat size as a qualitative restriction. The broken-line arrows of Fig. 6.3.1 clarify the qualitative restrictions that a material change in size may impose on Combank's use of state-of-the-art IS (information systems) technology and on the bank's operations flexibility.

Numerous indirect relationships exist in a causal map describing the system structure of a strategic situation. They emanate from the first-order relationships that the arrows disclose on a causal map. When the Boolean matrix corresponding to a causal map is squared, then it reveals second-order relationships, such as $i \rightarrow k \rightarrow j$.

When Combank's adjacency matrix is raised to the matrix power of $N=2$, then its entries denote the second-order paths of change transmission. Some of these change transmission paths can be verified by tracing them in Fig. 6.3.1. For example, it should be easy to see the second-order paths of

- operations flexibility $\rightarrow$ cost $\rightarrow$ profit, and
- functional efficiency of support services $\rightarrow$ cost $\rightarrow$ profit.

By computing consecutive powers of Combank's adjacency matrix, that is, matrix power $N= 3,4,\ldots,15$, allows identifying the number of influence paths of order $N= 3,4,\ldots,15$, respectively. These are third-, fourth-, and higher-order influence paths interconnecting the variables of Combank.

Yet, the lack of feedback loops in the comprehensive situation map of Fig. 6.3.1 ends the MICMAC computations quickly. The nonrecursive CSM reveals a single fifth-order effect just before the consecutive powers of Combank's adjacency matrix become perfectly stable for $N=6$, with all its entries driven to zero. Fig. 6.4.1 verifies that the higher-order matrices reduce to naught from matrix power $N=6$ onward.

Without feedback loops, the sum vectors along the consecutive powers of Combank's adjacency matrix cannot reveal the hierarchy of strategic variables. The stability of such a hierarchy would depend on the indirect (i.e., feedback) effects of a much higher order than $N=5$. The consecutive line plots of Fig. 6.4.1 show the behavioral patterns of change in the exposure and influence of Combank's strategic variables as the adjacency matrix power increases from $N=1$ to $N=15$. Both the exposure and influence values have been *normalized* in Fig. 6.4.1 to allow comparing the consecutive powers of Combank's adjacency matrix.

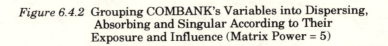

Figure 6.4.2 Grouping COMBANK's Variables into Dispersing,
Absorbing and Singular According to Their
Exposure and Influence (Matrix Power = 5)

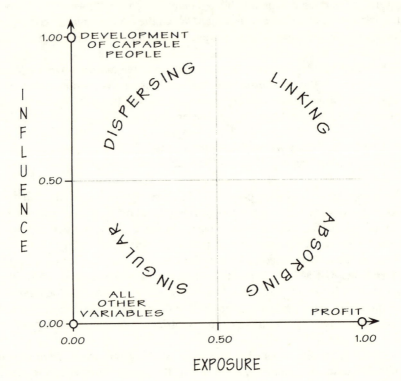

The normalized vectors for matrix power $N=5$ captured the overall influence and overall exposure of Combank's strategic variables in the CSM of Fig. 6.3.1. The plots of these values along the overall exposure and influence dimensions of Combank's strategic variables in Fig 6.4.2 show MICMAC's *intermediate anchoring* of variables into absorbing, dispersing and singular.

Together, Appendix C.3 and Fig. 5.4.1 define the four quadrants of Fig. 6.4.2. Briefly, singular variables cover isolated variables that both affect and are exposed to only a few strategic variables. Dispersing variables affect many but are exposed to a few, influencing other variables directly or indirectly. Absorbing variables affect a few, but are exposed to many. Lastly, linking variables are both highly exposed and highly influential.

The MICMAC results of Fig. 6.4.2 simply confirm the expectations of the Combank planing team, which are already captured in the CSM of Fig. 6.3.1. Typically, the network of relationships among strategic variables is complex and difficult to visualize without comprehensive mapping. Even if the information required for performing matrix multiplication might prove elusive in some cases, managers and planners would still benefit from a design team's efforts to assess the structural importance of strategic variables.

This type of analysis may add more value than the arbitrary assignment of weights to strategic variables. Undertaken within the principles underlying causal mapping, matrix multiplication is a defensible approach. Often, it helps to unearth hidden high-order effects, and it thereby improves strategy design.

These preliminary results conclude the case of Combank for now. Yet, they serve as an advance organizer for Part V, supporting the necessity of computing scenarios to enhance the plural rationality evolving in a management team. Part V presents environmental and decision scenarios computed both on the CSM (Chapter 9) and on computers through full-scale simulation models, both stochastic (Chapter 9) and deterministic (Chapter 10).

It may feel awkward to interrupt the presentation of scenario-driven applications, postponing the computation of scenarios until Part V. Often, however, both our project and our course participants require a mental pause between rough-cut mapping and scenario propagation. This pedagogical pause allows them to reflect on and internalize the diversity of worldviews involved in causal mapping. In itself, causal mapping is a learning experience, forcing participants to think not only about their business, but also about the way they think about their business.

SUMMARY

This second introductory application gradually shows how to implant scenario-

driven planning. Its aim is to enhance strategy design toward accomplishing a favorable strategic posture consistent with a firm's long-term goals. Our intervention at Combank helped a team of top managers refine and jointly formulate the firm's problématique or strategic decision situation. Combank's senior vice-president of strategic planning, and the vice-presidents of finance, marketing, operations and planning shared their divergent but complementary views of the bank. The case narrated the strategic situation coherently through a description that combines Combank's marketing- and technology-centered views.

In the process of implanting scenario-driven planning with Acar's CSM, we seek to surface relationships among variables that opposing schools of thought in a business firm find essential. Our project participants analyzed these relationships for accuracy of perception through a dialectical form of group dynamics. The consecutive use of three computation methods allows the propagation of three generations of change scenarios, analyzing the same relationships for possible future implications—what might happen on a what if basis.

Section 9.2 details Combank's computed scenarios. The insight gained from the scenario-driven planning process leads to the strategic recommendations listed in the Executive Summary.

Part IV

COMPETITIVE ADVANTAGE THROUGH SCENARIOS

Chapter 7

Competitive Intelligence Systems for the 1990s

How are Western firms addressing the challenges of the 1990s? Can they extricate themselves from a two-decade legacy of trailing behind the stunning performance of their Far Eastern competitors? Although morale and culture are important ingredients for success, a firm needs to have a grand design of where it is headed. This chapter addresses the issue of gaining control and managing strategic uncertainty through a scenario-driven competitive intelligence system. The chapter concludes with a warning about rushing impulsively into the most popular, but not necessarily most fruitful, form of scenario construction.

7.1   PRACTICAL CONSIDERATIONS: THE VIEW FROM THE TRENCHES

Forward-thinking managers try to design coherent strategies. Their implementation often resembles the original form, but all too often some designs run afoul of the external environment. So do empires. For example, Minorco had to concede defeat in its bid for the world's second largest gold miner, Consolidated Gold Fields. Failing to go global, Anglo-American, Minorco's parent company, found itself trapped in South Africa's gilded cage.

Conventional techniques of forecasting changes in the environment provide no cohesive way of understanding the effect of changes that have occurred and will occur in the future. In effect, managers have a difficult time separating real from trivial changes and effects. Deciding where action is called for can be even harder if preventive measures are missing.

Most external change effects are of intensity, not of kind. In his provocative book *Business NOT as Usual,* Ian Mitroff (1987) points out that changes in the environment do not merely happen and then go away. They have a lasting effect on business as usual. An example of such threats to business is the spreading environmental fervor. Environmentalist concerns affect industries that are directly involved in 'exploiting' the environment, such as the forest products and petroleum industries.

According to an essay in the *New York Times* by R. Suro (1989), a new form of environmental zeal is spreading throughout the United States. Thousands of people are banding together in small community groups against local industrial plants. These employers, once respected, are now reviled as *poisoners* of the neighborhood. People with no previous interest in environmental issues or other civic affairs are often the leaders of these grassroots efforts. Their targets are frequently the smokestacks visible from their front doors. The new protesters include working class people, in addition to more affluent people who can afford to live farther away.

In reaction, some executives and management theorists are engaging in a version of the popular television game shows which R. E. Freeman likes to call "Blame the Stakeholder." In *Strategic Management: A Stakeholder Approach* (1984), Freeman contends that the times are producing *scapegoatism*. In "Blame the Stakeholder," most contestants lead companies that have experienced changes in the environment. They are asked to pick a stakeholder group and to blame the position of their company on that group. Government is a favorite culprit, with special interest groups not too far behind. Engaging in such games generates little serious progress, no matter how good it makes us feel. At some point, firms must stop fighting the last war and take a careful look at the response options open to them. It is at that point that scenario-driven planning becomes relevant. Denial—

refusing to admit that the external environment is the way it is—provides but false comfort. Being kept busy fighting the last war, many firms refuse to admit that external stakeholder groups have a stake in business. They can make or break a firm.

Psychological projection occurs when we blame someone else or some external event for our own shortcomings. It is so easy to project a firm's inability to satisfy stakeholder needs on the group itself. Often, stakeholder groups and their concerns are called unreasonable or irrational (Freeman, 1984, p. 23; Freud, 1933).

Another response pattern is available. It is summarized in the comic strip *Pogo:* "We have seen the enemy and it is us." According to Abraham Zaleznik, the Konosuke Matsushita professor at the Harvard Business School, today's companies need leaders, not merely conciliators. Zaleznik believes that business leaders must accept and learn from failure to meet stakeholder needs (personal communication, 2/15/91).

Not all stakeholder needs can or should be met, and, of course, at times horrible mistakes cannot be avoided. Moreover, corporate social responsibility may be neither a necessary nor a sufficient condition for successful performance. Baron points out the lack of empirical support for the relationship between performance dimensions, such as competitiveness and profitability, and actions taken in the cause of ethics and corporate social responsibility: "Even if there were an empirical relationship, the direction of causality would have to be established. That is, does socially responsible behavior lead to superior performance or does superior performance allow a firm to take socially responsible actions?" (Baron, 1993, p. 502).

Yet, human fallibility is not much of an excuse for failing to acknowledge the inadequacy and complacency resulting from continually being busy fighting the wars of the past. Naturally, rough play requires talent. It is an art, but not necessarily one that is conducive to increasing productivity.

No matter how artfully bureaucratic, today's firms can no longer ignore changes in the global environment. These changes have given rise to a perplexing dilemma, and business leaders are faced with a severe psychic risk. On the one hand, the dilemma requires understanding each change individually to adjust a firm's strategic direction relative to each change in the environment. On the other hand, if several changes in the environment occur together with changes in a firm's strategy, then piecemeal tactics implemented in the prevailing style of management will amount to less than an adequate strategic response.

Deming states that we are "Living under the tyranny of the prevailing style of management" (1993, p. xi). Imagine the psychic risk of artfully political leaders who do not understand their firm's strategic situation. Direct communication, creative dialogue, and honest confrontation are replaced by manipulation. The creativity of the firm is diminished, people lose their zest for work, and valuable talent goes unexplored or moves elsewhere.

Power struggles? No, power fullness. Leadership contains power. Yet, the most important element of power is internalization. According to Pfeffer (1981), internalizing power means that managers "feel" right on the job, which in turn means that managers' mental capabilities and talents are reflected in decision making.

No matter how artfully concealed, an incomplete understanding of a firm's strategic situation will prevent subordinates from helping their leaders lead. In turn, the leaders will not be able to guide or to protect their subordinates. Low cognizance of the nature and structure of a firm's strategic situation leads to power loss. The informational base of power breaks off, and its moral foundation becomes shaky.

In its search for the secret of business excellence, the popular press bemoans US firms' stress on analysis and lack of leadership talent. In today's quest for business leaders as opposed to conciliators, any interest in scenarios shown by the strategist or executive should be welcomed. Yet, we need a clearer delineation of scenario-driven planning to make it a potentially rich field of practice and research—rich in the sense that it can foster effective or efficiently adaptive strategic management. Strategizing is a creative conceptual activity. If business leaders and management scholars are to take up the scenario challenge, they must base organizational learning on environmental analysis with scenario-driven planning.

This approach reflects the overriding goal of scenario-driven planning: to create the necessary conceptual framework for filtering the product of observation and extracting coherent information out of it, to be ready to better learn from experience. Having gathered experience on the job and in strategy design, the line manager can then rise above the ceiling of daily pains and its attendant information overload.

Computer scientists see a need for more data, but in reality most of us are flooded with data. What we need to do is learn to recognize patterns in the data and to compose relevant information for strategic turnaround. The view from the trenches is that time is of the essence. The corporate vehicle must keep rolling at full speed on the road to the future, all the while repairing itself.

7.2   THE COMPETITIVE ADVANTAGE OF SCENARIOS

Arthur Andersen & Co. (1984) emphasizes that, to be useful, scenario-driven planning should correspond to real-world circumstances. Scenarios must involve managers by provoking consideration of how subtle variations in a few key relationships can have profound consequences. Another observer claims that managers' active involvement in scenario-driven planning can lead to a powerful competitive advantage (Becker, 1982).

Traditionally, future trends and events have been projected as extrapolations of past events and data. Based on the premise that the future *is* the product of the past, planners have developed such forecasting techniques as trend extrapolation and econometric modeling. Elegant as these methods are, their performance in the last several decades has been far from satisfactory (Zentner, 1987). As a result, scenarios must provide some sense of the future environment that managers will encounter or create through their expectations. To be useful, each scenario should be built around a central theme that serves both to set the tone of the scenario and to create the organizing principle from which to construct it.

Despite their brevity and macroeconomic nature, the global predicament scenarios of Drucker (1986) and Marris (1985) afford a convenient framework in which to organize extensive data about the future of the world economy. Each scenario

- is built around a central theme that focuses attention on causal processes and decision points;
- provokes consideration of how small variations in a few relationships can have profound consequences;
- supports the necessity of integrating qualitative and quantitative information into a consistent picture;
- is not a simple forecast, but is built on the premise that the future is not the product of the past.

To provide a point of reference and an immediate example, the following section details a project undertaken by the Battelle Institute of Columbus, Ohio, for Goodyear Aerospace. Battelle/Goodyear Aerospace's scenario-driven planning project probably had a greater psychological than tangible impact. It challenged the conventional wisdom and, to some extent, complacency. Paul Schoemaker (1993) argues that the psychological benefit of scenario-driven planning may stem from the exploration of one set of conjunction fallacies to counteract another set, such as the overconfidence in a firm's current strategy.

Indeed, Goodyear Aerospace had been warned of potential market threats. In this regard, scenario-driven planning has a great psychological effect. It enables its participants to anticipate potential shocks to a business environment, and so it mitigates the damage of surprises. Our consulting experience with scenario-driven planning is similar to that of Millett & Randles (1986). We find that the propagation of strategic change scenarios stimulates much discussion, whereas computed scenarios creep into strategy in numerous subtle ways.

The Battelle/Goodyear Aerospace experience shows the importance of involving scenario users in selecting scenario themes and data, and in incorporating information into the scenarios. Like the scenarios of Drucker and Marris, the US defense expenditure scenarios of Millett & Randles (1986) integrate qualitative and quantitative information into a consistent picture of the defense industry. Built around a central theme, they focus on causal processes and provoke consideration of how variations in a few key relationships or values can have profound consequences.

A word of caution is in order here. Unless the managers who will be using the scenarios are involved in their development from the beginning, they will not understand them and will be reluctant to use them. In his account of the use of scenarios in the chemical industry, Zentner (1987) observes that most contemporary managers and graduate business students prefer a world of certainty, even though their experience suggests the contrary. Those with a scientific or engineering background find it especially difficult to plan with several alternative futures. They are capable of wasting considerable time on the inquiry, "Which is the most probable future?" Zentner argues that asking this question not only is unprofitable, but also shows lack of understanding of probability concepts.

It is interesting to observe how fast Goodyear Aerospace moved from a single forecast to a multiple-scenario platform. Several scenario experts point out that implanting scenario-driven planning is difficult. In dealing with cultural resistance, for example, Amara & Lipinski (1983, p. 198) satirically allude to the need for a corporate anthropologist who would describe tribal dances (i.e., decision-making meetings), tribal smoke signals (i.e., corporate communications), and the tribal power structure. Even Godet's modular and mechanistic method takes twelve to eighteen months to implement. At least half of that time is taken up with constructing the base. In Godet's scenario method (1987), the base is an image of the present state of the system, which serves as a starting point for the futures study. In the much cited case of Shell, it took *eight years* for scenario-driven planning to become fully accepted.

Chandler & Cockle (1982) express surprise that managers at the very top of the business tree could doubt the importance of scenario-driven planning. It can be surprising to those steeped in strategy design. The following two views represent the two ends of a spectrum of opinion on the use of scenarios. These perspectives were presented at a symposium for chief executives held in London in the early 1980s. About a dozen of the United Kingdom's top blue-chip corporations were represented. The representative of the oil sector spoke of his firm's use of scenario-driven planning: "Our planners have an international reputation. They've been doing this sort of thing now for a number of years and have persuaded our managers of the importance of their work by being right about many of the uncertainties" (Chandler & Cockle, 1982, p. 125). He went on to explain that this planning team had first crossed his path at a presentation overseas in the early 1970s, before the 1973 oil crisis. They had warned then of the likelihood of major oil price rises; they were heard politely, of course, but with little belief. Ten years later, their scenarios are viewed as an essential and integral part of the management process for the corporation. And yet: "That's fine for you," observed another from a more beleaguered industrial sector, "but it doesn't seem relevant when you're fighting for survival. People get cynical about planning at a time like this" (Chandler & Cockle, 1982, p. 125). Sir Joshua Reynolds once said: "Man is the animal who will spare no energy, no effort to avoid the problem of thinking" (cf. Amara & Lipinski, 1983, p. 200).

It is indeed amazing how most of us and some reactive managers as well, when busy fighting the last war, always find the time to fight planning. In today's complex and turbulent global environment, managers are paid to think ahead and to encourage long-term thinking. Yet, sometimes they heed the advice of those organization theorists for whom the environment is always unknowable and intractable. Drucker (1954) was quite right to declare that planning was "not a respectable human activity." Though a rather harsh indictment, Mintzberg (1993) concurs. Yet, any planning would be unnatural if it tried to inject a long-term perspective in an environment of short-term rewards (Amara & Lipinski, 1983).

Corporate cultures, which contain consensual views of the future, change neither quickly nor easily in large firms. Changes in the fundamentals, surprises, and discontinuities can all be perceived as very threatening, destabilizing, and costly. Yet, in Goodyear's Aerospace Division, it took less than a year for scenario-driven planning to become accepted. By the summer of 1985, "managers were thinking and planning in their own creative ways according to a unified expectation of future market conditions" (Millet & Randles, 1986, p. 71).

The purpose of scenario-driven planning is to force managers and planners to wrestle with realistic alternative futures in advance; to think of *contingencies* and alternative responses early. To achieve this goal, creative scenarios are needed, backed with plausible analyses of the propagation of change. In addition to having a central theme that involves their potential users early on, scenarios must be anchored into a methodologically sound and productive approach to strategy design. Often, the results are strategic flexibility and greater adaptability.

7.3 AN EXAMPLE OF THE STATE OF THE ART: BATTELLE'S STUDY ON US DEFENSE EXPENDITURES

In January 1984, the Goodyear Aerospace Company asked the Battelle Institute of Columbus, Ohio, to help it generate scenarios with its proprietary software BASICS (Battelle Scenario Inputs to Corporate Strategy) method. The Battelle Institute is a leader in methods of scenario generation. Its analysts, such as Honton, Stacey, and Millett, have written several brochures to describe these methods. The purpose of Goodyear Aerospace was to estimate global economic, political, and military conditions to 1995. These conditions were expected to affect US defense requirements and thereby the firm's products.

The project began by determining objectives and identifying sixteen key variables and trends, which Battelle calls *descriptors*. These descriptors included the Soviet-American strategic balance, arms control, international conflict, worldwide arms trade, defense technologies and US defense expenditures in their international context. They were selected for their importance to the company and their

significance for the future security of the United States, the firm's principal customer. Battelle prepared a five-page essay on each descriptor. These essays provided company managers with valuable insights into macro trends about which
they had been interested but not well informed. They also established a factual and
probabilistic foundation for integrating the trends into logically consistent sets of
descriptor states that could be expected by 1995.

BASICS builds scenarios through cross-impact analysis. Intuitive and purely
qualitative scenarios may be adequate for relatively simple decision situations in
placid environments, but even then, such scenarios lack the rigor that cross-impact
analysis brings to strategic decision making. In long-range, multifactor (i.e., complex), and highly uncertain environments, cross-impact analysis is believed to
provide a systematic and objective way of networking business trends into a coherent set of hypothetical sequences of probabilistic occurrence (Duval, Fontela, &
Gabus, 1975; Honton, Stacey, & Millett, 1985; Stover & Gordon, 1978). Godet's
MICMAC and SMIC methods bear a relationship to Battelle's cross-impact technique. For this reason, we explain cross-impact analysis in some detail and give an
example.

In BASICS, all descriptors and their alternative states are arrayed along the
rows and columns of a matrix. The hypothetical occurrence of each descriptor state
may cause the probabilities of occurrence of all other descriptor states to increase
or decrease. Proceeding down the columns of the matrix, each cell of the cross-impact matrix carries an index value of these estimated impacts, from +3=greatly increases to -3=greatly decreases. Figure 7.3.1 illustrates how BASICS represents
cross impacts through a one-descriptor by one-descriptor block of cells.

This 3×4 matrix is one block extracted from a 49×49 cross-impact matrix. The
larger, complete cross-impact matrix has 2,401 cells. These portray the impact values of US defense expenditures on the United States' strategic nuclear delivery
vehicles (SNDVs). The matrix is to be read as follows.

The probability of more than 2,400 SNDVs by 1995 is estimated at $p=0.10$. If
US defense expenditures were to be 9 to 13 percent of GNP by 1995, then that
would have a moderately strong impact, indicated by the "2" index entry, on the
probability that SNDVs will be more than 2,400. Similarly, it would have a moderately strong but negative impact, that is, the -2 entry, on SNDVs numbering less
than 1,700, including all strategic missiles and bombers.

Appendix C.4 gives a detailed technical summary of BASICS. Briefly here,
BASICS starts with initial probabilities of occurrence, known in statistical decision
theory as the *a priori probabilities*. Then, it recomputes all the cross-impact index
values and adjusts the initial probabilities, so that the given a priori probabilities of
the descriptor states are driven to one (i.e., will certainly occur), or zero (i.e., will
certainly not occur).

The program runs numerous simulations, which are scenario sequences of de-

Figure 7.3.1 **The Cross-Impact Matrix of Miller & Randles (1986)**

U. S. Strategic Nuclear Delivery Vehicles (SNDVs)	U. S. Defense Expenditures		
	9-13% of GNP	6-9% of GNP	3-6% of GNP
>2400 (p=0.10)	2	-1	-2
2000-2400 (p=0.30)	1	0	-1
1700-2000 (p=0.40)	-1	0	1
<1700 (p=0.20)	-2	-1	2

scriptor-state occurrence and nonoccurrence. They are based on BASICS' computational formula for probability adjustments. BASICS then organizes them into scenarios. In Battelle's approach, scenarios are aggregations of simulations with identically occurring descriptor states.

In the Goodyear Aerospace study, analysis of the total number of computer simulations and of the resulting scenarios produced a mainline, *most likely* scenario and a *principal alternative* scenario for the international environment until 1995. These were reported to middle managers in June and to upper-level managers in September 1984. In some respects, the mainline scenario portrayed a continuation of several trends for another ten years (1985-1995). In this most likely future, for example, the size of the US and Soviet strategic arsenals, the strategic arms limitation talks (SALT), and the strategic doctrine (i.e., deterrence with a triad of strategic forces), all were expected to endure.

Other results of the most likely scenario were surprising and disconcerting to Goodyear Aerospace managers. Based on the interactions with other descriptors, for example, of two different rates of deployment of new military technologies, the slower one occurred in most simulations. In other words, the environment was expected to retard the rate of new technology deployment rather than accelerate it. In retrospect, this surprising result now appears to be rather accurate.

Another surprising result was that US defense expenditures would most likely be 3 to 6 percent of the US gross national product (GNP) by 1995. There was an intuitive expectation that this descriptor would climb to 9 percent of GNP. Yet, this low state (3 to 6%) of the mainline scenario coincided with the stable strategic arsenal, the SALT regime, and the nonoccurrence of a major power projection by the US. The military buildup of the first Reagan administration had most likely peaked in 1984.

This scenario of defense expenditures received a hostile response from some middle-level managers. It was presented in the summer of 1984, when Reagan's reelection seemed inevitable. Real growth in defense expenditures had been as high as 27 percent in 1980-1984. Also, the real annual growth rate had recently been as high as 6 to 8 percent. Thus, several managers were confident that the rate of defense spending would continue for another four years.

By the summer of 1985, however, it was clear that Congress would not support Reagan's programs. The mainline scenario prepared in 1984 was already playing in the first year of its ten-year period, much to the skeptical delight of the Battelle analysts and Goodyear Aerospace planners.

Not all scenario-building techniques are based on cross-impact analysis. The importance of Battelle's study is that the managers who participated in this scenario-driven planning project were responsible for integrating the scenario implications into strategic plans for their products. Some found this responsibility easier to carry out than others, but all had been exposed to the alternatives for their customer, business environment, and product growth potential.

Meanwhile, top executives supported the approach enthusiastically. They appreciated their middle-level managers' thinking and planning in their own creative ways, according to unified expectations of future market conditions. Such expectations could *not* have been imposed on them by either top management or an outside consultant.

7.4   HASTE MAKES WASTE: A WORD OF CAUTION

Active engagement and support of senior managers are essential for scenario-driven planning to succeed. Both in Goodyear Aerospace and in the Royal Dutch-Shell Group of Companies, the scenario planning teams had gained support among top corporate policymakers (Millet & Randles, 1986; Schwartz, 1991; Wack, 1985a, 1985b).

Despite his guardian angel group, Pierre Wack, the chief planner at Shell UK (see Section 2.4), left some managers unconvinced that scenarios were necessary and a valuable input to planning. According to Arie de Geus, some of Shell's managers and planners were debating the scenarios' connection with actual decisions: "For most outside observers, this internal debate would have been an enigma" (1992, p. 2).

Wack himself made the following assessment of scenarios:

> Scenarios deal with two worlds, the world of facts and the world of perceptions. They explore for facts but they aim at perceptions inside the heads of decision makers. Their purpose is to gather and to transform information of strategic significance into fresh perceptions. This transformation process is not trivial—more often than not it does not happen. When it works, it is a creative experience that generates a heartfelt "Aha!" from your managers and leads to strategic insight beyond the mind's previous reach (1985b, p. 140).

Battelle's approach to scenario-driven planning is fundamentally different from Wack's. The managers of Goodyear Aerospace identified pertinent variables and trends in the firm's environment (i.e., Battelle's descriptors). In addition to getting managers involved early on, Battelle offered a specific method for generating environmental scenarios in a productive fashion. Although focusing on decision variables is extraneous to Battelle's scenario method, BASICS allows for a speedy computation of the resulting scenarios.

The eight-year lag to acceptance at Shell was partly due to the lack of a specific method for constructing environmental scenarios in a focused manner. According to Wack, scenarios were introduced to the planning process at Shell on an experimental basis. The use of scenario-driven planning initially stood a high risk of being emasculated by losing its credibility with line managers.

In addition to its lack of a clearly articulated method, scenario-driven planning at Shell was split off as a separate staff activity. Over time, scenario construction was increasingly seen as a participative alternative to forecasting, which did not involve line managers early on in the process. Despite the initial lack of a scenario construction method, the eight-year lag gave Wack a lot of time to reflect on the changing laws that govern managerial behavior at Shell. In his insightful analysis of scenario-driven planning, Wack notes that whether scenarios succeed or fail depends on the inner model of reality of the decision maker. This model is an organized set of assumptions that guides the decision maker's inner understanding of how and why the business environment is going to unfold. It incorporates critical external triggers of changes in the environment and critical internal change levers that decision makers pull or push, trying to gear into success. Such an inner model never blandly mirrors reality; it does more than that. It is always a construct, a negotiated perception of reality, focused on the causal structure of key external and internal variables in a strategic situation.

Karl Weick (1977, 1979) argues that the environment we see ourselves is mainly enacted, conjured up by our perceptions and imagination. In stable times, a reasonably good match can be had between this mental model and the unfolding reality and scenario-driven planning has less to offer than in troubled times. In times of rapid and unexpected change, however, one's mental model by itself is not as helpful. It is in such situations that scenario-driven planning has leverage, making the difference between good and bad decisions.

Because they are alternative ways of seeing the world, scenarios afford a systematic method of breaking out of a decision maker's single worldview. Scenario-driven planning offers another perspective and provides the ability to reperceive reality. In turbulent times, as Wack proposes, there is more to see than we normally perceive. Information potentially relevant to us is lying around unnoticed because, locked into our way of looking at things and change, we fail to see its significance. Not only should we take the time for "walking around" (Peters & Waterman, 1982), but also for *looking around* to check on our implicit assumptions and to correct them with properly filtered information. The next chapter discusses this issue further.

SUMMARY

In the face of today's societal shift from the industrial to the postindustrial era, the global environment is dynamically complex, discontinuous, and turbulent. No matter how perceived, this shift is a force that business clearly must handle. In times of rapid and unexpected change, logical incrementalism guided by mental models is not sufficient. It is in such situations that scenario-driven planning provides analytical power and consistency. It can make the difference between good and bad decisions.

Because they are alternative ways of seeing the world, scenarios afford a systematic method of breaking out of each decision maker's single worldview. Scenario-driven planning offers other perspectives of reality. Its rationality (i.e., its particular synthesis of perception and analysis) systematically expands the way managers think, learn, and feel about strategic situations.

Scenario-driven planning perhaps has more psychological than tangible punch. It challenges the conventional wisdom and, to some extent, complacency. Indeed, scenario-driven planning has a great psychological effect by anticipating potential shocks to a business environment and mitigating the damage of surprises. Thus prepared, managers can devote their energies to redirecting their firms, taking advantage of opportunities and attenuating threats. Scenario-driven planning contributes to a firm's capacity to anticipate, to prepare for, and to create its own future.

Chapter 8

Features of the Proposed Planning Process

The pursuit of competitive intelligence is not for the indolent or the fainthearted. It is not a lineal sequential process that can be achieved in one go, but an iterative and painstaking one. First, there is the chronic lack of reliable information. Then, there are the inevitable modeling or computational errors that will creep into the early iterations. Such considerations do not surprise seasoned practitioners or strategy researchers. Less understood is the degree to which strategic management depends on unstated assumptions—the planner's, the manager's, and society's. To show how scenarios can make the process more productive, this chapter revisits the crucial role of assumption analysis in strategic planning.

8.1   PREREQUISITES OF SCENARIO ANALYSIS

The Importance of Consistent Assumptions

Arie de Geus (1988) notes that managers increasingly view scenarios as sources of "new knowledge." Scenario-driven planning can become a firm's "tool for learning" about business and social systems. Because planning is directed toward the future, predictions of changes in the environment are indispensable components of it and an important source of information for strategic management.

Scenarios provide corporate intelligence and a link on the path from traditional forecasting methods toward interactive planning. Yet, even experts' predictive judgments are based on historical expertise. A *broadened* search for expertise would not detract attention from grasping creativity and intuition in newly encountered strategic situations.

Writers in the strategy field recognize that human cognitive limits affect strategic decisions. Those responsible for strategy design face an ambiguous task of extreme complexity. The conceptual framework of Fig. 4.2.1 shows only a few of the elements involved in the process of strategy design. The complexity of managing uncertainty through changes in strategy appears almost infinite, while the matching human and organizational information processing capability is usually limited. The concept of bounded rationality and the requirements it makes of organizational decision making can help firms appreciate the contribution of scenario-driven planning to managing strategic uncertainty.

Bounded rationality reflects people's cognitive limits (Simon, 1957). Individuals faced with complex choices are unable to make objectively rational decisions because

1. They cannot generate all the alternative courses of action.
2. They cannot handle all the information needed to predict the implications of choosing a given alternative.
3. They can neither value nor select among anticipated implications.

The wide range of feasible courses of action available and the large amount of information required to coordinate actions make organizational problems particularly complex. Often, good decisions are a consequence of simplified decision making. Organizations are designed to "transform intractable decision problems into tractable ones" (Simon, 1979, p. 501). Organizational members exhibit bounded rationality and make rational decisions under simplified conditions of choice. Herbert Simon (1979) describes the simplification of organizational deci-

sion making in terms of a psychological environment that adapts managerial decisions to organizational objectives, providing each manager with information to
make correct decisions.

Yet, this simplification is a double-edged sword (Morecroft, 1985b). It promotes seemingly rational and decentralized decision making, but it does not guarantee that managerial choices are either consistent or mutually supportive. The
most common organizational processes for simplifying decision making include
(1) authority and corporate culture; (2) factoring; (3) goals and incentives; (4) routine; and (5) cognitive biases (CBs).

Authority and corporate culture simplify decision making intangibly. They
transmit a firm's values and traditions to all its constituents. In turn, these values
and traditions permeate thinking in all decision functions, altering the assumptions
of decision makers and introducing bias and distortion into the interpretation of information. Forrester (1968a) shows how the president of a firm with a fast-growing
new product line insisted on a tight control over all capital expenditures, thereby
biasing the firm's capital renewal decisions. High backlogs were the outcome of
this bias, with customer orders having to accumulate to justify expansion. Forrester
incorporated this conservative facet of authority and corporate culture into a system dynamics model to show how a bias in orders for capital could cause sales to
stagnate even in a fast-growing market with a large sales potential.

Factoring simplifies decision making through a network of specialized decision
functions (Morecroft, 1988). This network handles the distribution of information
among a firm's decision functions. Each function receives only part of the available information, an amount small enough for timely processing and action. With
no decision maker having the whole picture, each has a unique but limited view of
a firm's strategic situation (Allison, 1971; Cyert & March, 1963).

Goals and incentives also simplify decision making. They focus managerial attention on specific dimensions of performance by determining what information is
important in making a decision (e.g., shipments against orders outstanding), and
what information can be ignored (e.g., quality). Frantic changes ensure that each
goal is met at the end of each quarter regardless of any strategic implications. This
is short-sighted decision making at work, but it is simple (Morecroft, 1985b).

Organizational routines simplify decision making by confining information
from predetermined sources processed with simple rules of thumb (Allison, 1971,
p. 83; Nelson & Winter, 1982, pp. 96-136). In magazine publishing, for example, a
prevalent routine is to link the number of pages of each issue to the number of advertising pages sold. More advertising pages result in a thicker magazine. This can
work, but it can also contribute to financial loss if production and distribution cost
exceeds revenue (Hall, 1976, p. 195).

Cognitive psychologists and behavioral decision theorists have identified a
wide range of cognitive biases (CBs) that simplify the decision makers' perceptions of a strategic situation, rendering strategy design manageable. Some behav-

ioral decision theorists prefer the term *heuristics* because the term *biases* suggests that these cognitive simplification processes have a negative effect on strategic decisions. Tversky & Kahneman, Winkler & Murphy, and others observe that CBs may actually improve decisions. Firms can display effective decision making despite people's cognitive limits and the overabundance of information (Morecroft, 1988; Simon, 1976; Tversky & Kahneman, 1974; Winkler & Murphy, 1973). Though useful, CBs sometimes lead to severe and systematic errors (Tversky & Kahneman, 1974, p. 1125).

Drawing on the expanding literature on CBs, Schwenk conjectures about cognitive simplification processes that are frequently encountered in problem forming and decision making under uncertainty. Schwenk assumes that the formulation of strategic situations begins with the recognition of gaps between expectations or standards and performance. These standards may be based on past trends, projected trends, standards of global competitors, expectations of internal and external stakeholder groups, and even normative strategy models.

In 1984 Schwenk published nine sets of cognitive biases, CB_1 through CB_9, and proposed the grouping shown in Table 8.1.1 according to the decision-making stage these biases affect. This long list of potential pitfalls for strategic thinkers reveals how difficult managerial planning and learning from experience have become. In a manager's day-to-day work, this sorry situation is further worsened by the lack of availability of pertinent and well-structured information.

Schwenk's purpose in discussing the effects of these processes on strategy design was not to criticize the quality of strategic decisions. Rather, he wanted to generate ideas about the ways decision makers actually deal with complexity, ambiguity, and uncertainty. His focus on processes encountered both in the laboratory and in field settings allows the selection of biases with a high probability of affecting strategic decision making.

A central feature of strategy design situations is their lack of structure. The strategic decision-making process is characterized by novelty, complexity, and openendedness (Mintzberg, Raisinghani, & Théorêt, 1976). Strategic decision makers begin with little comprehension of a situation and their understanding deepens as they work on its formulation.

Mason & Mitroff (1981) note the lack of structure and complexity of strategic situations. Strategic situations have no clear form, they state; it is extremely difficult either to describe them or to determine the criteria by which strategic alternatives should be judged. Managers are right to complain that strategy design situations are complex and involve environmental uncertainty and ambiguity.

These arguments suggest that it may be dangerous to draw situation-specific conclusions from the available expertise on scenario construction and analysis. Scenarios are directed at ill-structured strategic situations. Yet, it is striking how little attention is paid to the process of strategic situation formulation or problem forming. Among the phases of intelligence, design, choice, and implementation, many writers focus mainly on choice and implementation. Concerned authors, realizing this shortcoming, argue for the need to focus on intelligence and design. Among these authors is Godet, who comments on the complementary scenarios used to bring corporate futures into perspective: "Forecasting work operates in one direction but not in reverse: models have to be tested in the framework of the interplay of probable, *coherent hypotheses* supplied by the scenarios, and not the other way around" (Godet, 1987, p. 22; emphasis ours).

Table 8.1.1 Grouping of Cognitive Biases (CBs) Adapted from Schwenk (1984)

Decision-Making Stage I: GOAL/PROBLEM FORMULATION

CB_1 : *Prior hypothesis bias* and *adjustment and anchoring.* Influenced by these biases, decision makers perceive fewer gaps than their data indicate.

CB_2 : *Escalating commitment.* Under its influence, decision makers minimize the significance of gaps, and do not make full use of these gaps for changes in strategy. Strategic decision makers may even become more committed when they receive feedback indicating failure than indicating success.

CB_3 : *Reasoning by analogy.* Even if the significance of a gap is recognized, decision makers define the factors causing the gap through an analogy to a simpler situation.

Decision-Making Stage II: GENERATION OF ALTERNATIVES

CB_4 : *Single-outcome calculation.* In searching for a solution to a problematic situation, decision makers generate and bolster a single alternative rather than a few.

CB_5 : *Inferences of impossibility* and *denying value tradeoffs.* Decision makers deal with nonpreferred alternatives by denying that these serve any values better than the preferred alternative, and by overestimating the difficulties of their implementation.

CB_6 : *Problem set.* Under its effect, and that of unchallenged assumptions, decision makers who attempt to generate more than one alternative generate only a few.

Decision-Making Stage III: EVALUATION AND SELECTION

CB_7 : *Representativeness.* Under its influence, decision makers overestimate the accuracy of their predictions of the consequences of alternatives.

CB_8 : *Illusion of control.* Under its influence, decision makers overestimate the importance of their own actions in ensuring the success of alternatives.

CB_9 : *Devaluation of partially described alternatives.* Decision makers exhibit a preference for alternatives described in detail, even though partially described alternatives score higher on their evaluation criteria.

Within the context of defining critical internal and external variables in the scenario analysis phase, Hax & Majluf of MIT state: " The current state of knowledge in management precludes structuring this activity in a more solid scientific base we at least can submit managers to an orderly process aimed at extracting from them their vision of the firm and its environment" (Hax & Majluf, 1984, p. 158).

Little thought is given to the elicitation of assumptions governing the construction of scenarios. For example, the third step of the process of constructing industry scenarios proposed by Porter in *Competitive Advantage,* reads: " Make a range of *plausible assumptions* about each important causal factor" (Porter, 1985, p. 449).

Realizing Assumptional Consistency: A Synoptic View

Porter's work has revolutionized strategic management, but unfortunately, he does not provide a method for ensuring the consistency of events subsumed under each of his industry scenarios. Mason & Mitroff (1981) point out the importance of assumption surfacing and the generation of counterassumptions through dialectical debate. The name given to their method is SAST (strategic assumption surfacing and testing). Methodological vagueness can only help disguise biased planning under a cloak of logical self-consistency. Consistency in the conjuring up of plausible future events cannot be ensured without a coherent technique for computing the combined effects of changes in the environment and in strategy.

Underlying the literature in scenario analysis and construction is the premise that creative scenarios can be constructed through the mere aggregation of data. Chandler & Cockle (1982) and Godet (1987) present summaries of such case studies. The same applies to the case studies presented in works by Brauers & Weber (1988), Morris (1982), and Potts (1985). Typically, scenario works assume that more and better information will also lead to better scenarios and better forecasts. Godet views the construction of a database as an important prerequisite to the construction of scenarios.

Several large banks with headquarters in the United States, such as Bank of America, Chemical Bank, Citibank, Chase Manhattan, and Manufacturers Hanover Trust, currently scan and analyze the domestic and international environment. With three different units engaged in the process, Citibank probably has the most sophisticated intelligence system. One unit is charged with the task of detecting and analyzing economic trends, another focuses on political risk analysis, and the third concentrates on monitoring the sociopolitical environment. Prebble & Reichel (1988) show that many of Citibank's innovations have been attributed to these units.

The availability of data for scenario construction and strategic decision making is not being questioned. Rather, the scenario approach is mostly one of thinking about the relationships among selected variables. Then, one might apply statistical techniques to estimate values of parameters in these equations, or to perform sensitivity analyses (Bogue & Buffa, 1986). The common underlying hypothesis remains that these relationships will hold over time. They are assumed to describe a strategic situation in enough detail to construct creative scenarios or to obtain accurate forecasts through consensus.

With regard to the proper method of constructing scenarios, it is difficult to identify a generic framework. At one extreme is Ackoff (1981) who recommends the use of scenarios only through structured group processes or adaptive processes of learning and evolution. At the other extreme, most of the existing software packages for scenario construction, such as BASICS, INTERAX, KONMACA, SCENSIM, and SMIC, require hard data. Typically, these packages average judgmental estimates through a sophisticated mathematical algorithm. A generic example might be the analytic hierarchy process (AHP) formulated by Saaty (1987) whose advantage is stability in output from small variations in data input.

Yet, these packages are not conducive to a dialectical exploration, where a group viewpoint is not constrained to average out individual views. For learning and evolution to take place, scenario construction must drop any form of averaging and explore the causalities underlying a strategic situation. An interactive approach to scenario-driven planning intelligence might be preferable, particularly one with a built in divergence-convergence scheme (Acar, 1983; Ackoff, 1981; Lahr, 1983).

Several observations can be made about integrating scenario-driven planning into a firm's strategic management process. One line of research tries to assess organizational environments according to principles from cognitive psychology. One very strong group put together at the University of Bath has developed software to produce cognitive and concept maps. These follow the works of cognitive psychologists such as Kelly (1955) and Bannister & Fransella (1971). Yet, the generalizability of these principles to business situations is still low. In a related thrust, Daft & Weick (1984) recommend building up interpretations about the environment as a basic requirement of individual and organizational assessment.

As a polar extreme, the converse consideration deals with the relevance of computerized models to support the construction of scenarios. After the planner constructs a structural (i.e., mathematical) model of the environment and the strategic situation , (s)he normally chooses to translate it into a computer program. The reference and the contrasted scenarios can then be run faster, and modifications involving sets of different factors can be made more easily.

In the computerized approach, the intermediate step of pseudocoding can show the structure of intuitive logical alternatives and make programming easier. This pseudocoding step helps programmers obtain an agreement from the decision makers before any programs are fully coded. In system dynamics, for example, the pseudocoding of DYNAMO© (DYNAmic MOdels) may require diagramming the relationships among levels and rates (Forrester, 1961, 1969; Lyneis, 1980; Roberts et al., 1983). Even user-friendly programs, namely, iThink™ (Richmond, Peterson, & Charyk, 1992) and STELLA® (Richmond & Peterson, 1992a), are rather intricate for the initial problem-framing stage of scenario-driven planning. Managers and consultants may refrain from using them at the beginning of a dialectic among stakeholder groups.

The causal mapping method we advocate provides a convenient desktop tool. Part V will show how comprehensive situation mapping (CSM) blends additivity and transitivity properties into a technique for propagating change scenarios from variable to variable. These features of CSM allow the development of a method for analyzing complex strategic situations by generating change scenarios.

For the sake of completeness, the framework outlined by Godet (1987) does hint toward a dialectical debate between the most likely or *reference* scenario and the *contrasted* scenarios. His underlying hypothesis, however, is that relationships within the most likely scenario do hold, and the strategic situation is described in enough detail to provide decision support.

In line with the work pioneered by Ackoff (1970, 1981), Churchman (1968, 1971) and Mason & Mitroff (1981), and in sharp contrast to Godet's (1987), Acar's (1983) CSM allows intermeshing scenarios with dialectics. The causal mapping technique of CSM is a process contrast between convergence and divergence. This convergence-divergence scheme owes an intellectual debt to the SAST of Mason & Mitroff. Within CSM, however, assumption analysis is methodologically anchored in and supported by the causal mapping method.

Synoptic View of Comprehensive Situation Mapping (CSM)

In CSM, causal mapping and SAST are integrated into a single methodological continuum. In practical terms, this enables stakeholder groups to engage in a dialectical inquiry of potential problems. Thus, they can avoid problems or design strategy to turn problems into opportunities, while keeping a firm adaptive to new circumstances. For this reason, CSM could also be described as dialectical mapping. Comprehensive situation mapping represents an application to strategy design of the stakeholder theory of the firm, sketched out by Freeman and others (Acar, 1983; Acar, Chaganti, & Joglekar, 1985; Freeman, 1984).

We advocate this process because it offers the option of a single-perspective analytic with multiperspective dialectics. In the first or divergence phase of CSM, each decision maker's view of the nature and structure of a strategic situation is diagrammed separately from the perspectives of other decision makers. The implications of each view are then computed as change scenarios. This is CSM's *divergent-analysis phase*. It emphasizes the ability of scenario-driven planning to turn strategic management into a forward and outward looking process.

In the second or *convergence phase* of CSM, participants engage in a dialectical debate. This phase consists of presentations, minor and major assumption analysis, and a possible consolidation of the participants' comprehensive situation maps. The process requires direct communication, creative dialogue, and honest confrontation. This is CSM's *convergent-synthesis phase* of competing worldviews. It emphasizes the ability of scenario-driven planning to turn strategic management into a most creative, productive, fulfilling experience. While productivity increases, participants receive more fulfillment and zest from their work, and valuable talents and imagination emerge within the firm and among stakeholder groups.

Using the manual CSM or simulation takes scenario generation away from the mechanical manipulations of the BASICS and MICMAC methods. CSM builds substance and creativity into scenario-driven planning by presenting a formal mechanism for tapping into the ideas of stakeholder groups. Our experience is that it takes less than a day and a couple of good examples for managers and graduate business students to grasp the mechanics of CSM.

By propagating selected changes in the environment and in strategy throughout a causal map—all this can be done shorthand in CSM—divergent analysis investigates multiple what if questions by exploring pure and mixed scenarios. These scenarios are not merely based on assumptions about environmental events and trends.

In CSM, a first set of second-generation scenarios are built by activating a causal network's external change triggers. Changes in CSM's external change triggers allow computation of the combined effect of changes in the environment on a strategic situation.

A second set of second-generation scenarios are derived by activating the causal network's internal change levers. Changes in CSM's internal change levers permit computation of the combined effect of changes in strategy on the situation. These decision levers might be pulled by purposeful parties, or actors as they are called in this approach.

CSM helps managers and strategy students to understand complex decision situations. It allows them to compute the combined effects of changes in the environment and changes in a firm's strategy, taken together, on the firm's long-term performance. Thus, CSM allows accurate modeling of the nature and structure of a strategic situation, so that it enables participants to define and to examine change as a concrete and empirically observable phenomenon rather than a metaphor. Instead of merely stating that the environment and the organization are undergoing turbulent changes, it becomes possible to define and track their changes. Through CSM it becomes possible to reperceive an organization as a set of describable processes. Instead of saying there is a lot of change in the environment, one can say what, how much, where, and who will be affected or will have to become involved.

8.2   THE PROPOSED INTELLIGENCE SYSTEM: DESIGN MATTERS

> *People who described themselves as practical...*
> *proud to be uncontaminated by any kind of theory,*
> *always turned out to be the intellectual*
> *prisoners of the theoreticians of yesterday.*
> —John Maynard Keynes

Theoretical Underpinnings of the Business Intelligence Function

Part II found the business environment uncertain at many levels and in many ways. Combined changes in countries and firms worldwide increasingly move industries onto the transnational platform. In the process, customers, suppliers, products, markets, competitors, technology, and even industrial structures become global. Firms cannot retain their strategic initiative without appropriate intelligence systems. Scenario-driven intelligence systems provide a basis for anticipating changes in the new reality of global industries. This basis allows firms to anticipate the effects of changes in the environment on variables directly linked to long-term performance. It also enables managers to assess alternative strategic options, *given their firms' capability to take appropriate action.*

Scenario-driven intelligence systems can help managers circumvent two types of environmental uncertainty, both of which are potentially crippling. First, scenario-driven intelligence helps battle the uncertainty about the causalities involved in the transmission of change among environmental and decision variables. Second, it can help managers battle the uncertainty about their own as well as their firm's stakeholder values.

In formulating ill-structured strategic situations, the choices of a corporate microcosm and an interpretation or an interpretive paradigm of the environmental macrocosm are interrelated. They can serve as a point of departure for conceptualizing and forcing specificity. Problem forming generates disorderly and conflicting data. Managers have to transform these data into information and concrete ideas by using existing interpretive schemes or by formulating new ones. In this contest of competitive intelligence, a first line of attack is to focus on

- How and why certain environmental stimuli and data are searched out and selected.
- How they are synthesized into mental models or cause and effect perceptions.
- How they affect scenario construction.

This work addresses technical requirements, taken up in the COMBANK case study of Part V.

A line of greater immediate concern requires researchers and practitioners alike to explore the modeling process itself. For the sake of realism, in order to make negotiated perceptions of reality explicit, we need representations where managerial options and self-interest projections mold the way observations are interpreted and incorporated into strategy models. This is the unavoidable and most challenging path to tread if we want to build a dialectical debate into the process of strategy design.

Do we really want to? The answer is an unequivocal "Yes!" and for two reasons:

1. The dogma of the traditional hierarchical organization has been planning, managing, and controlling, whereas the new reality of the learning organization incorporates vision, values, and mental models. It entails training managers and teams in the full learning cycle originally conceived by John Dewey (1910, 1938; cf. Senge & Sterman, 1992):

$$
\begin{array}{ccc}
\textit{Reflect} & \longrightarrow & \textit{Discover} \\
\uparrow & & \downarrow \\
\textit{Produce} & \longleftarrow & \textit{Invent}
\end{array}
$$

2. The quality of organizational learning is determined by the quality of the inquiry system that mediates the restructuring of organizational theory in use (Schön, 1983).

The scenario construction frameworks of Acar (1983), Amara & Lipinski (1983), and Godet (1987) are combined and extended into a new one in Fig. 8.2.1. The proposed model integrates scenario research and practice into scenario-driven planning and suggests combining a firm's view of the world and of itself through its competitive intelligence function. It gives a concrete form to scenario-driven planning, and it clarifies its interface with organizational boundaries. A firm's evolving language and label system, as well as its organizational capability and knowledge, constitute such boundaries. To be effective, scenario-driven intelligence must be designed as an inquiry system.

Seen as a set of interrelated elements, a management inquiry system provides the methodological framework for the problem formulation-solution-implementation process. Scenario-driven planning can then be tailored to a specific strategic situation. One reason for choosing CSM is the lack of generalizability of softer approaches, such as Mason & Mitroff's, to deal with scenario construction explicitly. They do *not* provide ways of packaging situation-specific alternatives into consistent scenarios (Acar, 1983).

Another reason is that one must address *all* stages of problem forming, not only at the empirical problem-dependent level, but also at the conceptual level. Within a firm, the existing symbolism of the language and label system, and the existing capability and knowledge, are the initial building blocks used to understand and describe its decision situation.

According to Zeleny (1988), the language and label systems that managers initially use to coordinate their knowledge-derived choices are *imprecise* and *fuzzy*. In reality, initially fuzzy language is not only adequate and effective for managing uncertainty and interdependence, but also required. Decision makers must use it to overcome initial psychological barriers and Schwenk's grouping of cognitive biases in Table 8.1.1.

Within the tactical planning loop of Fig. 8.2.1, changes in the environment become environmental trends or event patterns, and changes in strategy, implemented through competitive and collective tactics, reflect managerial decisions. Together, they determine a firm's potential and actual performance. The actual performance of a firm is contrasted with stakeholder pressures, reflected in stated midterm objectives, to produce yet another gap between stakeholder expectations or standards and performance.

Depending on the firm's language and label system, and its organizational capability and knowledge, this gap may be defined for service, quality, or productivity. In some instances, it can match closely what is perceived to be the firm's unique advantage—a pivotal product or service characteristic affecting customers' purchasing decisions. In other instances, it may just lead to a new asymmetry, setting new directions for a firm in its strategic behavior.

The tactical planning loop of Fig. 8.2.1 corresponds to a firm's action-reaction moves, manifested as pure actions or pure communications over time. Also ranging from entirely coercive or competitive, to entirely accommodative or collective, these tactics determine its performance. Together, the firm's tactics and the transactional exchange of its goods or services for money convert the potential of yesterday's strategy into today's profits and dividends. Managers who purchase, fabricate, distribute, price, promote, advertise, or sell must have some experience with the processes described within this loop.

To address future profits, however, firms interact with the environment through an adaptive activity. This changes the markets they serve, the technology they offer, the products/services they sell, and the way they sell, promote, or advertise. To become efficiently adaptive, and to improve its organizational processes and capability, a firm must adjust its strategic posture and processes to changes in its environment.

Perhaps a good way of explaining the model construction and the competitive intelligence or scenario construction loops of Fig. 8.2.1 is by referring to Daft & Weick (1984). Their discussion of a firm's intrusiveness and environmental equivocality are relevant here.

Figure 8.2.1 Framework for Scenario-Driven Planning

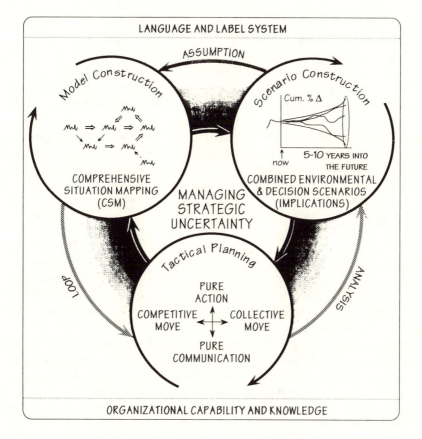

Daft & Weick emphasize that many events and trends in the environment are inherently unclear. Managers discuss such events and trends, and form mental models and visions expressed in a common language and label system. Within this process of enactment, *equivocality* relates to managerial assumptions underlying the analyzability of cause-effect relationships in the environment. A firm's *intrusiveness* determines how active or passive the firm is about environmental scanning and analysis. In this context, because the global environment has become increasingly more turbulent, active firms construct both causal models and scenarios to improve performance.

Managers of *active firms* combine the acquisition of new data with the creation of new interpretations about the environment and their firm's strategic situation. They reduce equivocality by assessing alternative futures through scenario construction and by acquiring more data about the environment. Frequent meetings and debates occur, some by videoconferencing or telecomputing, during which managers use the process of dialectical inquiry to guide themselves through the containing assumption analysis loop, which turns out to be the major strategic loop. Although often ignored, this loop provides active organizations with a strategic compass (Mason & Mitroff, 1981).

Conversely, *passive firms* do not actively seek data but reduce equivocality by establishing rules, procedures, and regular reports—reams of laser-printed paper with little or no pertinent information. Managers in passive organizations use the media to interpret events and trends in the environment. They obtain insight from personal contacts with significant others in their environment. Their data are personal and informal, obtained as the opportunity arises.

At best, managers of passive firms activate the model construction loop of Fig. 8.2.1. Sometimes, they do so unknowingly when, for example, they boot up electronic spreadsheets. Typically, these contain inside-out causal models, with all assumptions hidden deeply within their structure. At bootup, only the numbers show. Managers of passive firms use electronic spreadsheets to laser-print matrices with comforting numbers. They "twiddle a few numbers and diligently sucker themselves into thinking that they're forecasting the future" (Schrage, 1991). They do so only when rapid changes in the environment force them to stop playing Blame the Stakeholder. They stop fighting the last war for a while, artfully name the situation a crisis, and roll up their sleeves to discuss and to argue, but they quickly agree on some arbitrary interpretation of the situation to generate face-saving strategic options. Miller & Friesen (1983, pp. 225-227) show how rapid changes in the environment can lead to crisis-oriented decision making in unsuccessful firms. In contrast, successful firms respond to environmental dynamism by looking further into the future in designing strategies.

Together, these options and the negotiated interpretation of the environment, reflected in spreadsheet patterns, are filtered through the dominant logic or conceptual/mental model of the firm. Qualitative implications or performance implications are again contrasted with stakeholder values, reflected in long-term goals, to produce a gap. Because managers of all stripes of firms use the model construction loop of Fig. 8.2.1, this gap may suggest some next steps for action.

The Proactive Way

Managers of active firms enter the analytical/empirical model construction loop of Fig. 8.2.1 both consciously and conscientiously. In addition, they activate the competitive intelligence function through scenario construction as well as the assumption analysis loop. Instead of twiddling spreadsheet numbers, managers of active firms twiddle their models' fundamental assumptions.

Because the global environment has become more competitive and is rapidly changing, firms depend heavily on it for resources. So active firms develop multiple lines of inquiry (i.e., multiple scanning functions) into the environment to reduce strategic uncertainty and equivocality. As a firm gathers more data about the environment, its managers attempt to build analytical/empirical models of both the firm and its environment.

Model construction enables managers of active firms to stake, through a cognitive or causal map, their intuition about how they perceive the nature and structure of their firm's strategic situation. This perception's quantitative implications are then assessed through the process of scenario construction.

Through our approach to scenario-driven planning these implications can be captured quantitatively through the propagation of external and internal changes on the map itself. CSM allows computing the combined implications of both change triggers activated in the external environment and change levers that managers may decide to pull on internally to induce changes in strategy.

CSM also comprises a goal-modeling component. This allows contrasting the quantitative implications of changes in the environment and in strategy with stakeholder interests, reflected in resource allocation projections, to produce a gap. Again, this gap may suggest some next steps for management decisions leading to corporate action within the tactical planning loop of Fig. 8.2.1.

Having quantified the implications of their shared visions and claims about the structure of the firm's strategic situation, managers of active firms are more likely to reduce strategic uncertainty and equivocality. They can better manage strategic interdependence. Because a perception is the starting point of scenarios, by using the scenario construction loop, active firms have a better chance to become faster strategic learners.

The inquiry system proposed in Fig. 8.2.1 includes several contributions. First, by translating the environmental macrocosm and the corporate microcosm into a common context for conceptualization, the requisites of theory building can be addressed. Planning analysts no longer have to operate piecemeal. A theory and a dominant logic typically emerge from shared perceptions about a firm, its environment, and stakeholder values through model construction.

Second, the outputs of the various activities of the problem formulation-solution-implementation process build on each other as successive layers. In Fig. 8.2.1 the counterclockwise arrow follows the direction of multiperspective dialectics required for assumption surfacing, analysis, and testing. This process allows adjustment of individual and organizational theories and logic, leading to an evolutionary interpretation of the real system toward which managerial decisions are targeted.

Lastly, the inquiry system of Fig. 8.2.1 enables flexible support of all phases in the process of strategy design. In the proposed framework, problem finding or forming, or *situation formulation* receives equal attention as problem solving.

Within the domain of formal model building, a distinction should be drawn between simultaneous equations and causal or lagged equation models. Financial and forecasting models often posit functional relationships without explicit reference to reference behavior patterns. Even when under the scenario label, mathematical forecasting techniques gaze deeply neither inside the firm nor its markets, but in a sense treat them as black boxes. Conversely, lagged models incorporate realistic reference behavior patterns. They try to describe a sequence of *events* in a system of interrelated entities, each with an identifiable set of variables under its control. In this context, the process of scenario construction can relate to each variable the possible interaction paths among entities as well as the conditions under which these can be actualized. Depending on the application's domain, either a declarative or a procedural mode of computer simulation can be used.

Scenario-driven planning can and should be used to open up the black box of individual decision makers' mental models, and to specify the concepts and rules they apply. In the process, a firm's own language and label system, organizational capability and knowledge, and strategic decision processing system are enriched. Scenarios may bring about transformation rules that were not previously thought of as well as new variables and interaction paths.

As an entity, each decision maker has a local scope and deals only with specific variables and access paths to other entities. Yet, key success factors are not etched in stone. Often, we only observe a representative state of each entity, namely, locally meaningful variables and parts of a scenario. This representativeness can change dynamically in the process of scenario construction. Beyond the purely technical advantages of computing change scenarios, planning becomes interactive, and language and reference systems render themselves more adequate, effective, and precise. Their associated organizational capability develops even more. In addition, the minor and major assumptions underlying the mental models of individual decision makers can surface because scenarios specify the conditions under which variables incur change. In this fashion, an enhanced SAST process could be undertaken.

To conclude, by looking into the dynamics of strategic decision making and the resulting behavior of firms, the framework proposed in Fig. 8.2.1 can help managers, planners, and organization researchers see the tremendous potential of scenario analysis. They may choose to create scenario-driven intelligence systems to generate information for strategy design. They will be building real knowledge in the process, while developing their firm's capacity for institutional learning. According to Pascale (1984), this capacity to speed up institutional learning truly is a sustainable competitive advantage.

SUMMARY

Strategic situations are complex and involve uncertainty. Because planning is directed toward the future, predictions of changes in the environment are indispensable components of it. Conventional forecasting techniques provide no cohesive way of understanding the effect of changes that will occur in the future. Scenarios provide corporate intelligence and a link from traditional forecasting methods to modern interactive planning systems. In today's quest for managers who are more leaders than conciliators, any interest in scenarios on the part of the strategist or executive should be welcomed. A clearer delineation of scenario-driven planning is needed to make it a potentially rich field of application and research. Our approach recognizes that a piecemeal approach will not be adequate when changes in the environment and in strategy occur together. Dealing with such changes (both internal and external) calls for a radical rethinking of strategy design and methods.

The examples of the following chapters describe a number of scenario methods that can be used profitably for organizational learning and the management of uncertainty. One reason for our choice is the necessity of generalizability. Another is that we must address all stages of strategic formulation. The proposed scenario-driven intelligence system provides a theory of planning that rests on the notion of a collective inquiry system. This allows translating the environmental macrocosm and a firm's microcosm into a shared understanding of causalities. Informed discussion can then take place. Viewing scenario-driven planning as an inquiry system can help the outcomes of the sequence of problem formulation, solution and implementation stages build on each successive layer of learning activities.

In addition to the structural analysis and scenario construction processes, the intelligence system we propose incorporates multiperspective dialectics, which is essential for assumption surfacing, analysis, and testing. This process of assumption analysis leads to uncovering present assumptions and strategies, which in turn may lead to the discovery of new assumptions and strategies. Lastly, the proposed framework can support all phases of strategy design, where problem finding and problem solving should receive equal attention.

Part V

STANDARD APPLICATIONS

Chapter 9

Computing Scenarios

The Combank and Infoplus real-life case studies of Part III, Battelle's Goodyear Aerospace case of Chapter 7, and the prerequisites and design matters of the proposed planning system in Chapter 8, all suggest the computation of scenarios to enhance the plural rationality that typically evolves in a management team. Meanwhile, the interjection of the theory in Chapters 7 and 8 between Parts III and V allows us to reflect on and internalize both the theoretical and the practical aspects of planning with rough-cut causal mapping. This chapter first presents environmental and decision scenarios computed first with CSM and then by computer simulation through the estimation of stochastic cross-impact effects.

9.1   INFOPLUS (B)

Computing Scenarios on the CSM Causal Map

As shown in Fig. 5.3.1a, the influence diagram fails to resolve whether Info-plus' capacity and capability or its visibility will be more decisive in determining its demand for service. An influence diagram cannot reveal which path will domi-nate. This lack of guidance, which MICMAC may or may not resolve, depending on whether or not feedback loops are present, can mislead managers and planners into a naive or incorrect determination of critical decision variables in a strategic situation.

Conversely, comprehensive situation mapping (CSM) possesses simulationlike capabilities and thereby represents a good start toward strategic modeling and computer simulation. CSM's simulationlike capabilities allow the assessment of the complex effects of changes in external and internal variables that affect a firm's strategic situation in hard and soft ways.

CSM allows the propagation of multiwave change scenarios along quantified causal relationships (i.e., the double- and single-line arrows connecting the vari-ables on a causal map). Quantifying the relationships among variables in CSM yields a much deeper understanding of a decision situation's dynamic structure than the qualitative analysis of an ID. Statements of purpose can be linked directly to a firm's strategic goals because CSM captures the combined effects of changes both in the environment and in the firm's strategy.

Through CSM the causal effects produced through a particular channel of change can be combined with those resulting from other changes or channels of change. In CSM terminology, the effects caused by a single change in a single variable constitute a *pure scenario* of change transfer. The effects produced either by multiple changes in a single variable or by multiple changes in many variables make up a *mixed scenario* of change transfer. It is possible to compute mixed sce-narios by summing the cumulative percentage changes or effects of pure scenarios, resulting from *ceteris paribus* changes, that is, independently from other changes.

The analysis of causal linkages is a complex business that ideally requires com-puter modeling and simulation (Forrester, 1958; Roberts et al., 1983; Watson, 1981. (Chapter 10 gives a brief introduction to computer modeling and simula-tion). Yet, an approximation can be realized by some proper form of causal map-ping, such as the CSM method presented in the following example. This method captures the critical dimension of causality, namely, whether changes in one or several variables are necessary to produce a desirable effect (Ackoff & Emery, 1972). Pure and mixed scenarios capture and combine the complex effects of changes transmitted throughout the causal network of variables pertinent to a strategic decision situation.

Illustrative First-Generation or *Pure* Scenario

Figure 9.1.1 shows Infoplus' CSM map, now complete with change transmittance coefficients, time lags, and pure scenarios. Together, CSM's change coefficients and time lags help us explore Infoplus' alternative futures through the computation of scenarios on the causal map itself. Appendix C.2 as well as Sections 5.3 and 6.3 detail the components of CSM. For a more extensive treatment, see Acar (1983). For example, the double-line arrow on the left of the diagram connecting external funding with Infoplus' resources indicates that, a 10 percent increase in external funding at time $t = 0$ will cause a 10 percent increase in Infoplus' resources instantaneously, assuming there is no drastic change in GCB's support policy for Infoplus. The broken-line arrow connecting the initial support variable to Infoplus' resources signifies this condition of GCB's unchanged initial support.

In turn, this change in Infoplus' resources would cause its capacity and capability to rise proportionally with a three-month lag, that is, at time $t = 3$ months. The occurrence of this change assumes that Infoplus maintains its partial autonomy from GCB (the parent organization), without any significant increase in overhead charges. The broken-line arrow connecting partial autonomy to capacity and capability declares this assumption. (Table 5.3.1 in Section 5.3 explains the meaning of each variable name in Fig. 9.1.1.)

The change in Infoplus' capacity and capability will in turn induce a 10 percent increase in demand for service from its previous level, whatever that might be, with a five-month lag, that is, at time $t = 8$ months. This change in demand occurs independently from the full-channel effect of visibility.

By itself, the increase in Infoplus' capacity and capability is insufficient to cause a change in actual service. The two single-line arrows signify that *both* the capacity and capability and the demand for service must increase to coproduce a change in actual service. This change will occur at the latest time, computed from when both capacity and capability and demand for service changed from their previous levels. The magnitude of the change in actual service will be the least of the two changes arriving from the two single-line arrows in Fig. 9.1.1a.

Single-line arrows, CSM's partial channels, work together with one another to transmit a positive change in comprehensive situation mapping. Yet, the magnitude and the timing of the change transmittance are independent from each other. One partial channel may transmit the least change to its downstream variable, but another single-line arrow may determine the timing of that change independently from its magnitude. This is the *latest time* and *least change* or LL rule of CSM, applied to the transmission of positive changes (or increases), involving partial channels or single-line arrows.

Depending on the context, a negative change (a decrease) in a variable may be sufficient by itself to transmit a change to the receiver of a single-line arrow, inde-

Figure 9.1.1 INFOPLUS' Complete CSM with Change Transmittance
Coefficients, Time Lags and Scenarios

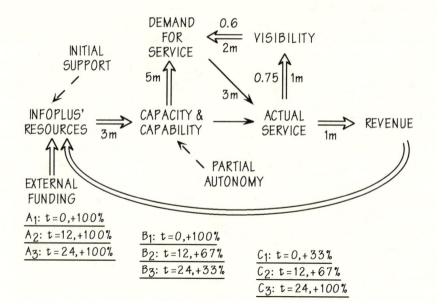

pendently from other single-line arrows. This is the situation described in Fig. 9.1.1a. A decrease in either the demand for service or the capacity and capability would cause a proportional decrease in actual service. A decrease in capacity and capability would show up immediately in Infoplus' actual service delivery, but Infoplus' service backlog can obscure a decrease in demand for service for at least three months. The three-month time lag next to the single-line arrow connecting demand for service to actual service declares this assumption. This asymmetry of increases and decreases has not been promptly dealt with by previous ID authors.

Let us return to our illustrative scenario, which we call Z. With both the capacity and capability and the demand for service increased, actual service will also rise 10 percent from its previous level, with a three-month time lag at time $t = 11$ months. In a little less than a year, Infoplus' director and the two GCB consultants expect to serve their local business community, helping the Mittelstand of New York City increase its information technology (IT) platform worldwide. This contribution should increase Infoplus' visibility by 7.5 percent ($3/4$ of $10\% = 7.5\%$) from its previous level, with a one-month lag to time $t = 12$ months. Two months later, at $t = 14$ months, the increase in Infoplus' visibility will increase the demand for its services by 4.5 percent from its previous level (i.e., $7.5\% \times 0.6$).

By itself, the increase in demand is insufficient to cause a change in actual service. Both demand for service and capacity and capability must increase to coproduce a change in actual service. Again, this change will occur at the latest time, when both capacity and capability and demand for service change from their previous levels. The magnitude of the change in actual service will be the least of the two changes arriving from the two single-line arrows in Fig. 9.1.1b.

Meanwhile, the 10 percent increase in Infoplus' contribution to its local business community through actual service will cause a 10 percent increase in its revenue, with a one-month lag, at time $t = 12$ months. This lag represents a one-month average collection period of service fees from new customers and established partners. According to the feedback loop or full channel of Fig. 9.1.1b, the 10 percent increase in revenue will increase Infoplus' resources both instantaneously and proportionally, causing in turn a proportional increase in capacity and capability, with a three-month time lag at time $t = 15$ months.

Again, with both capacity and capability and demand for service increased, actual service will also increase by 4.5 percent from its previous level, at time $t = 17$ months. Both the change transmitted to actual service and the associated time lag travel through the partial channel emanating from demand for service. Enabled by the change in capacity and capability, this change occurs three months after the 7.5 percent increase in Infoplus' visibility made its demand for service rise by 4.5 percent at time $t = 14$ months, therefore reaching actual service at time $t = 14 + 3 = 17$ months. Also, the change in actual service transfers a three-fourths change or 3.4 percent to visibility at time $17 + 1 = 18$ months. This re-

Figure 9.1.1(a) **INFOPLUS' Illustrative Example of Pure Scenario Z at t=11 months**

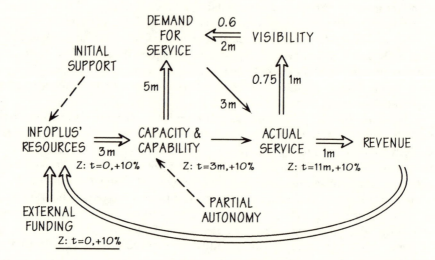

Z: t=8m,+10%

DEMAND FOR SERVICE 0.6 ◀══ 2m VISIBILITY

INITIAL SUPPORT

5m

0.75 1m

3m

INFOPLUS' RESOURCES ══▶ 3m CAPACITY & CAPABILITY ──▶ ACTUAL SERVICE ══▶ 1m REVENUE

Z: t=0,+10%   Z: t=3m,+10%   Z: t=11m,+10%

EXTERNAL FUNDING

PARTIAL AUTONOMY

Z: t=0,+10%

Figure 9.1.1(b) INFOPLUS' Illustrative Example of Pure Scenario Z
at t=20 months from the Initial +10% Increase in
External Funding

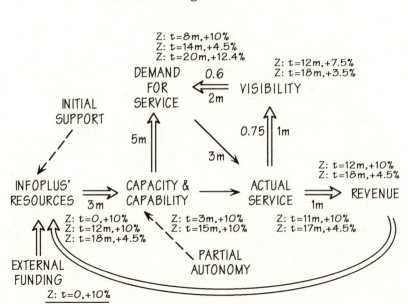

Figure 9.1.1(c) Cumulative % Changes Under Pure Scenario Z by
t=20 months from the Initial +10% Increase in
External Funding

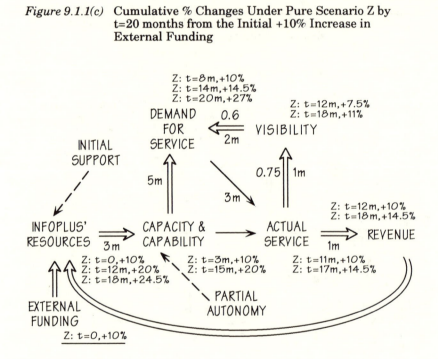

flects back on Infoplus' demand for service by 2.4 percent at time $t = 20$ m ($m =$ months).

The first-generation pure scenario Z shows how easy it is to manually compute scenarios on the causal map itself, with or even without the help of a four-function calculator. Often, all one needs is a pen and a piece of paper or a napkin. It is even easier than it looks if one records next to each variable both the magnitude and the time of each change sequentially. For example, if the percentage change effects were recorded shorthand next to demand for service, then the successive percentage change entries next to it would have been Z: $t=8m$, +10%, Z: $t=14m$, +4.5% and Z: $t=20m$, +12.4% (from Z: $t=20m$, +10% plus Z: $t=20m$, +2.4%), yielding the corresponding cumulative percentage change entries of Z_c: $t=8m$, +10%, Z_c: $t=14m$, +14.5%, and Z_c: $t=20m$, +27% of Fig. 9.1.1c. Accumulation is necessary, for in "a photograph or static view taken of the system," the cumulative percentage changes would have been the quantities that showed up (Wolstenholme, 1992, p. 125).

Once the managers concerned have been satisfied with the structure of the CSM and the quantified relationships between each pair of variables, it is very easy to pseudocode or macrocode the CSM model in a computer language or spreadsheet. Pseudocoding is the name typically given to the first- or macrolevel computer coding in some simulation languages. Many of our business policy students routinely use spreadsheets to compute scenarios on their comprehensive situation maps. We do not object. On the contrary, we encourage the pseudocoding of CSM because it reinforces the computing skills that business students acquire either in computer and information systems courses or in internship programs.

Depending on availability, a conventional spreadsheet or a special-purpose simulation package can be used to further calibrate the model. Section 10.2 gives a brief introduction to computer modeling and simulation. In addition, Appendix C presents some of the most well-known system dynamics simulation modeling languages that support scenario-driven planning.

Naturally, the computer speeds up the computation of change scenarios, especially complex mixed or combination scenarios, and allows sensitivity analyses to be performed. Yet, computing scenarios shorthand on a small transparent CSM often gives managers sufficient insight to shift the expectations that guide their decisions (Wolstenholme, 1992). After such a good start in the art of problem framing, using the computer may not always be necessary. And, when one is finally used, it often yields useful results because it no longer seems to take fanciful flights away from reality.

Infoplus' Second-Generation or Mixed Scenarios

Through CSM the causal effects produced through a pure scenario of change transfer can be combined with the changes propagated through other changes or channels of change. Again, the effects caused either by multiple changes in a single variable or by multiple changes in many variables make up a mixed scenario of change transfer. Mixed scenarios can be computed by summing the cumulative percentage effects of pure scenarios. Computing mixed scenarios of change transfer yields a much deeper understanding of a decision situation's dynamic structure.

Infoplus' director and the two GCB consultants were in the middle of negotiating with a consortium of funding agencies and networked public organizations over alternative funding schemes when we came aboard. One funding agent had already contemplated the possibility of gradually decreasing Infoplus' external funding over a period of three years. The underlying rationale was that Infoplus should be able to support itself gradually from revenue through actual service.

Conversely, another agent within the consortium net had already expressed a slight preference for gradually increasing Infoplus' external funding, again over a three-year period. The underlying rationale was that Infoplus would need time to identify its information technology (IT) needs more precisely, and thereby better serve its clients and partners.

Despite their differences in funding alternatives, the two agents had signaled a possible consensus on the time period that the consortium might be willing to provide funding for Infoplus. Naturally, this prompted the question of whether Infoplus would be able to stand on its own within three years from its inception, without any further support other than using the services of GCB's internal consultants. Under these circumstances, three mixed scenarios of change transfer were computed to assess the sensitivity of Infoplus' demand for service and revenue to external funding. Each mixed scenario was computed by summing the cumulative percentage effects of three pure scenarios. Table 9.1.1 details Infoplus' total scenario input.

Mixed scenario A is Infoplus' best-case sequence of pure scenarios. It assumes that external funding will increase three times by 100 percent from its base level at the beginning of three consecutive years, starting now at $t=0$. This scenario represents high external funding at a constant rate. The scenario could play if Infoplus' director and the two GCB consultants spent most of their time negotiating and lobbying over external funding schemes.

Regarding the B series of scenarios, pure scenario B_1 assumes that external funding will increase by 100 percent from its current level at $t=0$. Yet, pure scenario B_2 shows that external funding will increase by two-thirds from its original level at time $t=12$ months, and B_3 that external funding will increase by one-third from this status quo level at time $t=24$ months.

Mixed scenario B represents external funding at a decreasing rate, with the bulk of external funding arriving early. This scenario would play if the funding consortium adopted the position of the agent who believes in gradually decreasing Infoplus' external funding over three years because Infoplus should support itself from revenue through actual service.

Table 9.1.1 Infoplus' Scenario Input

Scenario		Time	
		t	External
Mixed	Pure	(months)	Funding
A	A_1	0	+100%
$(A_1+A_2+A_3)$	A_2	12	+100%
	A_3	24	+100%
B	B_1	0	+100%
$(B_1+B_2+B_3)$	B_2	12	+67%
	B_3	24	+33%
C	C_1	0	+33%
$(C_1+C_2+C_3)$	C_2	12	+67%
	C_3	24	+100%

Mixed scenario C is Infoplus' worst-case scenario in the funding delays it assumes. Its component scenario C_1 assumes that external funding will increase by one-third from its initial level now at time $t=0$. Pure scenario C_2 shows that external funding will increase by two-thirds from its original level at time $t=12$ months, and C_3 by 100 percent from its previous level at time $t=24$ months.

Infoplus' worst-case mixed scenario C represents external funding at an increasing rate, with the bulk of external funding arriving late. This scenario would play if the funding consortium adopted the position of the agent who believes in gradually increasing Infoplus' external funding over three years because Infoplus needs time to identify its precise IT needs.

Figure 9.1.2 shows Infoplus' computed scenarios. Mixed scenario A produces the highest cumulative percentage change both in demand for service and in revenue from actual service. Mixed scenario B is not too far behind, but mixed scenario C helps neither the demand for service nor the revenue accelerate as fast as they do under mixed scenarios A and B.

A comparison between mixed scenarios B and C shows that Infoplus' positive-loop CSM model is *not* equally sensitive to decreasing external funding, with the bulk of funds arriving early, and to increasing external funding, with the bulk of funds arriving late. During the first two years of mixed scenario B, Infoplus' demand for service and revenue increase as rapidly as they do under mixed scenario A, which represents high external funding at a constant rate. During the third year,

Figure 9.1.2 INFOPLUS' Computed Scenarios

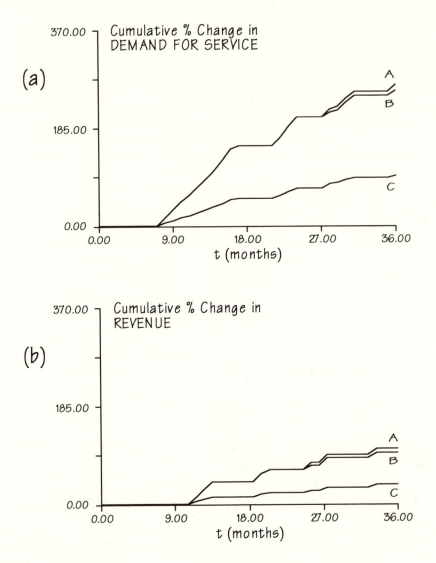

the funding scheme differences assumed under mixed scenarios A and B start showing up.

These differences are more pronounced in Fig. 9.1.2b than in Fig. 9.1.2a. The gradual decrease in external funding under mixed scenario B is detected earlier in Infoplus' revenue than in its demand for service. In Fig. 9.1.2b, the relatively lower magnitude of cumulative percentage change in revenue exacerbates the small differences between mixed scenarios A and B.

Yet, these are not as glaring as the reduced performance in Infoplus' demand for service and revenue under mixed scenario C. The initially tight external funding under scenario C makes Infoplus' capacity and capability as well as demand for service rise, but only marginally from their base levels. Just short of one year, Infoplus starts serving the *Mittelstand* of New York City, that is, small and medium-size firms, but its limited actual service turns Infoplus' visibility into a low profile. A low profile is hardly the thing for a startup organization to keep. Coupled with its low capacity and capability Infoplus' low visibility will cause demand for service and revenue to level off much faster under mixed scenario C. At the end of three years, the cumulative percentage increase in the two variables is just about one third of their corresponding increase under mixed scenarios A or B.

The mixed scenarios of Table 9.1.1 as well as their component pure scenarios (Fig. 9.1.1 and Table 9.1.1) assume no drastic change in GCB's support policy for Infoplus. In Fig. 9.1.1, the broken-line arrow connecting initial support to Infoplus' resources signifies GCB's required initial support. Similarly, these scenarios assume that Infoplus will maintain its partial autonomy from GCB, and there will be no significant increase in GCB's overhead charges. In Fig. 9.1.1, the broken-line arrow connecting partial autonomy to capacity and capability declares this assumption.

Figure 9.1.2(a) shows that under mixed scenario C Infoplus' demand for service heading toward an equilibrium of stress and strain, thereby creating the potential for low revenue in Fig. 9.1.2b. If mixed scenario C were to occur, even slight changes either in GCB's initial support or in Infoplus' partial autonomy from GCB could exacerbate Infoplus' problems. Needless to say, an increase in GCB's overhead charges would further reduce Infoplus' revenue and thereby cripple the capacity and capability required for managing the tension that Infoplus' matrix organization creates. (Section 5.2 describes Infoplus' organizational design.)

Infoplus' Third-Generation or *Accounting-for-Interdependence* Scenarios

The interdependence among the variables pertinent to Infoplus' strategic situation motivated the use of the classic BASICS (Battelle Scenario Inputs to Corporate Strategy) method (Honton, Stacey, & Millett, 1985). This is a commercially available stochastic simulation computer package to which we have made several references. It is used widely by Battelle and others in scenario-driven planning.

BASICS helps in assessing the posterior probability of occurrence of each state (i.e., high, medium, or low) that may occur in a firm's performance variables as a result of a corresponding state occurring in an external or environmental variable. The BASICS simulation algorithm combines each variable's predefined states into ten consecutively generated pseudorandom trials to estimate the stochastic frequency of possible outcomes that may occur in the future. (Appendix C.4 gives a detailed technical summary of BASICS.) Using BASICS (Battelle, 1988) gave us a balanced consideration to what might happen to Infoplus in the future.

Three sets of a priori probabilities assigned to the three possible states (high, medium, low) of each of Infoplus' crucial variables helped to estimate the final outcome probabilities. The three sets of the probabilistic weights assigned are:

- 0.60, 0.30, and 0.10 for the best-case scenario,
- 0.33, 0.34, and 0.33 for the reference scenario, and
- 0.10, 0.30, and 0.60 for the worst-case scenario, respectively.

The insight gained from the deterministic scenarios computed on the CSM and MICMAC in Section 5.4 helped us establish an occurrence cross-impact (CI) matrix for Infoplus' strategic situation. See also Section 5.4. Along with the above three sets of a priori state probabilities, the CI matrix served as input to the BASICS computational method.

The BASICS simulation algorithm estimated the posterior (i.e., postanalysis) probability of occurrence of each variable's state (high, medium, low), while taking the interdependence among Infoplus' variables into account. The algorithm combined each variable's predefined states into ten consecutively generated pseudorandom trials to estimate the stochastic frequencies of possible future states in funding, demand, and revenue of the Infoplus service.

The first set of a priori probabilities yields a most probable outcome that combines high levels of Infoplus' external funding, demand for service, and revenue. Under the best-case scenario of Fig. 9.1.3, the corresponding *posterior* probabilities of external funding, demand for service, and revenue are 0.83, 0.90, and 0.87, respectively. These estimates depict Infoplus' prospects for fast growth in view of its current situation. The BASICS computational method amplifies the existing differences in the first-estimate or a priori probabilities. These are transformed into posterior probabilities of variable states, while accounting for the cross impacts among possible future events.

Under the second set of a priori probabilities, the most probable outcome again combines high levels of Infoplus' external funding, demand for service, and revenue. Under Infoplus' reference scenario in Fig. 9.1.3, the posterior probabilities of external funding, demand for service, and revenue are 0.53, 0.50, and 0.53, respec-

Figure 9.1.3   INFOPLUS' Probabilistic Scenarios

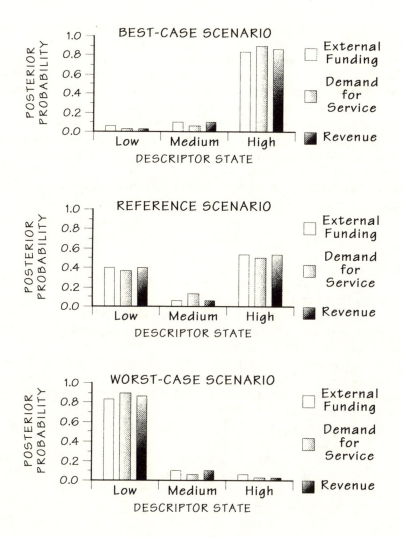

tively, with low-state posterior probabilities of 0.40, 0.37, and 0.40, respectively.

Lastly, under the third set of a priori probabilities, the most probable outcome finds Infoplus' external funding, demand for service, and revenue at low levels, with corresponding posterior probabilities of 0.83, 0.90, and 0.87, respectively. Although the worst-case scenario results are equiprobable to Infoplus' fast-growth prospects, the reference scenario of Fig. 9.1.3 positions the highest posterior probabilities in the high state of Infoplus' external funding, demand for service, and revenue.

These stochastic simulation results reinforce the conclusions reached from the deterministic scenarios computed on the CSM. Figure 9.1.2 shows that in the first two years of mixed scenario B, which represents external funding at a decreasing rate, with the bulk of it arriving early, Infoplus' demand for service and revenue increase as rapidly as they do under mixed scenario A, which represents high external funding at a constant rate (Fig. 9.1.1 and Table 9.1.1). The funding differences between scenarios A and B start showing only in the third year.

The BASICS stochastic frequencies of future outcomes, as well as the derived posterior probabilities that combine predefined states of Infoplus' descriptor variables, imply that in the worst case scenario Infoplus may not pass the acid test. Infoplus may not be able to stand on its own, within three years from its inception, without any further support other than that of GCB's internal consultants.

Conclusion

To evaluate a strategy design, its results must be anticipated and considered along with changes in the business environment. Given its current resource capability, stakeholder concerns, and organizational goals, Infoplus' future performance depends on the moves of multiple actors, such as the federal, state and city foundations as well as GCB's managers, internal consultants and spokespersons.

In such a situation, it is natural to focus on the potential benefits of opportunity. Yet, concentrating on success factors exclusively, while ignoring potential problems, can lead to mental blocks that are not only cognitive, but also social and emotional (Mitroff, Emshoff, & Kilmann, 1979; Ohmae, 1982). Actions or changes in the environment that may alter stakeholder support and power will determine the very survival of Infoplus.

The scenario-driven analysis of the potential GCB partnership with business aimed at gaining insight into the dynamics of the system. It shows exactly how the very existence of Infoplus will be determined by the moves of other actors and external stakeholder groups. Computing scenarios and discussing computed scenarios invariably create new information that can sensitize managers and planners to the dynamic implications of a strategic decision situation. Without information filtering and new-information creation, a decision process may lead nowhere

(Nonaka, 1988), unless there is a guide with a "superior vision over the maze" of a firm's problems in transition (Churchman, 1971, p. 176).

Infoplus' future is not totally predetermined; indeed, it remains open to multiple possible outcomes. The actors in the system possess various degrees of freedom which they will exercise through action to attain their personal and organizational objectives. Ultimately, they will create uncertainty about Infoplus' future, which is at once the issue and the consequence of predictable battles. This uncertainty alone supports the necessity of analyzing the actors' moves and confronting their aims and balance of power, as manifested in qualitative constraints and resources.

The deterministic scenarios computed on the CSM reveal Infoplus' sensitivity to the initial support for financial, human, and physical resources required for its growth and survival. The percentage of overhead claimed by GCB for its initial support and internal consultants may subsequently determine whether Infoplus will be able to stand on its own within three years from its inception.

The stochastic simulation results computed with BASICS— following the procedure detailed in Appendix C.4—reinforce the deterministic scenario conclusions. Yet, exactly what will happen to Infoplus depends on external actors, such as the federal, state, city and other foundations, GCB consultants and administration, and various spokespersons.

9.2   COMBANK (B)

Recall of First-Generation Scenarios of Section 6.3

In computing strategic scenarios, variables of interest typically relate to performance. Just by looking at a CSM diagram and noting the full channels of change transfer it contains, a manager can tell what variable changes are sufficient by themselves to cause a change in performance. Yet it can be equally important to know what variables need coordination to coproduce a change. These variables can readily be spotted by looking for the partial channels of the diagram. It is no less imperative to think about and to remember where to look for radical or significant departures from the *status quo*. These are signified on the CSM causal map by broken-line arrows, denoting qualitative conditions or restrictions on the transfer of change (see Fig. 6.3.1).

CSM's change transmittance coefficients and time lags allow quantifying the effects of the involved causalities and thereby providing a fairly accurate description or model of a firm's strategic situation. Naturally, this "model will be a simplification and an idealization, and consequently a falsification. It is hoped that the features retained for discussion are those of greatest importance" (Turing, 1952).

Although expressed in terms of relative changes, and thereby preempting the difficulty of dealing with different units, CSM's computational technique operates as a linearly additive and transitive model of the transmission of change (Acar, 1983). These features are pertinent to both strategy researchers and practitioners who are willing to integrate tangible and intangible variables in rough-cut mapping and modeling, which is a prerequisite to full-scale strategic modeling and computer simulation (Morecroft & van der Heijden, 1992; Richardson & Pugh, 1981; Wolstenholme, 1992).

In the case of Combank, the first generations of reference scenarios computed on each team's CSM gave the entire planning group a better sense of the long-term implications of each alternative view. The computed scenarios captured the behavioral patterns of profit growth, showing the potential synergy among Combank's services, volume capacity, and the importance of staying close to the customer. Combank's planning group started to anticipate the dynamic implications of its divergent models.

That first generation of pure and mixed scenarios caused minds to race, giving our project participants a better idea of the synergy between their future and existing services, such as custody, private banking, investment management, corporate trust, and employee benefits. Everyone got involved. Our project was off to a great start on scenario-driven planning.

Combank's Second Generation of Mixed Scenarios

Regardless of the direction the influx of foreign funds might take in the future, there are two basic threads in Combank's possible responses. The first involves raising revenues and thereby boosting the effectiveness aspect of Combank's CSM. The second possible response is the predictable counterpoint to just raising revenues. It addresses the efficiency aspect of Combank's strategy—streamlining operations. These response lines led to running four sets of mixed change scenarios on the integrated and now complete CSM map of Combank's *problématique* in Fig. 9.2.1. Ackoff (1981) calls such messy managerial problem situations "messes." Ozbekhan (1977) uses the less pejorative and more elegant term *problématique*.

Table 9.2.1 summarizes Combank's mixed-scenario input. The first mixed-scenario set (ACE or A + C + E) assumes a 100 percent increase triggered in the influx of foreign funds from its previous level, at times $t=0,12$, and 24 months, a 100 percent change in Combank's effort to increase its functional efficiency of support services from its current level, at times $t=0,12$, and 24 months, and a 100 percent increase in the development of capable people, again at times $t=0,12$, and 24 months. The mixed or combination scenario ACE is the best-case scenario of fast-growth potential within the bounds of Combank's present strategy.

Figure 9.2.1 COMBANK's Complete CSM with Scenario Input

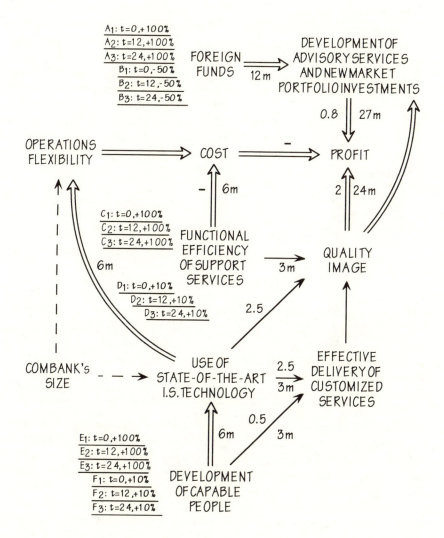

The second set (ADF) denotes, again, a 100 percent upward change in the influx of foreign funds from its original level, at times $t=0,12$, and 24 months, with a 10 percent change in Combank's effort to increase its functional efficiency of support services, at times $t=0,12$, and 24 months, and a 10 percent increase in the development of capable people, at times $t=0,12$, and 24 months. ADF represents Combank's reference scenario given its present parameters and strategy.

Table 9.2.1 Combank's Scenario Input

Scenario		Time t (months)	Foreign Funds	Functional Efficiency of Support Services	Development of Capable People
Mixed	Pure				
A $(A_1+A_2+A_3)$	A_1 : A_2 : A_3 :	0 12 14	+100% +100% +100%		
B $(B_1+B_2+B_3)$	B_1 : B_2 : B_3 :	0 12 14	-50% -50% -50%		
C $(C_1+C_2+C_3)$	C_1 : C_2 : C_3 :	0 12 14		+100% +100% +100%	
D $(D_1+D_2+D_3)$	D_1 : D_2 : D_3 :	0 12 14		+10% +10% +10%	
E $(E_1+E_2+E_3)$	E_1 : E_2 : E_3 :	0 12 14			+100% +100% +100%
F $(F_1+F_2+F_3)$	F_1 : F_2 : F_3 :	0 12 14			+10% +10% +10%

The third mixed-scenario set (BCE) infers a -50 percent change triggered in the influx of foreign funds at times $t=0,12$, and 24 months, a 100 percent increase in Combank's functional efficiency of support services at times $t=0,12$, and 24 months, and a 100 percent increase in the development of capable people, at times $t=0,12$, and 24 months. BCE is the scenario of slow or no growth given the bank's present situation and strategy.

Lastly, the fourth scenario set (BDF) assumes a -50 percent downward change in the influx of foreign funds from its previous level, at times $t=0,12$, and 24 months, with a 10 percent change in Combank's effort to increase its functional efficiency of support services, at times $t=0,12$, and 24 months, and a 10 percent increase in the development of capable people, at times $t=0,12$, and 24 months. BDF represents Combank's worst-case scenario.

Figure 9.2.2. imparts Combank's best-case (ACE), reference (ADF), slow-growth (BCE), and worst-case (BDF) computed scenarios on profit potential. The cumulative percentage change in profit under each scenario set unfolds a possible alternative future for Combank over a seven-year period, from time $t=0$ to $t=84$ months. The four scenarios capture the combined effects of changes triggered in the global economic environment, reflected by the influx of foreign funds on the one hand and Combank's efforts to manipulate its internal levers on the other.

Figure 9.2.2 displays the potential synergy among Combank's services, volume capacity, and the importance of staying close to the customer. The bank's efforts are reflected by changes either in the functional efficiency of support services or in the development of capable people, or in both. These variables portray the strategic levers at the disposal of Combank so far stemming from the dialectical process initiated by our intervention.

Combank does not appear to be equally sensitive to upward and downward changes in the influx of foreign funds because of the synergistic leverage of inter-nal decision variables on profit. Combank's strategic levers could keep it afloat even if the funds from overseas decreased by 50 percent. Figure 9.2.2 shows a slight growth in profit during the first three years into scenario BCE.

Yet, if Combank does not take advantage of the strategic leverage at its dis-posal, a downward change in the influx of foreign funds could cause an influx of red ink. Given Combank's current situation and reference parameters, if scenario B does play, the 10 percent increase in functional efficiency of support services and in the development of capable people will not vitalize profit.

Figure 9.2.2 allows a clean, almost lexicographic ordering of the visible cost (VC) observed under each scenario set when some other scenario set in fact plays. Ordering Combank's cost of lost opportunities at steady state yields

$$VC(ACE - ADF) < VC(ACE - BCE) < VC(ACE - BDF). \tag{1}$$

Combank will incur a real cost (RC) if another set of events turns out to be true in this strategic situation. Section 4.1 defines RC and VC in the context of assump-tional analysis. Their use in the above strict inequality (1) with Combank's com-puted scenarios of Fig. 9.2.2 represents a different but related context.

Combank would do reasonably well even under the slow-growth BCE scenario, if no major environmental disturbances occurred. To be on the safe side, a more energetic level of managerial planning would be appropriate.

Yet, growth-related acts and tactical moves must be executed with extreme cau-tion. The mixed scenarios of Fig. 9.2.2 as well as their component pure scenarios

Figure 9.2.2 COMBANK's Computed Scenarios

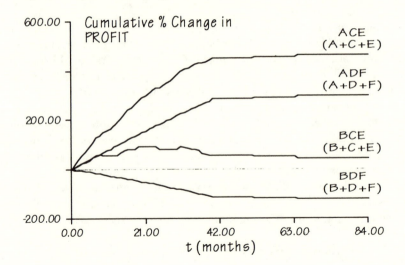

(Fig. 9.2.1 and Table 9.2.1) assume no drastic change in Combank's size. In Fig. 9.2.1, the broken-line arrows connecting Combank's size to the use of state-of-the-art IS technology and to operations flexibility designate this qualitative restriction. Its immediate implication is that Combank continues *outsourcing* its major information systems projects, while relying on its capable personnel for identifying quality suppliers who enjoy economies of scale of their own by serving many firms.

Other things being equal, creative reengineering of support services—see Davenport (1993) and Tobias (1991) for a candid treatment of process reengineering—through continuous-process improvement (CPI: cf. Richmond & Peterson, 1992a) will enable Combank to withstand potential price shakeouts, both locally and overseas. For an example, consider Combank's "tool-train workshop" from Section 6.2. Also helpful might be the selective outsourcing of major IS technology projects coupled with selection, training, and retention of top-notch personnel. Moreover, these activities give away Combank's high-quality image; let it keep on staying close to clients with a global presence; and guard its competitive advantage in the low-volume high-margin end of commercial banking.

Combank's Third-Generation or *Accounting-for-Interdependence* Scenarios

The interdependence among the variables pertinent to Combank's strategic situation motivated the use of BASICS (Battelle, 1988), the stochastic simulation computer package used widely by Battelle and others in scenario-driven planning (Honton et al., 1985). BASICS helped assess the posterior probability of occurrence of each state (i.e., high, medium, or low) that may occur in Combank's potential profit as a result of a corresponding state affecting the influx of foreign funds into the United States. The BASICS simulation algorithm combines each variable's predefined states into ten consecutively generated random trials to estimate the stochastic frequency of possible outcomes that may occur in the future. Appendix C.4 gives a detailed technical summary of BASICS. Using BASICS gave a balanced consideration to what might happen in Combank's future.

To estimate the final outcome probabilities, we assigned three sets of a priori probabilities to the three possible states (high, medium, low) of each of the variables that Combank's planning group deemed critical. The three sets of the probabilistic weights assigned are:

- 0.50, 0.33, and 0.17 for the best-case scenario or fast-growth potential,
- 0.33, 0.34, and 0.33 for the reference scenario, and
- 0.17, 0.33, and 0.50 for the worst-case scenario, respectively.

Figure 9.2.3   COMBANK's Probabilistic Scenarios

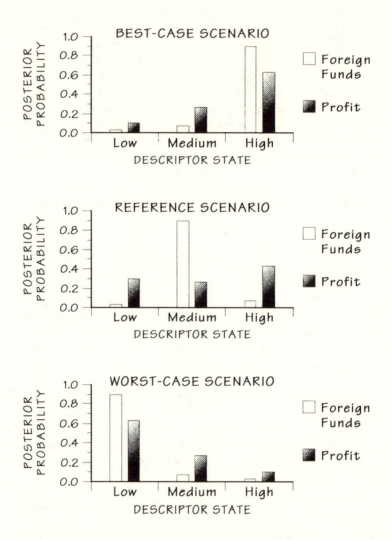

The insight gained from CSM's deterministic causal graphing helped to establish the cross-impact (CI) matrix for Combank's strategic situation. Along with the above three sets of a priori probabilities, the CI matrix served as input to BASICS, which confirmed the CSM results.

The BASICS simulation algorithm estimated the posterior probability of occurrence of each variable's high, medium, and low state, while taking the interdependence among Combank's variables into account. The algorithm combined each variable's predefined states into ten consecutively generated pseudorandom trials to estimate the stochastic frequencies of possible future outcomes in foreign funds and Combank's potential profit.

Again, BASICS amplifies the differences in the first-estimate or a priori probabilities. The BASICS program transforms these a priori probabilities into posterior probabilities of variable states, while accounting for the cross impacts among possible future events.

The first set of a priori probabilities yields a most probable outcome with both foreign funds and profit at high levels. Under the best-case scenario of Fig. 9.2.3, the corresponding posterior probabilities of high foreign funds and profit are 0.90 and 0.63, respectively. These estimates depict Combank's prospects for fast growth in view of the present snapshot of its situation.

Under the second set of a priori probabilities, the most probable outcomes combine a medium influx of foreign funds, while the variable descriptor of Combank's potential profit attains a relatively high state in its stochastic frequency. The reference scenario of Fig. 9.2.3 yields corresponding posterior probabilities of 0.90 for the medium influx of foreign funds and 0.43 for the high potential profit.

Under the third set of a priori probabilities, the most probable outcome finds foreign funds and profit at low levels, with posterior probabilities of 0.90, and 0.63, respectively. It is worth noting that the worst-case scenario results of Fig. 9.2.3 are equiprobable to Combank's fast-growth prospects, whereas the reference scenario of Fig. 9.2.3 yields the largest posterior probability in the high state of profit.

Conclusion

Our scenario-driven planning intervention at Combank combined three scenario methods to frame its strategic decision situation or *problématique:* the CSM causal diagramming, MICMAC, and BASICS. The analysis of Combank's profit potential aimed at gaining insight into the dynamics of its system. It showed how the very success of Combank's current strategy will be partially determined by the moves of external actors.

These moves include the US Federal Reserve policies for cushioning real economic activity from the stock market fluctuations, for increasing industrial production and reducing consumption, and for meeting the Gramm-Rudman targets to achieve a budget surplus. Scenario-driven planning and the group dynamics entailed in our CSM method combined a causal analysis of future events with a dialectical probing into implicit assumptions. This combination is helpful for generating a better understanding of Combank's strategic situation.

The first generation of pure scenarios undertaken at Combank, which we recalled at the beginning of this section (9.2), was based on Combank's marketing- and technology-centered views. The insight gained from these divergent but complementary views led to the second generation of scenarios. These captured Combank's three alternative futures, in addition to its Ackoff-Ozbekhan or reference scenario, expressed as the percentage and cumulative percentage change in profit over a seven-year period. These mixed scenarios were computed on Combank's aggregate CSM, capturing the combined effects of changes triggered in the global economic environment and in Combank's efforts to manipulate internal change levers.

The MICMAC analysis of the aggregate CSM in Chapter 6 helped to establish an occurrence cross-impact matrix of Combank's situation variables. This matrix served as input to the BASICS computational method, leading to Combank's third generation of probabilistic scenarios. These provide a balanced consideration of which one might dominate among Combank's alternative futures.

Analyzing Combank's potential moves, confronting its aims, and balancing its strategies in view of its constraints and resources through scenario-driven planning helped answer some basic questions about Combank's uncertain future. In the process of implanting scenario-driven planning with CSM, many underlying assumptions were unearthed through a succession of innovative ideas. These ideas were about the issues and consequences of predictable battles in the emerging transnational environment of financial services, where the distinctions between traditional types of financial ventures are beginning to blur.

Our scenario-driven planning intervention with its three consecutive scenario generations showed that whatever the influence and interconnections of Combank's situation variables, the company's future is not totally predetermined: it remains open to several possible scenarios. The firm's top managers possess various degrees of freedom which they will be able to exercise through action to attain their personal and organizational objectives.

The stochastic simulation results of BASICS reinforce the conclusions reached from the deterministic scenarios computed on the CSM. The potential synergy among Combank's services, volume capacity, and the importance of staying close to the customer provide a powerful strategic leverage at Combank's disposal.

If Combank does not take advantage of its strategic leverage and if the probabilistic reference scenario of Fig. 9.2.3 holds, a medium influx of foreign funds could anchor profit to its low descriptor state. The BASICS-derived stochastic frequencies of possible future outcomes verify that in the worst-case scenario Combank should expect a substantial decline in its profit (Fig. 9.2.2).

Conversely, if Combank pulls on its internal levers of functional efficiency of support services and development of capable people with zest and vigor, then it can shift the profit anchor to its high descriptor state. The deterministic scenario BCE of Fig. 9.2.2 shows how growth in Combank's profit can grow even if the funds flowing in from overseas decreased by 50 percent. Exactly what will happen depends in part on the specific decision made and its mode of implementation.

Future research into Combank's strategic options should be directed at exploring one of two alternative future paths. These stem from the bank's two basic views of itself, focusing on marketing and operations, respectively. To achieve synergy, the implications of divergent but complementary views must be refined and explored continuously by detailed scenario analyses toward full-scale strategic modeling and computer simulation. Implanting scenario-driven planning with CSM causal mapping should make the transition toward full-scale strategic modeling and simulation smoother or at least less bumpy.

The following chapter includes a classic example of what full-scale behavioral modeling and computer simulation can accomplish.

SUMMARY

The Infoplus case example shows how computing deterministic scenarios on the CSM can resolve the net effect of multiple paths of influence on relevant strategic variables. Computed scenarios invariably help organize or create new information that can sensitize managers and planners to the dynamic implications of a strategic decision situation. Without creating new information, a decision process may lead nowhere.

Similarly, the scenarios computed on Combank's CSM reveal its sensitivity to the influx of foreign funds, countered with its efforts toward the development of capable people. Combank's success in increasing the functional efficiency of support services may subsequently determine whether it will continue projecting a strong quality image. This image is necessary for Combank to sustain its competitive advantage within its strategic posture in the low-volume high-margin end of commercial banking.

Although expressed in terms of relative changes, and thereby preempting the difficulty of dealing with different units, CSM operates as a linearly additive and transitive model of the transmission of change. These features should interest strategy researchers and practitioners willing to integrate tangible and intangible variables into rough-cut causal mapping—a prerequisite to full-scale strategic modeling and computerized simulation.

These methods possess powerful features that firms can use.

Chapter 10

System Dynamics

Thus far we have focused on simple computational techniques and on comprehensive situation mapping (CSM), which can serve as a transition between problem framing and full-scale modeling. It wouldn't be fair to leave the reader in suspense forever, without allowing a glimpse of what full-scale modeling can do for scenario-driven planning. This chapter is a brief introduction to system dynamics modeling and simulation. It begins with a biographical sketch of Jay W. Forrester, the creator of system dynamics. Following that is a historical and gradual introduction to computer modeling and simulation. The last section, through the case of Datacom, shows how a description of the premises of decision making followed by computed scenarios can enhance the interpretation of a system dynamics simulation model.

10.1 BORN APPLIED

The 1989 International Meeting of the System Dynamics Society was special. For the first time, it took place in Germany, at the University of Stuttgart. It was also the society's first meeting after the retirement of its founder, Jay Wright Forrester, Germeshausen Professor at MIT's Sloan School of Management. The organizers of the meeting asked Forrester to share with the participants the history of system dynamics.

On that memorable evening of 13 July 1989, Forrester did not give a technical talk, but instead briefly sketched an autobiography of sorts. Two threads run through this man's life, which *is* the history of system dynamics. First, everything Forrester has ever done has converged to become system dynamics. Second, at critical moments of his life, whenever opportunity knocked, he explored "what was on the other side" (Forrester, 1989, p. 2). This section draws exclusively from the banquet talk Forrester gave at the 1989 meeting.

Forrester grew up on a cattle ranch in Nebraska, in the middle of the United States. On a cattle ranch, the economic forces of supply and demand, changing prices, and industry pressures become a personal part of daily life, and everyone works hard to get results. Life must be practical in an agricultural setting; it is neither theoretical nor conceptual. Indeed, on a cattle ranch, life is a full-time immersion in the real world.

In high school, Forrester was interested in practical activity—he built a wind-driven electric plant to provide electricity to his home for the first time. When he finished high school, he received a scholarship to go to the Agricultural College, but three weeks before enrolling, he decided it wasn't for him. Herding cattle in Nebraska's winter blizzards was simply not electrifying enough for him. Instead, he enrolled in the Engineering College at the University of Nebraska, which back then was the only academic field with theoretical dynamics at its core.

Finishing college brought another turning point. Forrester went to MIT, which offered him $100 per month for a graduate research assistantship. This was more than any other university offer. Also, as Forrester said, his mother had been a librarian in Springfield, Massachusetts, and so she knew there was a school called MIT. In the Midwest in those days, MIT meant "Massachusetts Investor's Trust," not an engineering school.

At MIT, Forrester worked for Gordon S. Brown, a pioneer in feedback control systems. During World War II, he worked with Brown on servomechanisms for the control of radar antennas and gun mounts. Again, this was research toward an extremely practical end during which he literally run from mathematical theory to the battlefield.

When the captain of the US carrier *Lexington* visited MIT, he saw an experimental unit, planned for redesign and scheduled to go into production a year or so later. The captain said, "I want that, I mean that very one. We can't wait for the production ones." He got it.

About nine months later, the experimental control unit stopped working, and so Forrester volunteered to go to Pearl Harbor. Having discovered the problem but not having time to fix it, the captain came to him and said they were about to leave port. The captain also asked if Forrester would like to go along to finish the job. Forrester went, having no idea what that meant at the time.

They were offshore during the invasion of Tarawa (now state capital of Bairiki, Kiribati), northwest of the Gilbert Islands in the Pacific Ocean, but later took a turn between the Sunrise and Sunset chains of the Northern Marshall Islands. The Japanese had fighter-plane bases on both island chains of the Marshall Islands, and they didn't like having a US Navy Task Force wrecking their airports. After dark, they dropped flares along one side of the ship and came in with torpedo planes from the other side. Finally, they hit the *Lexington* at 11 P.M., cutting off one of the four propellers and setting the rudder in a hard turn. Again, this gave a very practical view of how research and theory apply to the battlefield.

At the end of World War II, Forrester decided he would either get a job or start a business in feedback control systems until Gordon Brown intervened with a list of projects. Forrester picked from the list the project of building an aircraft flight simulator. This was similar to an aircraft pilot trainer, but so precise that it could take wind-tunnel data of a model airplane and predict the behavior of the real airplane before a prototype was built.

The simulator was planned as an analog computer. It took only about a year to conclude that an analog machine of that complexity could not do much more than solve its own internal idiosyncrasies. So, Forrester invented *random-access magnetic storage* or *core memory*. His invention went into the heart of Whirlwind, a digital computer used for experimental development of military combat information systems. This eventually became the semiautomatic ground environment (SAGE) air defense system for North America.

The SAGE system had about thirty-five control centers, each of which was 160 feet square, four stories high, and contained about 80,000 vacuum tubes. These computer centers were installed in the late 1950s, with the last decommissioned in 1983. They were in service about twenty-five years. The statistics show a 99.8 percent uptime, or less than twenty hours a year downtime. Even today, it is difficult to get such high reliability. The SAGE air defense system was another practical job, with theory and new ideas being only as good as the working results.

In 1956, Forrester, thinking that the pioneering days in digital computers were over, left engineering to go into management. That might seem surprising considering the major technical advances of the last thirty years. As it turn out, from 1946 to 1956 computers registered more improvements in speed, reliability, and storage capacity than in any other decade. At any rate, Forrester was in management already, with his project team having complete control of a multibillion dollar business. It wrote the contracts between each prime contractor and the Air Force, and it designed the computers and controlled their production. The SAGE project entailed managing an enterprise that involved the Air Defense Command, the Air Material Command, the Air Research and Development Command, Western Electric, AT&T, and IBM.

When James Killian, then president of MIT, told Forrester about the new management school being started at MIT. Killian suggested that Forrester "might be interested." Forrester's career turn into management was clearly no accident.

The Sloan School of Management was founded in 1952 with a grant of $10 million from Alfred P. Sloan, the man who built General Motors. Sloan expected a management school in a technical environment like MIT to develop differently from one in a liberal arts environment like Harvard, Columbia, or Chicago. Perhaps it would be better, too, but in any case it would be different. It was worth $10 million to run the experiment.

In the four years before Forrester joined the school in 1956, standard courses had done nothing about what a management school within an engineering environment might mean. After spending fifteen years in the science and engineering side of MIT, Forrester took the challenge of exploring what engineering could do for management.

Most people at Sloan assumed that an application of engineering technology to management would either advance the OR field, or explore the use of computers for handling management information. Forrester had a year free of other duties, so that he would decide why he was at Sloan.

With regard to the use of computers for management information, at that time manufacturers in the computer business, and banks and insurance companies were already using computers. A few engineers in a management school would not have any major effect because the momentum was already there. Forrester considered OR too but found it limited. It lacked the practical importance that had always appealed to him.

Chance intervened when Forrester found himself in conversation with people from General Electric. Their household appliance plants in Kentucky puzzled them. As they explained, those plants would work with three or four shifts for some time and then, a few years later, with half the people laid off. It was easy to say that business cycles caused fluctuating demand, but that explanation did not seem to be the entire reason. GE's managers felt that something was wrong.

After talking with them about their hiring, firing, and inventory policies, Forrester began to perform some simulation using pencil and paper on a notebook page. It started at the top with columns for inventories, employees, and customer orders. Given these conditions and GE's policies, one could decide how many people would be hired or fired a week later. This decision gave a new condition of employment, inventories, and production. It became clear that a system that was wholly determined internally had potential for oscillatory or unstable behavior. Even with constant incoming orders, as a consequence of commonly used policies, employment instability was possible. *That first inventory control system written with pencil and paper simulation marked the beginning of system dynamics.*

Out of that first dynamic analysis came the early beginnings of what are now the DYNAMO© compilers (Pugh & Carrasco, 1983). An expert programmer, Richard Bennett, worked for Forrester while he was writing his first system dynamics article (Forrester, 1958). Later, that article became Chapter 2 of *Industrial Dynamics* (Forrester, 1961). When Forrester needed computer simulation results for the article, he asked Bennett to code up some equations to run them on the computer.

Bennett, a very independent type, refused to code the program for that set of equations. Instead, he wrote a compiler that would create the computer code automatically. He called the compiler Simulation of Industrial Management Problems with Lots of Equations (SIMPLE). Bennett's insistence on creating a compiler accelerated later modeling, which rapidly expanded system dynamics. Jack Pugh has since extended the early system dynamics compilers into DYNAMO©.

At about the time system dynamics was starting, Forrester was asked to be on the board of the Digital Equipment Corporation. Kenneth Olsen and other founders of the company had worked with Forrester in the Whirlwind computer days. Forrester did not understand the nature of high-technology growth companies as well as he would like and undertook to model such companies to guide his own position on the board. His model gave insight into why high-technology companies often grow to a certain level and then stagnate or fail. Initially, the model dealt with the interactions among capacity, delivery delay, price, and quality.

Yet, the process of modeling corporate growth moved system dynamics out of physical variables, like inventory, into much more subtle considerations. Over 90 percent of the variables in that model lay in the top-management influence structure, including leadership qualities, character of the founders, creation of organizational goals, and the way an organization's past traditions determine its decision making and its future.

A turning point came in 1968 when system dynamics expanded to Germany after Gert von Kortzfleisch spent several months at MIT and took system dynamics back with him. Several of his students, including Erich Zahn and Peter Milling, who organized the 1989 International Meeting of the System Dynamics Society, are now leaders in the field. In 1970, Eduard Pestel, president of the Technical University of Hannover, arranged for the Volkswagen Foundation to support the research that produced *The Limits to Growth* (Meadows et al., 1972).

Forrester applied his knowledge of computer sciences and engineering feedback control processes to managerial and socioeconomic systems. The rest of his talk covered a thirty-year history full of outstanding, truly pioneering achievements. Most of them are well-known, documented beautifully in the preface of Forrester's monographs.[1] The talk concluded with the recounting of a recent trend in system dynamics, aimed at changing the mental models people use to represent the real world.

Forrester believes that exposure to systems thinking and dynamic behavior patterns should start at an early age, before people establish inflexible contrary patterns of thought. Both management consultants and teachers realize early on that unlearning is harder than learning. Empirical evidence shows that exposure to cause-effect feedback thinking and computer modeling can begin successfully in classes for 10-year-old children (Holt, 1970; Papert, 1980; Roberts et al., 1983; Senge, 1990).

Forrester's concept of management education has not changed over the years. His 1958 article concluded with the implications of systems dynamics for management education and practice. It is as relevant to management education and practice today as it has ever been:

According to Forrester (1958, p. 66), just as automation requires new skills at the worker level, so will improved planning methods require new abilities at the management level. The executive of the future will be

- concerned not so much with actual operating decisions as with the basis for wise operating decisions
- concerned not so much with day-to-day crises as with the establishment of policies and plans that minimize emergencies
- able to do these jobs with sophistication and skill
- capable of understanding the implications of market trends and the probable behavior of consumer demand
- capable of recognizing the ebb and flow of forces which interact to generate fluctuating economic conditions
- able to relate the changing factors in research, investment and marketing to the life cycle of a product
- able to relate different financing methods with their relative advantages and risks to the uncertainties of market and economic conditions
- of devising organizational forms that are efficient and encourage the creativity of people

---

1   Forrester's system dynamics work as well as other system dynamics books formerly published by MIT Press or Wright-Allen Press are now available from Productivity Press (541 NE 20th Avenue • Portland, OR 97232).

Forrester expected changes in various management responsibilities, including a merging of many line and stuff functions. Although the kind of system studies discussed in this book and in Forrester's 1958 article might be primarily the province of staff specialists, their conclusions are only as valid as the assumptions on which computed scenarios are based. Their answers are no more pertinent than the questions asked. Forrester concludes that systems planning must become the tool of the responsible manager for

> It is by nature a thoughtful process of weighing the past and present, not to reach the immediate decision of the moment but to derive guiding principles for the future (Forrester, 1958, p. 66).

Scenario-driven planning and full-fledged system dynamics models lead to a decisive integration of strategy making and operations, with the dividing line much lower in the organization than at present. The interaction among conventional functions can speed up the movement toward decentralized management. In the past, power had been concentrated at the top to improve integration and control. An increased understanding of a firm's business environment, strategy, operations, and their interdependencies, can lead to an improved definition of objectives and more pertinent standards for the measurement of managerial success. This in turn will permit managers at the lower levels to take on more operating responsibility.

> Senior executives will then be free to give more attention to product innovation, economic conditions, and the organizational changes that will enhance man's creativity (Forrester, 1958, p. 66).

10.2 INTRODUCTION TO COMPUTER SIMULATION

In the past, model formulation and problem framing compromised between realistic replicas of real systems and models whose mathematical analysis was tractable. There was no payoff in models that faithfully conformed to a system if they were impossible to analyze mathematically. Similar considerations led to concentration on asymptotic or steady-state results as opposed to the more useful ones on transient time (Ross, 1990).

Now, with fast and inexpensive computers available, a system can be modeled as faithfully as possible and simulation can be used to analyze it. A comprehensive history of mathematical modeling and simulation is well beyond the scope of this book. Very briefly, however, scientists and engineers have used both analog and symbolic machines to compute the behavior of models representing real systems.

Analog machines simulate (i.e., imitate, from the Latin *simulare*) a system by making a direct physical analogy between the machine and the system. An example of an analog computing machine is the slide rule, which maps real numbers to positions along two scales. This mapping allows multiplying and dividing by sliding the two scales. Analog machines vary continuously because the position of their elements changes continuously. They were used almost exclusively to simulate the behavior of real systems or processes before the invention of the *transistor*, an engineering breakthrough.

Symbolic machines use transistors to simulate through an equivalence between the discrete states of the machine and a system. An example of a symbolic computing machine is the abacus, with the position of the beads representing numbers. Their position can vary continuously, but the states of the abacus change discretely. John Napier's invention of the decimal point was the *notational* breakthrough that made the electronic computation of symbols possible (Belknap, 1991, p. 70).

Simulation involves some kind of model, a simplified representation of reality. During the course of a simulation, the model mimics important elements of what is being simulated. A symbolic or mathematical model represents both the important elements of a system and the structure of their interactions. Models can serve many purposes. They can help describe, understand, predict and control, that is, ma n - a g e, the behavior of a real system. System dynamics, for example, provides a structure for modeling real systems. Business models have witnessed a shift in emphasis in the last twenty to thirty years. Their emphasis has shifted from the well-structured problems at the tactical and operational levels of management to the ill-structured problems at the business and corporate levels. (Section 12.2 presents a unified view of problem framing and problem solving.) The fundamental distinction between computer simulation and other problem solving methods is that in computer simulation the data are gathered from a computer model as opposed to being gathered in the real world.

Often, it is reasonable to assume that all variables in a model behave in a predictable manner. Such a model is said to be *deterministic* because it does not permit any statistical variability in the relationships assumed among variables. This simplification of a complex problem in a deterministic model is warranted by the managers' knowledge of a particular activity. Complex problems cannot be solved without deep substantive knowledge of the problem at hand. No matter how skilled analysts may be in their respective fields, they will not be able to tackle problems involving economic issues, for example, unless they understand economic systems. According to Forrester: "In general, modeling what is found in formal academic economics will do rather little to explain the dynamics of economic systems. The modeling must start from an understanding of how business operates in the limited-information, non-equilibrium conditions of real economic behavior" (Personal communication, 28 June 1993).

Similarly, managers cannot solve a company's sales problem unless they understand what is going on within the firm. Managers know the important actors and variables affecting their business. They live with them on a daily basis, trying to deflect environmental threats or, better still, to turn them into business opportunities. Through systems thinking, modeling, and reflection, they can develop a tip-of-the-fingers' feeling about the relationships underlying a strategic situation. Yet, more than anyone, managers understand how the search for cause-effect relationships to explain system behavior sometimes gives way to a belief in random events. Then it becomes important to account explicitly for randomness in the behavior of one or more variables through a statistical model—*probabilistic* over a single time period or *stochastic* over several successive time periods. This is most appropriate when dealing with such uncontrollable variables as the monthly demand for computer spare parts or the daily arrivals for emergency aid in an emergency care unit.

The following section shows how to analyze a deterministic model through computer simulation. Chapter 9 has already given a taste of stochastic simulation through the implementation of BASICS on the deterministic scenarios of Combank and Infoplus.

In a statistical simulation model, whether probabilistic or stochastic, the computer is used to generate random or, more precisely, pseudorandom numbers, which determine the values of random variables from arbitrary statistical distributions. By using the concept of discrete events, random variables can generate the behavior of a stochastic model over time. By continually generating the behavior of the system, it is possible to obtain estimators of desired quantities of interest.

The statistical questions of when to stop a simulation and what confidence to place in the resulting estimators are beyond the scope of this book. Karian & Dudewicz (1991), Law & Kelton (1982), and Ross (1990) present a variety of ways to improve on the usual simulation estimators. They show how to use simulation in order to determine whether a stochastic model is consistent with a set of actual data and to deal with the important subject of variance reduction.

In a deterministic model, mathematical symbols or equations are used to represent the relationships in a system. To perform a simulation using a mathematical model, the calculations indicated by the model's equations are performed over and over to represent the passage of time—in one-month intervals, for example.

From Systems Thinking to System Dynamics Simulation Modeling

Model builders take different approaches to choosing the issues they model as well as the content of their models. This chapter focuses on one perspective for computer modeling and simulation, namely, system dynamics.

System dynamics applies feedback control principles and techniques to strategic decision situations in order to improve long-term performance through the (re)design of strategy and policy. Feedback loops exist whenever decision makers are affected by the implications of their own decisions over time. Through system dynamics models, it is possible to integrate the logic underlying a firm's decision functions with information feedback-loop structures and computer simulation techniques into a powerful strategic inquiry system (Fig. 10.2.1).

System dynamics provides a coherent structure for modeling the effects of feedback-loop structures underlying highly interconnected systems. This line of strategic inquiry offers a new way of thinking about organizational problems. Using basic concepts of system structure, especially interconnectedness through feedback loops, one can explain how structure determines organizational behavior patterns (Forrester, 1968b).

A system may be defined as a collection of interacting elements functioning together for a particular purpose. For example, a firm may be viewed as a system that produces and sells products, maintains inventories, hires employees and performs other functions to survive and grow economically. An airline is a system of personnel, as well as electrical, mechanical, and hydraulic components designed to transport passengers comfortably through the air.

The systems approach emphasizes connections among the various parts that constitute a whole; *systems thinking* is concerned with connectedness and wholeness. By its nature, a systems view of a problem cuts across disciplinary boundaries as defined in many traditional sciences, in a search to understand a problem from an integrated viewpoint.

For example, viewing a firm as a system might involve integrating the economics of the marketplace with the sociology of the employees' work environment and the technology of manufacturing. A systems view of a firm might involve aspects of political science, geography, economics, and sociology. Exactly how these various disciplinary perspectives can be integrated is of the major intellectual challenges of the systems approach.

System science emerged as a serious field of study after World War II. Originally, the field was rooted in the biological and engineering sciences; only more recently has it branched out to become involved with social and economic systems (Cavaleri & Obloj, 1993; Checkland, 1975; Churchman, 1969; Roberts, et al., 1983; Schoderbek, Schoderbek, & Kefalas, 1990; Senge, 1990; van Gigch, 1978). Early analyses of biological and engineering systems shared a common emphasis on the ways system components work together to perform some well-defined function. For example, the mechanism that the human body uses to maintain a constant body temperature of 98.6 degrees Fahrenheit resembles the control machinery designed to stabilize an airplane's altitude during flight. Both systems function to keep some quantity—blood temperature in one case and altitude in the other—within narrowly defined limits under a wide range of possible disturbances.

Figure 10.2.1 A Powerful Strategic Inquiry System

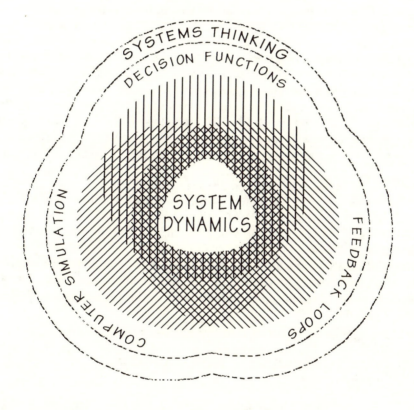

The pioneers in biological and engineering systems theory also considered the implications of their work for problems outside biology and engineering. In his early work, *Cybernetics* (1948), Norbert Wiener sketched the outlines of a new field of inquiry. Cybernetics became the study of how biological, engineering, social, and economic systems are controlled and regulated. Wiener proposed that the same general principles that control body temperature and the altitude of airplanes may be at work in the market mechanisms of economic systems, the decision-making mechanisms of political systems and the cognitive mechanisms of thought processes.

Wiener and other systems theorists argued that all aspects of human behavior, ranging from the economic to the political, the social, and the psychological, may be governed by a single set of governing principles. If this claim proved to be true, great advances in human knowledge could be made through the systematic study of those general organizing principles. This was the premise of the early system scientists (Beer, 1968; Checkland, 1975; Churchman, 1969; van Gigch, 1978). In the decades since these bold claims were first articulated, researchers have made impressive progress in applying a systems perspective in many diverse fields. For example, Karl Deutsch laid out a cybernetic view of political processes in his classic *The Nerves of Government* (1963). Herbert Simon (1957) proposed a cybernetic view of human intelligence, and Jay Forrester first applied the broad principles of cybernetics to industrial systems in his pathbreaking work, *Industrial Dynamics* (1958, 1961).

Forrester's initial work in industrial systems has been subsequently broadened to include other social and economic systems and, as noted earlier, is now known as the field of system dynamics. The field of system dynamics, one of several possible variants of the systems approach, forms the basis for the simulation model presented in Section 10.3.

Relying heavily on the computer, system dynamics provides a framework in which to apply the ideas of systems theory to social and economic problems. Appendix B presents a modeling process that can be used in a wide range of dynamic modeling situations.

Hardwiring Economic Rationality, Decision Making, and Cognitive Processes

Suppose that a firm's unit sales drop and its productivity declines. Is it reasonable to believe that the firm's managers deliberately designed a strategy to suffer losses? An alternative explanation is that a series of intendedly rational policies or tactics (i.e., intended to produce desirable outcomes) unexpectedly produced unwelcome results when combined.

A central idea of the systems view of organizations is that well-intentioned decisions can cause unfavorable behavior when combined (Churchman, 1969). This idea pervades the descriptive interpretations of decision situations encountered in both business (Hall, 1976) and government (Allison, 1971; Friend & Jessop, 1969). Yet, a gap between a model's assumptions and its computed scenarios requires a transient leap in logic, often undermining confidence in models of business and social problems (Bell & Senge, 1980). These considerations support the necessity of setting up an important task in the model and scenario construction phases of scenario-driven planning (Fig. 8.2.1). The task is to explain clearly how a model's underlying assumptions lead to its simulated behavior.

John Morecroft employs two different techniques for bridging the gap between model assumptions and simulated implications: premise description and partial model tests (Morecroft, 1983, 1985b). Premise description examines the bounded rationality in a model's assumptions, pointing out cognitive limitations in strategy making. Partial model tests expose the intended rationality of combinations of policies or tactics, showing management's judicious actions with respect to a model's assumptions. The contrast of partial and whole model simulations can clarify the causes and persistence of dysfunctional behavior in a firm's system.

Section 8.1.1 reviewed the requirements of bounded rationality for strategic decision making. Because of these requirements, Cyert & March (1963) used premise description to clarify the behavioral and cognitive assumptions of early simulation models. Objective rationality guides the process of laying open and describing assumptions and raises questions peculiar to the situation under consideration. Here are some examples:

- Why is some information available in a decision process and not in another?
- Why do delay and distortion occur in the transmission and interpretation of information?
- Why is bias present?

The answers to these questions point to empirically observed decision processes stemming from bounded rationality. Typically, the decision processes that a behavioral model captures may be intendedly rational within the bounds set by common managerial practice. At the same time, they can be far removed from objective rationality. Strategic decisions often *are* intendedly rational with respect to the assumptions made about the environment. Simon wrote: "It is precisely in the realm where human behavior is intendedly rational that there is room for a genuine theory of organization and administration" (Simon, 1976, p. xxviii).

Like premise description, partial model tests had long been used in simulation to debug model submodules, but Morecroft suggests using partial tests to expose the intended rationality of strategic decisions. Again, what justifies this new and important role of partial model tests is that decision making is rational within the context of assumptions or premises in the decision makers' thinking. Through this condition a complex simulation model can be decomposed into pieces, while expecting simulation runs of the pieces to reveal intuitively clear, plausible behavior. The partial tests should show that local decisions are well adapted to achieving local goals.

Yet, localized rationality in decision making does not ensure that the system's behavior is well adapted to a firm's multiple objectives. Dysfunctional behavior is possible as a systemic problem, resulting from the coupling of decisions. Firms often exhibit flaws in organizational design (Robey, 1982).

The strength of partial model testing becomes apparent when a full-scale model exhibits counterintuitive and highly ineffective behavior. The surprising behavior of the full-scale model can be traced to the interaction of many intendedly rational acts. The coupling of decision processes can violate the assumptions or conditions for rational adjustment among decisions. Then their system is integrated in such a way that the rationality of the parts cannot satisfy the objective rationality required for success of the system. The contrast of partial and full-scale model tests can explain the unfavorable behavior of the system.

Section 10.3 illustrates the usefulness of these techniques with a system dynamics model of a sales organization, in which sales force productivity is prone to decline. Morecroft derived this model from a classic intervention in the marketing strategy of a large firm selling advanced data communications equipment (see 1984, 1985b, 1990).

The original model describes many interlinked decision processes, covering customer purchasing, price perceptions, sales force time allocation, quitting, overtime, motivation, and sales objective setting. The large structure of the original model was developed through interviews and discussions with executives, managers, and staff of the data communications firm's sales marketing, and personnel functions.

The small derived model focuses on overtime adjustment, objective setting, and sales force motivation. The structure and parameterization of these processes remain virtually unchanged from the large model. The rationality of the small model preserves that of the large, empirically derived model. Simulations of the small model show the same declines in sales productivity that the large model did for reasons that the firm's managers and executives found both plausible and persuasive.

10.3   DATACOM (UNABRIDGED)

This section translates and extends Morecroft's (1985b) model into iThink™ (Richmond, Peterson, & Charyk, 1992) from the original DYNAMO© equations, which he kindly sent us. Again, this model was derived from a much larger model that was built during a system dynamics intervention in the sales organization of a large firm selling advanced data communications equipment. Hence the name we gave it: Datacom.

Following Morecroft's analysis (1985b), we trace the decline in Datacom's unit sales and productivity to the inauspicious interactions among sales objectives, overtime, and sales force motivation. Partial model testing shows how several decision processes work when their rational assumptions are not seriously violated. Partial tests are then compared with tests of the entire model to reveal the causes of dysfunctional behavior in Datacom's sales organization.

We reproduce and extend Morecroft's simulation results by running multiple environmental scenarios. In his 1985 *Management Science* article, Morecroft used a single environmental scenario throughout.

Datacom's Sales Organization Model

Figure 10.3.1 shows the four major feedback loops that summarize the connections among Datacom's decision processes. Underlying the structure of Datacom's system are the stock ☐ and flow ⟷ variables, combined into infrastructures and feedback-loop relationships through single-line arrow connectors ↖ and auxiliary or converter variables ◯ . In the middle of Fig. 10.3.1 is loop #1, where the effective sales effort (i.e., the hours the sales force spends with customers) generates monthly unit sales. Generated sales also depend on the sale time that the sales force needs to close a sale. More sales force hours generate more unit sales according to the average sale time required per unit sale.

Moving clockwise in Fig. 10.3.1, we find that the monthly sales commitment (SC) in loop #2 is an exponential smoothing of past monthly sales (Forrester, 1961, pp. 406-411), with an adjustment time constant $t=12$ months. The sales objective projects past trends in monthly unit sales.

Back in loop #1, sales performance compares current sales with the sales objective to help the sales force decide on overtime: more if performance is poor and less if it is good. Closing loop #1, overtime determines the effective sales effort, together with Datacom's stable sales force of 400 and its motivation.

In loops #3 and #4, the motivation index is the product of sales performance and overtime. This is an index of current working conditions that affect motivation, with a time lag of $t=3$ months. It takes time for the sales force to become demoralized. Either an increase in overtime or a decrease in sales performance can result in lower motivation three months later. Similarly, it takes time for Datacom's sales force to become fully productive once it is demotivated.

Figure 10.3.1 Feedback Loops of DATACOM's Sales Organization Model (Adapted from Morecroft, 1985)

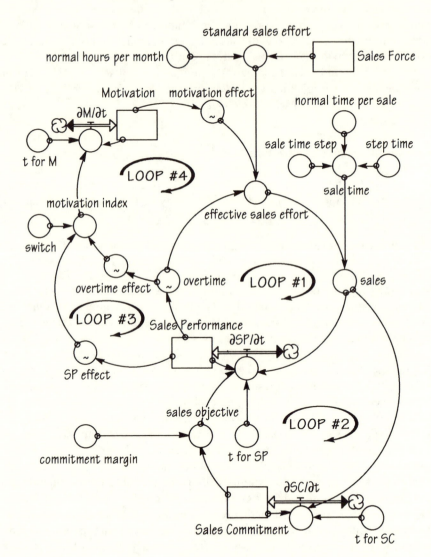

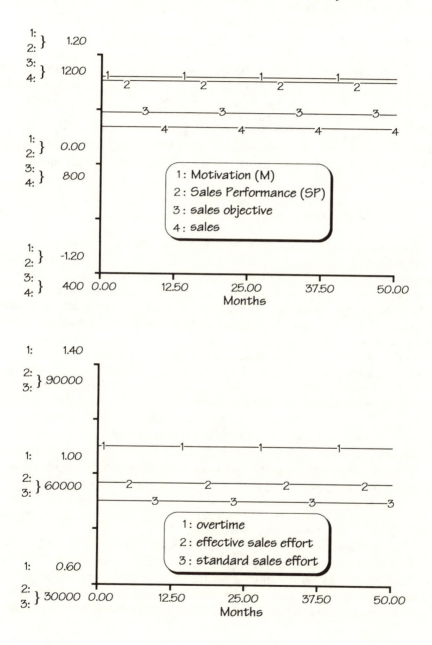

Figure 10.3.2 DATACOM's Sales Organization in Steady State

1: Motivation (M)
2: Sales Performance (SP)
3: sales objective
4: sales

1: overtime
2: effective sales effort
3: standard sales effort

The primary purpose of a system dynamics model, or any other simulation model, is to test the logic or reasoning behind it. Both in iThink™ and in STELLA© (Richmond & Peterson, 1992a; Richmond, et al., 1992), the basic progression of model testing is:

Idealized input→Parameter sensitivity→Reference pattern→Policy design

In nonrudimentary system dynamics simulation models, idealized input and parameter sensitivity are conducted in steady state. If initialized in steady state, then any subsequent behavior pattern that a model shows will be an artifact of the relationships operating within the model itself. If a model is not in steady state and a test is conducted, then it will be difficult to separate the response to a test input from a response to the model's initial imbalance. The output from iThink™ in Fig. 10.3.2 shows Datacom's sales organization model initialized in steady state.

Premise Description

Premise description draws attention to the decision processes of overtime adjustment and sales objective (Fig. 10.3.1). In loop #1, overtime is a nonlinear graphical function of sales performance. Like the table functions of DYNAMO and Vensim™, the graphical functions of iThink™ and STELLA© let the modeler relate one variable to another arbitrarily. If sales performance meets or exceeds Datacom's sales objective, that is, sales performance ≥ 1, then each salesperson works a standard of 130 hours per month and the overtime multiplier remains neutral at one. If sales performance falls below the objective, that is, sales performance < 1, then there is peer pressure to work harder to receive bonuses:

$$\text{overtime} = \text{GRAPH(Sales Performance)} \qquad (1)$$
$$(0.75, 1.40), (0.8, 1.40), (0.85, 1.35), (0.9, 1.25),$$
$$(0.95, 1.10), (1.00, 1.00), (1.05, 1.00), (1.10, 1.00)$$

A notable feature of the graphical nonlinear table function of overtime in Eq. 1 is its simplicity. It shows how at Datacom sales performance is the sole premise for overtime adjustments. No effort is made to maximize either personal or corporate income. That would entail a sophisticated intertemporal computation of sales, performance, compensation, and motivation.

Sales performance (SP) is an exponential smoothing of current performance, with an adjustment time constant of $t=3$ months. Current performance is the ratio of monthly sales to the monthly sales objective, capturing a natural judgmental smoothing process. A drop in unit sales must be sustained for a few months to convince Datacom's sales force to take corrective action. To fix ideas, the corresponding iThink™ equations are:

$$
\begin{align}
\text{Sales Performance(t)} &= \text{Sales Performance(t-dt)} + (\partial SP/\partial t)*dt && (2) \\
\text{Initial Sales Performance} &= 1/(1 + \text{commitment margin}) && (2.1) \\
\partial SP/\partial t &= (1/t \text{ for SP})*((\text{sales/sales objective}) - \\
&\quad \text{Sales Performance}) && (2.2) \\
\text{t for SP} &= 3 \text{ \{months\}} && (2.3)
\end{align}
$$

In loop #2, the sales objective is a good example of *bounded rationality*, a notion reviewed in Section 8.1. It shows the role that authority and corporate culture, routine, and cognitive biases play in forming the premises of decision making. The monthly sales commitment, inflated by a fixed 5 percent margin, determines the monthly sales objective. This formulation describes a political goal-setting process. Datacom's executives pressure middle management for cost-effective performance to spur their sales force. The 5 percent commitment margin provides security to market managers, while it pressures the sales force to improve on its past performance. The iThink™ equations are

$$
\begin{align}
\text{sales objective} &= \text{Sales Commitment}*(1 + \text{commitment margin}) && (3) \\
\text{commitment margin} &= 0.05 && (3.1)
\end{align}
$$

$$
\begin{align}
\text{Sales Commitment(t)} &= \text{Sales Commitment(t-dt)} + (\partial SC/\partial t)*dt && (4) \\
\text{Initial Sales Commitment} &= \text{sales} && (4.1) \\
\partial SC/\partial t &= (1/t \text{ for SC})*(\text{sales - Sales Commitment}) && (4.2) \\
\text{t for SC} &= 12 \text{ \{months\}} && (4.3)
\end{align}
$$

The exponential smoothing of past monthly sales in Eq. 4.2 shows Datacom's organizational routine of committing to sell in the near future just about the same amount sold in the recent past. This routine demands little detailed information, no sophisticated forecasts, and no market surveys.

Unlike the overtime and objective-setting processes, the model's nonlinear motivation functions express behavioral assumptions about Datacom's sales organization. The iThink™ equations for loops #3 and #4 of Fig. 10.3.1 are

$$
\begin{align}
\text{motivation effect} &= \text{GRAPH(Motivation)} && (5) \\
&\quad (0.00, 0.4), (0.2, 0.5), (0.4, 0.65), \\
&\quad (0.6, 0.85), (0.8, 0.95), (1, 1.00)
\end{align}
$$

$$
\begin{align}
\text{Motivation(t)} &= \text{Motivation(t-dt)} + (\partial M/\partial t)*dt && (6) \\
\text{Initial Motivation} &= \text{motivation index} && (6.1) \\
\partial M/\partial t &= (1/t \text{ for M})*(\text{motivation index - Motivation}) && (6.2) \\
\text{t for M} &= 3 \text{ \{months\}} && (6.3)
\end{align}
$$

$$\text{motivation index} = (\text{overtime effect*SP effect})*\text{switch}+(1\text{-switch}) \qquad (7)$$
$$\text{switch} = 0 \qquad (7.1)$$

$$\text{overtime effect} = \text{GRAPH(overtime)} \qquad (8)$$
$$(0.8, 1.00), (0.9, 1.00), (1.00, 1.00), (1.10, 1.00),$$
$$(1.20, 0.9), (1.30, 0.7), (1.40, 0.4), (1.50, 0.3)$$

$$\text{SP effect} = \text{GRAPH(Sales Performance)} \qquad (9)$$
$$(0.5, 0.4), (0.6, 0.45), (0.7, 0.6), (0.8, 0.75),$$
$$(0.9, 0.95), (1, 1.00), (1.10, 1.00), (1.20, 1.00)$$

The graphical nonlinear function in Eq. 5 shows how motivation affects Datacom's effective sales effort. If motivation is high (i.e., near one), then it will not depress the effective sales effort; if it drops bellow 0.8, then it will hurt the sales effort.

Equations 6 through 9 show how the motivation of Datacom's sales force depends on current working conditions. Although conditions of high overtime and poor sales performance can precipitate a drop in the motivation index in Eq. 7, Datacom's sales organization model is an optimistic one. Sales force productivity is higher than it would be if, for example, quitting or apathy were included (Mohr, 1982). The simulation results show how, despite this optimistic bias, the model results in dysfunctional behavior patterns.

Partial Model Test #1: Intended Rationality of Overtime Adjustment

Datacom's sales organization feedback loops allow the design of partial model tests of intended rationality. The first partial model test examines loop #1 of Fig. 10.3.1 in isolation. This test shows how Datacom adjusts the overtime of its sales force to a decline in monthly sales, independently of any changes in motivation and sales objective. To conduct the test, we disturbed the model from its steady-state equilibrium at month one, with a 50 percent increase in the average sale time, that is, from sixty to ninety hours per unit sold. We also held the sales objective fixed and neutralized motivation by setting the motivation index to one.

· The 50 percent increase in sale time represents a significant but plausible tightening of the market. In Morecroft's full-scale intervention model (1984), Datacom's customers were converting from the old to a new data communications technology. This migration era caused the average sale time to rise significantly once the easy-to-convince customers bought into Datacom's new technology, leaving the old technology to the die-hards. Naturally, it is very difficult to predict exactly when such a transition might occur in a market.

This simple test makes the model's simulated behavior easy to interpret. Figure 10.3.3 shows how monthly sales fall in response to the 50 percent increase in the

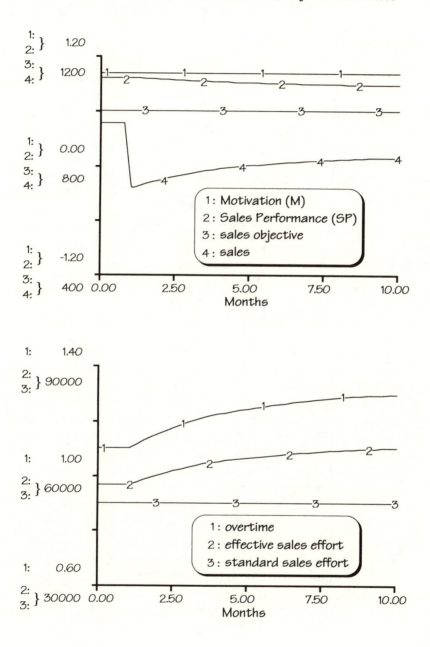

Figure 10.3.3 Test #1: DATACOM's Overtime Adjustment Process

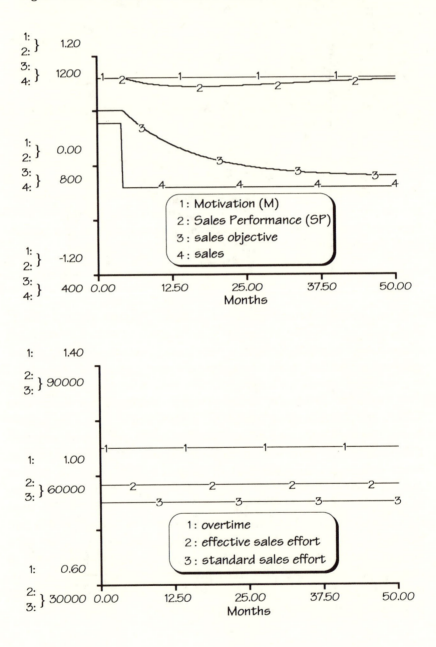

Figure 10.3.4 Test #2: DATACOM's Objective Setting Process

1: Motivation (M)
2: Sales Performance (SP)
3: sales objective
4: sales

1: overtime
2: effective sales effort
3: standard sales effort

average sale time. This causes overtime to increase. More overtime causes a greater effective sales effort and thereby more monthly sales. Within nine months from the initial increase in the average sale time, Datacom's sales organization reaches an equilibrium of stress and strain. The sales force now works long hours under pressure from an unyielding sales objective.

This partial model test shows that the model's assumptions produce intuitively correct behavior patterns. It is both natural and expected that as Datacom's sales drop more effort is elicited from its sales force. Similarly, the decision rules governing overtime changes are intendedly rational. Poor sales performance causes more overtime to improve it. Precisely this same rationality will be at work in the more complex full-scale simulation of the model. Let's remember that.

Partial Model Test #2: Intended Rationality of Objective Setting

This partial model test isolates the behavior of the causal linkage in loop #2 from monthly unit sales to Datacom's sales objective. To conduct the test, we again neutralized motivation and tipped off the model of Fig. 10.3.1 from its equilibrium through a 50 percent increase in sale time, this time at month 4. However, we kept overtime constant at 1.10, the equivalent of 10 percent, and increased the simulation length from 10 to 50 months.

Figure 10.3.4 shows how the drop in unit sales at month 4 causes the sales objective to fall. The tight market conditions make Datacom's market managers renegotiate their sales commitment with Datacom's executives. The time it takes to realize that the sales decline is permanent, rather than temporary, and to convince executives without losing face, can explain the gradual sales objective adjustment.

These results corroborate the effects of bounded rationality that Section 8.1 describes. Again, authority and corporate culture, goals and incentives, routine, and CBs all play a role, causing inertia in the sales objective adjustment. Forty-six months after the drop in unit sales, the sales objective is close to its new equilibrium. The adjustment is a rational one but incremental. This is the same rationality underlying the more complex full-scale simulation of the model. Let's be aware of this.

Bounded Rationality and Inefficiency in the Entire Model

In the final simulation experiment, we examine how Datacom's intended rationality holds up in the entire model of Fig. 10.3.1. Once again, following Morecroft's environmental scenario consistently, we disturb the model from equilibrium by a 50 percent step increase in sale time. Yet, this time all four loops are active. Setting the switch in Eq. 7.1 to one causes motivation to change along with

Figure 10.3.5 Productivity and Sales Traps in DATACOM's Sales Organization

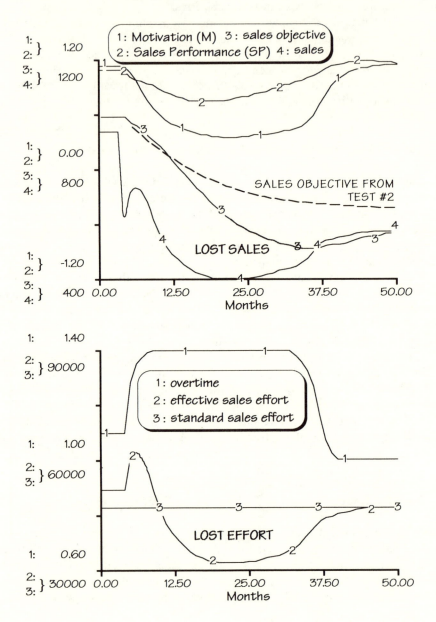

changes in overtime and sales performance.

Figure 10.3.5 shows the model's inefficient resulting behavior. Datacom's sales organization gets locked in a trap, with its unit sales below potential and its effective sales effort below what could be achieved with no overtime. The figure displays the difficulties of managing the complete system.

The sharp decline in monthly sales widens the gap between itself and the sales objective. Datacom's sales force puts in more overtime, increasing its effective sales effort to prevent a further decline in sales performance. This causes sales performance to level off between years 1 and 2. Thus far this behavior looks rational, but there are two problems with it.

First, the high overtime coupled with the low sales performance causes motivation to decline. Second, compounding this problem, the sales objective itself does not decline as rapidly as it did in Test #2. Initially, overtime masks the decline in sales performance, which it could not do when held constant at 10 percent (Fig. 10.3.4).

Pressured by the unyielding sales objective, Datacom's sales force continues to work long hours, but its effective sales effort continues to fall. This causes a further decline in sales. Datacom's managers are mixed up now. They have been lowering their sales objective incrementally, in response to tight market conditions. Yet, after month 9, sales decline even further.

The objective-setting process does not allow a distinction between the fall in sales caused by market forces and the fall caused by lowered motivation and effective sales effort, that is, productivity. The incremental downward adjustment of the sales objective keeps pressuring the sales force, thereby lowering rather than raising the effective sales effort. This is a complete breakdown in the rationality of Datacom's sales management system.

Two years later, Datacom's sales organization starts to recover from its productivity and sales traps. The sales objective has incrementally fallen enough to relieve the sales force from the pressure of a heavy workload. Yet, the damage is permanent. The shaded areas of Fig. 10.3.5 show both the lost sales and the lost effective sales effort that the breakdown in the intended rationality of Datacom's sales management system has caused.

From Downside Risk to Upside Potential of the Entire Model

The feedback structure of Datacom's sales organization, with its nonlinear interlocking loops can turn its management into a hazardous job. In a placid industry environment, there are only moderate changes. The overtime and objective-setting processes can work well together in the case of relatively mild environmental threats, operationalized by small (i.e., 25%) steps is sale time—the time a salesperson needs to close a sale.

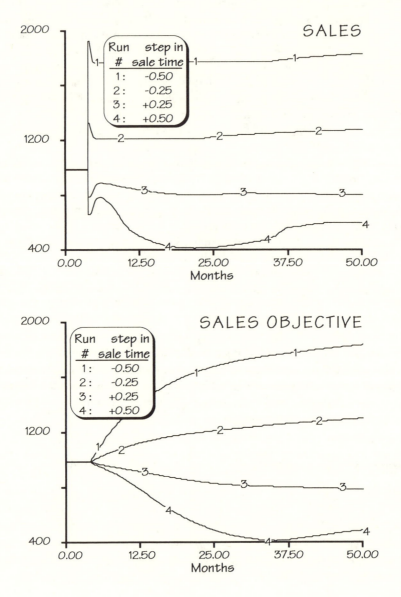

Figure 10.3.6 Sensitivity of DATACOM's Sales and Sales Objective to Multiple Environmental Scenarios

Figure 10.3.6 shows the sensitivity of Datacom's sales and sales objective to multiple environmental scenarios affecting the entire model of Fig. 10.3.1. These cover both increases and decreases in the average sale time. The incremental adjustment of the sales objective results in lost sales even in the case of a -50 percent step decrease in sale time.

In Fig. 10.3.6, a small increase in sale time will cause a temporary increase in overtime, followed by the usual incremental relaxation of the sales objective. Then, the productivity and sales trap signals will be too weak for Datacom's executives to notice.

The much larger 50 percent increase in sale time activates the nonlinear motivation loops which, once dominant, reverse the normal response of the sales force to pressures from the sales objective. Morecroft's scenario (run #4) represents Datacom's downside risk of violating the premises of the objective setting process. The intended rationality, however, of its decision functions imperils its upside potential even when environmental opportunities emerge.

The phase plot of Fig. 10.3.7 shows the relationship between Datacom's sales performance and sales force motivation under multiple environmental scenarios (i.e., run #1 through run #4). It is amazing how spirited the motivation stays under run #1. With sales performance above the sales objective, Datacom's sales force is experiencing a jolly hiatus for three years, while customers migrate to competitors.

Back in Fig. 10.3.6, the sales objective itself does change faster with a -50 percent step decrease in sale time because there is no overtime to mask the negative difference between sales and the sales objective. Because sales performance now exceeds Datacom's sales objective, each salesperson works a standard of 130 hours per month and the overtime multiplier remains neutral at one. No longer pressured by the sales objective, Datacom's sales force opts for a standard sales effort.

Three years later, the monthly sales objective starts climbing slightly above monthly sales. A mild pressure to exceed the standard sales effort starts building up, forcing the sales force to respond incrementally through overtime. Again, the objective-setting process does not allow distinguishing between the sharp rise in sales caused by market forces—a competitive asymmetry perhaps or the sudden death of die-hards—from the rise caused by spirited motivation and effective sales effort, that is, productivity without overtime.

Despite this sales growth opportunity for Datacom, the incremental upward adjustment of the sales objective keeps pressure off the sales force, thereby causing the stalemate of Fig. 10.3.6. The intended rationality of Datacom's sales management system breaks down completely, even in the face of opportunity. If opportunity loss is damaging, then the damage is again permanent, or at least prolonged.

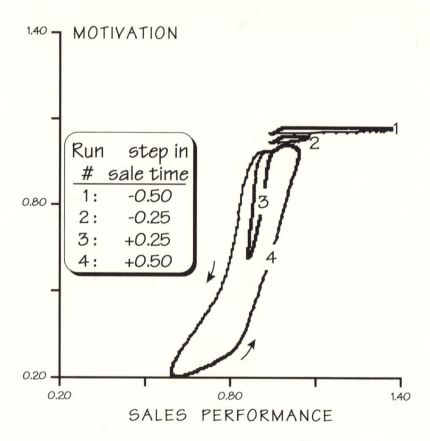

Figure 10.3.7 Sensitivity of the Relationship Between Motivation and Sales Performance to Multiple Environmental Scenarios

Conclusion

Often, model description and analysis can leave a large gap in logic between the assumptions embodied in individual equations and their simulated behavior. Premise description and partial model tests bridge this gap. Premise description and partial model testing are useful diagnostic methods for simulation modeling. They can improve the quality of model formulation and analysis and help clarify the theory implicit in the model to both academic and managerial audiences.

The understanding acquired from premise description and partial model testing can be helpful in justifying model formulations and selecting between alternative formulations. For example, the awareness of inertia and related negative implications in the objective-setting decision process naturally prompts the following questions:

- Why is a more rational process not in use?
- Why don't market managers learn more quickly about market conditions?
- Why don't they integrate their knowledge about the market into the sales objective?

Perhaps the information required to improve rationality (i.e., the synthesis of perception and analysis) is not available. Or the information is available, but ignored. Fear of renegotiating a sales commitment may block knowledge about changing market conditions.

Regardless of the correct answer, if there is only one, these questions prompt us to scrutinize the assumptions underlying a model. Premise description and partial model testing are helpful in policy design. An understanding of the conditions that cause a breakdown in the rationality of a decision process and a subsequent problem in the system may well point to the changes necessary to remedy the problem. Roger Hall reached the same conclusion in his simulation study of the fall of the old *Saturday Evening Post* (1976).

In Morecroft's sales model, for example, a policy change that assumes market managers know and act on motivation information greatly reduces the likelihood of being caught in the productivity and sales trap. Alternatively, a policy change that assumes market managers have some knowledge of market conditions, and use that knowledge to renegotiate their sales commitment avoids the trap.

SUMMARY

A basic tenet of systems thinking is that the dynamic behavior of a system is produced by the structure *of the system. Structure consists of the underlying stocks and flows combined into infrastructures, which then are outfitted with feedback-loop relationships. The feedback loops enable infrastructures to realize their full potential for generating dynamic behavior patterns. In particular, feedback relationships enable infrastructures to generate self-regulating behaviors as well as to produce counterintuitive responses to policy initiatives and other forms of human intervention.*

Morecroft's model of Datacom's sales organization provides a better feeling for how structure produces dynamic behavior. This knowledge serves well in preparing for designing processes, strategies, and policy initiatives that are capable of yielding improved performance.

Premise description relates the formulation of individual equations in a decision process to macro-organizational processes such as factoring, routines, traditions, and biases. Partial model tests relate the premises of decision making to simulated behavior. If organizational decision making is intendedly rational, then partial model tests should reveal behavior that is intuitively clear and consistent with the assumptions of a model's decision processes. A comparison of partial and full model tests provides an explanation for this disastrous or counterintuitive behavior.

When nonlinear feedback loops become dominant either in a model or in a firm's real system, then they reverse the normal response of actors, violating the premises or basic assumptions underlying objective setting processes. These circumstances can degrade the quality of managerial decisions.

Failing to meet a commitment, a decision maker may unwittingly set objectives that guarantee a still larger discrepancy between performance and commitment. Organizational decisions, though intendedly rational, sometimes are not sufficiently farsighted to compensate for large declines in productivity caused by highly nonlinear loops acting in concert.

Part VI

REPERCEIVING IN THE MULTIVERSE OF RATIONALITY

Chapter 11

Strategy Designs of the 1990s

> *Wandering between two worlds, one dead,*
> *the other powerless to be born.*
> —Alfred de Musset

In our increasingly transnational world economy, the interdependent business environments of countries determine its structural evolution. Nowhere else are the effects of this interdependence clearer than in the opening up of the former USSR. Its failing economy has made it impossible to maintain its rigid closed-market system. Our colleagues in Moscow and other universities in the newly formed Commonwealth of Independent States have begun soliciting our help with scenario-driven planning. Profiled in five dimensions, a set of five scenarios for the new Russia shows how internally consistent motifs allow building macroenvironmental scenarios. Equally striking in the business world is the emphasis that world-class firms place on overcoming in their strategies the integration-responsiveness dilemma pointed out by Prahalad & Doz (1987). The transnational archetype has emerged from their strategies, but other firms cannot drift into it either from a traditional or from the multifocal archetype. They must design the transformation because the longer a firm trades off global integration for local responsiveness, and vice versa, the more it alienates itself from transnationalism.

11.1 BACK FROM THE USSR: A COMMONWEALTH OF INDEPENDENT STATES

The earlier chapters have repeatedly made the point that, to compute decision scenarios, managers and their analysts have to input environmental scenarios into their modeling. Where do these scenarios come from? This chapter illustrates the task of generating environmental scenarios.

How abrupt the collapse of communism was in Eastern Europe! Assuredly, there had been uprisings and attempted breaks with Moscow before the 1990s, but all of them had been submerged. Then, within a year, under Mikhail Gorbachev's leadership the Soviet Union stopped intervening in Eastern European affairs. Soon noncommunist governments formed, the Berlin Wall came down, East and West Germany were united under the West German model, and experiments in moving to market economies began in all Eastern European countries.

Originally, *glasnost* (openness) and *perestroika* (restructuring) were launched simply to reform communism and make it work better. Even with these intentions, the policies met strong resistance from the entrenched party functionaries and bureaucrats. On the other side, radicals and noncommunists won election victories and began exerting pressure for the elimination of communism and its replacement by a market system.

George Shultz, the former US secretary of state, is reported to have been told by his Soviet counterpart, Edvard Schevardnadze, that the Chernobyl nuclear reactor accident made the Soviet leadership more fully appreciate the need for *glasnost*. The Kremlin leaders were unable to get reliable, timely information on the crisis through their bureaucratic channels. Instead, they found that the Cable News Network (CNN) broadcasting by satellite from the United States was their best source of information on a major event in their own country. This drove home to top government leaders that their closed system had to be opened for the benefit of the country.

Since 1987, political instability and strife have played an important role in foreign joint venture activity in the former USSR. Changes in the distribution of joint ventures by states have been affected by political and legal developments, the availability of natural resources, and concentration of human capital. For example, the 1991 failed coup led to enhanced trade between the West and the former Soviet Union. In these developments the new Soviet states parlayed a source of relief from economic distress .

Turning this threat into an opportunity, the West saw the situation as a growth opportunity in the light of stagnating markets at home. Moreover, Russian scientists with innovative ideas are willing to bargain. AT&T, Corning, General Atomics, Hewlett-Packard, IBM, Sun Microsystems, and United Technologies are among the US firms, for example, that are taking advantage of the existing brain power in the former Soviet Republics (Stead & Hof, 1993). While Western firms acquire exclusive rights in artificial intelligence, ceramics, fiber optics, magnetic-containment reactors, and computer-network architecture to minimize competition, they learn more about the risks of joint ventures in the region, including the accessibility of its markets to traditional Western marketing strategies and tactics.

Kublin (1991) outlines the obstacles to the formation of joint ventures with the former Soviet Union, including such factors as the inconvertibility of the ruble, tax laws, and motivation problems among Commonwealth workers. Similarly, Pettibone (1991) delineates potential risks, urging Western firms to screen their future partners thoroughly before entering into a joint venture. Nevertheless, little reliable information is available on foreign joint ventures that might be instructive to marketers wishing to explore these market opportunities (Kvint, 1990).

The fifteen new nations of the former Soviet Union are Armenia, Azerbaijan, Belarus, Estonia, Georgia, Kazakhstan, Kyrgyzstan, Latvia, Lithuania, Moldova, Russia, Tajikistan, Turkmenistan, Ukraine, and Uzbekistan. Yet, according to the Russian government and the Statistical Bureau of the Commonwealth of Independent States, in 1990 Russia still represented three-fourths of the foreign-host joint venture entities. The conditions in Moscow favored this state of affairs, a fallout from the changed political situation. Firms were released from state ownership in Moscow, with freedom to make their own economic decisions.

This situation was relatively unchanged in 1991, but the percentage traced to Moscow dropped considerably, from 54 to 46 percent. The joint venture population was seen to have difficulties with areas of Russia beyond Moscow and St. Petersburg. The increase in joint ventures within other areas of Russia was based on the greater wealth of natural resources and production facilities in these locations.

The transformation of the former USSR established Russia as the largest member of the new confederacy, but Russia is itself a federation of varying ethnic minorities, each vying for power. By 1992, the concentration of foreign joint ventures had shifted dramatically beyond Russia itself. Of the non-Russian locations, the Baltic states increased significantly between 1990 (9.8%) and 1991 (16.5%), but then leveled off in 1992 (15%) as a percentage of all foreign-host joint ventures (Kvint & Prince, 1992).

Russia's Alternative Futures

Also in 1992, Igor A. Portyansky, director of the Center for Independent Analysis in Moscow, and visiting scholar at the System Dynamics Group of MIT in Cambridge, Massachusetts, outlined certain principal gauges that may determine Russia's possible alternative futures. Combined with the Global Systems Spotlight described by Cavaleri & Obloj (1993, pp. 347-349), these scenarios give one more persuasive example of how macroenvironmental scenarios are built around internally consistent motifs.

Figure 11.1.1 illustrates these ideas with a set of five spiderweb graphs corresponding to five macroenvironmental scenarios. Nihon Chukuko (Japan Hollow Steel Company) uses similar composite-rating graphs to represent related dimensions in process control. Following Isuzu's process control system, Chukuko's plant manager connects the rating points of process dimensions with straight-line segments, "so that the composite rating resembles a spider web" (Schonberger, 1986, p. 28).

Figure 11.1.1 displays five of Portyansky's macroenvironmental scenarios for the new Russia, profiled in five dimensions:

- Business climate, ranging from favorable to unfavorable, depending on how foreign investors might perceive it.
- Government, ranging from a single-party utilitarian quasi-militia to a multiparty democracy.
- Inflation, ranging from low to high.
- Private ownership, ranging from low to high, depending on the number of private businesses.
- Ruble strength, ranging from low to high, depending on its stability, convertibility, and exchange rate, say, relative to the US dollar.

A *confusion era* will mark Russia's transition if its population splits into free market and communism supporters. The need to maintain political stability will then bring about a coalition government that will slow down the privatization of state-owned organizations, repel Western aid, increase price controls, and loosen Russia's monetary policy. Then, however, confusion reigns supreme as the reduced direct foreign investment and trade increase unemployment, with the resulting impoverishment fortifying Russia's communism supporters. A few private firms will offer a few goods and services. Combined with the loose monetary policy, the reduced market competition will push up inflation. The high inflation will reduce the ruble's stability and value, further reducing direct foreign investment and trade, which will in turn cause private ownership to decline further.

The *back to communism* scenario could always play in Russia. Military-backed totalitarianism and rampant nationalism could revive a single-party nonparliamentary government that would ban every market-oriented policy, leaving no privatization to speak of. On the contrary, nationalization and economic sanctions will confront direct foreign investment and trade. Without private firms, all goods and services will come from the state, which through its central economic planning politburo will provide lucrative new jobs, ample career opportunity and social security, set prices, and cut as many new rubles as needed. The state will also control inflation and adjust the ruble to equal the US dollar, without any need for currency

Figure 11.1.1 Russia's Alternative Futures in Five Dimensions

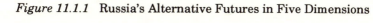

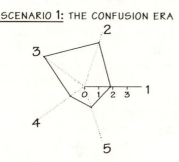

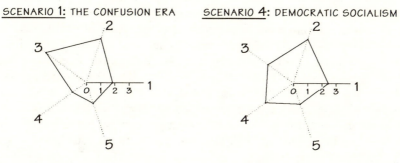

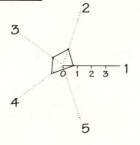

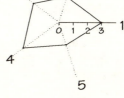

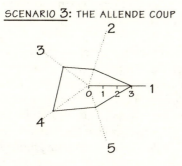

SCENARIO 1: THE CONFUSION ERA

SCENARIO 4: DEMOCRATIC SOCIALISM

SCENARIO 2: BACK TO COMMUNISM

SCENARIO 5: THE NEW TRIPOLAR

SCENARIO 3: THE ALLENDE COUP

DIMENSIONS

1 :	BUSINESS CLIMATE
2 :	GOVERNMENT
3 :	INFLATION
4 :	PRIVATE OWNERSHIP
5 :	RUBLE STRENGTH

hedging and swaps. National pride will thereby be restored, but the world's market forces will be totally ignored. Now, that is a good definition for a closed-market, centrally controlled totalitarian state.

Allende's coup in Chile in the early 1970s could explain (if one may use that verb) Russia's possible technical experiment of combining centralized economic planning with decentralized decision making. Portyansky augurs *glasnost's* and *perestroika's fin de siècle* through a military coup that might be witnessed by widespread bankruptcies, worker layoffs, unemployment, and impoverishment. Yet, the military-backed monarch in the style of President Salvador Allende will make reconstructionism especially prevalent after the spread of a new market-oriented elite to revive the Russian economy through a new wave of privatization. The privatized and politically stable economy will attract direct foreign investment and trade, while citizens will use state vouchers to purchase goods and services at world prices. Investment in the private sector will create new jobs, which in turn will reduce unemployment and thereby impoverishment. The elimination of price controls and import tariffs will cause inflationary tendencies, but increased market competition should counteract their negative effects on the ruble's stability and value, which should remain high.

Democratic socialism will spare private firms from themselves reengineering the socio-politico-economic infrastructure necessary for business to flourish. In the incredible torpor of a Scandinavian-style political system, no elite will impose its views on the Russian public. Then, however, the members of parliament might pay no greater service to their country than to lament over every issue, always groping toward a new tax to fund the expansion of a social program. Fairly balanced market- and protectionist-oriented policies will support the inflation-causing output of the state sector, but also acknowledge the need to maintain a favorable business climate that will entice direct foreign investment and trade. Investors and workers will share the stocks of privatized consumer-oriented firms which, along with wide-scale social programs, will create new jobs and somehow manage to keep unemployment and thereby impoverishment low. Competing firms in the consumer goods and services markets will hold inflation down and repudiate its negative effects on the ruble's stability and value, to keep it convertible into foreign currencies.

In the *new tripolar* scenario, the early twenty-first century again will mark *glasnost's* and *perestroika's* end, but with Russia's transition now complete. Its GNP will surpass Germany's, making Russia third in the world economy, following closely on the fortunes of the United States and Japan. A US-style two-party government will result from the years of germane tranquility and widespread affluence. The entirely market-oriented population will revive the Russian economy through privatization, with its politically stable economy attracting direct foreign investment and world trade. Investment in the private sector will create new job and career opportunities, which in turn will reduce unemployment and impoverishment. A few restrictions on imports, exports, and prices will remain, causing inflation, but Russia's competitive markets will suppress its negative effects on the ruble's high stability and value.

Potentially Expedient Levers

Milgrom & Roberts (1992) expect the new economies of the former USSR to face innumerable problems in moving to market-oriented systems. They delineate the following leverage points that the new economies of the Commonwealth of Independent States might choose to explore.

- Educate the public to the new rules of the game and gain acceptance for these rules.
- Decide on competition and regulatory policies and find a way to deal with the fact that simply privatizing giant inefficient state firms will yield a system of giant inefficient private monopolies.
- Decide how much to wean their industries from state subsidies and develop tax systems to finance government activities.
- Decide whether and when uncompetitive firms will be allowed to fail and create social service and support systems to handle the human costs of the dislocations that their economies are sure to face, both during and after the transition.
- Determine property rights and decide who will be allowed to own the privatized firms, how title will be transferred, and what prices will be charged.
- Design and set up capital markets and create banking, financial and monetary systems.
- Design meaningful accounting systems so that firms can be valued and their performance evaluated.
- Redraft laws to allow for new forms of economic organizations, new patterns of ownership, and new kinds of business transactions.
- Train managers to operate in a market system and to compete in a world market (Milgrom & Roberts, 1992, pp. 15-16).

All these tasks are interdependent and in need of coordination. Private enterprise will not work without the discipline of potential failure. Output markets are of no use without input markets, including those for capital, through which producers can obtain the resources they need. Neither of these is of much value without well-defined property rights and mechanisms for contract enforcement. All the parts have to come together and fit reasonably well for the system to work.

The worst outcome might be some halfway compromise or tradeoff between the old closed-market control system and the new private initiative and ownership system. A long tradeoff epoch might prove inescapable. The new economies of the Commonwealth of Independent States would therefore be fated to wonder between de Musset's two worlds. Then, a *back and forth to the USSR* scenario might play ad infinitum.

The potential negative effects that a tradeoff or halfway compromise can cause are best understood in the context of *internationalization*. Increasingly, Western firms are realizing that combining international, global, and multinational elements in their strategy designs may be an inadequate response to the transformation of the global economy into a transnational one. Transnationalism emerged from the synthesis of international, global, and multinational strategic archetypes, not as an undifferentiated identity, but as a concrete unity that affects the administrative, strategic-information, and strategic-management systems of world-class firms. It entails an attainable ideal and an aspiring reference structure (Drucker, 1989; Keen, 1991).

The emphasis that some firms put on overcoming the integration-responsiveness tradeoff is striking (DeMeyer et al., 1989). Motivated by the rich and fast-paced strategic trajectories of US, European, and Japanese world-class firms, Section 11.2 argues that the longer a firm trades off global integration for local responsiveness, and vice versa, the more it may be alienating itself from transnationalism.

11.2   REACHING FOR THE TRANSNATIONAL GESTALT

> *We are not going to be able to operate*
> *our Spaceship Earth successfully*
> *for much longer unless we see it as*
> *a whole spaceship and our fate as common.*
> *It has to be everybody or nobody.*
> —Buckminster Fuller

Traditionally, national differences prodded firms to create new markets, to make more profit, and to strengthen their strategic posture around the world. In the mid-1980s, however, environmental forces changed the nature of business worldwide. The traditional archetypes of internationalization can no longer offer an adequate response. Some firms, such as Ericsson, Matsushita, and Unilever combine international, global, and multinational elements in their strategy design. Unilever, for example, which used to focus on local responsiveness through autonomous subsidiaries, has recently introduced low-cost brands worldwide, thereby incorporating an element of global thrust in its strategy. It has also introduced learning and technology transfer, elements of an international strategy design.

Initially, new organizational forms manifest themselves as differences of degree. Over time, the cumulative effects of the forces underlying such transformations displace and propagate reference or aspiration structures, which in turn lead to differences in type. This enhances the firm's ability and preference to choose a strategy design or combinations of designs to decrease or to increase its distance from emerging archetypes.

Transnationalism emerged from the synthesis of international, global and multinational archetypes, not as an undifferentiated identity, but as a concrete unity that affects the administrative, strategic-information and strategic-management systems of world-class firms. It entails an attainable ideal and an aspiring reference structure that guide the arguments presented here. The rich and fast-paced strategic trajectories of US, European, and Japanese world-class firms show that, in the context of global environmental pressures and constraints, the longer a firm trades off global integration against local responsiveness, and vice versa, the more it might be alienating itself from transnationalism.

The transnational research data show how the strategic actions of firms give the world economy its transnational thrust (Drucker, 1989). Yet, firms should not expect to drift into transnationalism like the world economy does (Keen, 1991). The strategic management implications of this composite argument are alarming, but there may still be time and a way for firms to break through the region of compromise and to progress toward the transnational archetype. The transformation requires an assessment of how changes in strategy affect a firm's distance from, or proximity to, the transnational archetype.

Internationalization Archetypes

In our increasingly transnational world economy, the interdependence of countries' business environments determines an industry's structure (Porter, 1986). Interdependence is high in global industries, as opposed to multidomestic ones where changes in one country's environment have little or no effect on another. Industry structure in turn determines a firm's strategy along two dimensions: the geographically concentrated or geographically dispersed configuration of its value-added chain of activities (Porter, 1985), and subsidiary interdependence in integrating these activities (Jarillo & Martínez, 1990).

The value-added chain is an interesting twist in the internationalization literature, aimed at resolving the global integration and local differentiation tradeoff by standardizing some links of the value-added chain and differentiating others. In most cases, however, the differentiated links entail downstream activities and focus on final goods markets. Hence, they ignore the benefits of learning and technology transfer, which increase the strategic value of operating assets in a *"multination network"* (Kogut, 1989).

Taking a slightly different view, Bartlett & Ghoshal (1989), Jarillo & Martínez (1990), and Prahalad & Doz (1987) argue that the responsiveness of firms to customer and host government needs to localize foreign assets may determine Porter's geographical-configuration dimension. Their integration-responsiveness grid of Fig. 11.2.1 yields five archetypes, each implying its own internationalization strategy design or behavior pattern.

1. *The international archetype* characterizes export-oriented firms, with most of their sources of core activities geographically concentrated, that rely on decentralized marketing, and they emphasize the worldwide transfer and adaptation of parent-firm knowledge and capabilities, for example, Ericsson of Sweden.

2. *The multinational archetype* characterizes firms that are seeking to capitalize on their ability to differentiate their products in each country to satisfy local tastes and national interests. Responding to customers on a country-by-country basis, firms in multidomestic industries do not seek to coordinate or to integrate geographically dispersed activities. Through autonomous and self-sufficient subsidiaries they emphasize building strong market presence through sensitivity and response to national differences. This approach has been typical of US and European firms, such as Nestle, Philips, and Unilever. It is also typical of the hardwired multinationals that developing regions form to internalize both country needs and trade in internal markets, hoping to reduce transaction costs and to enable price discrimination across markets (Georgantzas, 1989).

3. *The global archetype* characterizes firms that are oriented toward carefully chosen markets (Ohmae, 1989). They seek cost advantages through geographically concentrated activities, and they emphasize standardized product design, global-scale manufacturing and distribution, and highly centralized coordination and integration. Japanese firms such as Matsushita are good examples of this archetype (Smothers, 1990).

4. *The multifocal archetype* characterizes firms that are not yet sensitized to the interplay of economic, organizational, and political forces of transnationalism. Prahalad & Doz (1987) describe this archetype extensively, with the normative implication of focusing managerial attention on aspects that simultaneously require global integration, such as products, and demand local responsiveness, such as geographical regions. The data of Morrison (1991) empirically support the archetype but leave internationalization highly dependent on situational factors. Morrison concludes that, although emphasis on quality (i.e., being responsive to customers through quality) persists

Figure 11.2.1   Internationalization Archetypes on the Integration-
Responsiveness Grid

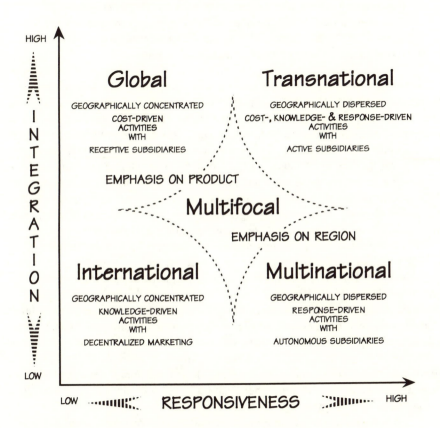

Adapted from the framework Jarillo & Martinez (1990) proposed in
order to characterize the different roles that subsidiaries of MNCs
can play within a firm's overall strategy

in most designs, each firm emphasizes different strategy dimensions because each interprets its industry differently.

5. *The transnational archetype* characterizes firms that are poised to combine global efficiency with local responsiveness through learning and technology transfer. They coordinate their geographically dispersed activities to obtain economies of both scale and scope, while they emphasize learning from and transfer technology to their active subsidiaries. They thereby build strong market presence through sensitivity and response to national differences as well. Reflecting on the transformations of 236 US, European, and Japanese firms, Bartlett & Ghoshal (1989) present this archetype as the preferred model for strategy design and implementation.

This diversity of response is consistent with the contingency theory's notion of equifinality (Van de Ven & Drazin, 1985). Similar environmental pressures produce different consequences, and the interactive effects of internal and external pressures determine a firm's trajectory of changes toward the multifocal archetype.

The concise encapsulation of the multifocal tradeoff raises the fascinating possibility that the lack of fit causes multinational firms to integrate and to coordinate their value-added chain of activities regardless of home-nation pressures (Cvar, 1986). Conversely, the same lack of fit causes global firms to differentiate their value-added chain of activities geographically, according to home-nation pressures, and to depend for coordination on autonomous subsidiaries.

Whether or not a firm adopts a tradeoff perspective toward the multifocal archetype of Fig. 11.2.1 depends on how it interprets its industry environment (Morrison, 1991; Porter, 1985). Then the firm's strategy design or trajectory of behavior patterns fall into two cases.

In the first case, a firm interprets the system of forces equivalent to the integration-responsiveness dimensions of Fig. 11.2.1 to be in equilibrium. Thus, the multifocal archetype emerges, supporting the contingency theorist's search for coherent-trajectory configurations or archetypes (Miller & Friesen, 1978, 1984). If a firm assumes that the system of forces equivalent to the integration-responsiveness dimensions is in equilibrium, then, naturally, it will opt for the multifocal archetype in its strategy design.

In the second case, a firm interprets the system of forces equivalent to the integration-responsiveness dimensions of Fig. 11.2.1 to be in disequilibrium. Then, a nonzero resultant force has to emerge from this interpretation, which the firm may choose to ignore or to probe and to exploit further.

- If the firm ignores the resultant force, a product of its own interpretation, then again it will opt for the multifocal archetype in its strategy design.

- If, however, the firm chooses to probe and to exploit the resultant force further, then the attendant challenge will be to create or to adopt a new management technology, resulting in processes that foster cross-cultural collaboration throughout the firm, without a tradeoff between integration and responsiveness.

Firms that adopt the tradeoff perspective may be alienating themselves from the transnational archetype, regardless of their ability to trade off global integration against local responsiveness, and vice versa. The multifocal archetype cannot remove the ancestral conflict between efficiency and flexibility (DeMeyer et al., 1989, p. 143). On the contrary, it drains them both to create an unfortunate era of transition, a transitional value crisis of sorts. Firms that adopt it should not expect to drift into transnationalism because that is impossible (Keen, 1991).

At best, their efforts will replicate the trajectory caused by the behavioral patterns of a vector sliding up and down between the global and multinational archetypes of Fig. 11.2.1. The attendant challenge of creating or adopting processes that foster cross-cultural collaboration throughout the firm, without a tradeoff between integration and responsiveness, will be forever lost.

It is plain to see "the perils of losing focus" in Yamaha's international strategy archetype (Schlender, 1993). In years past, the firm's export-oriented decentralized marketing, with most sources of core activities geographically concentrated, emphasized the worldwide transfer and adaptation of parent-firm knowledge and capabilities. This brought Yamaha out of focus and into a multitude of sidelines, causing a 30 percent decrease in profit from 1990 to 1992.

Seisuke Ueshima, president of Yamaha Corporation, is now trying to reorient the firm's strategy toward more carefully chosen markets. Constrained by Japan's tradition of lifetime employment, Ueshima is still seeking cost advantages through geographically concentrated activities and highly centralized coordination. Yet, the behavioral pattern of Yamaha's sales may soon resemble a vector sliding up and down as the firm trades off versatility for market discretion.

Toward the Transnational Breakthrough

To emphasize a fundamental departure from the integration-responsiveness grid's conventional representation in Fig. 11.2.1, let us consider Koopmans' (1951) extension of Pareto optimality to productive efficiency. Figure 11.2.2 should help the reader to understand the centrifugal forces leading to the transnational archetype.

The productive efficiency-flexibility frontier $x^1 x^s x^2$ of Fig. 11.2.2 represents a state in which a firm's responsiveness and integration have been so organized that, within its limitation of resources and current management technology, there is

Figure 11.2.2 **The Transnational Breakthrough Transformation**

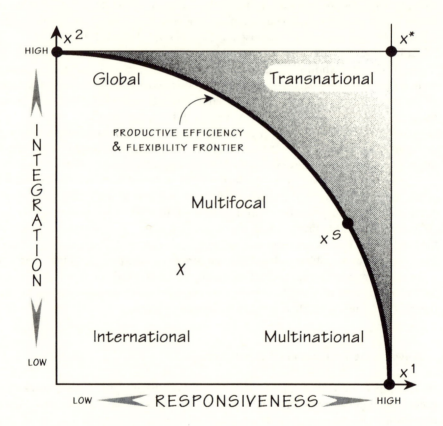

no way of becoming more locally responsive without reducing its global integration, and vice versa.

Figure 11.2.2 also encapsulates the transnational breakthrough, a prominent strategic alternative x^* which some firms either have not yet discovered or treat as nonexistent. DeMeyer et al. (1989) attribute its absence from their data on Europe and North America to the fact that most European and North American firms have not yet focused on overcoming the traditional conflict between efficiency and flexibility. Conversely, DeMeyer et al. find the emphasis that Japanese firms put on overcoming the integration-responsiveness tradeoff striking.

In Fig. 11.2.2, the heavily traced boundary of X represents a "region of compromise," a bargaining set representing only a temporary disguise of the absence of x^* (Zeleny, 1982, p. 118). A compromise alternative x^S, including the extremes x^1 and x^2, is incapable of either removing or resolving the underlying conflict.

At any multifocal point x^S located on the heavily drawn boundary of X, there is at least one customer, government, parent firm, or subsidiary that remains unsatisfied with respect to what is actually achieved through a multifocal strategy. For example, even if a firm persuades a host government to accept the multinational alternative x^1, and even if the host government is genuinely convinced that such a negotiated outcome is the best for both the country and the firm, the conflict still exists. Soon the suppressed perceptions and value judgments will claim their toll. Conflict will emerge again, hasty agreements will not be honored, and deceit and treason will appear.

The culturally based and deeply entrenched sets of preferences and values do not change overnight. The strategic performance trajectories of Japanese firms toward the transnational archetype entail translating economic might into clout in Washington, into research contracts to US schools, and into building a philanthropic image (Holstein, 1988). Such tactical moves intrigue managers, journalists, and strategy researchers who are not-yet-sensitized to the ideal-seeking dynamic process of strategy design toward transnationalism.

Smothers' (1990) focus on the linkages between patterns of Japanese strategy is a useful start. Yet, firms will not understand the transnational archetype without understanding the process leading to it. For it is the progress toward the transnational archetype, not its absolute attainment, which creates the instrumentality of values needed to assess a firm's progress toward transnationalism.

The strategic dimensions of global integration or efficiency and local responsiveness or flexibility may be the primary determinants of a firm's value within a multination network (Kogut, 1989). Yet, a firm's internationalization strategy should enable learning and technology transfer (Anon., 1989; Smothers, 1990; Teece, 1987), geographical and product diversification (Geringer, Beamish, & da Costa, 1989; Rumelt, 1974), and subsidiary autonomy and activation (Jarillo & Martínez, 1990).

By itself, size does not determine a firm's profit (Drucker, 1989; Keen, 1991). Rather, it is the way the firm adjusts to size, copes with it, and capitalizes on the opportunities that size offers that determine profitability (Poensgen & Marx, 1985).

A family of distance-membership functions could help a firm determine the proximity of its strategy design or combination of designs x^k from the transnational archetype x^* as follows:

$$L_p(l,k) = \sqrt[p]{\sum_{i=1}^{n} l_i^p (1-d_i^k)^P} .$$ (1)

In Eq. 1, $l = (l_1, \cdots, l_n)$ would be equivalent to a firm's "strategy-dimension attention vector," and $p \in (0, \infty)$ a distance parameter (Zeleny, 1982, p. 165). Depending on industry structure, and the firm's specific situation, its strategy design x_i^K would place different emphasis l_i on each strategy dimension i. $L_p(l,k)$ would then determine the distance between the firm's ideal strategy design d^*, leading to the transnational archetype x^*, and the actual vector of proximity induced by an alternative design d^k.

An increase in p gives more emphasis to the largest deviation $(1-d_i^K)$. As $p \rightarrow \infty$, the largest deviation completely dominates a strategy design, and the firm assigns comparable importance to all of the design's dimensions. Hence, p weights the deviations of alternative strategy designs according to their magnitudes and across their strategy dimensions, while l_i weights their deviations according to their strategy dimensions, regardless of their magnitudes.

If $p=1$, the minimization of $L_p(l,k)$ would reflect a firm's complete disregard for a design's individual deviation magnitudes; it is their total sum it would be after. Conversely, if $0<p<1$, because the $d_i^k s$ are normalized between zero and one, the emphasis would be reversed. A decrease in p from one to zero would emphasize the smallest deviation relatively more in the total sum, while adjusting the larger deviations relatively slightly.

The Transformation Prerequisites

Concocting a family of distance-membership functions like Eq. 1 could help in assessing the proximity of a firm's strategy design or combination of designs to the transnational archetype. The assessment would be neither purely descriptive nor purely normative. It would carry normative implications toward changes in the firm's strategy. Whether or not these are considered in strategy making might in turn depend on whether eroding competitiveness, declining productivity growth, and explosive environmental changes produce the familiar litany of strategic uncertainty, sufficient to threaten traditional organizations and management practices.

Figure 11.2.3 The Transnational Transformation Requirements

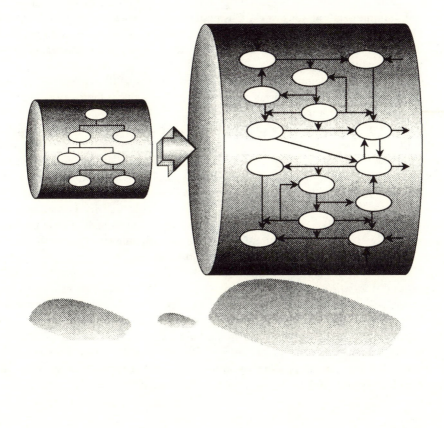

Firms facing environmental pressures coupled with strategic uncertainty usually work hard to clarify their mission, visions, and values. Some seek growth through locally controlled *and* globally responsive structures, themselves the outgrowth of new worldviews and organizational mind-sets.

Changes in management technology can lead to new organizational mind-sets. These may in turn improve a firm's innovation capability by encouraging new and more frequent patterns of social interaction. Figure 11.2.3 shows how the adoption of a new management technology (i.e., scenario-driven planning) can propel business growth through administrative innovation (i.e., changes in structure), redirecting flows of authority, control, and communication.

The transnational transformation will never fly, and it may not even stand in firms that merely overlay new technology on their conventional flows of authority control, communication, and work. Cosmetic approaches to the renewal of business and management systems are doomed to repeat the historically high unsatisfactory performance of firms that tried to improve efficiency not through quality, but through a quality bypass.

Again, hard times require new organizational mind-sets. Ill-conceived cosmetics are hardly a remedy when firms must retool and reengineer their strategic management systems to compete for their future.

Computed scenarios will reveal transformation rules and social interaction paths that were not previously thought of. As an individual entity, each decision maker in each country has a local scope and deals only with specific variables and access paths to other entities worldwide. (S)he only observes a representative state of each entity, that is, those parts and variables in a strategic situation which are locally meaningful. Yet, this representativeness (Table 8.1.1 defines the representativeness CB, i.e., cognitive bias) can change dynamically in the process of computing scenarios either on a CSM or on the computer using a full-fledged simulation model (Georgantzas & Acar, 1989, p. 264).

Without computed scenarios, it is highly likely that the *core operating policies*, as opposed to *espoused policies* (Argyris & Schön, 1978) guiding organizational behavior will remain unchanged. Efforts to improve strategic management flounder because new strategies and tactics threaten traditional habits, norms, and assumptions. Part of the problem lies in the failure to recognize the importance of prevailing mental models. The laudable goals of empowering and enabling individuals will prove counterproductive unless, of course, a firm's managers can at once act locally and think globally (Senge & Sterman, 1992).

Conclusion

In the process of internationalization, firms face challenging technical, regulatory, political, and organizational changes. While trying to adapt to them, inadvertently a firm may adopt the multifocal archetype, misinterpreting the need for simultaneous integration and responsiveness as a need for a tradeoff between the global and multinational archetypes. Yet, the attendant challenge of transnationalism is to create processes that foster cross-cultural collaboration throughout the firm, without a tradeoff between integration and responsiveness. The strategic trajectories of US, European, and Japanese firms show that, in the absence of mindset renewal, global environmental pressures and local constraints can easily prolong the integration-responsiveness dilemma, and thereby alienate firms from transnationalism.

International strategy researchers should pay more attention to how firms emphasize and combine these dimensions in their performance trajectories toward the transnational archetype. Geringer et al. (1989) show that the loci of the strategy dimensions that maximize profitability may not necessarily lie at extreme anchor points; also plausible is the existence of multiple loci or anchor values. Measuring the proximity or progress of firms toward the transnational archetype, through the family of distance membership functions in Eq. 1, should help researchers assess the texture and validity of internationalization archetypes as patterns of relationships among structure, systems, and meaning.

It should also help improve practitioners' decision quality, which is negatively affected by the complexity of strategic-decision situations. Creating alternative strategy designs to bring a firm's trajectory closer to the transnational archetype requires the design and coalignment of tactics that combine competitive and collective moves (Fig. 8.2.1). Gemünden & Hauschildt (1985) elaborate on the process of designing such alternatives to counterbalance the challenges of complex strategic decision situations.

The proximity of Japanese firms to the transnational archetype shows how the complexity of strategy designs positively affects the quality of strategic decisions. It is important to realize that the transnational archetype emerged from such designs. Yet, it is impossible for a firm to drift from a traditional or the multifocal archetype into transnationalism. That is,

each firm must design its own transformation.

The transnational imperative demands rethinking the role that new management technology can play in strategy making. A firm's potential payoff may be lost if its current management technology cannot afford to diagnose its strategic situation explicitly. In Boulding's (1956) terminology, the *dynamic clockwork*, as opposed to a *static framework*, of the following chapter considers the interrelationships among important variables that affect the process of developing a new management technology. Its development can lead to productivity improvements that create and, more importantly, sustain a competitive posture.

SUMMARY

In our increasingly transnational world economy, the interdependence among countries' business environments may determine its structural evolution. Nowhere are the effects of this interdependence clearer than in the opening up of the former USSR. Its failing economy simply made it impossible for the country to afford its rigid closed-market system.

Thus far, political instability and strife have played an important role in foreign joint venture activity in the former USSR, while the West has seen the situation as a growth opportunity in the light of stagnating markets at home. Western firms that do not practice scenario-driven planning are still trying to learn about the risks of joint ventures in the region, including the accessibility of these markets to traditional Western marketing strategies and tactics.

The fifteen new nations of the former Soviet Union face great problems in moving toward market-oriented systems. These all entail interdependent tasks that need coordination. All the parts have to fit reasonably well together for the system to work. The worst outcome might be some halfway compromise or tradeoff between the old closed-market system and the new private initiative and ownership structure.

The potential negative effects of tradeoffs and halfway compromises are best understood in the context of internationalization, where transnationalism emerged from the synthesis of international, global, and multinational strategic archetypes. Transnationalism has become a concrete force affecting the administrative and strategic management systems of world-class firms. It entails an attainable ideal (Fig. 11.2.2), and an emerging reference structure (Fig. 11.2.3).

The strategy designs of world-class firms emphasize overcoming the integration-responsiveness dilemma. The longer a firm trades off global integration against local responsiveness, and vice versa, the more it is alienating itself from transnationalism. The transnational archetype emerged from the strategy designs of individual firms. Yet, managers should not expect to drift from a traditional or multifocal archetype into transnationalism. They must design the transformation.

Chapter 12

Planning Technology for the 1990s

Firms often view innovation and new technology as the means to superior quality, productivity, and profitability. For example, automation implies increased quality, productivity, and profitability, but requires managing the rapidly advancing technology of organizational learning. Transnational competition demands rethinking the role that new management technology can play in strategy making. A firm's potential payoff may be lost if its management technology does not explicitly diagnose its strategic situation. This chapter considers the interrelationships among important variables that affect the development of new management technology. Investing in new management technology can lead to productivity improvements that often help create and, more importantly, sustain a superior strategic posture.

12.1   IT PAYS TO THINK GLOBALLY, BUT WHEN IN ROME...

Planning Organizational Learning

Organizational innovation combines the development and implementation of new ideas, systems, and products or services (Damanpour, 1991). Administrative innovations embody the adoption of internally generated or purchased administrative programs, processes, and techniques new to the adopting organization. Autonomous work groups, contingent compensation schemes, and scenario-driven planning are examples of administrative innovations.

Technological or technical innovations incorporate the adoption of internally developed or purchased devices, production processing systems, and techniques new to the adopting organization. Examples of technical innovations are robots, computer-integrated manufacturing, and scenario-driven planning.

Organizational researchers examine the effects of new management technology on performance from administrative and technical perspectives. Unintentionally perhaps, they treat administrative and technical innovation separately or emphasize the distinctions between the two (Daft, 1978). There is a technical school in organizational sociology (Perrow, 1967; Woodward, 1965), but it has been concerned primarily with the effects of extant technology on organizational structure than with innovation. Proponents of the administrative perspective emphasize the effects of administrative innovations, that is, changes in organizational structure. They focus on patterns of social interaction and on the amount, rate and permanence of innovation (Damanpour, 1991). This perspective suggests that changes in a firm's management technology determine its innovation capability by encouraging new and more frequent social interaction. The changes in structure that constitute administrative innovations redirect the existing flows of authority, control, and communication. Often, these changes yield an *organic* structure and promote more innovation.

Proponents of the technical perspective concentrate on the combined effects of market forces and new management technologies on the type, i.e., product versus process, and the rate of innovation within firms (Utterback & Abernathy, 1975). This perspective suggests that changes in a firm's technology affect its capability of technical innovation by encouraging new and more frequent response patterns to markets' pull and technical push. Highly specialized, as opposed to flexible, management systems constrain a firm's future choices. Technical innovations, that is, changes in management technology, can increase a firm's productivity and simultaneously increase its technical capability. Often, these changes yield an increased technico-economic feasibility and promote more innovation.

Administrative and technical innovations are interdependent in effect, if not by design (Scott, 1987). Kimberly (1981) points to the synergistic effects of administrative and technical innovations. The adoption of one type of innovation enables the adoption of another. The data of Fennell (1984) support the synergistic effects hypothesis, but also call for research to disentangle the complexity of these effects. Both researchers and practitioners should try to understand exactly how administrative along with technical innovations affect organizational performance (Collins, Hage, & Hull, 1988; Georgantzas & Shapiro, 1993).

Scenario-driven planning is a new management technology. Often, it is the technology behind the superior performance of world-class firms (de Geus, 1988; Godet, 1987; Merten, 1991; Morecroft & van der Heijden, 1992; Nonaka, 1988; Senge, 1990; Senge & Sterman, 1992; Tobias, 1991). Their managers use scenarios to articulate their mental models and thereby make better decisions. Their performance is a consequence of continuously improving their strategy designs, which scenario-driven planning enhances through a tireless renewal of organizational mind-sets. Computed scenarios can help a management team produce an insight that is much richer than that expected from a single-point forecast.

Typically, the context of strategy making is an ill-structured, uncertain one in which decision makers continuously try to broaden their perceptions, to improve their understanding, to articulate, and to improve their mental models of the relationships among variables relevant to the decisions they have to make. Strategic decisions are not and should not be made by simply eliciting information from managers and engineers (Remus & Kottemann, 1987).

The following section describes the interrelationships among important variables that affect the process of developing new management technology. Investing in new management technology can lead to productivity improvements that often create and, more importantly, help sustain a superior strategic posture.

Modeling Organizational Learning

A firm's management technology can be a determining factor for its future. It is not so much a matter of using portfolio matrices to come up with a strategy *for* management technology, but of designing strategy *through* management technology. The strategic thrust of new management technology adoption (i.e., organizational learning) is increasingly recognized in technology-management research and practice (Cavaleri & Obloj, 1993; de Geus, 1992; Istvan, 1992; Merten, 1991; Schwartz, 1991).

Figure 12.1.1 shows our modified version of a technico-economic development model (Myrdal, 1957). Its circular causation vision stems from two hypotheses: (1) a positive loop of growth with a low stationary point; and (2) multiple effects of social variables in technico-economic development. The model's self-sustained characteristics of growth at high revenue agree with contemporary ideas about economic growth (Kuznets, 1966).

Naturally, Fig. 12.1.1 does not exhaust the variables relevant to new management technology development planning, but it does incorporate some of the criteria suggested in the organizational innovation and learning literatures. Acar (1983) deals extensively with the consensus or dialectical processes necessary for constructing comprehensive situation maps like the one of Fig. 12.1.1. Similarly, Appendix C.2 as well as Sections 5.3 and 6.3 detail the components of CSM.

Our CSM model of Fig. 12.1.1 shows that, under a pure scenario of change transfer, a 10 percent increase in a firm's productivity would cause a relative 20 percent increase in its revenue, lagged three years. This one change would immediately cause a relative one-fifth growth in the firm's financial resources, and a relative four-fifths increase in market demand. The 10 percent increase in productivity would show up as a 16 percent increase in market demand three years later, with a 4 percent increase in financial resources, both from the previous levels of these variables.

These linkages are consistent with the research results of Bao & Bao (1989), who examined the association between firm value (i.e., security price) and productivity (i.e., added value), in twenty-nine US oil refining and twenty-eight apparel firms, for the 1973-1985 period. They found a strong association between firm value and productivity, suggesting that productivity can affect a firm's investment resources. This provides evidence supporting the disclosure of added-value information. Perhaps soon financial managers may use officially disclosed productivity data to analyze a firm's performance.

Chakrabarti (1990) assessed the relationship between organizational innovation and productivity in the chemical, textile, and machine-tool industries. Although the relationship between new management technology and productivity was found to be complex and dynamic, in the chemical industry the decline in productivity coincided with a significant decline in innovation. Chakrabarti noted an opposite trend in the textile industry, while in the machine-tool industry the increase in innovation coincided with a decrease in productivity. Chakrabarti concluded that cyclical fluctuations in demand may have created problems in small firms producing special-purpose tools.

Within the broad context of international competitiveness, technical knowledge and administrative capability differences among countries can play a central role in explaining output differences between them (Badulescu, 1991; Georgantzas & Madu, 1990). Prudent managers must understand the effect of change in order to visualize the chains of events that could lead to possible alternative futures (Tushman & Anderson, 1986).

Figure 12.1.1 CSM of Organizational Learning

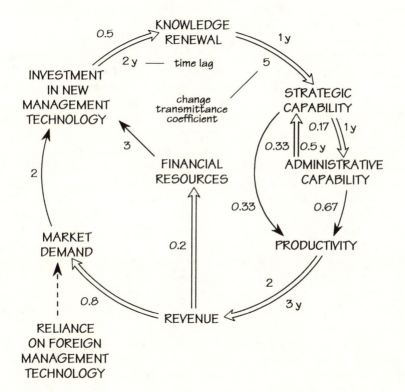

Organizational Learning Scenarios

CSM handles both hard and soft as well as external and internal variables, and it possesses computer simulationlike capabilities. CSM thus represents a good first step toward computer modeling and simulation. Starting from the CSM map of Fig. 12.1.1, a range of scenarios can explore possible alternative futures. In Fig. 12.1.1, assume that investment in new management technology increases by 75 percent, at time t = 0. Let us call this scenario pure scenario A. Similarly, let us assume a pure scenario B, involving a 5 percent decrease in the investment in new management technology at time t = 3. Each of these changes will cause a ripple of effects that CSM can capture quantitatively.

Parts (a) and (b) of Fig. 12.1.2 show the resulting dynamic behavior of the investment in new management technology, productivity, and revenue under pure scenario A and pure scenario B, respectively. The two scenarios show that the positive loop model responds differently to positive and negative changes in the investment in new management technology.

During the first seven years of pure scenario A, investment in new management technology and revenue increase rapidly, while productivity does so only during the first three years. After three years in the same scenario, productivity becomes constant, while after seven years, investment in new management technology and revenue increase at a declining rate. Conversely, during the first seventeen years of pure scenario B, the investment in new management technology, productivity, and revenue follow a fairly smooth downward trend, but their decline accelerates thereafter. The CSM model of new management technology shows how its development planning can turn into a vicious circle.

CSM's mixed scenarios enable the changes produced through multiple change channels to be combined. Figure 12.1.2c shows the dynamic behavior of the investment in new management technology, productivity and revenue under mixed scenario AB. Each line represents cumulative percentage change over twenty-one years.

During the first seven years of this mixed scenario, both investment in new management technology and revenue follow an upward trend, with productivity increasing more rapidly than investment, while revenue does so during the first three years only. After three years in the same scenario, that is, after time t = 10 years, investment in new management technology faces downward, while productivity continues rising, but at a declining rate. After the first seventeen years under mixed scenario AB, investment in new management technology, productivity, and revenue follow accelerating downward trends, changing at different rates.

The phase plots of Fig. 12.1.3 capture the synergistic effects of administrative

Figure 12.1.2 Organizational Learning Scenarios

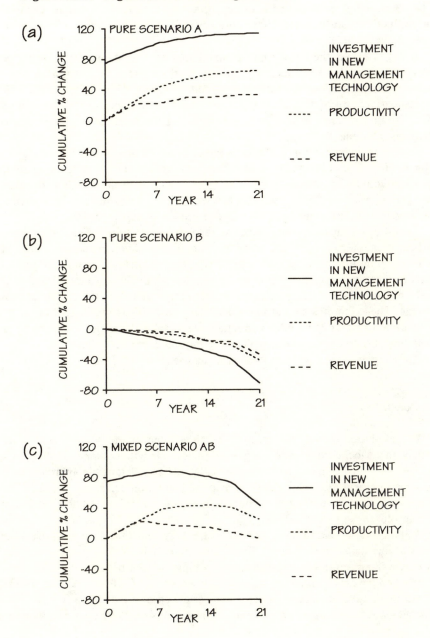

and strategic capability on productivity, thereby supporting the synergistic effects hypothesis (Fennell, 1984; Georgantzas & Shapiro, 1993; Kimberly, 1981). The adoption of one type of new management technology enables the adoption of another. Assuredly, the synergistic effects of administrative and strategic capability on productivity are positive under pure scenario A but negative under pure scenario B.

In Fig. 12.1.3c, the phase plot of mixed scenario AB shows that a firm's performance against the productivity objective falls rapidly as investment in new management technology diminishes by a mere 5 percent. This slight erosion makes it progressively more difficult to repeat the good performance of revenue and productivity under pure scenario A, thereby creating the potential for lower productivity and revenue.

Even a slight reduction in the investment in new management technology can exacerbate a firm's problems. It is difficult to attain not only revenue goals but also productivity objectives. Performing poorly on both usually leads to decreased motivation and adaptability, and to a further decline in a firm's administrative capability, that is, of managing its diversity of professional perspectives.

This illustration shows that CSM can resolve the net effect of multiple paths of influence on relevant variables, when there are both positive and negative net paths of intervening effects. Dealing with relative changes, that is, cumulative percentage changes, bypasses the difficulty of dealing with different units. In addition, CSM operates as a linearly additive and transitive model of the transmission of change. These features should interest strategy researchers and practitioners who are willing to integrate tangible and intangible variables in rough-cut mapping and modeling, a prerequisite to full-scale modeling and computer simulation.

These are powerful features that firms can use.

Conclusion

Process-based models can complement the content-based development of new management technology. The integration of process with content should provide decision support to management teams. CSM offers a defensible approach to the new management technology development and adoption decisions. It can be used alone, or it can accompany the better-known decision-making techniques of conflict resolution and idea analysis.

Yet, decision-making tools for new technology selection must consider all aspects of the managerial decision. They must embody performance measures, such as maximizing return on investment and getting the best possible combination of features on the new technology at the least possible cost (Offodile & Acar, 1993).

An illustrative example was presented for the case of the vicious circle of new management technology development planning. This example does not attempt to

Figure 12.1.3 Relationship Between Investment in New Management Technology and Productivity

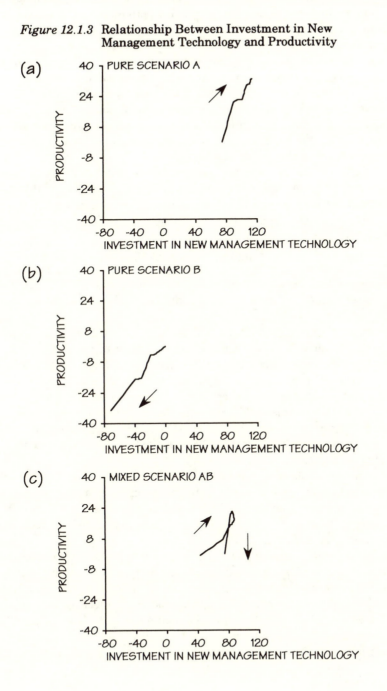

generate an ultimate solution to the new management technology adoption issues, and in no way does it exhausts these issues. The purpose is simply to show how researchers and practitioners can integrate and apply existing models in new management technology adoption decisions.

Comprehensive situation mapping extends the power of cognitive mapping. When time lags and transmission coefficients among pairs of variables are estimated from a database, subsequent what if analyses of the map can provide correct evaluation of various variables. Yet, effective planning support requires more than simply having a formal model of the situation under consideration. It is vital to use the model in dialogue and discussion within the management team responsible for investments in new management technology.

To be effective, CSM and computer simulation models must be used interactively to support and to challenge intuition. In this dialectic role, CSM and computer simulation are removed from the pedestal of the infallible black box to occupy a more modest and appropriate position as complements to the powers of deductive thinking and reasoning.

It must, of course, be noted that the scenarios emanating from a CSM are only as good and challenging as the map itself. Variables pertinent to a firm's specific situation should not be omitted. In addition, the change-transmittance coefficients and time-lag estimates should not be fanciful but, as in any modeling approach, should gradually improve (Eden, 1988).

Processes for obtaining them, such as the nominal group and the Delphi techniques ensure neither accuracy nor consistency. Their contribution has been refuted in the decision-making literature (Linstone, 1981; Linstone & Turoff, 1975; Mason & Mitroff, 1981). Dialectical inquiry and the "devil's advocate" methods have been proposed as superior alternatives (Acar, 1983; Ackoff, 1981; Chanin & Shapiro, 1985; Churchman, 1971; Cosier, 1981a & 1981b; Georgantzas, 1990; Mason, 1969; Shapiro & Chanin, 1987). This section shows the type of model, CSM or computer simulation, that can be integrated in a dialectical inquiry system to facilitate negotiation.

Scenario-driven planning is the new management technology that can enhance institutional learning and facilitate negotiation among managers and planners. Computing environmental and decision scenarios can sensitize a firm's management planning team to the dynamic implications of managerial and technological change (Georgantzas & Acar, 1989).

Even if the quantitative information necessary to draw a full causal diagram might prove elusive in some cases, a management planning team will still benefit from being confronted with different categories of available information. Knowing the relative importance of intangible and second-order effects of new managerial practices or technological shifts can hold a central role in explaining differences in productivity growth between firms, or within one firm over time.

Undertaken within scenario-driven planning, CSM is a good first step toward modeling and quantitative analysis. Methodologically, it becomes a defensible approach to the surfacing of critical assumptions, the recognition of prominent CBs (cognitive biases), and the appraisal of strategic or technological alternatives. CSM allows a welcome new kind of planning calculus and cost-benefit accounting, the kind that does not disregard indirect effects and intangible variables.

12.2 PRODUCTIVITY AND ORGANIZATIONAL LEARNING

We close with a unified view of problem framing and problem solving. It is a biased view that regards problem solving as the ultimate goal of problem formulation or framing. This is a bias for action aimed at closing the gap between qualitative and quantitative analysis in problem framing and problem solving.

Strategy researchers deal with the plural rationality of problem formulation, most of them drawing sharp distinctions between problem framing and problem solving (Chanin & Shapiro, 1985; Gilmore et al., 1982; Grauer, Thompson, & Wierzbicki, 1984). This stream of research distinguishes five subareas in the field:

- Cognitive processes
- Managerial problem solving
- Problem-solving methods
- Improving human input to decision-aiding technologies
- Management science methodology.

This grouping is descriptive and unbiased, and therefore useful for presenting a first-level rationale of problem framing.

Chanin & Shapiro (1985) discuss the relationship between problem framing and dialectical inquiry, providing another linkage between problem framing and scenario-driven planning. The common thread among these reviews of the field is their striving toward an ideal of impartiality, acknowledging the traditional view of problem solving as a *phased* process, with problem framing its starting point.

An emerging rationale views a well-framed problem as a problem half solved. This trend has been more partial to problem framing as a rewarding activity in its own right. It is called *problem framing* at the Wharton School (Gilmore et al., 1982), *problem structuring* at London's Tavistock Institute (Fach, 1972), *problem defining* by Eden (1978) and his colleagues formerly at the University of Bath, and *problem forming or setting* by other authors. This rationale takes problems as abstractions extracted from experience through analysis. What we actually experience are messy tangles of variables, along with their effects and constraints. What matters is the way we initiate our understanding of the problem situation. Eden et al. (1979), Checkland (1975), and Mason & Mitroff (1981) show how theorists of managerial problem solving have been preoccupied with problem framing.

Yet, most psychologists and interpersonal group facilitators attribute real-world problems to psychological constructs or to communication difficulties. Problem framers describe messy situations according to their intrinsic structural features. In stark contrast, process and organizational development consultants believe that either the lack of communication or the divergence of objectives causes most malfunctions, and they thereby see the search for structural features and situational parameters as an academic exercise (Blake & Mouton, 1964; Schein, 1969).

Among problem framers is the heavy phalanx of the dour problem solvers, who are heavily armed with quantitative weapons of a forbidding appearance. There is a sprinkling of less formidable logical problem solvers in their ranks (Kepner & Tregoe, 1965; Tregoe & Zimmerman, 1980), but the overwhelming majority belongs to some mathematical persuasion or discipline. In recent years, a new specialty has appeared within OR—operational research or, alternatively, operations research/management science (OR/MS)—with problem solving at the core of its vocation.

The Root Metaphor

OR's formidable mathematical apparatus has alienated most managers, process consultants, and problem framers from its contributions. Often, they undertake behavioral research projects with little or no connection to extant decision-making theory. Most practitioners perceive OR/MS as a set of tools in a foreign language. Yet, to those who have submitted themselves to its rigor even for a short while, OR is not just a bag of tricks but a methodical attempt to recognize problem structures under diverse circumstances. The arched gateway of Fig. 12.2.1 acknowledges OR as the art of problem solving par excellence.

The undisguised bias of our approach provides enough information to allow typing the subareas of problem framing according to a progressive order. Figure 12.2.1 presents problem sensing, problem framing, and problem solving as gradations along a continuum—that is, a progression along which each type (i.e., approach or academic discipline) moves us along the range of sub-areas.

Let us keep in mind that one of the end points of this spectrum is its original anchor: a focal strategic situation under investigation. Usually, modelers refer to this starting point as the *reality-out-there* or *focal system*. At the other end of the spectrum lies in waiting the potential solution set to the problem situation.

Following Acar (1987a), the model of the problem-framing process we propose here is that of a bridge, an arched gateway between the strategic situation and potential solutions to its ills. Two groups of qualitative approaches rest on the left abutment of the bridge in Fig. 12.2.1.

The closest to the focal strategic situation is the approach dealing with cognitive processes (Bannister & Fransella, 1971; Eden, 1988; Hall, 1984; Kelly, 1955)

Figure 12.2.1 Elements of an Arched Gateway Bridging the Gap
Between a Focal Strategic Situation and its Solution Set

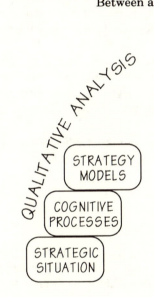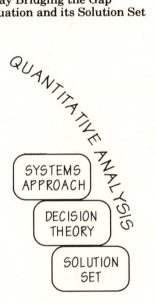

or with pure process consultation (Schein, 1969). Although the basic psychological research is increasingly more quantitative, its associated interventions tend to be very qualitative. One step to the right takes us in Fig. 12.2.1 to the strategic consultancy box. Here we find such authors as the classical strategy writers (Henderson, 1979; Porter, 1980, 1985) and some behavioral scientists (Hogarth, 1980; Tversky & Kahneman, 1974), but also some organization theorists (Mintzberg, Raisinghani, & Théorêt, 1976).

At the other end of the spectrum, next to the set of solutions, lies the solid-line box of the formal decision theory models and optimization algorithms. This is the field of OR/MS; its methodology is described in OR/MS texts (Ackoff & Sasieni, 1968; Bellman, 1961; Drenick, 1986; Marschak & Randers, 1972; Zeleny, 1982). Next to it in Fig. 12.2.1, one finds the box of systems analysis. This is the 'hard' systems or cybernetics approach (Ashby, 1963; Forrester, 1961, 1968a, 1968b; Sterman, 1989; Wiener, 1948). OR/MS has recently recognized the necessity of adopting a systems view that allows analyzing and representing a firm's manufacturing or service production engine as a complex system comprising many interdependent elements (Parnaby, 1986).

A systems view of a firm might involve aspects of political science, geography, economics, and sociology. Exactly how these various disciplines can be integrated is one of the major intellectual challenges in systems analysis. Its integration with OR/MS yields a comprehensive range of quantitative methods and techniques for analyzing what is made or served and how. These well-known and well-developed approaches are used extensively in manufacturing and service systems reengineering (Davenport, 1993; Tobias, 1991). They are depicted by the solid-line boxes at the right-hand side of the spectrum of Fig. 12.2.1.

Bridging the Gap

Right now, there are the two entrenched cultures at each end of the spectrum, and very little is fully operational in the middle. As conventional wisdom has it, there is no middle ground: problem framing is predominantly qualitative as of now, and problem solving is predominantly quantitative.

Some procedures do take short-cuts (Fig. 12.2.2). Yet, the cost is an unintentional but unavoidable loss in decision quality or accuracy. The flatter the short-cut line is in Fig. 12.2.2, the less valuable the solution will be. For example, process consulting is more effective than intuition-based managerial decision making (Schein, 1969), and dialectical inquiry is more effective than pure process consultancy (Mason & Mitroff, 1981).

The three keystone boxes of our symbolic arch are shown in gray lines because they are in the making. A number of efforts have been made in this regard, though

Figure 12.2.2   Short-Cut Solutions

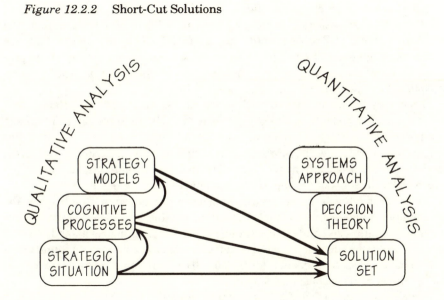

they have not been totally successful (Checkland, 1975; Eden, 1978, 1979, 1988; Hall, 1976 & 1984; Morecroft, 1988; Richardson & Pugh, 1981). Eden's work is too close to cognitive mapping, yet it has opened important vistas (Eden, 1979, 1988). Mason & Mitroff's SAST (strategic assumption surfacing and testing) is top-heavy toward the dialectical end; yet it teaches us a very important lesson about process. Nadler's work was pathbreaking, but it appears to have been stifled by its excessive quest for computational simplicity and conceptual symmetry (Nadler, 1970).

Qualitative problem framing and formal problem solving are being bridged through the development of these frameworks. They all pertain to the problem-framing paradigm, but none of them develops a rigorous way of modeling causalities in order to study the dynamics of the system underlying a strategic situation's evolution.

Eden's work is an exception (Eden, 1978, 1979, 1988). It entails developing lengthy and wordy scenarios, but it is a strong incentive in the right direction. The scenarios of the SAST procedure (Mason & Mitroff, 1981) are weaker. They are merely the aggregates of plausible hypotheses, without the plausibility check provided by a rigorous computation of the dynamics of change (Acar, 1983). Its assumptional analysis concept, however, needs to be retained.

System dynamics is another exception, but, as discussed, it pertains more properly to the systems analysis type than to problem framing from scratch (Forrester, 1958, 1961). (Chapter 10 gives a brief introduction to the field of system dynamics and shows how Morecroft combines premise description and partial model tests with system dynamics modeling and simulation to bridge the gap between Datacom's model assumptions and simulated implications.)

Model description and analysis can often leave a large gap in logic between the assumptions embodied in a model's equations and their simulated behavior. Implanting scenario-driven planning through CSM can help managers and strategy students make the transition from the conventional case approach, by argumentation alone, to full-scale modeling for learning. The transition is no longer an option for US firms; it has become mandatory.

Developing a general or future manager's ability to reperceive strategic situations systemically and dynamically, and improving a manager's mental models, support the need for managers to themselves become the modelers. The separation of knowing from doing (i.e., knowledge from action), in the sense of "some know and some act," like the separation of managers (controllers) from doers (workers), is a self-inflicted wound of modern management (Zeleny, 1991).

Used either individually or in teams, comprehensive situation mapping can challenge and improve a manager's mental models of strategic decision situations. Implanting scenario-driven planning through CSM can speed up the transition to modeling for productive learning (Acar, 1983, 1987b; Georgantzas & Acar, 1989).

Figure 12.2.3   Scenario-Driven Planning Can Bridge the Gap Between
a Focal Strategic Situation and its Potential Solutions

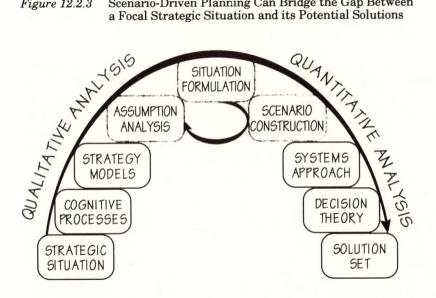

Researchers in systems dynamics and elsewhere have experimented with many processes to catalyze systems thinking in management teams. Typically, effective learning processes are both *iterative* and *flexible* (Randers, 1980). These two characteristics make a learning process attractive, but also "somewhat slippery and elusive" (Roberts et al., 1983, p. 7).

Senge & Sterman recommend that business schools form collaborative action research partnerships with firms, develop new tools to accelerate learning, and test the effectiveness of those tools in real organizations, where managers face pressing issues. Senge & Sterman disclose the three stages of an effective learning process:

- *Mapping mental models*—explicating and structuring assumptions via systems models.
- *Challenging mental models*—revealing inconsistencies in assumptions.
- *Improving mental models*—continually expanding and testing mental models (1992, p. 140).

Similarly, Acar presents seven conditions that an effective problem framing approach ought to meet (Acar, 1983, 1987b). CSM fulfills all of Acar's criteria, incorporates the three stages of an effective learning process that Senge & Sterman delineate, and thereby meets the conditions for the three keystone boxes of our arch diagram. Figure 12.2.3 uses the arched-bridge analogy to situate the vital role that CSM could play in bridging the gap between qualitative descriptions and quantitative modeling of strategic decision situations.

CSM combines two features that are rarely, if ever, associated together in a single scenario-driven planning method.

From Ackoff's interactive planning concept and the Mason-Mitroff SAST, CSM borrows the notion of assumptional analysis and of a dialectical debate and planning system (Ackoff, 1981; Mason & Mitroff, 1981). It melds them together in a powerful combination denoted by its divergence-convergence cycle. (Section 5.3 elaborates on CSM's divergence-convergence cycle; see also Appendix C.2.) This is a rather formalized mode of assumptional analysis of the SAST type, but it is anchored to a causal mapping technique. Assumptional analysis is the part of CSM which abuts the classical qualitative problem-framing approaches.

CSM also includes features of the quantitative type which brings it beyond the influence diagramming (ID) of Diffenbach (1982), Hall (1984), Maruyama (1963), Ramaprasad & Poon (1985), Richardson & Pugh (1981), and Weick (1979). ID is content to combine signed influences, without consideration of their magnitude. Its analysis is based solely on connectedness and on consideration of the number of negative signs and loops. Acar (1983) shows the danger of such algebralike manipulations in a nonalgebraic context. CSM allows computing and tracking both the magnitude of relationships among variables and the time lags in a system.

Also carefully built into CSM is the distinction between the necessary or partial channel and the sufficient full-channel linkages for the transmission of change.

These features provide a simple yet powerful internal structure to CSM. They endow its users with the ability to capture the intrinsic structure of complex strategic situations. With CSM's computational properties, it can be used as a shorthand simulation of the propagation of change.

Once an environmental trigger or a firm's internal lever, or both, have changed from their previous levels, CSM's scenario computation feature allows testing the dynamic implications or consequences of strategies and tactics fairly rapidly. Meanwhile, CSM users can revert to the assumptional analysis mode whenever the problem-framing process requires it.

Conclusion

The intellectual dichotomy between qualitative and quantitative approaches to strategic management should not prevent us from seeking to bridge the gap between them. Problem framing might reveal itself to be a continuum, along an arch as presented here, and not as a mere phase of a process in one extreme interpretation or a be-all in others. A number of procedures and methods are coming on stream to help us with problem framing. CSM is a promising approach.

SUMMARY

Scenario-driven planning is in many ways a fickle management technology. Given enough time, it may adapt itself to a variety of organizational cultures, allowing itself to be embellished by all sorts of meretricious gadgetry. Like a true democratic courtesan, it flatters the inexpert suitor with a simulation of submission. Naive suitors, however, ecstatic over simple spreadsheets, may be missing the joy of organizational learning and its attendant benefit—competitive advantage.

"Seek out real knowledge and thou shalt not be deceived." Perhaps because scenario-driven planning does allow such liberties to be taken for the sake of commercial gain, it reserves long-term benefits for firms whose concern about the future matches their passion for excellence. Their mature leadership is nourished by the rational pluralistic subtlety of scenarios

The readers who have made it this far into this book draw their persistence from the very heart of the organizations they manage. Similarly, the wide range of scenario examples in this book reveals—with intricate clarity—how firms manage to make scenario-driven planning tell the truth about themselves and their possible alternative futures. That's what modern management is capable of when it is not coerced into flamboyance.

For the past two decades, leading-edge firms have recognized that the combination of lucidity in strategic thinking and passion for proaction makes scenario-driven planning unique among strategy design tools. Through the present volume, the rest of us are now offered a chance to see this opinion reinforced. Major facets of corporate life are its pursuit of excellence in creating the future through subtle leadership and its focus on dealing with strategic uncertainty through organizational learning.

Part VII

APPENDIX

Theoretical Foundations of Scenario-Driven Planning

The earlier chapters and examples have presented the state of the art in scenario methods. The stage is now set for an in-depth appraisal of where the field is going by discussing some of the underlying principles involved. We now step back to appraise the state of the art of scenario-driven business intelligence, and we take stock of the methodological principles underlying the growing spectrum of scenario methods. This discussion of general principles and recent contributions to the field, though somewhat technical, gives a good sense of where planning with scenarios is headed.

A.1   A COMMONSENSE APPROACH TO SCENARIOS HAS COME OF AGE

Background: Qualitative Versus Quantitative Scenarios

Kahn & Wiener (1967) define scenarios as the hypothetical sequences of events built to focus attention on causal processes and decision points. In the 1960s and early 1970s, researchers often asked what new insight into business and social problems could be gained from modeling and simulation that could not be had from conventional methods.

In a book dedicated to the application of system dynamics simulation to business, James Lyneis (1980) observes that firms often isolate policy designs from environmental scenarios. They base strategy computation or design on the most likely or most recently devised environmental scenario. An important aim of future research related to strategy is to improve the quality of dialogue and debate among decision makers, and between decision makers and the models they use (Morecroft, 1988, 1992; Senge, 1990; Senge & Sterman, 1992).

The scenario method originally advocated by futurology researchers such as Kahn and Wiener in 1967 was the least structured. It simply involved applying reasoned judgment and intuition in describing alternative futures to represent specific themes, or simply to capture pessimistic, most likely, and optimistic assumptions.

The newer approaches we discussed involve structured steps for identifying scenario elements, grouping them, and then assembling them into compatible sets of assumptions to form scenarios (Vanston, 1977). Examples of these procedural methods are the dialectical approach (Churchman, 1969; Mason & Mitroff, 1981)—cf. Section 4.1 on SAST; the trend scenario approach (Bonnicksen, 1985; Durand, 1972), which tries to trace progression of events following predetermined themes; and the Battelle BASICS method.

Before proceeding further, we should outline the range of possible methods. At the other far end of the spectrum are the quantitative, structured algorithms, and simulation models of operational research/management science (OR/MS). They are part of the curriculum of most business schools and can be subsumed under the collective name of *mathematical modeling*. The basic idea of mathematical modeling is to capture the relationships with a set of equations that could serve as an explicit model of the firm. Then, one reasons on the model. The corporate model (lower part of Fig. A.1.1) becomes a simplified mirror, an artificial reality that gives the planner the opportunity to reason and even carry out mathematical computations.

Figure A.1.1 Corporate Planning Framework
(Adapted from Amara & Lipinski, 1983)

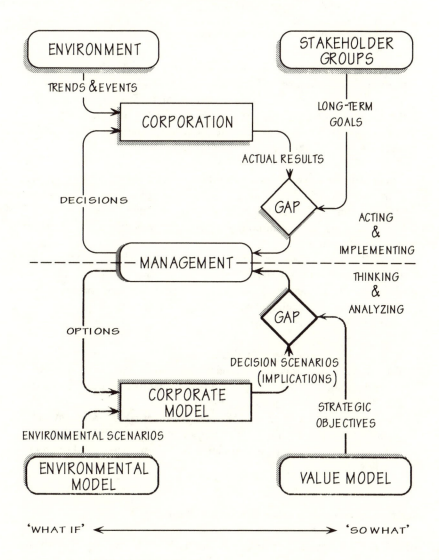

Amara and Lipinski's (1983) synthesis of the OR simulation modeling literature shows how the OR/MS scientific approach provides a vehicle for capturing
environmental trends and events (upper part of Fig. A.1.1) in modules or submodules (lower part of Fig. A.1.1) whose role is to input environmental scenarios
into the model of the firm. In turn, the consequences of computations with the corporate model become the *decision* scenarios to be considered.

At the same far end of the spectrum are mathematical-combinatorial approaches
that are more sophisticated than BASICS. Typically but not exclusively of the
probabilistic variety, these share the following characteristics.

- They generate scenarios from combinations of values (i.e., events)
  representing a given set of variables.
- They obtain each scenario's likelihood from subjective estimates of
  the likelihood of each event, singly and as affected by other events.
- For simplicity, often they complete the methodological analysis with
  pairwise, instead of composite, event interactions.

Yet, one may not have to become quite so sophisticated to do good work in
practice. In-between those two extremes of the purely hypothesized first-generation
scenarios of Kahn and other futurists and the computed scenarios of OR/MS
simulation modeling, lies the middle ground of the *procedural scenarios*, which
are now the most common.

Millett & Randles (1986) agree that procedurally generated scenarios provide a
good middle ground between relying totally on informal, intuitive techniques and
being bound by the demanding methodological constraints of formal models and
other highly quantitative techniques. They argue that scenarios provide an excellent planning tool for three reasons:

1. They can be rigorous, systematic, and factual.
2. They need modest amounts of time and resources. (Scenarios demand
   more data and calculations than purely subjective models, but less
   than statistical and econometric models.)
3. They can provide a direct link between the external environment and
   corporate strategy by allowing strategy makers to formulate, debate,
   and appraise their company's situation in its competitive and regulatory environments.

Reference Scenarios Versus Interactive Planning

Russell Ackoff argues that firms have four basic modes for coping with changes
in the environment. The first mode, *inactivity*, involves ignoring the changes and

continuing business as usual. The second mode, *reactivity*, involves waiting for something to happen and responding to that change; here, the response must be stimulated by an outer force. The third mode, *preactivity*, involves trying to predict external changes and positioning the firm before they happen; this *prea*ctive mode is anticipatory. The fourth mode is the proactive or interactive mode. *Proactivity* calls for interactive involvement with the outer forces and pressures that seeks to create the future for stakeholder groups.

Though proper for certain sets of circumstances, each of these responses presumes a basic attitude for dealing with changes in the environment, even the quiescent mode. Essential differences between the reactive, preactive, and interactive modes of planning result from differences in managerial orientation toward the past, present, and future (Ackoff, 1970, 1978 & 1981).

In this context, Ackoff uses the term *reference scenario* to refer to the combination of reference projections a firm would most probably have if there were no significant changes in its behavior and that of its environment. Furthermore, he asserts that a reference scenario best reveals a firm's strategic decision situation or "mess." Ozbekhan (1977) makes the same point in his study on the future of Paris. The point is that, for Ackoff, one does not have to go all the way with computerized simulation; many consultants believe that procedural models can generate reference scenarios. Moreover, Ackoff's call for strategic turnaround starts with an idealized scenario of a desirable future. To be effective, such a scenario should be interesting and *provocative*. It should show what to change to evade the mess of problems facing a firm's strategic situation.

It is critical that a scenario *not* be presented as a forecast of what will happen; its purpose is strictly to show the implications of a firm's current behavior and assumptions about its strategic decision situation. This point should become better understood in managerial practice. Overselling scenarios can undervalue them.

In a recent book (1991), Flood & Jackson wonder whether the theory of interactive planning equips us adequately for all strategic decision situations. Their critique of Ackoff's work begins by asking what systems metaphors interactive planning does not employ and what assumptions it does not make about strategy contexts. Following this line of critical assault, Flood & Jackson conclude that interactive planning fails to take account of the possible existence of coercive situations, such as simple-coercive and complex-coercive strategy contexts.

Yet, in *Creating the Corporate Future*, Ackoff does not present interactive planning alone but jointly with scenarios (Ackoff, 1981). Flood & Jackson's critical assault falls flat on its metaphorical face once metaphor, simile, and analogy have stepped aside to make some elbow-room for Ackoff's *provocative scenario* idea. Without strategic scenarios, interactive planning may indeed fail to take into account organizational conflict. (Section 1.1 elucidates the potential failure of strategic considerations grounded exclusively on the psychology of participation.) Conversely, scenario-driven interactive planning provokes participants, inviting conflict between clashing worldviews in both simple and complex strategic situations.

Nonetheless, Flood & Jackson present a comprehensive survey of planning methods that should be required reading for anyone interested in gauging the broad scope now attained by formal planning methods—some of which is quite sophisticated. Flood & Jackson are rightly concerned with organizational conflict. Ignoring incompatible goals in strategy making is dangerous as was made clear in the Bhopal, India, disaster. In that instance, the interplay of *tight coupling* (i.e., errors in a subsystem quickly affected the entire system) and *social isolation* (i.e., the plant was cut off from the corporate system) led to crisis (Shrivastava, 1988). System failures, such as in Bhopal, the Challenger disaster, or Chernobyl, will continue unless the capability of stakeholder groups to change their mental models improves through multiple computed scenarios.

As discussed in the earlier chapters, Mason & Mitroff (1981) and Schwenk (1984) are correct when they maintain that stakeholder groups must negotiate and expand their worldviews though productive conflict (see also Litterer, 1966; van de Vilert, 1985). Equipped with scenarios, the process of conflict resolution creates new *bargaining windows* that make innovative solutions acceptable (Radford, 1980; Robinson, 1988). With its sources and intensity understood through causal modeling and computed scenarios, conflict can motivate and lead to effective strategy design and implementation. Indeed, conflict is necessary for a system to progress (Cosier & Rose, 1977). Alternative conflicting scenarios provide the means for stakeholder groups to respond both comprehensibly and comprehensively to a system's limitations, so that they can improve its performance over time (Georgantzas & Madu, 1990).

Point Estimates Versus Probabilistic Scenarios

A quandary presented in the scenarios literature concerns the misuse of probabilistic scenario models when, officially, no probabilities should exist. Given that single-point forecasts have not fared well during the past two decades (Schnaars, 1989), with environmental and strategic uncertainty increasing, upper and lower bounds frequently accompany single-point estimates (Schnaars & Topol, 1987), "so that one is highly confident the actual outcome will fall within that range" (Schoemaker, 1993, p. 198). Schoemaker correctly emphasizes "the actual outcome" because, oddly enough, there is no longer any probability concerning whether a point estimate lies in a confidence range or interval. Either it does or it does not.

To fix ideas, consider a sample of size n taken from a firm's sales or other data. *Before* the data are observed, the theoretical sample mean $\bar{X}$ and standard deviation S are such that the point estimate $E[\bar{X}] = \theta$ of the firm's average sales will lie in the estimation interval $\bar{X} \pm 1.96(S/\sqrt{n})$, with probability of 0.95. *After* the actual sample values of $\bar{X}$ and S are observed to equal $\bar{x}$ and s, respectively, at the 5 percent significance level one would be 95 percent confident that θ will lie in the $\bar{X} \pm 1.96(S/\sqrt{n})$ interval. Yet, *after* the fact, "there is no longer any probability concerning whether θ lies in the interval $\bar{X} \pm 1.96(S/\sqrt{n})$ for either it does or it does not" (Ross, 1990, p. 101).

This apparent paradox clarifies our American consulting tradition and the established paradigms of our most prominent learned societies, whose monothematic primacy has been prodding every US firm to function according to a single official scenario. Consequently, the basis for defining scenarios has been shifting in the literature from concerns about what a scenario ought to be to the mechanics entailed in manipulating subjective probability estimates.

Frequently asked questions concern scenario components and usage patterns (Dembo, 1991; Robinson, 1991; Schoemaker, 1991), thereby shifting managerial attention from a more crucial question: What development process is necessary? This shift is described in the next section.

Propagated along the network of causal relationships underlying a strategic situation, computed scenarios explicitly deal with uncertainty either within or across themselves, or both. This is plainly seen in the real-life cases of Infoplus, Combank and Datacom presented in Chapters 4, 5, 9, and 10 as well as in the dynamic clockwork of new management technology presented in Chapter 12. The behavior patterns that their deterministic models exhibit represent systemic variation produced by the relationships underlying each strategic situation, under different scenarios. The models and the associated scenarios capture the environmental and strategic uncertainties prominent in each case by downplaying the random variations of conventional wisdom that chance events can produce over a large number of repeated occurrences. Managers understand from experience how the search for cause and effect relationships that explain system behavior sometimes gives way to a belief in irrationally random events. Increasingly, their economists concur.

Can plain knowledge, the world's new form of capital (Drucker, 1989; Zeleny, 1991), ever offer strategic management less choice than the appearance of sophistication? It is plain utopia to pretend that modeling to predict the future can offer better solutions to strategic management problems than modeling for learning from it or from the past. In Chapter 9, BASICS' stochastic scenario frequencies make the probabilistic nature of scenarios more explicit, but only to reinforce the causal interdependence among the variables pertinent to the strategic situations of the Combank and Infoplus examples, and not to bother with estimating probabilities of confidence intervals themselves, no matter how appealing these appear to be to some practitioners.

Computing Scenarios for a Decision Situation

Focal elements are represented as either inputs or outputs of the modeling process (Fig. A.1.1). Inputs are either controllable by the decision-making team or uncontrollable. Let us begin with the uncontrollable inputs. Some may appear as *constants*. We assume that the values of constants are fixed at all times.

Another type of uncontrollable input is an *exogenous variable*, the value of which is determined by forces external to the model of the situation under consideration. The value of an exogenous variable may be different under various circumstances and thereby subject to manipulation by the modeling team during simulation. If the value of the exogenous variable is known, then it is a *deterministic exogenous variable*. If the value is not known or is subject to variation, then it is a *stochastic exogenous variable*. Its value is then generated for the model either arbitrarily or randomly from a probability distribution. A model with deterministic variables and inputs is a deterministic model. Stochastic variables require accounting explicitly for randomness in the behavior of one or more variables through a probabilistic model for one time period or a stochastic model for successive time periods.

Some inputs to a model correspond to elements under the decision-making team's control. These are included in the model of a situation as *decision variables*. Decision makers can test alternative courses of action by assigning different values to these variables. The objective of a simulation run is to simulate precisely the causal effects of one input variable on endogenous variables in order to arrive at a better understanding of the dynamic (i.e., changing over time) behavior patterns produced by a system by means of observing how its variables interact.

The outputs of a simulation model represent those elements of the reference system that are of greatest interest to the decision-making team. The output or results of a model are produced by the structure of the relationships among its *endogenous variables*. The numerical values that its endogenous variables take on are determined by that structure. If a model outputs a single value, then it is characterized as possessing deterministic endogenous variables. If, instead, the model outputs a range of values corresponding to a probability distribution, then it is characterized as either a probabilistic model for one time period or a stochastic model for successive time periods. Probabilistic and stochastic simulation models usually entail the generation of pseudorandom numbers.

Computing the dynamic behavior of a mathematical model simulates the behavior of a system over time. From the behavior patterns or trends produced by a dynamic model, we can draw inferences about the behavior of the real system. We refer to changes that occur in a system over time as *events*. Models are initially formulated for the general case. Yet, the real advantage of a model occurs when its quantified variables result in a set of simulated events.

In OR/MS modeling, a *scenario* is a representation of an interconnected sequence of trends/events describing an internally consistent future" (Amara & Lipinski, 1983, p. 5). Given a plausible set of values for the exogenous variables, a decision-making team may try in each run some combination of values for the decision variables. Each combination of values for the decision variables, given a plausible set of values for the exogenous inputs, is a *scenario run*.

A.2 SOME RECENT THEORETICAL CONTRIBUTIONS

Amara and Lipinski's 1983 must-read book deals with planning for an uncertain future. They define scenario as a representation of an interconnected sequence of trends/events describing an internally consistent future. The generation of scenarios capturing the essential elements of the external environment is the starting point for preparing separate forecasts for each principal factor or variable.

In *Techniques of Scenario Planning,* Chandler & Cockle (1982) also define scenarios as the coherent pictures of different possible events in the environment, whose effect on a set of businesses should be tested through linked models. Each picture is of a small part of the universe—a consistent set of assumptions and their consequences. The mechanism by which vague assumptions are translated into projected values of, for example, wholesale prices, gross domestic product (GDP), or consumer expenditures, involves manipulating macroeconomic models to represent the effect of each scenario.

In his 1985 landmark book *Competitive Advantage,* Porter claims that scenarios traditionally used in strategic planning have stressed macroeconomic and macropolitical factors. He posits that in competitive strategy the proper unit of analysis is the industry, and he refers to industry scenarios as the primary, internally consistent views of how the world will look in the future. Porter gives an extensive example of his conception of scenarios for the chainsaw industry, ranging from a favorable assumption, the "casual user saws are a fad," to an unfavorable one, the "casual user market never materializes" (Porter, 1985, p. 472).

Regarding the process called for in building these scenarios, Porter oversimplifies its essence by coupling two loops, the minor one—industry analysis—being embedded in a major loop of building industry scenarios (1985, p. 449). Contrary to Porter's view, Wack's argument is that scenario builders must wide-angle first to capture the big picture and then to zoom in on the details. Although industry focused scenarios can help analyze particular aspects of a business, a narrow focus start will probably miss key dimensions and cast scenarios in the wrong way. A premature focus ought to be avoided to give the process a chance (Wack, 1985a, 1985b).

This book repeatedly emphasizes that scenario technology entails methods for converting environmental or first-generation scenarios into computed decision scenarios. It is also imperative to involve management, both top and middle.

An example of the sophistication the practice of planning may bring in the 1990s is Godet's 1985 prize-winning book. Translated in English in 1987, it defines scenario as the description of a future situation emerging from the consistent progression of events. It covers two very different categories: *situational scenarios* or images, which describe future situations; and *development scenarios*, which describe the sequence of events that lead there (Godet, 1987). This distinction is an important theoretical contribution.

In the detection process of environmental threats, Godet further distinguishes between the *trend-based scenario*, which is the most likely scenario, and the *contrasted scenario*, which is the exploration of a purposely extreme theme based on the a priori determination of a future situation. In this respect, he builds a bridge between Cosier and Schwenk's devil's advocacy method and scenario analysis.

In the detection process of strategic opportunities, Godet also proposes using a *horizon* or *normative scenario*, in which one examines the feasibility of a desirable future by working backward from the future to the present. This proposal echoes Ackoff's call for starting corporate turnaround by an idealized design of a wanted future (Ackoff, 1981).

Godet's is a sophisticated approach to scenario building that tries to surpass Battelle's BASICS method presented in Section 5.3. He distinguishes the main components of scenario-driven planning:

- The building of a database
- The building of scenarios
- The generation of forecasts by scenarios
- The definition of corporate strategies
- The choice of strategic choices

This modular approach reflects Godet's perception that the goal of scenario building is to bridge the gaps between the multicriteria methods he surveys. The full names of his techniques give an idea of their tenor: the analysis of each actor's role; the experts' method, performed via the system and matrix of cross impacts (SMIC) survey (Godet, 1987); and the cross-impact matrix multiplication applied to classification (MICMAC), described in Appendix C.3.

With the database one tries to create an image of the present state of the system that will serve as a starting point of the future's study. Building the data base involves three phases: (1) the delimitation of the system studied and the general environment (economic, political, technological, etc.); (2) identification of the key internal and external variables; and (3) retrospective and actors' strategies.

In this framework, scenario construction calls for a division of the planning horizon into successive subperiods, with intermediate future images. Then, the challenge is to describe the pathway from the present situation to the final images chosen from the trend-based or most probable scenario and the contrasted scenarios by working backward. Godet's mechanistic but sophisticated approach to scenario-driven planning includes several interrelated steps such as systems analysis, retrospective actors' strategies, and elaboration of descriptive and normative scenarios.

Godet maintains that the factors, trends, and seeds of change in the database set in motion his scenario method by having evolutionary mechanisms intervene and by confronting the *actors'* strategies—as decision makers are called in the scenario literature. Godet uses the SMIC method to choose the final developmental possibilities characterized by n hypotheses. This method relies on consulting experts and allows a hierarchy of 2^n possible images because of the probabilities assigned to the hypotheses ranked in order of decreasing chance.

Equally sophisticated is the approach proposed in 1988 by Brauers & Weber. It has three basic phases: analysis, description of future states of environmental subsystems, and synthesis. The analysis phase reaches an exact definition for the entity under investigation, so that organizational participants develop and share a common understanding of the problem. Based on this consensus, the problem can be further bounded and structured.

To help participants pick a few representative influencing factors in the first analysis phase, Brauers & Weber recommend the use of *soft* creative methods such as morphological analysis, brainstorming, brainwriting, and the Delphi procedure. In the second phase of scenario analysis—description of future states of environmental subsystems—they define possible development paths of the influencing factors chosen in the first phase. In the third phase—synthesis—they consider existing interdependencies between these factors to build different scenarios through the synthesis of different future states. Lastly, to implement these three phases, Brauers & Weber propose the use of the computer system KONMACA (Compatible Scenario Matrix Generator for Linear Programming and Cluster Analysis).

By now, the scenario bandwagon has a technical base (Helgason & Wallace, 1991; Robinson, 1991; Rockafellar, 1991). Computer-based systems use available information technology to improve the effectiveness of managerial and professional planning activities. User-friendly software is being increasingly produced under the forecasting-with-scenarios label that promises to increase the scope and flexibility of forecasts by plugging in a variety of figures to create choice scenarios as the sales pitches intimate. Disciplines like accounting, finance, and marketing are also now positioning themselves to take fuller advantage of scenario-driven planning.

A.3 WHERE ARE WE HEADED IN SCENARIO ANALYSIS?

Amara & Lipinski (1983) suggest that a less mechanistic framework may be more successful. They believe that is crucial for scenarios to provide a description of the environment in which a firm competes. The goal of scenario building is for managers to capture and to analyze essential elements of the environment as described in Fig. A.1.1; to develop greater intuition and a better feel for their environment.

Amara and Lipinski separate the managerial activity of thinking/analyzing from the organizational activity of acting/implementing. The kernel of their framework is the interplay between environmental scenarios and management choices. That is, the evaluation of the expected corporate performance under each option—a particular candidate for the allocation of financial, physical and human resources vis-à-vis each possible scenario. The Fig. A.3.1a through Fig. A.3.1d series has been adapted from Amara and Lipinski to show the graded sequence of planning methods that has taken place over the years. In their view, the factor that drives the process is that component which most directly affects decision making.

The gradation starts in Fig. A.3.1a, whereby objectives are believed sufficient to drive final decisions. After World War I, the development of accounting science pointed to the fact that decisions were budget driven as in Fig. A.3.1.b. The post-World War II curricular development in business emphasized the leading role of strategic options, which led to the strategy-driven planning of Fig. A.3.1c. The symbolism of Fig. A.3.1(d) illustrates how, for Amara & Lipinski, it is the outcome of each scenario that should be seen as the *driver* of the planning process.

Lastly, in Fig. A.3.2 we show how the environmental scenarios input to the strategic planning process results in (computed) strategic scenarios that drive the process. Figure A.3.2 is a simplified rendering of the more elaborate framework for scenario-driven planning we proposed in Fig. 8.2.1.

Figure A.3.3 describes a theoretical approach to scenario-driven planning inspired from OR/MS. This approach conceives scenarios as the various branches of a decision tree. Interestingly, Amara & Lipinski's espoused theory is that they subscribe to this method, but their detailed prescriptions do not completely agree with the normative model of Fig. A.3.3. Yet, this model highlights an important concern in the description of the environment surrounding an organization. It is the selectivity skill that guides the identification of thorny interrelated issues lavished to furnish the achievement of strategic goals or the goodness (success or failure) of managerial choices.

The framework we propose brings scenarios closer to strategic issue diagnosis (SID). Dutton, Fahey & Narayanan (1983) suggest that SID is not only pervasive but also central to strategic decision making. Strategic decisions, when compared with tactical or operational decisions, are messy. They are typically more complex, novel, and open-ended, exhibiting "interconnectedness . . . complicatedness uncertainty . . . ambiguity . . . conflict . . . societal constraints" (Mason & Mitroff, 1981, pp. 12-13) SID creates a variety of issue-specific outputs such as assumptions, cause and effect understandings, predictive judgments, and a language and label system.

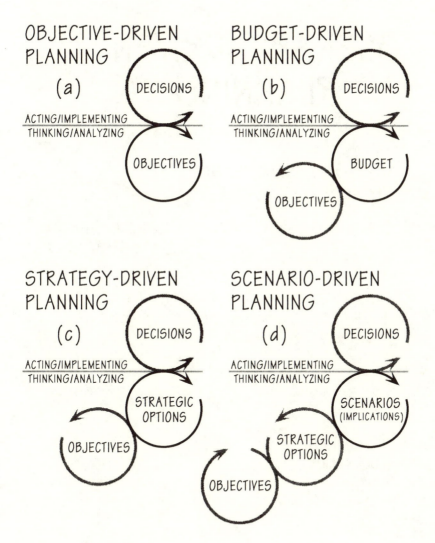

Figure A.3.2 Proposed Model (Adapted from Amara & Lipinski, 1983)

SCENARIO-DRIVEN PLANNING

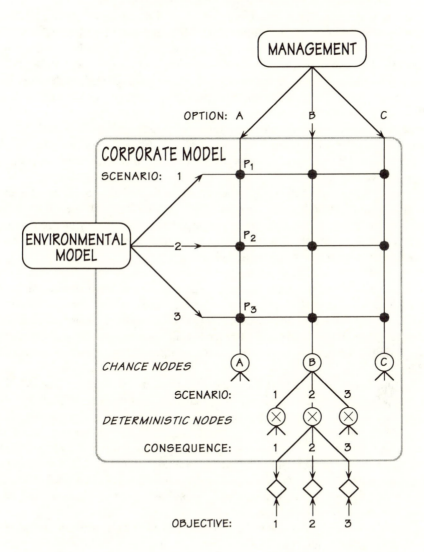

Figure A.3.3 Stochastic Modeling and Simulation in Scenario-Driven Planning (Reproduced from Amara & Lipinski, 1983)

To characterize the process that generates these outputs, Dutton, Fahey, & Narayanan use the terms: *recursiveness* (the interactive sequence of impressions and interpretations of data); *retroactivity* (the alternation or interplay of deductive and inductive modes of thinking); and *heterarchy* (the cycling back and forth between management and employees during SID). Furthermore, strategic issues generate disorderly and conflicting data that managers have to translate into information by using existing interpretive schemes or by formulating new ones.

Hence, three input factors become connected in the process of strategic issue diagnosis: mental associations, political interests, and issue characteristics. Colin Eden and his associates have shown that all three elements can be captured in a problem-solving thrust based on the use of cognitive maps (Eden, 1978, 1979, 1988). More recently, Eden describes the process of strategic options development and analysis (SODA), with computer support from a cognitive mapping package called COPE (Eden, 1989, 1990).

Scenario building has not yet been much addressed within SID itself. We do acknowledge the contributions of Coates et al. (1986) on the process of strategic issue management and tracking. In this line of work, however, scenario-driven intelligence systems are taken for granted and receive marginal treatment.

To systematize strategy design, the second author of this book developed a causal mapping method in his doctoral work at Wharton with Ackoff's group. Here, we use his method (CSM) to expand on and to improve the scenario building processes of Kahn, Wack, Ackoff, Amara & Lipinski and Porter, and to compute *strategic* scenarios through modeling and simulation.

Comprehensive situation mapping is a useful strategic situation formulation tool that can help practicing managers, consultants, and business students in strategy design from the initial situation conceptualization phase to strategic situation analysis to full-fledged system dynamics simulation modeling. Conceptualization and strategic situation analysis must precede traditional system dynamics simulation modeling to provide a powerful and flexible strategy design (Morecroft, 1985a).

The approach we borrow from Acar was used in our real-life case studies (Chapters 5, 6, and 9). It is a variety of systems analysis that can help identify requirements in each of the three major components of strategic issue diagnosis (Acar, 1983). CSM combines the advantages of cognitive mapping with an integrative desktop tool. It incorporates principles of system dynamics and systems thinking whereby relationships between strategic variables are not modeled piecemeal, but entire *situations* are captured at once. The idea is not to arbitrarily decompose strategic decision situations into problems, but to represent and then perceive them visually at a glance.

CSM acknowledges that the main parties involved in a situation are purposeful actors who can manipulate controllable levers or decision variables. Modeling the dialectical argumentation process is an essential component of direct or computerized group decision-support systems (Heintz & Acar, 1992). More sophisticated yet more mechanistic scenario-building tools, such as Battelle's BASICS and Godet's MICMAC and SMIC, could benefit from the dialectical debate feature incorporated in CSM to be used with causal mapping. These properties are fully compatible with the recommended scheme of Fig. A.3.3 and actually develop it further.

CSM has computational capabilities. By propagating change shorthand throughout the causal diagram, CSM investigates what if scenarios. It allows shorthand simulation of multiwave change scenarios throughout a causal network of environmental and firm-specific actors, factors and variables. These computational properties of CSM presage the power of scenario analysis and show the type of results managers could expect from the better scenario methods.

CSM clarifies the difference between pure and mixed scenarios of change transfer. A pure scenario can track the chain reaction of change caused by a single source within the network representing a firm's strategic situation. A mixed scenario is the result of triggers of change originating in several nodes, which fire all at once or with a time lag. These simulated events cause a variety of downstream changes in instrumental strategic variables. CSM shows how the overlay of several pure scenarios could have the same multidimensional effect as a mixed scenario. This property allows the generation of valid and sound strategic options.

Blended with its computational properties, such as the *additivity* and *transitivity* of the propagation of change (Acar, 1983) illustrated in the case studies of Parts III and V, these CSM features allow the diagramming of complex strategic situations and the computing of scenarios of changes in the environment and in a firm's strategy. These are not just loosely based on assumptions but are the computational results of propagating change through an elegant yet simple modeling technique. This technique simulates the way environmental sources affect a firm's situation by activating external triggers of change and the way internal levers might be pulled on decisively by a firm's management team.

Such scenarios simplify complex strategy designs and their implications for organizational performance and stakeholder goals. They also serve as a reminder that one could follow the road all the way to full-fledged modeling for better, more germane planning. Thus far, CSM remains a simplified, manual simulation technique for managerial convenience. Yet, it has features of the practical or low-church game theory that Shubik calls for (1987).

Because CSM has features akin to computer simulation, it can serve as a bridge between qualitative thinking and quantitative OR/MS simulation modeling. In qualitative thinking, scenarios are primarily environmental stories or hypotheses to be fed into strategy. In OR/MS simulation models, scenarios are the results of computing. This breach mirrors the "two-culture gap" of C. P. Snow; CSM and simulation techniques can bridge it.

Figure A.3.3 encapsulates the scenario modeling process. Essentially, modeling methods use both environmental scenario studies, such as Kahn's, and decision scenarios. An environmental scenario is a first-generation sequence of events and becomes an input to the computation of second-generation decision scenarios. In scope as well as in relevance, these computed scenarios surpass the environmental scenarios of Kahn and the industry scenarios of Porter. Computed scenarios are second generation because they accumulate sequences of events that are computed to be coherent, and based on the input supplied by the first-generation scenarios. This duality is implicit in Battelle's BASICS and in Godet's MICMAC methods, but it is most evident in simulation modeling methods—among which is CSM.

SUMMARY

Scenario generation is particularly helpful for the analysis of crucial, long-term investment decisions because it does not necessarily require translating the resulting events into their cash-flow implications. The power of the method resides in the fact that scenarios simply depict the events resulting from a strategic decision.

Aside from its positive effects on formulating strategic decisions productively, fostering institutional learning, and challenging psychological barriers and complacency, scenario-driven planning supports the organizational domain of strategic issue diagnosis (SID). Drawing on the work of Acar, Amara & Lipinski, Godet, Honton, Stacey, & Millet, Mason & Mitroff, and others, scenario analysis can be approached from a realistic viewpoint that should help business leaders and their planning analysts manage corporate uncertainty and strategic interdependence.

Our approach to scenario-driven planning yields a flexible yet productive method for strategy design. We define a scenario as the hypothetical sequence of events showing what can happen—not what will happen. Such event patterns are caused by the multiwave propagation of changes from the status quo, throughout a causal network of environmental change triggers and organizational decision levers.

The causal network of CSM is a visual representation of the perceived reality. This network is, in essence, an educated hunch or entrepreneurial statement about the nature and structure of a firm's strategic decision situation. Propagating change scenarios becomes the means of exploring the future implications of that vision. The overriding goal of scenario-driven planning is to create the necessary conceptual framework for filtering the product of observation and extracting coherent information from it, to make ready to learn from experience.

The Art of Organizational Learning

> *The successful executive of the 1990s,*
> *instead of merely adjusting to new paradigms,*
> *is actually going to create them.*
> —Werner Erhardt

Socrates argued that virtue is knowledge; Ackoff concurs. The act of engaging in modeling for learning is one of the main benefits of scenario-driven planning. Scenario undertakings that convey an effective description of their causal diagrams, or full-fledged simulation models, can help an organization learn from experience. Yet a gap between a model's assumptions and computed scenarios may require a quantum leap in logic and thereby undermine confidence in modeling strategic situations; for the logic underlying the composition of macroenvironmental scenarios can be quite elusive. The prescientific state of the art in modeling social systems may account for this hurdle. The second part of this appendix reflects on the valuable suggestions that independent consultant Peter Schwartz has made on the connection between the art of the long view and scenario-driven planning.

B.1   MODELING: PRELUDE TO ORGANIZATIONAL LEARNING

People often begin their business career with little quantitative maturity, along with little interest in and great resistance to the art of rough-cut mapping and modeling of strategic situations. Deeply held prejudices against anything quantitative surface quickly at work, inevitably blocking some otherwise brilliant career paths. This is unfortunate because in today's business every real-world event, action, and dynamic behavior pattern can easily relate to the unfolding art of modeling strategic decision situations. In a sense all of us, general managers, strategy students, and business policy professors, are already expert modelers, for we all carry in our heads our own models of the past, present, and future (Ingvar, 1985). These mental models reside somewhere between our ears to help us deal with uncertainty, frustration, criticism, and success. Being the product of our daily contact with reality, mental models determine how we deal with what we don't know and how we employ what we do know. A mental model is a prerequisite for formulating an explicit model of a firm's strategic situation.

An explicit or formal model still is a selective representation of the manager's daily contact with the reality of business. The modeling process provides a different way of seeing business problems, a different mind-set for thinking about strategic situations and for learning faster from their experiential ramifications. The relevance of modeling for learning to today's general manager and strategy student has much to do with their daily struggle to define, refine, and reperceive their contact with reality (de Geus, 1992; Senge, 1990; Senge & Sterman, 1992; Sterman, 1985, 1989; Zeleny, 1991).

Modeling What?

Modeling a strategic situation entails discovering and studying the intended rationality that is usually embedded in a firm's decision functions. Often, it requires capturing unknown and unknowable aspects of a social system that may be neither easy to observe nor easy to measure. Yet, the process of modeling can help a firm better understand itself, its strengths and weaknesses, its long-term goals and the strategy it must design to attain those goals (Forrester, 1992).

Modeling strategic situations is not a narrow specialty, but the admission of a firm's strategic limitations and of environmental complexity and turbulence. Modeling and computed scenarios can help today's modern organizations understand what they don't know. "We model what we do *not* know, not what we know" (Eppen, Gould, & Schmidt, 1991, p. xviii). Modeling serves many purposes on many organizational levels. One is to help a firm improve its decision-making quality, its management capability. To do this, general managers and strategy students learn and use the new technology of scenario-driven planning.

Increasingly, managers are also viewing computed scenarios as sources of new knowledge and as "intelligence amplifiers" that stimulate creativity and institutional learning (de Geus, 1988, 1992; Istvan, 1992; Merten, 1991; Senge, 1990; Senge & Sterman, 1992). Scenario-driven planning developments include

- Improvements in the symbols and software for mapping and modeling of strategic situations.
- Behavioral decision theory ideas for capturing the knowledge of decision makers into causal models.
- Improvements in simulation and scenario analysis that let modelers and model users gain better insight into firms' dynamic behavior.
- Emphasis on mental models, games, and dialogue between mental models and computed scenarios (Hurst, Rush & White, 1989; Morecroft, 1988).

Management teams now use system dynamics to create *microworlds* or *knowledge incubators* (Papert, 1980), which allow structuring informed debates about changes in strategy, in a process where mental models and computed scenarios become an integral part of debate and dialogue (Hall, 1984; Morecroft, 1992).

As in other areas of learning, even such esoteric areas as car racing and bar tending, scenario-driven planning requires learning a new language. Good racecar drivers are also good mechanics. Similarly, a good understanding of a firm's strategic situation comes, among other things, from an understanding of the mechanics in modeling tools, from the rough-cut mapping of influence diagramming (or ID) to full-fledged modeling and computer simulation (system dynamics).

Comprehensive situation mapping can help a firm make the transition from rough-cut mapping to modeling a strategic situation (Acar, 1983; Acar, Chaganti, & Joglekar, 1985; Georgantzas & Acar, 1989; Offodile & Acar, 1993). This transition is necessary, for US firms must stop inflicting wounds on themselves by separating knowledge from action. To move productively forward, we submit that those who know must become those who act, and vice versa.

Although improving strategic decision quality, and thereby productivity (Deming, 1986), is a prudent goal for any firm, the true purpose of improving quality and productivity in strategic management lies in the benefit of personal improvement through the modeling of strategic situations. To paraphrase Robert Pirsig's (1974) art of motorcycle maintenance, the real model a management team is working on is the model of itself. In other words, modeling forces clear thinking.

There are two traps to avoid in modeling a firm's strategic situation. The first has to do with managers whose longtime immersion in a particular system may prevent them from distinguishing the system as it is from the system they wished it were. Both wishful thinking and strong prejudices are hazards to successful modeling of strategic situation and dynamic analysis. The second trap has to do with outside consultants whose concealed prejudices or insufficient firmness with causal modeling may lead them to modeling the strategic situation that was initially thought to be present or was wished to be present (Forrester, 1961 p. 452).

The following section presents a modeling process that can be used in a wide range of modeling efforts. It also highlights some common mistakes that novices tend to make (Randers, 1980).

The Modeling Process

In the early phases of modeling a strategic situation, it may be helpful to try modeling a business or social process rather than a business or social system. Generally, it is more productive to identify a social process and ask about its cause than to slice a chunk of the real world and ask what kind of dynamic behavior pattern it will generate. Distinguishing between a social system and a social process is roughly equivalent to distinguishing between a system's underlying structure and its dynamic behavior patterns.

Jørgen Randers defines a *social system* as a set of cause and effect relationships, with its model structure being a causal diagram, a map of the real-world chunk chosen for study. A *social process* is a dynamic behavior pattern of events evolving over time. The simulation results of full-fledged system dynamics models usually portray such chains of events as they might occur in the real world (Randers, 1980, p. 120).

An example of a social system (structure) is the set of rules and practices that a firm might enact when dealing with swift changes in demand, along with the communication channels used for transmitting information and managerial decisions. A corresponding social process (behavior pattern) might be the stop-and-go pattern of capital investment caused by a conservative bias in the firm's corporate culture. Forrester (1968a) incorporates such a conservative facet of corporate culture in his model of a firm's fast-growing new product line. Sales stagnated because considerable back orders had to accumulate to justify expansion. The firm's president insisted on personally controlling the approval of all capital expenditures.

The common tendency is to begin by describing system structure; it seems to arise from its tangible nature as opposed to the elusive character of its dynamic behavior pattern. In addition, modelers usually present model structure before model behavior in their final reports. Ultimately, the goal in modeling a firm's strategic situation is to link system structure and behavior. Yet, in the early stages of modeling, it is preferable to start with a description of a system's dynamic behavior pattern and then proceed with the identification of underlying causes.

The Ackoff-Ozbekhan reference scenario (i.e., the development over time of a social process a firm would have had if there were no significant changes in its strategy and environment) often serves as a tangible manifestation of the social process portrayed by the model output. Using this reference scenario or behavior pattern helps identify the smallest possible set of cause-effect relationships among the variables pertinent to the firm's strategic situation capable of producing the reference scenario. A firm's strategic situation is best portrayed in such a reference scenario (Ackoff, 1981; Ozbekhan, 1977), while the small network of cause-effect relationships among the variables pertinent to the firm's strategic situation plays a crucial role in understanding its nature and underlying system structure (Randers, 1980, p. 121).

The modeling process itself is recursive in nature. The path from real-world events, trends, and negligible externalities to an effective formal model usually resembles the curve of Fig. B.1.1, which is irregularly oscillating both in frequency and in amplitude (width).

An effective formal model can only be produced through effective conceptualization, which focuses the modeling effort by establishing both the time horizon and the perspective from which a strategic situation will be framed. Typically, strategic situation models require adopting a long-term horizon, over which the likely effects of changes in policy and in the environment are assessed by computing strategic change scenarios.

Effective formulation is another requirement to effective modeling. Casting the chosen policy perspective into a formal representation entails postulating a detailed structure, a diagramming description precise enough to propagate images of alternative futures (i.e., scenarios), "though not necessarily accurate" (Randers, 1980, p. 118).

The detailed model structure will vary depending on the modeling method used. In comprehensive situation mapping, for example, all nodes represent *level* variables that accumulate the change transmitted to them over time. Yet, CSM distinguishes between *full channels* and *partial channels* of change transfer through double-line (⟹) and single-line (⟶) arrows, respectively, while it accounts for strategic limitations qualitatively through broken-line (- - ➤) arrows. Both time lags and change coefficients accompany each double- and single-line arrow in CSM to quantify the transmission of change throughout the causal network of interrelated variables over time.

Casting the chosen policy perspective into a system dynamics model entails postulating a detailed structure of stock □, flow  and auxiliary or converter ○ variables, combined into infrastructures and feedback-loop relationships

Figure B.1.1 The Recursive Nature of Strategic Situation Formulation

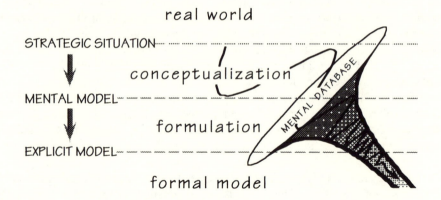

through single-line information connectors ↖₀ . "Only information leads into a decision function" (Forrester, 1961, p. 82).

The full-fledged modeling method of system dynamics requires a more detailed selection of parameter values and algebra than CSM. On the other hand, the built-in and graphical table functions of accompanying computer simulation languages and packages allow testing a model's behavior and sensitivity to changes in strategy and environmental perturbations.

Formulating a firm's strategic situation requires selecting parameter values and algebra in system dynamics simulation, and change transmittance coefficients and time lags in CSM. These allow propagating multiwave change scenarios of alternative futures by capturing the combined effects of changes in both the environment and the firm's strategy.

Quantifying the relationships among the variables pertinent to a strategic situation adds specificity to a model and thereby yields a much deeper understanding of a situation's nature and structure than qualitative conceptualization alone. There is a *big* difference between quantifying and measuring things. Everything can be quantified (or translated into numbers) for the sake of specificity, including the relationship between two variables pertinent to a strategic situation. But measuring is another story. There are a few things that we actually measure in our daily lives. Most of us never bother to measure the density of heat in a room, for example, but manage it quite effectively by using the arbitrarily quantified level of alcohol or mercury in a glass tube as a rough indicator of temperature. Yet, the process of modeling a firm's strategic situation should never downplay the managers' mental database and its information content as the management and social sciences often do. Effective modeling always draws on the mental database (Forrester, 1987, 1992).

The heavily traced hyperbolas of Fig. B.1.1 suggest that the quantity of information may decrease, by orders of magnitude, while the required quantification of the relationships among variables pertinent to a strategic situation changes the character of the information content as one moves from mental to written to numerical information. Perceptibly, a smaller quantity of information remains, but it is most pertinent to the nature and structure of the real-world strategic situation.

Mental, written, and numerical information plays different roles in shaping the formal model of a firm's strategic situation. The dominant role that the mental database plays in modeling will be appreciated if we visualize what would happen if a firm's managers let written policies and numerical information alone guide their actions. This going strictly by the book might be perceived as equivalent to a strike in some parts of the world. The mental database provides the raw material for modeling. In turn, the art in modeling expands, refines, and thereby improves the mental database. This is the fine art of modeling as a prelude to organizational learning in scenario-driven planning.

B.2   THE ART OF PLOT COMPOSITION

Macroenvironmental scenarios are an essential part of the input to scenario-driven planning. They describe how environmental forces might plausibly behave in the future. Often, the same set of driving forces behave in different ways, according to different possible plots. Macroenvironmental scenarios explore alternative futures on the basis of written plots or combinations of plots.

What is finding a plot line really like? Worth considering is the answer provided by Peter Schwartz (1991). This section draws almost exclusively on Schwartz's work, *The Art of the Long View*.

> Here is how it works in nearly every scenario situation in which I have taken part. We gather a team together who are aware of the decision that we are considering. Each member has done his or her research. We sit around talking for a day, developing ideas in response to these questions:
>
> • What are the driving forces?
> • What do you feel is uncertain?
> • What is inevitable?
> • How about this or that scenario?

For Schwartz, characters are the limiting blocks of scenarios. He illustrates the importance of characters by recounting what happens next. When he and his co-participants get to a point where ideas are churning, they break off for the night. The next morning, someone walks in with an idea for a scenario. Although the author of the scenario idea proceeds to describe it, someone else across the table may venture to elaborate some complementary notions.

Intriguingly, Schwartz compares this part of the scenario process to writing a movie script. He stresses that, although scriptwriters frequently begin with an idea, they soon develop characters. For example, in a film about car racing, shouldn't at least one character be a hot racer? One may want to see him race his childhood friend. Other characters may include the girlfriend, a crusty old mechanic, and other auxiliaries.

Schwartz pursues this analogy in his writing on scenarios. Having decided on the escape film characters, he creates a plausible setting for them: all four characters have gathered at the Indianapolis Speedway. What will happen next? Now the scriptwriters finally are in a position to consider several possible plots. Maybe the story will be based on rivalry over the championship and the girl. If so, conflict and competition become part of the deal. Predictable ending without a scenario? Schwartz throws this thought in:

> But what if the real thrust is the old man's education of two young drivers?

Then it's a plot about the challenges these young people deliberately face, and how they learn to develop prowess. A more interesting movie might combine both plots, or throw in a sudden and unexpected (but possible) event: halfway through the movie, one of the car racers is abruptly crippled.

Next, we summarize Schwartz's suggestions and recommendations.

Schwartz's Macroenvironmental Scenario Rules of Thumb

1. Schwartz warns against ending up with three scenarios because people may be tempted to identify one of the three as the "middle" or "most likely" scenario and then treat it as a single-point forecast. Then all the advantages of multiple scenarios might be lost.
2. Similarly, computing too many scenarios might blur the differences among them, so that they can lose their meaningful distinctions as decision-making tools.
3. Assigning probabilities to scenarios might be tempting, but it is dangerous. It is natural to consider seriously only the scenario with the highest probability. Schwartz recommends developing a pair of equally highly probable scenarios and a pair of potentially high-impact but relatively low-probability or "wild card" scenarios.
4. If probabilities must be used, one should never compare the probability of an event in one macroenvironmental scenario to the probability of another event in another macroenvironmental scenario. The two events are assumed to take place in radically different contexts, and the assignment of probabilities depends on entirely different assumptions about the future.
5. Vivid and memorable names may help macroenvironmental scenarios make their way into a firm's decisions. Schwartz recalls how Shell's world of internal contradictions (WIC) scenario survived for more than a decade because its name evoked a "powerful and evocative concept."
6. According to Schwartz, four major considerations should guide the selection of a scenario development team:
   a. Support and participation from top management is essential.
   b. Those who make and implement decisions should be involved in the creation of macroenvironmental scenarios.
   c. A broad range of functions and divisions should be represented on the scenario development team.
   d. Imaginative people with open minds who can work well together as a team should be selected.

7. Schwartz considers macroenvironmental scenarios effective when

   a. They are both plausible and surprising.
   b. They have the power to break old stereotypes.
   c. Their makers assume ownership of them and put them to work.
   d. Scenario-driven planning is intensely participatory, otherwise it fails.

Schwartz's Steps to Developing Macroenvironmental Scenarios

STEP 1: *Focal Issue or Decision*. Schwartz recommends starting "from the inside out" rather than "from the outside in," with a specific decision or issue and then build out toward the environment. Also, he recommends asking what decision makers in the firm will be thinking hard about in the near future as a prelude to investigating those decisions that will have a long-term effect on the firm's fortunes.

We agree with his assessment that scenarios developed on the basis of differences in the macroeconomy, that is, high versus low growth, may not highlight differences that make a difference to a particular company. He cites the example of a movie studio. Clearly, to a movie studio different approaches to product diffusion or new distribution technology would generate more useful scenarios than simple variations on economic growth. One could also think of other examples: a person buying a home will want to think about interest rates and the housing market; a construction firm might want to look at scenarios that differ around the number of housing starts; a defense contractor will conjure up scarecrow peace scenarios, and so on.

He also recommends, and here we concur with less enthusiasm, starting with important decisions and the mind-set of the managers making them. Most of all, "What is it that keeps me awake at night?"

STEP 2: *Industry Forces*. The second step follows logically from the first. Once a focal issue or decision has been identified, Schwartz suggests listing the variables affecting the success or failure of each decision—for example, facts about customers, suppliers, and competitors. He considers the questioning to be three-pronged:

   • What will decision makers want to know when making each decision?
   • What will they see as success or failure?
   • What considerations will shape those outcomes?

Clearly, however, it is the third question that is of great interest; the principal merit of the first two is to bring it up.

STEP 3: *Environmental Forces.* Although Schwartz's approach is more procedurally than methodologically based, it is valuable in that it aims at digging deeper. Its third step consists of listing the driving trends in the macroenvironment affecting the variables identified earlier. In addition to the checklist of socioeconomic-political, environmental, and technological forces, another route to the relevant aspects of the macro environment is the question: What are the forces behind the microenvironmental forces identified in step two?

Usually, these forces entail either predetermined demographics or uncertain public opinion. One has to agree with Schwartz that it is useful to know what is inevitable and necessary and what is unpredictable and still a matter of choice.

Research is usually required to adequately define the driving forces. It may cover new markets, technology, political issues, economic forces, and so on. One is searching for major trends and for breaks in major trends. The trends are the most difficult to find because novelty is difficult to anticipate—but read on.

STEP 4: *Importance and Uncertainty Ranking.* The purpose here is to identify two or three environmental trends that are most important and most uncertain. Scenarios cannot differ over predetermined elements, such as demographics or resource constraints, because these have to be the same in all scenarios. According to Schwartz as well as his predecessors, environmental variables and driving trends should be ranked on the basis of two criteria:

1. The importance for the success of the focal issue or decision identified in step one.
2. The uncertainty surrounding factors and trends.

STEP 5: *Scenario Logic.* Ranking the most pertinent variables and principal environmental trends indirectly indicates the primary dimensions along which the scenarios will differ. It is important to determine the location of each scenario along these "axes." According to Schwartz, the goal is to end up with just a few scenarios whose differences make a difference to decision makers. Yet, it might be more productive to end up with a set of parameters or scenario drivers, which can be skillfully combined to generate the highly relevant limit-case scenarios.

Once the fundamental axes of uncertainty have been identified, it is useful to present them as a continuum (unidimensionally), a matrix (bidimensionally), or a volume (tridimensionally) in which different scenarios can be identified and their details filled in. The logic of a given scenario will be characterized by its location in the matrix of most significant macroenvironmental scenario drivers.

One may have to watch out for an exponential increase in the total number of scenarios. To function as useful learning tools, scenarios must relate to the success of focal decisions. Fundamental differences or scenario *drivers* must be limited to a few, in our opinion, to avoid writing scenarios around every possible uncertainty. Many things can happen, but only a few scenarios can be developed in detail; otherwise the process dissipates.

In the end, macroenvironmental scenario logic may boil down to changes in a few variables, but the process for getting there is neither simple nor mechanical. It is more like reflecting on a set of basic or core issues until you have reshaped and regrouped them in such a way that a logic emerges and meaningful stories can be told.

Schwartz's own example makes our case for us. In his example, if an automobile company determines that fuel prices and protectionism are two of the most important scenario drivers, there will be four basic scenarios:

1. High fuel prices in a protectionist environment: in which case domestic suppliers of small cars have an advantage.
2. High fuel prices in a global economy: in which case fuel-efficient imports capture the low end of the market.
3. Low fuel prices in a protectionist environment: in which case American gas guzzlers have a good market at home but not abroad.
4. Low fuel prices in a global economy: in which case there is intense global competition for fuel-efficient models, but larger cars enjoy strong foreign markets.

Schwartz concludes his series of recommended steps by remarking that, once the macroenvironmental scenarios have been fleshed out and their implications determined, it may be worth spending time and imagination on identifying a few indicators to monitor further. For a firm can gain an edge on its competition by knowing what the future might hold for its industry and how the future might affect changes in the strategies of incumbent firms.

In Schwartz's experience, if the macroenvironmental scenarios have been built according to the previous steps, then they will be able to translate the movements of a few leading indicators into an orderly set of industry-specific implications. One may come to see how the logical coherence built into the scenarios may lead to plausible implications of leading indicators under each macroenvironmental scenario.

SUMMARY

The goal in modeling a firm's strategic situation is to link system structure and behavior. Modeling and computed scenarios can help today's modern organizations understand what they don't know, if they model what they don't know as opposed to what they do know. The modeling process provides a different way of seeing business problems, a different mind-set for thinking about strategic situations and for learning faster from their experiential ramifications. The relevance of modeling for learning to today's general manager and strategy student has much to do with their daily struggle to define, to refine, and to reperceive their contact with reality.

Modeling serves many purposes on many organizational levels. A good understanding of a firm's strategic situation depends on an understanding of the mechanics in modeling tools, from rough-cut mapping (ID) to full-fledged modeling and computer simulation (system dynamics). Comprehensive situation mapping can help a firm make the transition from rough-cut mapping to modeling a strategic situation. This transition is necessary for US firms to stop inflicting wounds on themselves by separating knowledge from action.

Quantifying the relationships among the variables pertinent to a strategic situation yields a much deeper understanding of a situation's nature and structure than qualitative conceptualization alone. This is not to downplay the managers' mental database and its information content, for the mental database provides the raw material for modeling. In turn, the art in modeling expands, refines, and thereby improves the mental database. This is the organizational learning that scenario-driven planning generates.

The art in constructing macroenvironmental scenarios entails weaving the pieces of environmental scanning and analysis together in narrative plots. Macroenvironmental scenarios should be built around a firm's strategic situation to rehearse its future. Ultimately, the value of scenario-driven planning stems from its ability to determine what changes in a firm's strategy can make it adaptable and productive if the desired future does not show signs of materializing.

Appendix C

Intelligence-Amplifying Tools

Increasingly, managers are viewing the developments in scenario-driven planning as a source of new knowledge and are using them to stimulate creativity and institutional learning. The management teams of world-class firms use formal problem-solving tools ranging from influence diagramming to system dynamics models to create microworlds or knowledge incubators, in a process where mental models and computed scenarios become an integral part of debate and learning. Future-oriented firms use full-fledged computer simulation models and compute both environmental and strategic scenarios in order to structure informed debates about changes in strategy. This appendix presents a synoptic overview of the intelligence-amplifying techniques used in this book.

C.1   INFLUENCE DIAGRAMMING (ID)

Background: Early Developments

It is often said that a picture is worth a thousand words. Whereas ancient and medieval texts, even treatises on natural science subjects, were almost entirely devoid of illustrations, recent centuries have seen an increasing reliance on (more or less abstract) diagrams to complement verbal descriptions in textbooks, essays, lectures, and so on. Modern authors or lecturers, generally familiar with some elements of geometry and set theory, abundantly punctuate their delivery with diagrams and doodles of one type or another. Even the idea of a pattern in anthropology, under the pen of a contemporary author such as Diesing (1971, pp. 157-164), sometimes takes the meaning of a network of attitudes and behavior elements connected by lines or arrows.

The diagramming conventions used are seldom made explicit. The implicit meaning can sometimes be gathered from the fact that either the elements of the diagram or the links among them appear to have a single possible interpretation, as in the case of the diagram in Fig. C.1.1a. More often than not, the elements and linkages of the diagram belong to different categories as in the case of the diagram in Fig. C.1.1b.

The links of the diagram in Fig. C.1.1a appear to be of a causal-chronological nature, while its elements are all events in some sense. Yet, the elements of Fig. C.1.1b cannot be as easily classified under the same category:

- Element #1 could be viewed either as a quantified variable or as an event.
- Elements #2 and #3 could be events or evaluations.
- Element #4 could be a qualitative variable or a constraint.
- Element #5 is clearly a decision rule.

Similarly, the interpretation of the links of Fig. C.1.1b is ambiguous because its elements cannot be subsumed under the same type.

Actually, ambiguity may be desirable during the initial phases of problem framing through causal mapping, while the participants are still searching for those elements they would like to include in their framing of the situation under consideration. Zeleny (1988) concurs that the language and label systems that managers initially use to coordinate their knowledge-derived choices are both *imprecise* and *fuzzy*. Initially fuzzy language, Zeleny states, is not only adequate and effective for managing strategic uncertainty and interdependence, but also required.

Figure C.1.1 Diagrams whose Elements may Possess
(a) a Single Interpretation, or
(b) Varying Interpretations

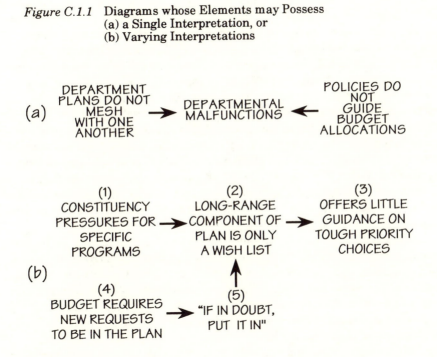

The assumptional analysis that takes place as the problem-framing process unfolds, however, can be facilitated if the participants manage to understand one another. This does not prevent participants from clinging to their own views of the situation. A minimal level of understanding requires that everyone present understand the language used. Specifically, the supporting causal mapping must evolve from a free-form doodling, favoring creativity through self expression, to a more disciplined diagramming, following shared conventions, to favor analysis.

In order for diagramming support to clarify an issue or to illustrate a situation, the diagramming convention has to be made explicit. What makes diagramming valuable in formulating decision situations is that it can serve as a simplified *model* of the situation, a model that can lend itself to some form of analysis. It then becomes all the more important to know how the model maps out the real situation into the diagram on which one ends up working.

Many authors have devised procedures for diagramming situations by means of systematic conventions (Hall, 1978, 1984). Some of them have attempted a causal orientation (Acar, 1983). For example, Hennessey et al. (1978) recommend using a fishbone diagram to represent the many visible symptoms attributable to a few causes to be agreed upon by the problem framing session participants.

The fishbone structure of Hennessey's cause-symptom-effect diagram is similar to the one advocated by Inoue & Riggs (1971). It is a structure that helps perform what is becoming known as the *backstep analysis* of a problem. This is a procedural aid to problem formulation in which one proceeds from a problem backward to its presumed causes. The search process of backstep analysis entails writing down the perceived problem as the end point of a converging treelike diagram, and working backward by writing down all the elements that could possibly lead to this end point.

In Fig. C.1.2, for example, of which many variants circulate in the problem framing literature, starting with city air pollution as an end point, one would write down *emissions* and *the weather* as possible contributors to city air pollution. Looking at emissions, one might write down *automobile, industrial,* and *other* as clusters of the potential emission sources, and so on. The complete diagram of Fig. C.1.2 becomes a model of the multitude of causal influences that combine to generate a particular problematic effect.

In this sense, backstep analysis is germane to the idea that it takes several coproducers to produce an effect. Also, the chainlike view of causality implicit in the procedure emphasizes the oft-forgotten fact that every cause conjured up can itself be viewed as the effect of some more distant cause. This brings in a useful influence for seeing things in context, which is largely what problem framing is about.

Backstep analysis is eminently amenable to group problem formulation. In such a setting, an additional advantage can be gained by making use of teamwork for brainstorming the likely causes of a problem at first and then testing whether they are reasonable and selecting among them.

Figure C.1.2   Backstep Analysis Diagram

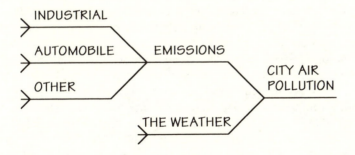

The above advantages of backstep analysis can accompany any problem-framing method that entails a causal diagramming procedure. The fact that most problem-framing methods attempt something of the kind is not purely coincidental.

Influence Diagramming (ID)

One of the major drawbacks of backstep analysis, however, is that it lacks adequate methodological controls. Generally, the causal interpretation is not uniform throughout cause and effect diagrams except in a very loose sense. In Fig. C.1.2, for example, *emissions* and *the weather* are contributors to city air pollution. Yet, *automobile* and *industrial* can be viewed as classes of emissions as well as contributors to them. The same haziness as to the exact interpretation of the implied causalities plagues the fishbone diagramming of Inoue & Riggs (1971). These authors label "causal analysis" a backstep diagramming procedure that has a similar fishbone-like structure, but in which the branches represent variable clusters, that is, factors, rather than major causes.

Although the representation of Hennessey et al. (1978) is more causally oriented than that of Inoue & Riggs (1971), it still presents problems. The solution to the excessive ambiguity of loosely defined causal maps does not reside in specifying its topography, but in classifying its symbolism and in a stricter connection with causal concepts. The majority of causal mapping authors appear to perceive this notion, for they depart from the representation of causes tapering into a single end point (the "problem") characteristic of backstep analysis. For example, Inoue & Riggs (1971) recommend extending their "causal analysis" diagram by another tree, starting with the problem as its root and then expanding into the downstream of effects and their consequences. They label their expanding tree effect analysis diagram.

Gilmore et al. (1982) extend this idea even further. Once the tree of causes and the tree of effects have been drawn, they recommend also examining and specifying the direct links among causes and effects so as to detect the presence of vicious circles. In other works performed by Wharton's Management and Behavioral Science Center, a flexible free-form diagramming structure is followed to allow focusing on the totality of the situation under consideration, as opposed to starting with an imputed problem.

Maruyama adopted the free-form diagramming layout in his work on deviation-amplifying mutual causal processes (1963), and later (1979) Weick followed suit. Echoing Forrester's (1975) point on the *non*intuitive nature of social systems, Weick states that managers can literally be said to "get into trouble because they forget to think in circles." He advocates causal diagramming because causalities are seldom unidirectional. If one looks for *the* cause of an event or a phenomenon, it will not be found because it is not there.

Figure C.1.3   Influence Diagram (ID) of a City's Health and Migration Management Situation (Adapted from Maruyama, 1963)

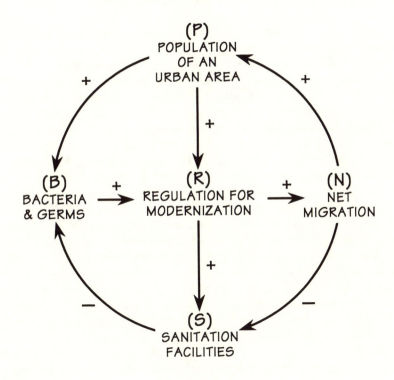

The influence diagramming (ID) example on which both Maruyama (1963) and Weick (1979) base their discussion has been adapted in Fig. C.1.3. Because the elements in the diagram are quantified variables, it is meaningful to talk of changes in them, in the form of increases or decreases in their levels.

These variables are connected by directed links (arrows), each qualified by a plus or minus sign. The ID of Fig. C.1.3 is a rough-cut model diagram linking elements of a specified kind with links of a specified nature: a + sign next to each arrow indicates that the two variables it connects change similarly, and a − sign indicates that the variables connected move in opposite directions.

The diagram indicates that an increase in sanitation facilities (S) generates a decrease in disease-causing bacteria and germs (B). Such a system has a number of loops. Maruyama points out that loops indicate mutual-causal relationships because in each loop the change in a variable comes back to affect it through other variables.

Simply looking at an influence diagram of a situation gives a qualitative idea of its structure. The ID identifies the elements abstracted from the situation, as well as the directions and signs of the influences among them. For example, it can be seen that the regulation for modernization node R increases the amount of sanitation facilities, but the effect of net migration (N) is to make them decrease in proportion to their previous relative level.

Maruyama also points out that additional information can be gathered from examining the loops. For example, loops $N \cdot P \cdot R \cdot N$ and $N \cdot P \cdot B \cdot R \cdot N$ indicate that an increase in the population of a city increases its modernization regulation, which increases migration to the city. This in turn increases the population of the city. Yet, path $P \cdot B \cdot R \cdot S \cdot B$ indicates that an increase in population causes an increase in bacteria & germs, which increase the disease control and sanitation facilities, which cause a decrease in deadly diseases. The negative sign next to the N·S arrow indicates that an increase in net migration strains the resources of and renders the existing sanitation facilities inadequate by making them proportionately smaller than before such a positive change in N occurs.

An increase in population causes a further increase in population through modernization and immigration, but also a decrease in population through garbage, bacteria, and disease. $P \cdot R \cdot N \cdot P$ is thus a deviation-amplifying loop, and $B \cdot R \cdot S \cdot B$ is a deviation-counteracting one.

Chapter 5 gives another detailed example of influence diagramming, describing the rough-cut mapping and modeling experience of Infoplus (A) with ID.

Cognitive Mapping at the University of Bath

A large research effort appears to be ongoing at the University of Bath about problem formulation in teams (Eden, 1988). For the conceptual underpinning of the modeling they are proposing, the Bath authors turn to the theory of personal constructs proposed by cognitive psychologists Kelly (1955) and Bannister & Fransella (1971). In this theory, a person's conceptual construction of the world is seen as composed of a finite number of dichotomous constructs, each having two poles. According to Eden (1979), such bipolar constructs can become the building blocks for strategic problem framing through *cognitive mapping*.

Most cognitive mapping varieties seek to understand exactly how people associate concepts in their minds. Applications of cognitive mapping are associated with research aimed at uncovering people's perceptions or mental models. Cognitive mapping thus differs from MS/OR modeling, in which a model of the dynamic structure underlying a decision situation is not meant to be an accurate representation of it, but simply an acceptable approximation for analysis (Ackoff, 1978).

A number of sophisticated computer programs are being developed at the Center for the Study of Organizational Change and Development, School of Management, University of Bath, to express cognitive modeling. The main idea is to elicit the set of linguistic constructs that managers use to define and redefine a set of variables pertinent to a strategic decision situation. Eden et al., (1981) discuss in some detail how this is done with unipolar and bipolar elements. Coding an individual's beliefs and values about a problematic situation and then running Eden's computer program allows us to obtain the individual's cognitive map of the situation. A detailed example of exactly how this is done can be found in Eden & Radford (1990) and in Flood & Jackson (1991).

The work of the Bath School of Management group is vast and still progressing. The importance of giving concrete formulation to the cognitive mappings of Kelly, Bannister & Fransella, and Hinkle is evident to psychology researchers. And one cannot help but be impressed by the magnitude of the task undertaken and the amount achieved. Although not all the achievement is in the line of problem framing, we concur with Eden et al. (1981) on the capability of consulting to represent field-dependent data diagrammatically as structured situations.

Yet, Kelly's authority notwithstanding, does the diagrammatic representation of strategic situations have to follow the route of psychological mapping? Do the links of a cognitive map represent causal relationships or simply mental associations among bipolar connected concepts? Causality has a specific and restricted meaning: It implies time precedence, necessity, and sufficiency (Ackoff & Emery, 1972).

Not all forms of psychological associations among mental constructs imply the perception of a causal linkage. Throughout a consulting intervention, cognitive mapping is useful for the participants to acquire a sense of each other's cognitive processes. The types of mapping developed by the Bath group are very useful in this regard as auxiliary rough-cut mapping tools. Yet, they may not be the most effective and efficient way to model strategic decision situations.

Some cognitive mapping authors have revived a sociometric notion developed in the 1950s and early 1960s and thereby attach a significant interpretation to what sociometrists called the in-degree and out-degree of a node in a directed graph of "digraph" (Harary, Norman, & Cartwright, 1965). *In-degree* is the number of lines or vectors leading into a node, whereas *out-degree* is the number of lines emanating from it. Some cognitive mappers use the out-degree to measure the effect of a particular variable on other variables of a digraph. This notion is intuitively appealing. Yet, there is no theoretical basis for construing the out-degree as either a measure or even a correlate of the importance of a variable.

Diffenbach (1982) and Ramaprasad & Poon (1985) use the sociometric concept of total influence, which they compute by summing up the number of direct and indirect nth-order relationships (Harary et al., 1965). Though more sophisticated than Weick's generalizations stemming from mere inspection of causal loops, this treatment also presents problems. First, it ascribes a real interpretation to the arrows linking variables. Second, it assumes that all elementary links are of equal importance; to compensate, this calls for the added burden of weighing the links at or up to the nth-step of an aggregation procedure.

The basic worldview of most mapping techniques is that some order may be extracted from situations that may appear unstructured. Whether this order is inherent to the situation, as some OR/MS positivists believe, or in the eye of the beholder, according to pragmatists, has been debated (Churchman, 1968). Be that as it may, we need not ascribe a positivist interpretation to the causal mapping approach of the following section because our concern is to explore the analytical advantage gained by certain modes of diagrammatic representation.

We retain from the Bath approach the idea of situation mapping as the means to problem defining and that of running scenarios as a way to explore implications. The mapping we propose is both defined unambiguously and linked explicitly to causality. In the original spirit of MS/OR, we view a causal map as a temporary model of a situation for the purpose of analyzing it and exploring its implications. Our device for accomplishing this modeling is Acar's (1983) comprehensive situation mapping (CSM).

C.2   COMPREHENSIVE SITUATION MAPPING (CSM)

Background: Systems Concepts

Decision tools using diagrams to cope with complexity are not new. Precedence diagrams, such as PERT (program evaluation and review technique) and CPM (critical path method), are well-known business planning tools. A range of mapping techniques, somewhat imprecisely referred to as *causal mapping*, is well established and benefits from a growing literature. One such mapping tool is Acar's comprehensive situation mapping (CSM).

Closely linked to the development of signal flowgraph analysis (Hall, 1962; Huggins & Entwisle, 1968; Lorens, 1964), CSM belongs to the cognitive mapping (Eden, 1988) family of diagramming representations. A sophisticated extension of the influence diagramming (ID) described in the preceding section, CSM overcomes the limitations of ID without introducing undue complexity (Acar, 1983; Acar, Chaganti, & Joglekar, 1985).

Churchman (1969, 1971) presents the systems approach as a continuing debate between attitudes of mind with respect to society. Within the vast systems thinking movement (Churchman, 1971; Forrester, 1958; Senge, 1990; Senge & Sterman, 1992; Sterman, 1985; Weick, 1979), a number of concepts and theories are emerging. A problem-framing method should make use of, or be compatible with, some systems concepts.

The *first* concept is that of a *system* and the notion of causality it entails. The Renaissance and post-Renaissance eras viewed nature as comprising small comprehensible parts in which it is ultimately decomposable. The process of inquiry most congruent with this view is analysis. For the analysis of a whole consists of disassembling it into parts, examining the parts and trying to understand the whole in light of the parts. According to Ackoff (1981), this reductionism was accompanied by a deterministic view of causality. Specifically, it was assumed that examining the parts is sufficient to understand the whole and that considering the environment is not necessary for this purpose. The causal relationship implicit in this view is the simple cause and effect relationship between two variables.

In contrast, the contribution of the recent systems worldview is not limited to telling us that a system has parts and is itself a part of a suprasystem, but is a rich concept of what a system is. A system is now viewed as a set of two or more elements, each of which has an effect on the whole system, and the effect of each element depends on the effects of the other elements as well. A system thereby has properties that none of its parts have, and the parts may themselves lose their properties if separated.

The first consequence of systems thinking is that a system cannot be properly understood simply by dissecting it, that is, by analysis alone. To understand a system fully, one must identify the whole in which the system is a part, explain the behavior of the whole, and then explain the behavior of the system in this light. A systems inquiry must proceed synthetically as well as analytically.

The second consequence of systems thinking is the interconnectedness of the parts of a system. *Interconnectedness* renders the simple binary cause and effect relationship insufficient for explaining the behavior of either the system or its parts. A system element does not operate in a vacuum, but in conjunction with other subsystems and their environment.

The causal model underlying this view is an effect production model in which several coproducers are each necessary but insufficient for the generation of their effect. Only the set of coproducers taken collectively is the cause of the product. Singer (1959) and Ackoff & Emery (1972) have called this new causal model *producer-product*. The producer-product type of causality can account for the role of the environment because it views both the producer and its environment as coproducing their product (Bellman, 1961). A method of problem framing should allow its user to deal with necessary as well as with sufficient causal links.

The *second* systems concept of importance for problem framing is the notion of *homeostasis*, a process in which negative feedback helps reduce deviation from a norm and thereby secure stability. Beltrami (1987), Clark (1988), Forrester (1968b), Richmond, Peterson, & Charyk (1992), Richmond & Peterson (1992b), Roberts et al. (1983), Senge (1990), and van Gigch (1978) explain the mechanisms by which system performance sometimes varies exponentially and sometimes tends to a limit.

They also explain why these dynamic behaviors may occur as a result of monotonic convergence or as a result of oscillatory behavior patterns. System dynamicists consider the feedback loop as the basic structural element in a system. Typically, system dynamics models show that dynamic behavior is generated by feedback loops of circular causality coupled with corrective delays (Richardson, 1991). Therefore, it is important that a problem-framing method keep track of the direction of causal linkages so as to account for direct, indirect, and feedback effects, as well as to track the time lags needed for these effects to be felt.

Elsewhere in this book, we conclude that progress in problem formulation appears to be contingent on the theoretical developments in causal mapping and assumptional analysis of situations. We now posit that the initial rough-cut mapping and modeling effort should be free-form so as not to inhibit creativity of expression. Subsequent iterations should steadily bring in a tightening of the initial representation. This second, diagramming phase, may be better aided by specifying the interpretation of the situational model obtained than by its topological appearance. The situational model should result in a clearly interpretable diagram, preferably indicating the direction, sign, strength, and lag of each quantified effect.

Is this conclusion bringing us back to the full-fledged system dynamics modeling that we recommend and present in Chapter 10 and Appendix C.5? Only in a sense. What is needed for problem formulation is a causal diagramming aid that would be manual and quick so as to lend itself to debate. Yet, compatibility with system dynamics modeling is a desirable feature.

Comprehensive Situation Mapping (CSM)

This said, let us return to one of the central points of the preceding discussion.

Problem formulation is linked to situational mapping. Situational mapping should be a flexible and imaginative effort lending itself to a critical review or debate of the major assumptions about the situation at hand. It can be aided at some point by diagramming the situation so as to clearly represent the perceived causal effects. Yet, this causal diagramming should not be time consuming or cumbersome. It should not create a disincentive for the participants to backtrack and reanalyze their assumptions several times during the problem-framing process.

In his seminal 1975 text on causal analysis, Heise formalized causal diagramming into an algebra of path analysis. His formal model complements the incompletely specified influence diagramming (ID) and tidies up some of its loose ends. Although linked to statistical theory, it is very close to the diagramming solution envisaged by Acar (1983).

Heise's original model is one in which a causal arrow directed from variable X to variable Y signifies that Y is a linear function (or a linear transform) of X of the form

$$X \overset{a}{\Rightarrow} Y \Leftarrow b \qquad \text{meaning} \qquad Y = a \cdot X + b \qquad (1)$$

Differentiating Eq. 1 yields $dY = a \cdot dX$. This means that a change in X automatically results in a change in Y scaled (in its own units) by the algebraic coefficient a. Depending on whether a is larger or smaller than unity, the change in Y will be relatively larger or smaller than the change in X, assuming that no unit conversion is necessary in the process. Similarly, the sign of the induced change in Y is either the same with or opposite to the sign of change in X, depending on whether the sign of a is positive or negative.

In short, the linearity assumption implies that any change in an upstream variable X automatically generates a proportional change in those downstream and adjacent variables, such as Y. The proportion is the structural coefficient a, called change-transfer coefficient or simply *transfer coefficient*. Ignoring the constant term b lightens the notation and the causal diagram of Eq. 1 reduces to the binary relationship equivalent to $Y = a \cdot X$ or $dY = a \cdot dX$ in equation form.

Based on Heise (1975), Acar (1983) proposes the following equivalence between the diagramming and analytic notations:

$$X \overset{a}{\Rightarrow} Y \quad \approx \quad Y = a \cdot X \quad (\text{or } dY = a \cdot dX). \qquad (2)$$

Both Heise (1975) and Acar (1983) omit the constant terms to lighten the notation at no cost to the calculus of change. The differentials of Eqs. 1 and 2 remain the same—they are both equal to $a \cdot dX$.

Our focus on causality as a structural relationship expressing linearity, and thereby the proportionality of change among variables, has a computational payoff:

Eq. 2 is a transitive relationship. This is easy to see. Consider the three-node causal chain $X \overset{a}{\Rightarrow} Y \overset{c}{\Rightarrow} Z$. It is equivalent to the set of two equations:

$$Z = c \cdot Y \qquad \text{and} \qquad Y = a \cdot X. \tag{3}$$

Combining them, we obtain $Z = c \cdot Y = c(a \cdot X) = a \cdot c \cdot X$.

This is a strong interpretation of causal linkage whereby a change in X automatically generates a change in Z as a consequence of its generation of a change in Y. The direct causal relationships between X and Y, and between Y and Z, generate a causal relationship between X and Z. In this sense, the three-node diagram $X \overset{a}{\Rightarrow} Y \overset{c}{\Rightarrow} Z$ can be reduced to a two-node one, that is,

$$X \overset{a}{\Rightarrow} Y \overset{c}{\Rightarrow} Z \qquad \text{reduces to} \qquad X \overset{a \cdot c}{\Rightarrow} Y \tag{4}$$

In this example, X can be viewed as an independent or exogenous variable, and Y and Z as dependent or endogenous variables (i.e., variables whose changes are determined by the causal system and its inputs). These inputs are the changes in X, which are then automatically channeled through the network of relationships. The origin node of the network, node X, becomes the source of change for endogenous node Z, but then the relationship $Z = a \cdot c \cdot X$ becomes a black box model, the output of the change in Z. What the detailed causal diagramming can do is to *open up the black box* and thereby reveal the operating causalities.

The advantage of structural over black box modeling becomes more evident when we consider more complex, nonlinear, that is, nonchainlike, arrangements. Consider, for example, the following diagram in which two separate sources X and Y feed into the same sink Z.

$$X \overset{a}{\Rightarrow} Z \overset{c}{\Leftarrow} Y \qquad \approx \qquad Z = a \cdot X + c \cdot Y \tag{5}$$

Heise (1975) points out that, in such a case, the level of Z might be due to either one of the separate influences exerted on it. He reasons that an advantage of the assumption of linearity among levels is the result in the linearity and additivity of the changes in the levels. Differentiating (5) yields:

$$dZ = a \cdot dX + c \cdot dY \tag{6}$$

In addition to providing his model with useful computational properties, additivity appears to Heise to be an implication of his notion of causality.

Most sociometric authors as well as Heise call a relationship causal if the occurrence of a first event is only a sufficient condition for the occurrence of a later event. They reason that the causal transmutations of events operated by material structures are neither unique nor impossible to decompose. A causal relationship can thus be effected by a causal operator embedded within different structures.

A causal operator consists of organized components, which themselves are often operators. Understanding how such operators function corresponds to the understanding of relationships in a causal model. The dissection of causal operators and relationships often is an important aspect of understanding the modeling of strategic situations.

This modular view of causal operators explains why they are often aggregated or synthesized, letting indirect causal effects be thought of as causal effects—the transitivity property expressed by Eq. 4.

The conjunction of changes and operators can generate subsequent changes. In turn, these changes will produce new changes, if they are coordinated with new operators. Heise (1975) conceives of change events as homogeneous flows subject to augmentation and diminution, but sometimes, for brevity and convenience, these are modeled as states or levels. The homogeneity of change-constituting flows implies that a flow has the same effect regardless of the subflows that constitute it.

The first implication is that flows are additive. This is what Eq. 5 shows, implying that the accumulation of effects resulting from different changes can be modeled in a consistent way. The second implication is that the flow levels can be ordered quantitatively, expressed along the time interval scale over which the results have been derived.

Additional CSM Features

The analysis of causal linkages and their implications is a complex business. Ideally, it requires modeling and simulation (Forrester, 1958; Roberts et al., 1983; Watson, 1981). However, an approximation can be realized by the proper form of causal mapping, such as Acar's modeling system, described above and now denoted as CSM (comprehensive situation mapping). This method's simulationlike features help capture the critical dimension of causality, namely, whether changes in one or several driver variables are necessary to produce a desirable effect (Ackoff & Emery, 1972). The case studies and diagrams of Chapters 5, 6, and 9 demonstrate exactly how pure and mixed scenarios computed on the CSM can capture and combine the complex effects involved in the transmission of change throughout the network of interrelationships among the variables pertinent to a strategic situation.

To sum up the previous section, in CSM a short name represents each variable that may cause change in itself and in other variables, or that may prevent the transmission of change. Three types of arrows connect variables in CSM. A double-line arrow (i.e., $\Longrightarrow$) connects a sender and a receiver of change, if a change in the sender is sufficient by itself to transmit a change to its receiver. If two or more senders must vary to coproduce a change in a receiver, then a single-line arrow (i.e., $\longrightarrow$) links each sender with the receiver of change. A broken-line arrow (i.e., $-\rightarrow$) connects a sender and a receiver if the sender can prevent the transmission of change to the receiver.

If change is transmitted with a *time lag*, or if the change induced in a receiver is not comparable either in sign or in proportion to the change in the sender, then both the time lag and a change transmittance coefficient written next to an arrow capture these quantitative relations. Each change transfer coefficient expresses the ratio of the induced percentage change to the one generating it.

This technical summary of CSM is of necessity very sketchy. A complete treatment of CSM and the derivation from its antecedents are given by Acar (1983). CSM is used here because it possesses modeling flexibility as well as computational capability that can assist managers in complex strategic decision situations. As noted in the text, CSM allows the causal effects propagated through a particular channel of change to be combined with the changes propagated through other channels of change. The effects caused by a change in a single variable constitute a pure scenario of change transfer. The causal effects caused by changes in multiple variables make up a mixed scenario of change transfer. It is possible to compute mixed scenarios by summing the cumulative percentage changes or effects of pure scenarios, which result from changes in variables that can change independently.

In summary, CSM allows diagramming the web of interrelationships relevant to describing a complex decision situation. It can make the dynamics of the interrelationships visible, explicit, and comprehensible. CSM is a desktop tool that both managers and planners can use individually and collectively. In addition to diagramming the network of causal effects or interrelationships, this method permits their quantitative consequences or implications to be traced by computing combined environmental and decision scenarios.

CSM allows propagating multiwave change scenarios. Section 9.1 gives an illustrative first-generation or pure scenario example. In the process of computing scenarios, the quantification of causal relationships, required for computing possible alternative futures under conditions of change, yields a much deeper understanding of a decision situation's dynamic structure than the qualitative analysis of an influence diagram (ID). Statements of purpose can be linked directly to a firm's long-term strategic goals because CSM captures the combined effects of changes in both the environment and the firm's strategy. To conclude this section, we append a summary of CSM's mapping conventions.

CSM's Mapping Conventions

A short name represents each variable that changes itself or may cause change in other variables. CSM also provides for those variables which, if they were to change radically, may prevent the transmission of change.

Three types of arrows connect variables in CSM.

1. A *double-line arrow* (i.e., $\Rightarrow$) is used to connect a sender and a receiver of change, if a change in the sender variable is sufficient by itself to transmit a change to the receiver of the arrow.
2. A *single-line arrow* (i.e., $\rightarrow$) links each sender to a receiver of change if two or more senders must vary to coproduce a change in the receiver.
3. A *broken-line arrow* (i.e., $--\blacktriangleright$) connects a sender and a receiver of change if the sender is a variable that can prevent the receiver from changing, regardless of all other effects.

In CSM, both time lags and change coefficients accompany each double-line and single-line arrow to quantify the transmission of change throughout the causal network over time. Every single- and double-line arrow bears a change transmittance coefficient written either above or next to it. This coefficient quantifies the relationship between two variables connected with an arrow. If the change induced in the receiver of the arrow is not comparable either in sign or in proportion to the change in its sender, then the change transmittance coefficient expresses the ratio of the induced percentage change to the one generating it.

For example, the $X \underset{3m}{\overset{-2}{\Rightarrow}} Y$ notation signifies that a relative change of 10, 15, or 20 percent originating in variable X, and counted from its base level, is transferred to variable Y with a three-month time lag. There, it causes a relative change of -20, -30, or -40 percent in the value of Y. When downstream-transferred changes are proportional to the upstream changes causing them, and of the same sign, then the multipliers may be omitted from the map.

Single-line arrows, CSM's partial channels, work together with one another to transmit a positive change. Yet, the magnitude and timing of the change transmittance are still independent of each other. One partial channel may transmit the least change to its downstream variable, but another single-line arrow may determine the timing of that change independently from its magnitude.

This is the latest time and least change or *LL rule* of CSM, applied to the transmission of positive changes (or increases), involving partial channels or single-line arrows. Depending on the context, a negative change (a decrease) in a variable may be sufficient by itself to transmit a change to the receiver of a single-line arrow, independently from other single-line arrows.

Every single- and double-line arrow bears a time lag. Written either below or to the right of each arrow, along with explicit time units, the time lag coefficient clearly specifies changes transmitted with a time lag (Acar, 1983). The CSM diagrams of Infoplus (Fig. 9.1.1), Combank (Fig. 9.2.1), and organizational learning (Fig. 12.1.1) show exactly how CSM's diagramming conventions are used to capture and to combine the complex effects involved in the transmission of change, throughout the network of interrelationships among the variables pertinent to a strategic situation.

C.3   CROSS-IMPACT MATRIX MULTIPLICATION APPLIED TO CLASSIFICATION: THE MICMAC METHOD

In practical applications, the analysis of relationships among variables frequently rests on simplified or heuristic procedures. These assess a system's behavior from the relative strengths of its feedback loops, qualitatively, without computing either scenarios or equilibrium states. Appendix C.1 explains how some heuristic procedures often lead to errors.

Through MICMAC (Matrice d'Impacts Croisés Multiplication Appliquée à un Classement: Cross-Impact Matrix Multiplication Applied to Classification) second-third-, and higher-order interaction effects can be assessed among the variables on a causal map pertinent to a firm's strategy design. The illustrative examples of Part III show exactly how this simple analytical approach enhances the limited capability of the human mind to trace and to interpret the effects of multiple interdependencies among strategy design and tactical variables, even qualitatively.

Matrix manipulation offers a disciplined way of relating the variables of a causal map. Although it helps define the role of each variable in the structure of relationships underlying a strategic situation, MICMAC entails both straightforward and efficient computing. It was developed between 1972 and 1974 by J. C. Duperrin & M. Godet (Godet, 1987, p. 38) and is summarized below.

Practical heuristic procedures for the sake of simplicity work well in determining the effects of variables when they are not interrelated. Yet, systems with interrelated variables exhibit interdependencies that simplified procedures may ignore. Then, managers and planners can easily overlook the indirect effects of interrelated variables, particularly when strategic situation descriptions neglect, as they often do, multiple interactions among variables.

Thinking of the variables pertinent to a strategic situation as means i and ends j helps to explain how the MICMAC principle works. Typically, the strategic ends include performance variables, such as sales, market share, and profit, while the means include environmental and decision variables, such as exchange and interest rates, raw material purchases, and personnel training.

An adjacency matrix $\mathbf{Q} = [q_{i\,j}]$ allows defining the relationships perceived among the variables on a causal map pertinent to a strategic situation. In this matrix, $q_{i\,j}$ indicates the presence of a relationship between variables i and j.

The relationship matrix $\mathbf{Q}$ can be augmented by specifying $\mathbf{C} = [c_{i\,k}]$, the matrix of interactions among strategic means, where $c_{i\,k}$ gives the interaction between means i and k. In tactical and operational planning, for example, the first-order relationships among variables are often captured on the "house of quality" chart (Georgantzas & Hessel, 1991; Hauser & Clausing, 1988). This chart is used widely in process design and reengineering for quality and lets production managers and engineers see the big picture (Fortuna, 1988).

Let K denote the set of strategic means and L the set of strategic ends. Then, $\mathbf{Q} = [q_{i\,j}]$, where $i \in K$ and $j \in L$, and $\mathbf{C} = [c_{i\,k}]$, where $i, k \in K$. If $q_{i\,j} \neq 0$, then the strategic means i affects the strategic end j directly. We refer to this direct effect as a first-order effect or path and denote it by $i \rightarrow j$.

If $\mathbf{C} \neq 0$, then the strategic means i affects means k directly and the strategic end j indirectly. We denote this effect by $i \rightarrow k \rightarrow j$ and refer to it as a second-order effect or path. This path is a special case of higher-order effects, where transitive sequences of direct first-order effects yield multiple paths of indirect higher-order effects.

DEFINITION 1

a. The Boolean matrix of the relationships among strategic means and ends $\mathbf{Q}^B = [q_{i\,j}^B]$ satisfies

$$q_{i\,j}^B = 1 \quad \text{for all } i \in K \text{ and } j \in L, \text{ such that } i \rightarrow j, \text{ and}$$
$$= 0 \quad \text{otherwise}$$

b. The Boolean matrix of the relationships among strategic means $\mathbf{C}^B = [c_{i\,k}^B]$ satisfies:

$$c_{i\,k}^B = 1 \quad \text{for all } i, k \in K, \text{ such that } i \rightarrow k, \text{ with } i \neq k, \text{ and}$$
$$= 0 \quad \text{otherwise}$$

c. The Boolean matrix of the relationships among strategic ends $\mathbf{E}^B = [e_{j\,p}^B]$ satisfies:

$$e_{j\,p}^B = 1 \quad \text{for all } j, p \in L, \text{ such that } j \rightarrow p, \text{ with } j \neq p, \text{ and}$$
$$= 0 \quad \text{otherwise}$$ ∎

DEFINITION 2

The composite Boolean matrix of all the relationships among strategic means and ends is

$$\mathbf{M} = [m_{i\,j}] = \begin{bmatrix} \mathbf{E}^B & 0 \\ \mathbf{Q}^B & \mathbf{C}^B \end{bmatrix}.$$

Accordingly, if the relationship matrix $\mathbf{Q}$ has k rows and n columns, then the composite Boolean matrix $\mathbf{M}$ is a $(k+n) \times (k+n)$ matrix satisfying the following conditions:

$$
\begin{aligned}
m_{i\,j} \quad &= \quad 0 \text{ or } 1 \quad &&\text{for all } i,j \\
&= \quad 1 \quad &&\text{if and only if } i \rightarrow j \\
&= \quad 0 \quad &&\text{for all } i = j
\end{aligned}
$$ ■

Let $\mathbf{M}^2 = [m_{i\,j}^2]$, where $m_{i\,j}^2 = \Sigma_k m_{i\,k} m_{k\,j}$. If $m_{i\,j}^2 \neq 0$, there is at least one $k \neq i$, such that $m_{i\,k} \times m_{k\,j} = 1$. That is, there is at least one second-order path of the form $i \rightarrow k \rightarrow j$. If $m_{i\,j}^2 = r$, then there are r second-order paths from i to j via a single intermediary. Similarly, $\mathbf{M}^3$ shows all third-order paths form i to j, such as $i \rightarrow k \rightarrow p \rightarrow j$; $\mathbf{M}^4$ shows all fourth-order paths; and so on.

Also, let $d_i^n = \Sigma_j m_{i\,j}^n$, and $p_j^n = \Sigma_i m_{i\,j}^n$, where d_i^n is the number of all nth-order paths originating at variable i, and p_j^n is the number of all nth-order paths ending at variable j. Then, $D_i^N = \Sigma_1^N d_i^N$ is the number of all paths no longer than N originating at i, and $P_j^N = \Sigma_1^N p_j^N$ is the number of all paths no longer than N ending at j. D_i^N depicts the overall nth-order effect or influence of means i, while P_j^N depicts the overall nth-order effect on, or exposure of end j.

If $\mathbf{C}^B = 0$ or $\mathbf{E}^B = 0$, then strategic means and ends either affect or are exposed to other ends and means, but not both. Depending on the situation of a particular strategy design, it is possible to identify pure means that affect ends and other means but are not exposed to any means. Similarly, it may be possible to identify pure strategic ends exposed to other ends and strategic means but not affecting any other ends.

If $\mathbf{C}^B \neq 0$ and $\mathbf{E}^B \neq 0$, however, then there are strategic means exposed to other means, and ends affecting other ends, respectively. In both cases, assessing the role of each means and end in a causal network of strategic relationships entails computing the overall influence and exposure of each strategic means and end.

Assuredly, the influence and exposure of strategic means and ends change according to the order of effects considered. As n increases, the behavior of $\mathbf{M}^n$ becomes crucial in analyzing the interaction among strategic ends and means, and in assessing their influence and exposure. In a related but different context, Georgantzas & Hessel (1991) delineate two plausible cases.

If a causal map does not contain any closed paths of the $i \rightarrow j \rightarrow k, \ldots, \rightarrow i$ form (i.e., the map involves a straightforward description of a simple situation), then there exists N, such that $\mathbf{M}^N = 0$. In this case, both the influence and the exposure of each end and means can be assessed directly via the following proposition:

PROPOSITION 1

If there is N, such that $\mathbf{M}^N = 0$, then $\mathbf{M}^n = 0$ for all $n \geq N$. That is, all strategic ends and means have finite influence and exposure. Conversely, if the design problem contains at least one closed path of the $i \rightarrow j \rightarrow k, \ldots, \rightarrow i$ form, then $\mathbf{M}^n \neq 0$ for all n, and the influence and exposure of some strategic ends or means will be infinite. ∎

The following proposition allows ergodic ranking of strategic means and ends, according to their influence and exposure (Godet, 1987, p. 38).

PROPOSITION 2

For most matrices $\mathbf{M}$ there exists c, such that if $D_i^c \geq D_k^c$ and $P_j^c \geq P_k^c$, then $D_i^n \geq D_k^n$ and $P_j^n \geq P_k^n$, for all $n \geq c$. ∎

This ranking becomes stable quickly and allows an assessment of the role that strategic means and ends play in the network underlying the causal structure of the strategic situation under consideration. It also allows grouping strategic variables according to their overall influence and exposure.

As shown in Fig. 5.4.1, singular strategic ends and means include isolated ends and means that influence and are exposed to a few ends and means. Singular ends and means allow changes to be propagated cleanly, without any repercussions for the rest of the causal map. However, the effects of changes in nonsingular ends and means are not as clean. Dispersing ends and means affect many strategic ends and means but are exposed to a few of them, influencing other ends and means directly or indirectly. Depending on the situation, there may be dispersing means affecting other means, or multiple ends, or a few ends with confounding effects on other ends.

Absorbing strategic ends and means affect a few ends and means, but are exposed to many. They depict ends met through multiple means, but their high exposure makes them vulnerable even to small changes in a causal map. Linking strategic ends and means are both highly exposed and highly influential. They transmit the effects of changes in a strategy design throughout a causal network of ends and means.

The following examples from Part III should make concrete the abstract notions and the mathematical formalism presented here.

Combining MICMAC with Infoplus' CSM

The direct or first-order relationships among seven of Infoplus' strategic variables allowed us to formulate the square adjacency matrix **M** as

$$
\begin{array}{r}
\\
\text{1. External Funding} \\
\text{2. Infoplus' Resources} \\
\text{3. Capacity \& Capability} \\
\text{4. Demand for Service} \\
\text{5. Actual Service} \\
\text{6. Visibility} \\
\text{7. Revenue}
\end{array}
\mathbf{M} =
\begin{array}{ccccccc}
1. & 2. & 3. & 4. & 5. & 6. & 7. \\
0 & 1 & 0 & 0 & 0 & 0 & 0 \\
0 & 0 & 1 & 0 & 0 & 0 & 0 \\
0 & 0 & 0 & 1 & 1 & 0 & 0 \\
0 & 0 & 0 & 0 & 1 & 0 & 0 \\
0 & 0 & 0 & 0 & 0 & 1 & 1 \\
0 & 0 & 0 & 1 & 0 & 0 & 0 \\
0 & 1 & 0 & 0 & 0 & 0 & 0
\end{array}
\begin{array}{c}
D_i = \\
1 \\
1 \\
2 \\
1 \\
2 \\
1 \\
1
\end{array}
$$

$$
P_j = \begin{bmatrix} 0 & 2 & 1 & 2 & 2 & 1 & 1 \end{bmatrix}
$$

M lists the relationships among the variables that Infoplus' planning team thought were pertinent to its strategic situation. Again, only seven of the nine variables of Table 5.3.1 are included in the matrix because the Infoplus team chose not to quantify the effects of the initial support and partial autonomy variables, but to treat them as qualitative restrictions. The broken-line arrows on the CSM of Fig. 5.3.1b help to clarify the qualitative condition of these two variables.

M shows the first-order effects among the strategic variables pertinent to Infoplus' strategic situation. For example, $m_{2,3} = 1$ denotes the single first-order path of change transmission originating at Infoplus' resources and ending at its capacity and capability. In the D_i vector, which gives the number of all paths no longer than $N=1$ originating at i, $d_3 = 2$ shows that two first-order paths originate at capacity and capability. Similarly, in P_j, which shows the number of all paths no longer than $N=1$ ending at j, $p_2 = 2$ signifies the two first-order paths ending at Infoplus' resources.

So far, there is nothing peculiar about these results. One could establish these relationships by merely inspecting the comprehensive situation map of Fig. 5.3.1b. A straightforward examination of the CSM should reveal the first-order effects directly. Yet, mere inspection of the map may not immediately uncover all the indirect relationships among the variables pertinent to Infoplus' strategic situation, which the consecutive powers of matrix $\mathbf{M}$ can capture, that is,

$$
\mathbf{M}^2 = \begin{bmatrix}
0 & 0 & 1 & 0 & 0 & 0 & 0 \\
0 & 0 & 0 & 1 & 1 & 0 & 0 \\
0 & 0 & 0 & 0 & 1 & 1 & 1 \\
0 & 0 & 0 & 0 & 0 & 1 & 1 \\
0 & 1 & 0 & 1 & 0 & 0 & 0 \\
0 & 0 & 0 & 0 & 1 & 0 & 0 \\
0 & 0 & 1 & 0 & 0 & 0 & 0
\end{bmatrix}
\begin{matrix}
D_i^2 = \\
1 \\
2 \\
3 \\
2 \\
2 \\
1 \\
1
\end{matrix}
$$

$$
P_j^2 = \begin{bmatrix} 0 & 1 & 2 & 2 & 3 & 2 & 2 \end{bmatrix}
$$

$$\vdots$$

$$
\mathbf{M}^{14} = \begin{bmatrix}
0 & 6 & 5 & 9 & 10 & 7 & 7 \\
0 & 7 & 6 & 12 & 14 & 10 & 10 \\
0 & 10 & 7 & 16 & 18 & 14 & 14 \\
0 & 6 & 4 & 9 & 10 & 8 & 8 \\
0 & 8 & 6 & 12 & 13 & 10 & 10 \\
0 & 4 & 3 & 7 & 8 & 6 & 6 \\
0 & 6 & 5 & 9 & 10 & 7 & 7
\end{bmatrix}
\begin{matrix}
D_i^{14} = \\
44 \\
59 \\
79 \\
45 \\
59 \\
34 \\
44
\end{matrix}
$$

$$
P_j^{14} = \begin{bmatrix} 0 & 47 & 36 & 74 & 83 & 62 & 62 \end{bmatrix}
$$

Although the entries of $\mathbf{M}$ are the direct, single-step links between variables or map nodes, the entries of $\mathbf{M}^2$ are the two-step or second-order linkages among them. In the 1950s and 1960s sociometrists showed that these links could be computed directly on the adjacency matrices—and therefore could be computerized. For example, $m^2_{5,2}$ indicates that there is but one path of length two (or a one two-step causal linkage) from node 5 (actual service) of the map of Fig. 5.3.1b to node 2 (Infoplus' resources). This much can be derived from $\mathbf{M}^2$ without direct inspection of the map.

Also in $\mathbf{M}^2$, $d^2_5 = 2$ denotes that two second-order paths of change transmission originate at actual service, and $p^2_5 = 3$ signifies the three second-order paths ending at the same variable. We could verify some of these change transmission paths by tracing them in Fig. 5.3.1b. For example, it should be easy to see the second-order paths of

- actual service → revenue → Infoplus' resources
- actual service → visibility → demand for service

In $\mathbf{M}^{14}$, however, tracing or at once keeping track of all eighty-three fourteenth-order paths of change transmission ending at actual service ($p^{14}_5 = 83$), may not be as straightforward. Helping its users mechanize this laborious work is one way MICMAC can be useful. It allows an assessment of the role that strategic variables play in the network of feedback loops underlying the causal structure of a strategic situation. The identification of indirect effects through the mere inspection of a CSM can be laborious. Yet, the computationally efficient powers of $\mathbf{M}$ can easily capture all indirect effects throughout a causal map. Simple routines that carry out matrix multiplication are routinely available in most spreadsheet programs.

In addition, if one thinks of the variables pertinent to a strategic situation as means and ends, or, alternatively, as *driver* and *dependent* variables (Godet, 1987, p. 44), then MICMAC leads to a grouping of these variables according to their overall influence and exposure. Figure 5.4.1 shows exactly what the outcome of this efficient procedure might look like.

The successive powers of the adjacency matrix $\mathbf{M}$ and the vectors numerically derived from its successive powers $\mathbf{M}^2$ through $\mathbf{M}^{14}$ can provide useful information about the structural role that each strategic variable plays in a comprehensive situation map. The emerging picture of overall effects among variables in the CSM of Fig. 5.3.1b is that of a hierarchy of strategic variables, according to their direct and indirect (i.e., feedback) effects on each other.

The consecutive line plots of Fig. 5.4.2 show the behavioral patterns of change in (a) the exposure and (b) the influence of Infoplus' strategic variables as the matrix power N of $\mathbf{M}^N$ increases from $N=1$ to $N=15$. Both the exposure and influence values have been *normalized* in Fig. 5.4.2 to allow comparing directly the powers of matrix **M**. The normalized values show how the exposure and influence vectors, P_j^N and D_i^N respectively, become stable after $N= 8$.

Along $\mathbf{M}^{14}$, the normalized D_i^{14} and P_j^{14} vectors capture the overall influence and exposure of Infoplus' strategic variables, which are otherwise expressed in the CSM of Fig. 5.3.1b. Most of the MICMAC results confirmed the initial expectations of the Infoplus team. Yet, the grouping of strategic variables according to their overall exposure and influence in Fig. 5.4.3 generated new discussion. It was interesting to observe how Infoplus' capacity and capability, which moved up the hierarchy considerably, captured the project participants' attention. They had initially thought that the most influential variable would be external funding. Similarly, actual service became the most exposed variable, with revenue ranking second.

The MICMAC classification indicated that Infoplus should carefully manage the transformation of external funds and other resources into capacity and capability. The classification of variables given by Fig. 5.4.3 reinforced the necessity of new capacity additions to strengthen Infoplus' capacity and capability and to manage the tension that its matrix organization creates.

Combining MICMAC with Combank's CSM

The case study of Infoplus has already shown that numerous indirect relationships may exist in a causal map describing the system structure of a strategic situation. Indirect relationships emanate from the first-order relationships which the arrows disclose on a causal map. When the Boolean matrix corresponding to a causal map is squared, then it reveals second-order relationships, such as $i \rightarrow k \rightarrow j$.

Indeed, when $m_{ij}^2 \neq 0$ in $\mathbf{M}^2 = \mathbf{M} \times \mathbf{M} = \{m_{ij}^2\}$, with $m_{ij}^2 = \Sigma_\kappa m_{ik} \cdot m_{kj}$, then there is at least one k with $m_{ik} \times m_{kj} = 1$, that is, there is at least one intermediate variable k that variable i affects directly, which (k) affects variable j directly. A second-order path goes from i to j via k.

If $m_{ij}^2 = n$, then there are n second-order paths, connecting i to j through n intermediate variables. Computing $\mathbf{M}^3$, $\mathbf{M}^4$,..., $\mathbf{M}^N$ allows identification of the number of influence paths of order $3, 4, ..., N$, respectively. These are the higher-order paths interconnecting the strategic variables on the causal map. Each time this procedure is repeated, a new set of influences can be deduced until $\mathbf{M}^N$ becomes stable.

Through the first-order relationships among 10 of the variables in Combank's strategic situation, the square matrix **M** is formulated as

	1.	2.	3.	4.	5.	6.	7.	8.	9.	10.	$D_i =$
1. Foreign Funds	0	1	0	0	0	0	0	0	0	0	1
2. Advisory Services	0	0	0	0	1	0	0	0	0	0	1
3. Operations Flexibility	0	0	0	1	0	0	0	0	0	0	1
4. Cost	0	0	0	0	1	0	0	0	0	0	1
5. Profit	0	0	0	0	0	0	0	0	0	0	0
6. Functional Efficiency	0	0	0	1	0	0	1	0	0	0	2
7. Quality Image	0	1	0	0	1	0	0	0	0	0	2
8. Use of I.S. Technology	0	0	1	0	0	0	1	0	1	0	3
9. Effective Delivery	0	0	0	0	0	0	1	0	0	0	1
10. Capable People	0	0	0	0	0	0	0	1	1	0	2

$$\mathbf{M} = \quad\quad P_j = \begin{bmatrix} 0 & 2 & 1 & 2 & 3 & 0 & 3 & 1 & 2 & 0 \end{bmatrix}$$

M shows the first-order effects specified by the team members in Combank's aggregate CSM of Fig. 6.3.1. Once more, only 10 of the 11 strategic variables of Fig. 6.3.1 are in Combank's adjacency matrix because its planning group chose not to quantify the effects of size—a qualitative condition. In CSM notation, broken-line arrows signify qualitative restrictions. In Fig. 6.3.1, a material change in size may impose on Combank's use of state-of-the-art IS (information systems) technology as well as on the bank's operations flexibility.

M shows the first-order effects among the strategic variables pertinent to Combank's strategic situation. For example, $m_{3,4} = 1$ denotes a single first-order path of change transmission that originates at Combank's operations flexibility and ends at cost. In the D_i vector, $d_3 = 1$ shows the same first-order path, while in P_j, $p_2 = 2$ signifies the two first-order paths ending at Combank's advisory services, the first one emanating from foreign funds and the second from the bank's quality image.

One could verify these relationships by merely inspecting the CSM of Fig. 6.3.1. A straightforward examination of the causal map should reveal the first-order effects directly. Yet, computing $\mathbf{M}^3$, $\mathbf{M}^4$,..., $\mathbf{M}^N$ helps identify the number of influence paths of order $3, 4,..., N$, respectively. These are second-, third-, and higher-order influence paths interconnecting the variables of Combank. The consecutive powers of **M** evolved as follows:

$$
\mathbf{M}^2 =
\begin{bmatrix}
0 & 0 & 0 & 0 & 1 & 0 & 0 & 0 & 0 & 0 \\
0 & 0 & 0 & 0 & 0 & 0 & 0 & 0 & 0 & 0 \\
0 & 0 & 0 & 0 & 1 & 0 & 0 & 0 & 0 & 0 \\
0 & 0 & 0 & 0 & 0 & 0 & 0 & 0 & 0 & 0 \\
0 & 0 & 0 & 0 & 0 & 0 & 0 & 0 & 0 & 0 \\
0 & 1 & 0 & 0 & 2 & 0 & 0 & 0 & 0 & 0 \\
0 & 0 & 0 & 0 & 1 & 0 & 0 & 0 & 0 & 0 \\
0 & 1 & 0 & 1 & 1 & 0 & 1 & 0 & 0 & 0 \\
0 & 1 & 0 & 0 & 1 & 0 & 0 & 0 & 0 & 0 \\
0 & 0 & 1 & 0 & 0 & 0 & 2 & 0 & 1 & 0
\end{bmatrix}
\begin{matrix}
D_i = \\[2pt]
\begin{bmatrix}
1 \\ 0 \\ 1 \\ 0 \\ 0 \\ 3 \\ 1 \\ 4 \\ 2 \\ 4
\end{bmatrix}
\end{matrix}
$$

$$
P_j = \begin{bmatrix} 0 & 3 & 1 & 1 & 7 & 0 & 3 & 0 & 1 & 0 \end{bmatrix}
$$

$$\vdots$$

$$
\mathbf{M}^5 =
\begin{bmatrix}
0 & 0 & 0 & 0 & 0 & 0 & 0 & 0 & 0 & 0 \\
0 & 0 & 0 & 0 & 0 & 0 & 0 & 0 & 0 & 0 \\
0 & 0 & 0 & 0 & 0 & 0 & 0 & 0 & 0 & 0 \\
0 & 0 & 0 & 0 & 0 & 0 & 0 & 0 & 0 & 0 \\
0 & 0 & 0 & 0 & 0 & 0 & 0 & 0 & 0 & 0 \\
0 & 0 & 0 & 0 & 0 & 0 & 0 & 0 & 0 & 0 \\
0 & 0 & 0 & 0 & 0 & 0 & 0 & 0 & 0 & 0 \\
0 & 0 & 0 & 0 & 0 & 0 & 0 & 0 & 0 & 0 \\
0 & 0 & 0 & 0 & 0 & 0 & 0 & 0 & 0 & 0 \\
0 & 0 & 0 & 0 & 1 & 0 & 0 & 0 & 0 & 0
\end{bmatrix}
\begin{matrix}
D_i = \\[2pt]
\begin{bmatrix}
0 \\ 0 \\ 0 \\ 0 \\ 0 \\ 0 \\ 0 \\ 0 \\ 0 \\ 1
\end{bmatrix}
\end{matrix}
$$

$$
P_j = \begin{bmatrix} 0 & 0 & 0 & 0 & 1 & 0 & 0 & 0 & 0 & 0 \end{bmatrix} .
$$

Here, for example, the digit 1 in the first row, fifth column, of the $\mathbf{M}^2$ matrix indicates the second-order effect of foreign funds on profit. This digit means that there is a circuit of length 2 going from the influx of foreign funds to profit. Similarly, the second-order effects of functional efficiency of support services on profit, by way of cost and quality image, are indicated clearly by the numeral 2 in the sixth row, fifth column, of $\mathbf{M}^2$.

The lack of feedback loops in the comprehensive situation map of Fig. 6.3.1 end the MICMAC computations quickly. The nonrecursive CSM reveals a single fifth-order effect just before the consecutive powers of Combank's adjacency matrix become perfectly stable for $N = 6$, with all entries of $\mathbf{M}^6$ driven to zero, that is, all $m_{ij}^6 = 0$. Figure 6.4.1 verifies that the higher-order matrices reduce to naught from $\mathbf{M}^6$ onward.

Without feedback loops, the sum vectors along the consecutive powers of $\mathbf{M}$ cannot reveal the hierarchy of strategic variables. That would depend on a much higher order of direct and indirect (i.e., feedback) effects. The consecutive line plots of Fig. 6.4.1 show the behavioral patterns of change in the exposure and influence of Combank's strategic variables as the matrix power of $\mathbf{M}^N$ increases from $N=1$ to $N=15$. Both the exposure and influence values have been normalized to allow comparing the powers of the adjacency matrix directly.

Along $\mathbf{M}^5$, the normalized D_i^5 and P_j^5 vectors capture the influence and exposure of Combank's strategic variables in the CSM of Fig. 6.3.1. The plots of these values along (a) the overall exposure and (b) the overall influence dimensions of strategic variables in Fig. 6.4.2 show MICMAC's intermediate anchoring of variables into absorbing, dispersing, and singular.

The MICMAC results of Fig. 6.4.2 simply confirm the expectations of the Combank planning team, already captured in the CSM of Fig. 6.3.1. This type of analysis may add more value than the arbitrary assignment of weights to strategic variables. Undertaken within the principles underlying causal mapping, matrix multiplication is a defensible approach. Often, it helps to unearth hidden high-order effects, and it thereby improves strategy design.

C.4   BATTELLE SCENARIO INPUT TO CORPORATE STRATEGY (BASICS)

Cross-impact analysis emerged from the need to better understand the complex effects of interrelated factors and variables on the business environment. Since the mid-1960s, when cross-impact analysis originated, its computational procedure has been refined, but it still entails processing judgment about how particular events affect the occurrence of other events in the business and economic-sociopolitical environment. Here we draw primarily on Battelle's Economics and Policy Analysis Occasional Paper Number 44, authored by Honton, Stacey, & Millett (1985), and on BASICS–PC™: Battelle's Scenario Development Software Package for the

Personal Computer (Battelle, 1988).

Since the mid-1970s, Battelle's cross-impact analysis computer program called BASICS has been applied to many strategic situations. The program is available on both mainframes and personal computers, running in an interactive mode. Its computational procedure involves straightforward and uncomplicated mathematics.

The elements of cross-impact analysis include

- Initial probabilities for events relevant to a firm's economic-sociopolitical, and industry environments.
- Cross-impact information in the form of a cross-impact matrix that defines how the initial or *a priori* probabilities might change as other events occur.

Cross-impact analysis is particularly useful because it allows focusing on interrelated events and quantifying their interrelationships. It provides the flexibility required for organizing and using "judgment and opinion more readily than other more traditional operations research and econometric techniques" (Honton, Stacey, & Millett, 1985, p. 2).

BASICS starts with the initially estimated probabilities of occurrence, known in the language of statistical decision theory as the a priori probabilities. Then, it recomputes all the cross-impact index values and adjusts the initial probabilities so that the given a priori probabilities of the descriptor states are driven to either 1 or zero. New information is created by readjusting the probabilities. The computational procedure of BASICS investigates the long-term possibilities of some events occurring almost certainly. Other events see their chances of materializing decline and gradually vanish.

The program executes numerous computer runs or, in our language, *simulations*. These simulations are scenario sequences of descriptor-state occurrence or nonoccurrence. They are based on BASICS' computational formula for probability adjustments. BASICS then organizes them into scenarios. In Battelle's approach, a scenario is an aggregation of simulations with identically occurring descriptor states.

BASICS is a procedural program requiring input (data) on which it applies a cross-impact algorithm (its computational procedure) to produce simulation results (output). Figure C.4.1 shows the throughput, that is, input-process-output, of Battelle's computational method implemented in the BASICS computer program. The following subsections detail the procedural steps involved in using BASICS.

Figure C.4.1   The BASICS Computer Program

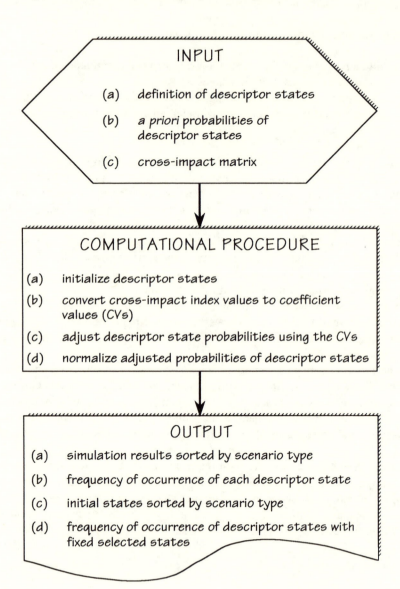

INPUT

(a)   definition of descriptor states

(b)   a priori probabilities of descriptor states

(c)   cross-impact matrix

COMPUTATIONAL PROCEDURE

(a)   initialize descriptor states

(b)   convert cross-impact index values to coefficient values (CVs)

(c)   adjust descriptor state probabilities using the CVs

(d)   normalize adjusted probabilities of descriptor states

OUTPUT

(a)   simulation results sorted by scenario type

(b)   frequency of occurrence of each descriptor state

(c)   initial states sorted by scenario type

(d)   frequency of occurrence of descriptor states with fixed selected states

BASICS' Input

The input to the Battelle BASICS procedure consists of (1) defining descriptor states; (2) assigning an a priori probability to each descriptor state; and (3) defining a cross-impact matrix.

A descriptor may be an environmental trend, event, development, variable, or attribute that serves to describe a firm's strategic situation. Frequently, the descriptors used in BASICS are proxies for variables, or sets of variables (factors), pertinent to a strategic situation. Each descriptor entails one or more descriptor states that represent alternative possible future outcomes. In most applications, however, two to four states characterize each descriptor. By definition, these states are mutually exclusive and collectively exhaustive.

At the end of the simulation, each descriptor is characterized by one of its states occurring and the other states not occurring. Once the outcomes of all descriptor states have been computed, then scenarios about alternative futures are constructed.

BASICS also requires obtaining and recording a priori judgment about future outcomes or descriptor states. The a priori probability estimates represent the best intuitive judgment of the likelihood of occurrences of alternative descriptor states ceteris paribus, that is, before taking into account the interaction among descriptors. Later, however, using its computational algorithm, the program adjusts these initial judgment estimates according to how descriptors might interact with one another in the future.

The sum of the a priori probabilities for all the states of a descriptor must always be equal to 1 because one of these states will occur with absolute certainty at some future date. Often, the a priori probabilities are established by combining trend analysis and expert opinion. Judgment must be exercised about the way the occurrence of a descriptor state affects the probability of occurrence of every other state.

Once descriptors are defined by the user, BASICS assigns all of them and their states to the rows and columns of a cross-impact matrix. Then judgment about the effect of the occurrence of a descriptor state on the probability of occurrence of all other states must be recorded in the appropriate cell of this *occurrence* cross-impact matrix, using an index value from Table C.4.1.

While working with the index values of Table C.4.1, in one column of the occurrence cross-impact matrix at a time, sets of indices are used to record judgment on the question: "If the jth descriptor state were to occur, how would this affect the probability that the ith descriptor state will occur?" (Honton, Stacey, & Millett, 1985, p. 5). In this question, index *i* refers to row states, and the index *j* refers to column states. In answering the question, the program users may exercise judgment by taking into account the direct relationships among descriptor states.

Yet, judgment must also be used to indicate how the nonoccurrence of a descriptor state affects the probability of occurrence of all other descriptor states. All this sounds complicated and time consuming, but the BASICS program can automatically generate the nonoccurrence matrix once the user has supplied the input required for the occurrence matrix. The program generates the nonoccurrence matrix by computing the average of all other state index values in the occurrence matrix, excluding the state it is calculating for, rounded up to the nearest integer.

Table C.4.1 Index Values Used in Defining BASICS' Cross-Impact Matrices

Index Value		Meaning
− 3	:	Significant decrease
− 2	:	Decrease
− 1	:	Slight decrease
0	:	No effect
1	:	Slight increase
2	:	Increase
3	:	Significant increase

The diagonal cells of both the occurrence and the nonoccurrence cross-impact matrices are filled with zeros because cross-impact analysis does not allow for any causal reciprocity effects among states within the same descriptor. The BASICS input requires judgment on a priori probabilities and on relevant cross-impact effects in order to distinguish among relevant descriptor states. Yet, judgment is needed only for descriptor states relevant to BASICS, not for irrelevant ones. Causal reciprocity effects, for example, with embedded time lags or delays, are valid feedback loops but the realm of full-fledged system dynamics simulation modeling, not of BASICS.

Battelle's Computational Procedure

The computational procedure of the BASICS program adjusts the a priori probabilities of descriptor states according to the occurrence and nonoccurrence of other events until each descriptor state's probability is driven either to one, indicating that the state will occur, or to zero, indicating that it will not occur. The outcome of each descriptor is one of its states occurring, with the remaining states not occurring. In the end of the BASICS simulation, each descriptor state either occurs or it does not occur. Hence, the BASICS computational procedure starts by initializing each descriptor state, say i, either to occur ($P(i) = 1$) or not to occur

$(P(i)=0)$. This implies that a given outcome, that is, a descriptor state initialized to one, will occur in the future.

Next, the BASICS program calculates new values for the a priori or initial probabilities, say $P(i)$, for $i = 1,2,\ldots,N$ descriptor states in the occurrence and nonoccurrence cross-impact matrices, according to the cross-impact index values of Table C.4.1. Again, ranging from -3 = significant decrease to +3 = significant increase, the table's index values, say $j = -3,-2,\ldots,3$, signify judgment about how the occurrence of a particular descriptor state might affect the probability of occurrence of all other descriptor states.

To adjust the initial probabilities, first, the BASICS algorithm converts each index value $j = -3,-2,\ldots,3$ in the occurrence and nonoccurrence cross-impact matrices into a relevant coefficient value though the following formula:

$$cv(j) = \text{If } (j \geq 0, |j| + 1, \frac{1}{|j| + 1}) \text{ for } j = -3,-2,\ldots,3 \qquad (1)$$

where: If (condition, return if true, return if false) or, alternatively,

$$cv(j) \quad = \quad |j| + 1 \quad for\ j \geq 0, \atop = \quad \frac{1}{|j| + 1} \quad otherwise. \Bigg\} \qquad (2)$$

Using Eq. 1, for example, BASICS will convert the occurrence and nonoccurrence cross-impact index value $j = 2$ to $cv(2) = 3$ and $j = -1$ to $cv(-1) = 1 / 2$.

Second, the program uses the initial probability $P(i)$ of each descriptor state $i = 1,2,\ldots,N$ in the occurrence and nonoccurrence cross-impact matrices, along with the converted coefficient values from Eq. 1 to compute new adjusted probability, say $P(i,j)$, sets using the formula:

$$P(i,j) = \frac{P(i) \cdot cv(j)}{1 - P(i) + \left[P(i) \cdot cv(j)\right]}, \text{ for } j = -3,-2,\ldots,3 \qquad (3)$$

Honton, Stacey, & Millett (1985) give a four-page justification for using Eq. 3 to compute the adjusted probability $P(i,j)$ for each descriptor state $i = 1,2,\ldots,N$ in the occurrence and nonoccurrence cross-impact matrices of BASICS. There would be no justification for repeating their arguments here, but it should suffice to show the relationship between the a priori or initial probability $P(i)$ of each descriptor state and its new adjusted probability $P(i,j)$, along the cross-impact matrix index values $j = -3, -2, \ldots, 3$. Figure C.4.2 shows exactly how the BASICS program adjusts each initial probability $P(i)$, in absolute terms, given its a priori judgment value and an index value $j = -3, -2, \ldots, 3$ in the occurrence and nonoccurrence cross-impact matrices.

Starting with an initial probability of $P(i) = 0.4$, for example, and an index value of $j = 2$, the graph of Fig. C.4.2 shows that the adjusted probability value is $P(i, j) = 0.67$. Conversely, the adjusted probability value for an index value of $j = -2$ is $P(i, j) = 0.18$. All values in the graph are probabilities, so they are naturally bounded by zero and one.

Given that the BASICS program requires all descriptor states to be mutually exclusive and collectively exhaustive, the sum of the probabilities for all states of each descriptor must add up to unity. After all the probabilities have been adjusted in the occurrence and nonoccurrence cross-impact matrices by using Eq. 3, Battelle's computational method normalizes the adjusted probabilities of each set of descriptor states so their sum is one.

The adjusted probabilities, for example, for a three-state descriptor might have been computed from Eq. 2 to be 0.50, 0.46, and 0.20. The sum of these probabilities does not add up to one, but to 1.16. When this occurs, and it does so frequently, the BASICS program normalizes the state probabilities of each descriptor. Normalizing would have made the three-state descriptor probabilities of our example equal to 0.43, 0.40 and 0.17, respectively, so their sum would have been equal to one. Indeed, that it is.

The BASICS simulation is complete once all the required adjustments have been made, including the normalizing of all sets of the descriptor state probabilities in the occurrence and nonoccurrence cross-impact matrices. BASICS continues computing until a single state per descriptor is set to occur or not to occur. The probabilities of all remaining descriptor states are adjusted accordingly. If a tie occurs, then BASICS uses a random number generation subroutine to select one state per descriptor.

BASICS' Output

At the end of the simulation, the BASICS program presents the user with the complete simulation results in a sequence of matrix tables. In these tables, all probabilities have been set to either zero or one, while the bottom row of each table always gives the final results. These results provide insight regarding the likelihood that a descriptor state might occur in the future.

To facilitate the analysis of the simulation output, BASICS groups together identical simulation results according to their frequency of occurrence. In each table, these frequencies are expressed as a posteriori probabilities, so they can be

Figure C.4.2 Relationship Between the Initial Probability P(i) and
the Adjusted Probability P(i,j) Along the Cross-Impact
Index j=–3,–2,...,3

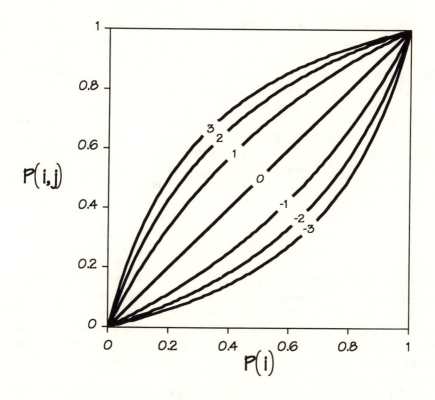

Source: Honton, Stacey & Millett, 1985. Reproduced by permission
of Battelle Institute, Colombus, Ohio.

compared with the a priori probability estimates.

In Chapter 9, the real-life case studies of Combank and Infoplus did use BA-SICS-derived frequencies of posterior probabilities. Each case provides a concrete example of how the BASICS output might be used to give a balanced consideration to what might happen to a firm's future.

Last, but not least, the BASICS program can print all these results in plain English rather than in matrices filled with zero and 1 digits.

Conclusion

Implemented through the BASICS computer program, Battelle's computational method is most pertinent to computing macroenvironmental scenarios. The value of the BASICS program stems from forcing the user into eliciting, organizing, and processing judgment and opinion for the specific purpose of synthesizing pertinent macroenvironmental scenarios.

Yet, our use of BASICS in Combank and Infoplus shows how Battelle's computational method can also work well in combination with other scenario-driven planning methods. BASICS can complement causal and full-fledged modeling in computing stochastic or accounting-for-interdependence strategic scenarios. These can provide managers, planners and strategy students with further insight regarding the likelihood of decision outcomes and their associated strategic, not merely environmental, uncertainty.

C.5   SYSTEM DYNAMICS SIMULATION MODELING SOFTWARE

Since Forrester's inaugural 1958 paper in the *Harvard Business Review*, most system dynamics applications and research studies have incorporated computer models written in special-purpose simulation languages. The field has grown along with an increasing interdependence between its modeling methodology and computer software. This unique interdependence has promoted new developments in system dynamics software, binding its developers to offering innovative features that enhance the quality of the modeling process.

Part 4 of the 1992 special issue of the *European Journal of Operational Research*, titled *Modelling for Learning*, contains a collection of short articles on software design. Guest Editors J.D.W. Morecroft and J. D. Sterman successfully compiled a set of diverse articles on software architecture and design matters in order to show the emphasis that developers place on mapping, graphics, documentation, simulation diagnostics, and gaming. The articles avoid abstract description by incorporating material specific to the software and its uses, and thereby effectively convey "the look and feel of each package" (Morecroft, 1992, p. 26). Together, these articles show how the nature of system dynamics simulation modeling is changing. The new generation of system dynamics software is increasingly rendering obsolete the technical barriers that in times past barred managers, strategy students, and their teachers from testing assumptions about the dynamic implications of a strategic situation on a computer. Now, even those managers and strategy students who lack technical expertise and modeling proficiency can think about strategy design with the help of a gaming simulator, such as the MicroWorld Creator™ (Diehl, 1992a; Diehl, 1992b), for example.

The need to make system dynamics simulation models more accessible to the general user led to the development of MicroWorld Creator™. Traditionally, once a system dynamics model of a firm's strategic situation was complete, a consultant had to translate the insight gained from the modeling process to the rest of the firm's managers. This proved to be a time-consuming process and unsatisfying, for written reports never deliver desirable effects.

A better way of recreating the model-building experience is to let managers interact directly with a system dynamics simulation model implemented as a microworld. Using MicroWorld Creator™ to design a microworld's computer interface creates an effective experiential approach to organizational learning (Senge & Sterman, 1992). With such an interface, system dynamics simulation "models which once appeared on computer screens as sinister skeletons of algebra are now fleshed out with text and clothed in color graphics" (Morecroft, 1992, p. 26).

The Zorbalander's College Fund: An Illustration of DYNAMO©, DYSMAP2, iThink™, STELLA®, and Vensim™

To illustrate Morecroft's point, here is an example of such an algebraic sinister skeleton:

$$\text{College Fund}(t) = \text{College Fund}(t{-}dt) + (\text{gain} + \text{deposits} - \text{loss} - \text{withdrawals}){*}dt \tag{1}$$

Initial College Fund = 0 {ZBLD$}

$$\text{gain} = \text{interest rate}{*}\text{College Fund} \quad \{\text{ZBLD\$/year}\} \tag{1.1}$$

$$\text{deposits} = 5000 - \text{STEP}(5000,2011) \quad \{\text{ZBLD\$/year}\} \tag{1.2}$$

$$\text{loss} = \text{inflation rate}{*}\text{College Fund} \quad \{\text{ZBLD\$/year}\} \tag{1.3}$$

$$\text{withdrawals} = 0 + \text{STEP}(\text{college expenses},2011) \quad \{\text{ZBLD\$/year}\} \tag{1.4}$$

$$\text{inflation rate} = 0.06 \quad \{\text{dimensionless}\} \tag{1.5}$$

$$\text{interest rate} = 0.1125 \quad \{\text{dimensionless}\} \tag{1.6}$$

$$\text{college expenses} = 40000 \quad \{\text{ZBLD\$/year}\} \tag{1.7}$$

This algebra is the skeleton of the structure underlying the situation facing the parents of a baby born in 1993 on the mythical island of Zorbaland (hence the ZBLD dollar bills). The baby's parents wish to secure the financial resources required for their child's future college education, which they anticipate will begin in the year 2011 (1.4) and last four years.

To establish the college fund of Eq. 1, they start saving ZBLD$5,000 a year (Eq. 1.2), in a special account that pays 11.25 percent interest per year (Eq. 1.6), compounded annually, with the time step for calculations set at periodic intervals of $dt = 1$ year. Zorbaland's Exalted King Zorba VIII has announced that over the next twenty-one years the inflation rate will average 6 percent annually (Eq. 1.5). This will place annual college expenses roughly in the neighborhood of ZBLD$40,000 (Eq. 1.7), for years 2011 through 2014.

Figure C.5.1 shows how a systems diagram might flesh out this personal finance situation to help the parents of the newborn Zorbalander assess the college fund's sensitivity to their annual deposits (Eq. 1.2) easily and quickly. If their baby had been born back in 1961, then they would have had to sketch the flow diagram of Fig. C.5.1a, following the instructions in Forrester (1961, Chapter 8).

In 1961, one would have to display diagrammatically the system interrelationships of the college fund situation simultaneously with the development of Eqs. 1 through 1.7. To the noninitiate, the flow diagram of Fig. C.5.1a appears cumbersome, but Forrester's diagramming convention is fairly easy to learn. To most people, it can become far simpler and easier to use than the equations for communicating the structure of the personal finance situation.

In 1993, most managers on the mythical island of Zorbaland as well as other real-world users of the mainframe DYNAMO© language (Pugh & Carrasco, 1983) and DYSMAP2/386 (Dangerfield, 1992) software still have to draw flow diagrams like the one shown in Fig. C.5.1a, and then code and enter the actual equations after the mapping process. In coding a DYNAMO© or a DYSMAP2/386 system dynamics model, the time postscripts J, K, and L represent the past, present, and future, respectively, providing the necessary rigor to safeguard against "absurd formulations" (Dangerfield, 1992, p. 205).

Conversely, users of iThink™ (Richmond, Peterson, & Charyk, 1992) and STELLA®, that is, Systems Thinking Experiential Learning Laboratory with Animation, (Richmond & Peterson, 1992b) can display diagrammatically on the glass of a computer screen the system interrelationships of the college fund situation, simultaneously with the development of Eqs. 1 through 1.7. The word "simultaneously" is used literally here. Although the user is creating the flow diagram of Fig. C.5.1b, the software automatically generates the difference equation structure required for simulation. The equations window allows the review and printing of a model's equations, but "there is never a need to write a difference equation" (Peterson, 1992, p. 199).

iThink™ and STELLA® users can create elegant flow diagrams like the one

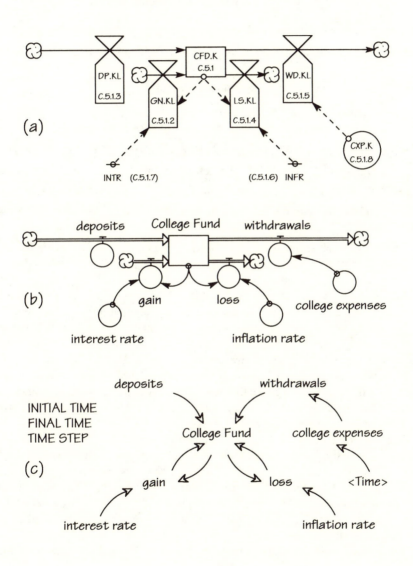

Figure C.5.1 System Dynamics Simulation Modeling Flow Diagrams:
(a) DYNAMO© & DYSMAP2, (b) iThink™ & STELLA®
and (c) Vensim™

shown in Fig. C.5.1b by choosing structural building blocks from a work-tool palette, by clicking on them with the mouse, and positioning them within the diagram window. The palette's four structural building blocks include

- The stock ☐ , which accumulates "stuff," such as material, orders, money, or personnel.
- The flow ⇥ or ⇤ , which transfers the "stuff" into and out of stocks.

Users combine these into feedback loop structures and infrastructures, using

- The single-line arrow information connector ↖.
- The converter ◯ .

Recent versions of iThink™ and STELLA® distinguish between *uniflow* ⇥ and *biflow* ⇤ variables. The default specification is the uniflow, which takes on nonnegative values only, while the biflow takes on both positive and negative values (Richmond & Peterson, 1992b; Richmond, Peterson, & Charyk, 1992).

Underlying each stock, flow, and converter is a repository for storing the algebra and documenting modeling assumptions. Each building block's repository opens up in a dialog window by double-clicking on the building block with the mouse. In Fig. C.5.1b, for example, double-clicking on withdrawals would open up a dialog window showing college expenses as a required information input.

The college expenses parameter is a required input to withdrawals because it has been so indicated by the single-line arrow information connector on the model diagram of Fig. C.5.1b. This is how the iThink™ or STELLA® system dynamics simulation software enforces a one-to-one correspondence between a model's flow diagram and the underlying equation logic that drives the simulation. Underlying each building block is a set of formal model building rules to prevent syntax errors in model structure (Peterson, 1992).

Converters are often used for parameters, time series input, and algebraic conversions implicating other variables, which also allow for straightforward graphically constructed table lookup functions. Connectors indicate informational, logical, or causal connections among the elements of a system dynamics simulation model. Once a situation has been mapped and its underlying relationships have been defined with equation logic, users can compute its dynamic implications by computing alternative scenarios.

The iThink™ and STELLA® software packages incorporate animation technology to help users improve their qualitative, nonnumerical, intuitive grasp of the behavior of a dynamic system. This auditory-kinesthetic-visual appreciation for the dynamic behavior of a system develops as users watch stocks fill and drain (↑ ▓▓ ↓), and flow and converter magnitudes animated as needle gauges ⊘ . Similarly, pictures and movies, which are less abstract than stock-and-flow diagrams or equations, often "provide a conceptual bridge between" the user's mental model and a formal system dynamics simulation model (Peterson, 1992). Yet, the software's animated time-series graphs and scatter phase plots are the locus for the graphical display of simulation output, while tables are just a mouse click away if the analysis of a decision situation requires "a more precise numerical representation of model output" (Peterson, 1992, p. 201).

Each stock rectangle represents the cumulative level of a variable that changes through the movement of its associated flow(s). Flows feed stuff into and drain stuff out of' a stock through double-line arrows (i.e. pipes), showing the direction of the flow to and from the stock. Often, flows feed into or emanate out of sinks and sources, respectively, that is, the clouds (⬡) of Fig. C.5.1, which define the boundaries of the system under consideration. Sink and source clouds are created automatically whenever a flow either does not feed into a stock or does not emanate out of a stock, respectively.

In Fig. C.5.1b, the outflow icon of monetary loss (Eq. 1.3) from inflation (Eq. 1.5) is a composite symbol. It consists of

- A directed double-line arrow or pipe ⇒ , within which stuff moves.
- A T-shaped spigot that regulates flow size or volume.
- A flow regulator ○ attached to the spigot.
- A sink (⬡).

A decision function in the repository of the flow regulator often determines the rate of a flow. Only information can feed into a decision function or flow equation through single-line arrow connectors. Flow regulators receive information input through connectors to determine the flow rate. In a feedback loop representation, the required sequence of connection is

Stock → Information (or causal influence) → Decision function (or action) → Stock

(see Morecroft, 1992, p. 19). In Fig. C.5.1b, for example, the outflow of monetary loss from inflation receives information about both the current inflation rate and the current level of the college fund stock, and then acts on their product (Eq. 1.3). This simple decision rule determines the annual rate of monetary loss from inflation. Similarly, the inflow of monetary gain from the annually compounding interest rate receives information about the interest rate and the level of the college fund, and then acts on their product (Eq. 1.1). This decision function determines the annual rate of monetary gain from interest income.

Generic feedback-loop structures appear consistently throughout system dynamics simulation models, creating qualitatively similar behavior patterns across a large variety of situations. In Fig. C.5.1b, for example, the feedback-loop structure from the college fund stock, to the monetary gain flow regulator and back to the college fund stock, if isolated, will always produce an exponential growth pattern as long as its external input (here the interest rate) to its flow regulator remains a positive constant. Similarly, the feedback-loop structure from the college fund stock, to the monetary loss flow regulator and back to the college fund stock, in isolation, will always produce an exponential decay pattern as long as its external input (now the inflation rate) to its flow regulator remains a positive constant.

In Fig. C.5.2, the exponential growth patterns in the college fund are produced by the dominating feedback loop of the net monetary gain of 5.25 percent per year (interest rate minus inflation rate), from 1993 through 2010. In the year 2011 the deposits stop, while the 18-year-old Zorbalander makes the first ZBLD$40,000 withdrawal to cover the first year's college expenses.

In 2011, the simulation interrupts the deposits made by the baby's parents by stepping deposits down to zero (Eq. 1.2), while it simultaneously starts the withdrawals stream by stepping withdrawals up from zero to match the ZBLD$40,000 college expenses per year (Eq. 1.4). Both Eqs. 1.2 and 1.4 take advantage of the STEP(<height>,<time>) built-in function, which generates a one-time step change of specified height occurring at a specified time. Special built-in functions (such as steps, ramps, Boolean operators, statistical distributions, etc.) are available in all the system dynamics simulation modeling software listed in Fig. C.5.1.

Back to Fig. C.5.2, the sensitivity test runs #1 through #3 show the sensitivity of the college fund to annual deposits in a systematic progression. These tests were conducted by computing three decision scenarios (run #1, #2, and #3), which correspond to incremental changes in the deposits parameter numbers of Eq. 1.2, from ZBLD$5,500 to 5,000 to 4,500, respectively.

The iThink™ and STELLA® software allows the set up of a sensitivity analysis through its sensitivity analysis window. In this window the user can direct the software to vary parameters incrementally, arbitrarily, or according to a statistical distribution function. In the year 2014, the baby Zorbalander, now a college senior, makes the fourth and last withdrawal of ZBLD$40,000 to pay college expenses, leaving ZBLD$1,467.32 in the college fund account for a small graduation gift.

Like the generic feedback-loop structures, feedback-loop infrastructures or *archetypes* also appear consistently throughout many business or other social systems, creating very similar qualitative behavior patterns. Senge (1990, Appendix 2) as well as the iThink™ and STELLA® software manuals (Richmond & Peter-

Figure C.5.2   Sensitivity to Annual Deposits

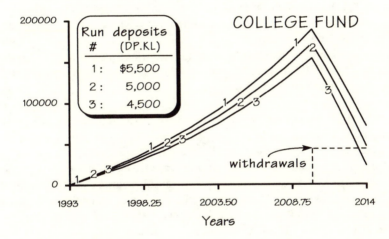

son, 1992a, 1992b) present several feedback-loop infrastructures because a rather "small number of these archetypes are common to a very large variety of management situations" (Senge, 1990, p. 94).

In Fig. C.5.2, for example, the shark-fin-shaped dynamic behavior pattern is common among personal-finance valuation situations. One could easily convert the college fund model of Fig. C.5.1 into an individual retirement account (IRA) by simply changing some variable names and adjusting for the desired annuity or uninterrupted stream of equal payments to occur annually upon retirement. A Zorbalander, for example, would have to substitute College Fund with IRA and college expenses with retirement income.

Interesting to note in Fig. C.5.1c is how the creators of Vensim™ have chosen an influence diagramming technique for displaying diagrammatically the network of interrelationships underlying a situation. Running only on Microsoft® Windows, Vensim™ provides a visually oriented mouse-driven system dynamics modeling environment (Eberlein & Peterson, 1992).

Like iThink™ and STELLA®, Vensim™ also permits diagramming simultaneously with the development of model equations, but it requires using its integral built-in function to simulate the calculus operation of integration rather than automatically generating a difference equation to specify the accumulation of stuff in a stock. Instead of automatically generating Eq. 1, for example, Vensim™ would require using its INTEG(<required input>,<initial value>) built-in function to specify that college fund is a stock as follows:

$$\text{College Fund} \ = \ \text{INTEG(gain + deposits } - \text{loss } - \text{withdrawals, 0) \{ZBLD\$\}}, \quad (2)$$

where 0 (zero) in Eq. 2 is the initial college fund, as in Eq. 1.

Upper case characters are significant in Vensim™ because they let the user visually distinguish stock accumulations in a causal diagram. Alternatively, as an option, the software allows placing rectangles and circles around variable names to distinguish stocks from flows and auxiliary converters.

As in iThink™ and STELLA®, Vensim™ users can create their causal flow diagrams like the one in Fig. C.5.1c by choosing tools from a work-tool palette, by clicking on them with the mouse, and by positioning them within the sketch window. The *sketch window* is just one of Vensim's many work tools that users can select from the program's workbench-toolbox palette. Unlike iThink™ and STELLA® which provide access to their unit of time, their initial and final time, time step (*dt*), and integration method in a time specs window, Vensim™ places these parameters as well as the variable <Time> in its sketch window. In iThink™ and STELLA® , ' TIME ' is accessible from the list of built-in functions.

Under Vensim's *workbench-toolbox* is a complex arrangement of model creation, structural, output analysis, and summary tool windows that the user can choose to review and to print. Vensim's complexity and multiple sophisticated options make the workbench-toolbox metaphor necessary for letting users "get views of parts and subassemblies, and [see] how they connect under different operating conditions" (Eberlein & Peterson, 1992, p. 217).

Vensim's advanced features that support complex causal networks include system dynamics modeling optimization for the purposes of parameter calibration, sensitivity testing, and policy analysis. The software was created to increase the modeling capabilities and productivity of already skilled system dynamicists, with functionality that improves the quality and understanding of models. As in CSM, the causal-tracing features of Vensim™ could enhance human effort, permitting fast dissemination and understanding of the complex causal networks typically underlying complex strategic situations.

SUMMARY

However tentative, a general conclusion can be drawn from our explorations of the intelligence amplifiers or modeling tools used in this book.

The basic approach and fundamental techniques of system dynamics simulation modeling, from rough-cut influence diagramming (ID) to comprehensive situation mapping (CSM) to the sensitivity analysis afforded by full-fledged computer models can indeed be applied fruitfully to problematic decision situations. Assuredly, the more exact procedures permit us to state our results with a degree of precision that could not be attained otherwise.

Yet, it is the process of framing a decision situation that permits actual numbers to be inserted for the construction of specific rules that apply, with a considerable degree of realism, to the particularities of the situation under consideration. It is the process of modeling that stimulates intuition, creativity, and institutional learning. In the process of modeling a strategic situation, mental models and computed scenarios become an integral part of debate and dialogue.

That is why management teams of world-class firms use modeling to compute both environmental and strategic scenarios. Structuring informed debates about changes in strategy through scenario-driven planning enables learning—specifically, learning to manage strategic uncertainty.

Bibliography

Abrahamson, E. (1991). Managerial fads and fashions: The diffusion and rejection of innovations. *Academy of Management Review, 16* (3): 586-612.

Acar, W. (1983). *Toward a Theory of Problem Formulation and the Planning of Change: Causal Mapping and Dialectical Debate in Situation Formulation.* Ann Arbor, MI: UMI.

Acar, W. (1984). What's a problem? In *Proceedings of the 1984 Annual Meeting of the American Institute for Decision Sciences (now Decision Sciences Institute)*, 23-25 Nov., Toronto, ON: 28-30.

Acar, W. (1987a). A biased view of problem formulation. In *Proceedings of the Annual Meeting of the Decision Sciences Institute*, 23-25 Nov., Boston: 449-451.

Acar, W. (1987b). Toward a consistent terminology for management theory building. *Systems Research, 4* (2): 119-125.

Acar, W. & Booth, D. E. (1987). Easier quality control: Combining problem classification with time-series analysis. *Production and Inventory Management, 28* (3): 53-58.

Acar, W., Chaganti, R. & Joglekar, P. (1985). Models of strategy formulation: The content-focused and process-focused models can and must meet! *American Business Review, 2* (2): 1-9.

Acar, W. & Howard, G. S. (1987). Dialectical inquiry and comprehensive situation mapping in DSS information requirements analysis. In *Proceedings of the North American Conference of the International Business School Computer Users and Groups (BSCUG)*, (July), Flint, MI: 122-126.

Ackoff, R. L. (1967). Management misinformation systems. *Management Science, 14* (4): B147-B156.

Ackoff, R. L. (1970). *A Concept of Corporate Planning.* New York, Ny: Wiley.

Ackoff, R. L. (1978). *The Art of Problem Solving.* New York: Wiley.

Ackoff, R. L. (1981). *Creating the Corporate Future.* New York: Wiley.

Ackoff, R. L. & Emery, F. E. (1972). *On Purposeful Systems*. Chicago: Aldine
    Atherton.
Ackoff, R. L. & Sasieni, M. W. (1968). *Fundamentals of Operations Research*.
    New York: Wiley.
Aguilar, F. (1967). *Scanning the Business Environment*. New York: Macmillan.
Aldrich, H. (1979). *Organizations and Environments*. Englewood Cliffs, NJ: Pren-
    tice-Hall.
Allison, G. T. (1971). *The Essence of Decision*. Boston: Little, Brown & Co., pp.
    79-81.
Amara, R. & Lipinski, A. J. (1983). *Business Planning for an Uncertain Future:
    Scenarios & Strategies*. New York: Pergamon.
Anderson, C. & Paine, F. (1975). Managerial perceptions and strategic behavior.
    Academy of Management Journal, 18: 811-823.
Andrews, K. (1987). *The Concept of Corporate Strategy* (revised ed.). Homewood,
    IL: Irwin.
Anonymous (1986). Business fads. *Business Week* (Special Issue, Jan. 20), .
Anonymous (1989). The ideas business: Economy of the mind. *The Economist* (22
    Dec.): 99-102.
Anonymous (1991). Global custody: Let us do your paperwork. *The Economist* (13
    Apr.): 76.
Ansoff, H. I. (1965). *Corporate Strategy*. New York: McGraw-Hill.
Ansoff, H. I. (1984). *Implanting Strategic Management* (Ansoff & McDunnel,
    1990, 2nd ed.). Englewood Cliffs, NJ: Prentice-Hall International.
Ansoff, H. I. (1985). Conceptual underpinnings of systematic strategic manage-
    ment. *European Journal of Operational Research, 19* (1): 2-19.
Anthony, W. P., Bennett, R. H. III, Maddox, E. N. & Wheatley, W. J. (1993). Pic-
    turing the future: Using mental imagery to enrich strategic environmental as-
    sessment. *Academy of Management Executive, 7* (2): 43-56.
Argyris, C. & Schön, D. (1978). *Organizational Learning: A Theory of Action Ap-
    proach*. Reading: Addison-Wesley.
Arthur Andersen (1984). *The future of oil prices: The perils of prophecy* . Arthur
    Andersen & Cambridge Energy Research Association.
Ashby, W.R. (1963). *Introduction to Cybernetics*. New York: Wiley.
Aupperle, K.E., Acar, W. & Booth, D.E. (1986). An empirical critique of "in
    search of excellence": How excellent are the "excellent" companies? *Journal of
    Management, 12:* 499-512.
Badulescu, P. (1991). International technological knowledge differences and eco-
    nomic growth comparisons: USA versus West Germany and Sweden versus
    Norway, 1963-1988. *Applied Economics (UK), 23* (1B): 263-282.
Bannister, D. & Fransella, F. (1971). *Inquiring Man: The Theory of Personal Con-
    structs*. London: Penguin.
Bao, B.-H. & Bao, D.-H. (1989). An empirical investigation of the association

between productivity and firm value. *Journal of Business Finance & Accounting (UK), 16* (5): 699-717.

Baron, D. P. (1993). *Business and its Environment.* Englewood Cliffs, NJ: Prentice-Hall.

Barr, P. S., Stimpert, J. L. & Huff, A. S. (1992). Cognitive change, strategic action and organizational renewal. *Strategic Management Journal, 13* (Summer Special Issue): 15-36.

Bartlett, C. A. & Ghoshal, S. (1989). *Managing Across Borders: The Transnational Solution.* Boston: Harvard Business School Press.

Battelle (1988). *BASICS-PC™: Battelle's Scenario Development Software Package for the Personal Computer.* Columbus, OH: Battelle.

Becker, H. (1982). Constructing and using scenarios: An aid to strategic planning and decision-making. *World Future Society Bulletin* (September-October): 13-24.

Beer, S. (1968). *Management Science: The Business Use of Operations Research* (2nd ed.). New York: Doubleday.

Beer, S. (1981). *The Brain of the Firm* (2nd ed.). Chichester, UK: Wiley.

Belknap, S. (1991). The Chicago kinetic simulator: A tool for the simulation and optimization of mathematical models. *The Mathematica Journal, 1* (4): 68-86.

Bell, J. A. & Senge, P. M. (1980). Methods for enhancing refutability in system dynamics modeling. In A. Legasto Jr., J. W. Forrester, & J. M. Lyneis (Eds.), *TIMS Studies in the Management Sciences: System Dynamics,* 14 (pp. 61-73). New York: Elsevier Science (North Holland).

Bellman, R. (1961). *Adaptive Control Processes.* Princeton, NJ: Princeton University Press.

Beltrami, E. (1987). *Mathematics of Dynamic Modeling.* London: Academic Press.

Benveniste, G. (1989). *Mastering the Politics of Planning.* San Francisco, CA: Jossey-Bass.

Bigelow, J. (1982). A catastrophe model of organizational change. *Behavioral Science, 27:* 26-42.

Birnbaum, P. & Ottensmeyer, E. (1984). *Responding to Federal Regulations: The Process of Strategic Choice.* Working Paper, Graduate School of Business, Indiana University.

Blake, R. R. & Mouton, J. S. (1964). *Managerial Grid.* Houston, TX: Gulf.

Bogue, M. C., III & Buffa, E. S. (1986). *Corporate Strategic Analysis.* New York: Free Press.

Bonnicksen, T. M. (1985). Initial decision analysis (IDA): A participatory approach for developing resource policies. *Environmental Management, 9* (5): 379-392.

Boulding, K. (1956). General systems theory—The skeleton of science. *Management Science, 2* (4): 197-208.

Boulton, W., Lindsay, W., Franklin, S. & Rue, L. (1982). Strategic planning: Determining the impact of environmental characteristics and uncertainty. *Academy of Management Journal, 25* (3): 500-509.

Bourgeois, L. J. (1980). Strategy and environment: A conceptual integration. *Academy of Management Review, 5* (1): 25-39.

Bourgeois, L. J. (1985). Strategic goals, environmental uncertainty and economic performance in volatile environments. *Academy of Management Journal, 28* (3): 548-573.

Bourgeois, L. J. & Eisenhardt, K. M. (1988). Strategic decision processes in high velocity environments: Four cases in the microcomputer industry. *Management Science, 34* (7): 816-835.

Bourgeois, L. J., McAllister, D. & Mitchell, T. (1978). The effects of different organizational environments upon decisions about organizational structure. *Academy of Management Journal, 21* (3): 508-514.

Bower, J. L. (1982). Business policy in the 1980s. *Academy of Management Review, 7:* 630-638.

Bowman, E. H. (1982). Risk seeking by troubled firms. *Sloan Management Review, 24* (3): 33-42.

Brauers, J. & Weber, M. (1988). A new method of scenario analysis for strategic planning. *Journal of Forecasting, 7* (1): 31-47.

Burgelman, R. (1983). Corporate entrepreneurship and strategic management: Insights from a process study. *Management Science, 29* (12): 1349-1364.

Burns, T. & Stalker, G. (1961). *The Management of Innovation.* London: Tavistock.

Campbell, D. (1969). Variation and selective retention in sociocultural systems. *General Systems, 14:* 69-85.

Casson, J. J. (1982). Enhancing the economic forecast. *Planning Review, 10* (2): 36-39, 46+.

Cavaleri, S. & Obloj, K. (1993). *Management Systems: A Global Perspective.* Belmont, CA: Wadsworth.

Chakrabarti, A. K. (1990). Innovation and productivity: an analysis of the chemical, textile and machine tool industries in the US. *Research Policy (Netherlands), 19* (3): 257-269.

Chandler, J. & Cockle, P. (1982). *Techniques of Scenario Planning.* London: McGraw-Hill.

Chanin, M. N. & Shapiro, H. J. (1985). Dialectical inquiry in strategic planning: Extending the boundaries. *Academy of Management Review, 10* (4): 663-675.

Checkland, P. B. (1975). The development of systems thinking by systems practice: A methodology from an action research program. *Progress in Cybernetics and Systems Research, 2:* 278-283.

Christensen, C. R., Andrews, K. R., Bower, J. L., Hamermesh, R. G. & Porter, M. E. (1987). *Business Policy: Text and Cases* (6th ed.). Homewood, IL: Irwin.

Churchman, C. W. (1968). *Challenge to Reason.* New York: McGraw-Hill.

Churchman, C. W. (1969). *The Systems Approach.* New York: Dell.

Churchman, C. W. (1971). *The Design of Inquiring Systems.* New York: Basic Books.

Clark, R. (1988). *System Dynamics and Modeling.* Arlington, VA: ORSA.

Coates, J. F., Coates, V. T., Jarratt, J. & Heinz, L. (1986). *Issues Management: How You Can Plan, Organize and Manage for the Future.* Mt. Airy, MD: Lomond.

Collins, P. D., Hage, J. & Hull, F. M. (1988). Organizational and technological predictors of change in automaticity. *Academy of Management Journal, 31* (3): 512-543.

Copeland, M. T. (1958). *And Mark an Era.* Boston: Little, Brown & Co. (Chapter IX: The case method of instruction).

Cosier, R. A. (1981a). Dialectical inquiry in strategic planning: A case of premature acceptance? *Academy of Management Review, 6:* 643-648.

Cosier, R. A. (1981b). Further thoughts on dialectical inquiry: A rejoiner to Mitroff and Mason. *Academy of Management Review, 6:* 653-654.

Cosier, R. A. & Rose, G. L. (1977). Cognitive conflict and goal conflict effects on task performance. *Organizational Behavior and Human Performance, 19:* 378-391.

Cvar, M. (1986). Case studies in global competition: Patterns in success and failure. In M. E. Porter (Ed.), *Competition in Global Industries,* Boston: Harvard Business School Press.

Cyert, R. M. & March, J. G. (1963). *A Behavioral Theory of the Firm.* Englewood Cliffs, NJ: Prentice-Hall.

Daft, R. L. (1978). A dual-core model of organizational innovation. *Academy of Management Journal, 21* (2): 193-210.

Daft, R. L. & Weick, K. E. (1984). Toward a model of organizations as interpretation systems. *Academy of Management Review, 9:* 284-295.

Damanpour, F. (1991). Organizational innovation: A meta-analysis of effects of determinants and moderators. *Academy of Management Journal, 34* (3): 555-590.

Dangerfield, B. (1992). The system dynamics modelling process and DYSMAP2[©]. *European Journal of Operational Research, 59* (1): 203-209.

Davenport, T. H. (1993). *Process Innovation: Reengineering Work through Information Technology.* Boston: Harvard Business School Press.

Davis, D. D. & Holt, C. A. (1993). *Experimental Economics.* Princeton, NJ: Princeton University Press.

Davis, S. M. & Lawrence, P. L. (1977). *Matrix.* Reading: Addison-Wesley.

DeCarlo, P. F. & Irwin, P. H. (1981). Tactics and techniques for making the tough decisions. *Planning Review, 9* (4): 20-24, 44+.

de Geus, A. P. (1988). Planning as learning. *Harvard Business Review, 66* (2): 70-

74.

de Geus, A. P. (1992). Modelling to predict or to learn? *European Journal of Operational Research, 59* (1): 1-5.

Dembo, R. S. (1991). Scenario optimization. *Annals of Operations Research, 30* (2): 63-80.

DeMeyer, A., Nakane, J., Miller, J. G. & Ferdows, K. (1989). Flexibility: The next competitive battle—The manufacturing futures survey. *Strategic Management Journal, 10* (2): 135-144.

Deming, E. W. (1986). *Out of The Crisis.* Cambridge: MIT Press.

Deming, W. E. (1993). *The New Economics.* Cambridge: MIT/CAES.

Dess, G. & Beard, D. (1984). Dimensions of organizational task environments. *Administrative Science Quarterly, 29:* 52-73.

Deutsch, K. W. (1963). *The Nerves of Government.* New York: Free Press (Chapters 11 and 12 give an excellent presentation of feedback loops).

Dewey, J. (1910). *How We Think.* New York: D.C. Heath.

Dewey, J. (1938). *Logic: The Theory of Inquiry.* New York: Holt, Rinehart & Winston.

Diehl, E. W. (1992a). *Microworld Creator™ 2.0: Shedding New Light on Old Business Problems.* Cambridge: MicroWorlds.

Diehl, E. W. (1992b). Participatory simulation software for managers: The design philosophy behind MicroWorld Creator™. *European Journal of Operational Research, 59* (1): 210-215.

Diesing, P. (1971). *Patterns of Discovery in the Social Sciences.* Chicago: Aldine Atherton.

Diffenbach, J. (1981). A compatibility approach to scenario evaluation. *Technological Forecasting & Social Change, 19:* 161-174.

Diffenbach, J. (1982). Influence diagrams of complex strategic issues. *Strategic Management Journal, 3:* 133-146.

Donaldson, L. (1992). The Weick stuff: Managing beyond games. *Organization Science, 3* (4): 461-466.

Downey, H. K., Hellriegel, D. & Slocum, J. (1975). Environmental uncertainty: The construct and its application. *Administrative Science Quarterly, 20:* 613-629.

Drenick, R. F. (1986). *A Mathematical Organization Theory.* New York: Elsevier Science (North Holland).

Drucker, P. F. (1954). *The Practice of Management.* New York: Harper & Row.

Drucker, P. F. (1986). The changed world economy. *Foreign Affairs, 64* (4): 768-791.

Drucker, P. F. (1989). *The New Realities.* New York: Harper & Row.

Duncan, R. B. (1972). Characteristics of organizational environments and perceived environmental uncertainty. *Administrative Science Quarterly, 17:* 313-327.

Duperrin, J. C. & Godet, M. (1975). SMIC 74: A method for constructing and ranking scenarios. *Futures, 7* (4): 302-312.

Durand, J. (1972). A new method for constructing scenarios. *Futures, 4* (4): 325-330.

Dutton, J. E., Fahey, L. & Narayanan, V. K. (1983). Toward understanding strategic issue diagnosis. *Strategic Management Journal, 4:* 307-323.

Dutton, J. E. & Freedman, R. D. (1985). External and Internal Strategies: Calculating, Experimenting and Imitating in Organizations. In R. Lamb & P. Shrivastava (Eds.), *Advances in Strategic Management,* 3 (pp. 39-47). New York: JAI Press.

Duval, A., Fontela, A. & Gabus, A. (1975). Cross-impact analysis: A handbook on concepts and applications. In M. M. Baldwin (Ed.), *Portraits of Complexity: Applications of Systems Methodologies to Societal Problems,* Columbus, OH: Battelle.

Dyson, R. G. (Ed.) (1990). *Strategic Planning: Models and Analytical Techniques.* Chichester, UK: Wiley.

Eberlein, R. L. & Peterson, D. W. (1992). Understanding models with Vensim™. *European Journal of Operational Research, 59* (1): 126-219.

Eden, C. (1978). Operational research and organizational development. *Human Relations, 31* (8): 657-674.

Eden, C., et al. (1979). Images into models: The subjective world of the policy maker. *Futures* (Feb.): 56-62.

Eden, C. (1988). Cognitive mapping. *European Journal of Operational Research, 36* (1): 1-13.

Eden, C. (1989). Using cognitive mapping for strategic options development. In J. Rosenhead (Ed.), *Rational Analysis for a Problematic World,* Chichester, UK: Wiley.

Eden, C. (1990). Managing the environment as a means to managing complexity. In C. Eden & J. Radford (Eds.), *Tackling Strategic Problems: The Role of Group Decision Support,* London: Sage.

Eden, C., Jones, S., Sims, D. & Smithin, T. (1981). The intersubjectivity of issues and issues of intersubjectivity. *Journal of Management Studies, 18* (1): 37-47.

Eilon, S. (1984). *The Art of Reckoning: Analysis of Performance Criteria.* London: Academic Press.

Emery, F. E.&.Trist, E. L. (1965). The causal texture of organizational environments. *Human Relations, 18:* 21-32.

Eppen, G. D., Gould, F. J. & Schmidt, C. P. (1991). *Introductory Management Science* (3rd ed.). Englewood Cliffs, NJ: Prentice-Hall.

Fach, W., et al. (1972). *Problem Structuring: A Methodological Approach to Organization for Positive Coordination in Planning.* London: Institute for Operational Research, Tavistock Institute of Human Relations.

Farmer, R. N. (1973). Looking backward at looking forward. *Business Horizons*

(Feb.): 21-36.

Farris, F. (1990). For US, a total surprise. *International Herald Tribune* (3 Aug.), pp. 1 & 6.

Fayol, H. (1972). *General and Industrial Management*. New York: Pitman. First French ed., 1916.

Fennell, M. L. (1984). Synergy, influence and information in the adoption of administrative innovations. *Academy of Management Journal, 27* (1): 113-129.

Flood, R. L. & Jackson, M. C. (1991). *Creative Problem Solving: Total Systems Intervention*. Chichester, UK: Wiley.

Fombrun, C. J. (1986). Structural dynamics within and between organizations. *Administrative Science Quarterly, 31:* 403-421.

Fombrun, C. J. & Ginsberg, A. (1986). Enabling and disabling forces on resource deployment. In *Proceedings of the Annual Meeting of the Decision Sciences Institute* (23-25 Nov.), Honolulu, HI: 1249-1251.

Forrester, J. W. (1958). Industrial dynamics: A major breakthrough for decision makers. *Harvard Business Review, 36* (4): 37-66.

Forrester, J. W. (1961). *Industrial Dynamics*. Cambridge: MIT Press.

Forrester, J. W. (1968a). Market growth as influenced by capital investment. *Sloan Management Review, 9* (2): 83-105.

Forrester, J. W. (1968b). *Principles of Systems*. Cambridge: MIT Press.

Forrester, J. W. (1969). *Urban Dynamics*. Cambridge: MIT Press.

Forrester, J. W. (1975). Counter-intuitive behavior of social systems. In J. W. Forrester (Ed.), *Collected Papers of Jay W. Forrester* (pp. 211-237). Cambridge: MIT Press.

Forrester, J. W. (1976). Business structure, economic cycles and national policy. *Futures* (Jun).

Forrester, J. W. (1987). Lessons from system dynamics modelimg. *System Dynamics Review, 3* (2): 136-149.

Forrester, J. W. (1989). *The Beginning of System Dynamics*. July 13, Stuttgart, FRG: Banquet Talk at the International Meeting of the System Dynamics Society.

Forrester, J. W. (1992). Policies, decisions and information sources for modeling. *European Journal of Operational Research, 59* (1): 42-63.

Fortuna, R. M. (1988). Beyond quality: Taking SPC upstream. *Quality Progress, 21* (6): 23-28.

Fredrickson, J. W. (1984). The comprehensiveness of strategic decision processes: Extension, observations, future directions. *Academy of Management Journal, 27* (3): 445-466.

Freeman, R. E. (1984). *Strategic Management: A Stakeholder Approach*. Boston: Pitman.

Freud, S. (1933). *The Complete Introductory Lectures on Psychoanalysis*. New York: W. W. Norton.

Friend, J. K. & Jessop, W. N. (1969). *Local Government and Strategic Choice.* London: Tavistock.

Friesen, P. H. & Miller, D. (1986). A mathematical model of the adaptive behavior of organizations. *Journal of Management Studies, 23:* 1-25.

Fushimi, T. (1989). Profitability analyses of yen appreciation. In Y. Monden & M. Sakurai (Eds.), *Japanese Management Accounting: A World Class Approach to Profit Management* (pp. 229-240). Cambridge: Productivity Press.

Galbraith, C. & Schendel, D. (1983). An empirical analysis of strategy types. *Strategic Management Journal, 4:* 153-173.

Galbraith, J. (1973). *Designing Complex Organizations.* Reading: Addison Wesley.

Galer, G. & Kasper, W. (1982). Scenario planning for Australia. *Long Range Planning, 15* (4): 50-55.

Gammon, J., III & Labuszewski, J. W. (1986). How to adjust risk in short covered calls. *Futures: The Magazine of Commodities Options, 15* (4): 72-74.

Gemünden, H.G. & Hauschildt, J. (1985). Number of alternatives and efficiency in different types of top-management decisions. *European Journal of Operational Research, 22* (2): 178-190.

Georgantzas, N. C. (1989). Share in: The missing link of MNE global strategy and structure. *Management International Review, 29* (3): 19-34.

Georgantzas, N. C. (1990). Cognitive biases, modeling and performance: An experimental analysis. In *Proceedings of the Annual International System Dynamics Conference* (9-14 July), Boston: 410-424.

Georgantzas, N. C. (1991). MNE competitiveness: A scenario-driven technology transfer construct. *Managerial and Decision Economics, 12:* 281-293.

Georgantzas, N. C. (1992). *Timing Changes in Strategy.* Working Paper, New York: Fordham University.

Georgantzas, N. C. & Acar, W. (1989). Scenario-driven interactive planning: A critical review. In D. L. Stone & E. F. Stone (Eds.), *Proceedings of the 32nd Annual Meeting of the Midwest Academy of Management,* 13-15 April, Columbus, OH: 260-264.

Georgantzas, N. C. & Acar, W. (1993). Scenario-driven technological development planning: A process view. In C. N. Madu (Ed.), *Management of New Technologies for Global Competitiveness,* 12 (pp. 243-260). Westport, CT: Quorum Books.

Georgantzas, N. C. & Hessel, M. P. (1991). The intermediate structure of designs for quality. In *Proceedings of the First International Meeting of the Decision Sciences Institute,* 24-26 June, Brussels, Belgium: 240-243.

Georgantzas, N. C. & Madu, C. N. (1990). Cognitive processes in technology management and transfer. *Technological Forecasting & Social Change, 38:* 81-95.

Georgantzas, N. C. & Shapiro, H. J. (1993). Viable theoretical forms of synchronous production innovation. *Journal of Operations Management, 11*: 161-183.

Gérardin, L. A. (1975). *L'Industrie et la Société, des probèmes en masse et un noeud de conflicts*. Paris, France: Rapport au Commissariat au Plan.

Gérardin, L. A. (1979). A structural model of industrialized societies: Evolutions, stability, policies, governability. In C. Renfrew & K. L. Cooke (Eds.), *Transformations: Mathematical Approaches to Culture Change* (pp. 299-325). New York: Academic Press.

Geringer, J. M., Beamish, P. W. & da Costa, R. C. (1989). Diversification strategy and internationalization: Implications for MNE performance. *Strategic Management Journal, 10* (2): 109-119.

Ghoshal, S. & Westney, D. E. (1991). Organizing competitor analysis systems. *Strategic Management Journal, 12* (1): 17-31.

Gilmore, T. N., et al. (1982). *Problem Framing*. Philadelphia, PA: Management and Behavioral Science Center, Wharton School, University of Pennsylvania.

Ginsberg, A. (1988). Measuring and modelling changes in strategy: Theoretical foundations and empirical considerations. *Strategic Management Journal, 9:* 559-575.

Gleckman, H., Carey, J., Mitchell, R., Smart, T. & Roush, C. (1993). The technology payoff. *Business Week* (14 June), pp. 56-68.

Glover, J. (1966a). *Innovation and evolution of the environment. Part I: Innovation* (Teaching Note No. 8-367-020). Graduate School of Business, Harvard University.

Glover, J. (1966b). *Innovation and evolution of the environment. Part II: Evolution* (Teaching Note No. 8-367-021). Graduate School of Business, Harvard University.

Gluck, F., Kaufman, S. & Walleck, A. S. (1980). Strategic management for competitive advantage. *Harvard Business Review, 58* (4): 154-161.

Glueck, W. F. & Jauch, L. R. (1984). *Business Policy and Strategic Management*. New York: McGraw-Hill.

Godet, M. (1987). *Scenarios and Strategic Management: Prospective et Planification Stratégique* (D. Green & A. Rodney, Trans.). London: Butterworths.

Godiwalla, Y. M., Meinhart, W. A. & Warde, W. A. (1981). General management and corporate strategy. *Managerial Planning, 30* (2): 17-23, 29.

Grauer, M., Thompson, M. & Wierzbicki, A. (Eds.) (1984). *Plural Rationalities and Interactive Decision Processes*. Berlin, FRG: Springer Verlag.

Gross, A. D. (1984). How Golf Oil deals with uncertainty. *Planning Review, 12* (2): 8-13.

Hall, A. D. (1962). *A Methodology for Systems Engineering*. Princeton, NJ: Van Nostrand.

Hall, R. I. (1976). A system pathology of an organization: The rise and fall of the old *Saturday Evening Post*. *Administrative Science Quarterly, 21:* 185-211.

Hall, R. I. (1978). Simple techniques for constructing explanatory models of complex systems for policy analysis. *Dynamica, 4* (3): 1-14.

Hall, R. I. (1984). The natural logic of management policy making: Its implications for the survival of an organization. *Management Science, 30:* 905-927.

Hamada, K. & Monden, Y. (1989). Profit management at Kyocera Corporation: The amoeba system. In Y. Monden & M. Sakurai (Eds.), *Japanese Management Accounting: A World Class Approach to Profit Management* (pp. 197-210). Cambridge: Productivity Press.

Hannan, M.T. & Freeman, J. (1984). Structural inertia and organizational change. *American Sociological Review, 49:* 149-164.

Harary, F., Norman, R. Z. & Cartwright, D. (1965). *Structural Models: An Introduction to the Theory of Directed Graphs.* New York: Wiley.

Harrigan, K. R. (1985). *Strategic Flexibility.* Lexington: Lexington Books.

Hartley, R. F. (1976). *Marketing Mistakes.* Columbus, OH: Grid Press.

Hartley, R. F. (1983). *Management Mistakes.* Columbus, OH: Grid Press.

Hatten, K. J. & Hatten, M. L. (1987). *Strategic Management: Analysis and Action.* Englewood Cliffs, NJ: Prentice-Hall.

Hauser, W. & Clausing, D. (1988). The house of quality. *Harvard Business Review, 66* (3): 63-73.

Hawken, P., Ogilvy, J. & Schwartz, P. (1982). *Seven Tomorrows: Seven Scenarios for the Eighties and Nineties.* New York: Bantam Books.

Hax, A. C. & Majluf, N. S. (1984). *Strategic Management: An Integrative Perspective.* Englewood Cliffs, NJ: Prentice-Hall.

Hayes, R. H., Wheelwright, S. C. & Clark, K. B. (1988). *Dynamic Manufacturing: Creating the Learning Organization.* New York: Free Press.

Heintz, T. J. & Acar, W. (1992). Toward conceptualizing a causal modeling approach to strategic problem framing. *Decision Sciences, 23* (5): 1220-1230.

Heise, D. R. (1975). *Causal Analysis.* New York: Wiley.

Helgason, T. & Wallace, S. W. (1991). Approximate scenario solutions in the progressive hedging algorithm: A numerical study with an application to fisheries management. *Annals of Operations Research, 31* (2): 425-444.

Helmer, O. (1983). *Looking Forward.* Beverly Hills, CA: Sage.

Henderson, B. C. (1979). *Henderson on Corporate Strategy.* Cambridge: Boston Consulting Group.

Hennessey, P., et al. (1978). *Managing Nonprofit Agencies for Results.* San Francisco, CA: Public Management Institute.

Hessel, M. P., Mooney, M. & Zeleny, M. (1988). Integrated process management: A management technology for the new competitive era. In M. K. Starr (Ed.), *Global Competitiveness: Getting the US Back on Track* (pp. 121-158). New York: W. W. Norton.

Hiromoto, T. (1988). Another hidden edge: Japanese management accounting (Special report: How control systems support manufacturing excellence). *Har-*

vard Business Review, 66 (4): 22-26.

Hitt, M. A. & Tyler, B. B. (1991). Strategic decision models: Integrating different perspectives. *Strategic Management Journal, 12:* 327-351.

Hogarth, R. M. (1980). *Judgment and Choice.* New York: Wiley.

Holling, C. S. & Goldberg, M. A. (1971). Ecology and planning. *Journal of the American Institute of Planners, 37* (4): 224-229.

Holstein, W. J. (1988). Japan's clout in the US. *Business Week* (11 July): 64-66.

Holt, J. (1970). *How Children Learn* (2nd ed.). Harmondsworth, UK: Penguin.

Holt, J. (1982). *How Children Fail* (Revised ed.). New York: Dell.

Holt, J. (1991). *Learning All the Time* (3rd ed.). Reading, MA: Addison Wesley.

Homer, J. B. (1985). Worker burnout: A dynamic model with implications for prvention and control. *System Dynamics Review, 1* (1): 43-62.

Honton, E. J., Stacey, G. S. & Millett, S. M. (1985). *Future scenarios: The BASICS computational method* (Economics and Policy Analysis Occasional Paper No. 44). Columbus, OH: Battelle.

Hopwood, A.& Stuart, T. (1987). Future scenarios for the profession. *Accountancy, 100* (1128): 101-103.

Huggins, W. H. & Entwisle, D. R. (1968). *Introductory Systems and Design.* Waltham, MA: Blaisdell.

Hurst, D. K., Rush, J. C. & White, R. E. (1989). Top management teams and organizational renewal. *Strategic Management Journal, 10* (Summer Special Issue): 87-105.

Huss, W. R. & Honton, E. J. (1987). Scenario planning: What style should you use? *Long Range Planning, 20* (4): 21-29.

Imundo, A. (1986). Are you optimizing returns on your check processing dollar? *Bank Systems & Equipment, 23* (9): 76-78.

Inoue, M. S. & Riggs, J. L. (1971). Describe your system with cause and effect diagrams. *Industrial Engineering* (April): 26-31.

Ingvar, D. H. (1985). Memory of the future: An essay on the temporal organization of conscious awareness. *Human Neurobiology, 4:* 127-136.

Istvan, R. L. (1992). A new productivity paradigm for competitive advantage. *Strategic Management Journal, 13* (7): 525-537.

Jarillo, J. C. (1988). On strategic networks. *Strategic Management Journal, 9* (1): 31-41.

Jarillo, J. C. & Martínez, J. I. (1990). Different roles for subsidiaries: The case of multinational corporations in Spain. *Strategic Management Journal, 11* (7): 501-512.

Jemison, D. B. (1981). Organizational versus environmental sources of influence in strategic decision making. *Strategic Management Journal, 2* (1): 77-89.

Jones, S. T. (1985). Multiple scenario planning: Atlantic Richfield's experience. *Journal of Business Forecasting, 4* (3): 19-23.

Kahn, H. & Wiener, A. J. (1967). The next thirty-three years: A framework for speculation. *Daedalus, 96* (3): 705-732.

Karian, Z. A. & Dudewicz, E. J. (1991). *Modern Statistical, Systems and GPSS Simulation.* New York: W.H. Freeman.

Keen, P.G.W. (1991). *Shaping the Future: Business Design through Information Technology.* Boston: Harvard Business School Press.

Kelly, G. A. (1955). *The Psychology of Personal Constructs.* New York: W.W. Norton.

Kennedy, J. A. & Sudgen, K. F. (1986). Ritual and reality in capital budgeting. *Management Accounting, 64* (2): 34-37.

Kepner, C. H. & Tregoe, B. B. (1965). *The Rational Manager.* New York: Mc-Graw-Hill.

Kilmann, R. H. (1989). *Managing Beyond the Quick Fix.* San Francisco, CA: Jossey-Bass.

Kimberly, J. R. (1981). Managerial innovation. In W. Starbuck & P. Nystrom (Eds.), *Handbook of Organizational Design* (pp. 84-104). New York: Oxford University Press.

Klein, H. E. & Linneman, R. E. (1984). Environmental assessment: An international study of corporate practices. *Journal of Business Strategy, 5:* 66-84.

Kogut, B. (1989). A note on global strategies. *Strategic Management Journal, 10* (4): 383-389.

Kojima, H. (1989). The relationship between environment and budgeting systems in Japanese corporations. In Y. Monden & M. Sakurai (Eds.), *Japanese Management Accounting: A World Class Approach to Profit Management* (pp. 475-486). Cambridge, MA: Productivity Press.

Kono, T. (1992). *Long-Range Planning of Japanese Corporations.* Berlin, FRG: Walter de Gruyter.

Kono, T. & Suzuki, Y. (1989). The transition of long-range planning systems: The case of NEC Corporation. In Y. Monden & M. Sakurai (Eds.), *Japanese Management Accounting: A World Class Approach to Profit Management* (pp. 241-259). Cambridge, MA: Productivity Press.

Koopmans, T. C. (1951). *Activity Analysis of Production and Allocation.* New York: Wiley, pp. 33-97.

Korsan, R.J. (1992). Fractals and time series analysis. *The Mathematica Journal, 3* (1): 39-44.

Kublin, M. (1991). Obstacles to Soviet-American joint ventures. *Journal of Consumer Marketing (The), 8* (3): 47-56.

Kuznets, S. (1966). *Modern Economic Growth: Rate, Structure and Spread.* New Haven, CT: Yale University Press.

Kvint, V. (1990). Integrating a government economy into the global marketplace takes more than exchangeable currency, stock markets and commercial banks. *Journal of Accountancy* (Nov.): 114-121.

Kvint, V. & Prince, M. (1992). Risks and prospects of joint ventures in the Soviet region with the participation of foreign companies. In *Creating and Managing Joint Ventures With European Enterprises Workshop*, Nov. 12, Chicago.

Lahr, M. L. (1983). Interactive planning. *Long Range Planning, 16* (4): 31-38.

Law, A. M. & Kelton, D. W. (1982). *Simulation Modeling and Analysis.* New York: McGraw-Hill.

Lawrence, P. & Lorsch, J. (1967). *Organization and Environment.* Homewood, IL: Irwin.

Leavy, D. P. (1986). Crisis communications: A planning checklist. *Credit, 12* (2): 13.

Leibenstein, H. (1976). *Beyond Economic Man: A New Foundation for Microeconomics.* Boston: Harvard University Press.

Lenz, R. & Engledow, J. (1986). Environmental analysis: The applicability of current theory. *Strategic Management Journal, 7* (4): 329-346.

Leontiades, M. (1980). *Strategies for Diversification and Change.* Boston: Little, Brown & Co.

Levi, I. (1984). *Decisions and Revisions.* Cambridge, MA: Cambridge University Press.

Lindblom, C. E. (1959). The science of muddling through. *Public Administration Review, 19:* 79-88.

Linneman, R. E. & Klein, H. E. (1983). The use of multiple scenarios by US industrial companies: A comparison study, 1977-1981. *Long Range Planning, 16* (6): 94-101.

Linstone, H. A., et al. (1981). The multiple perspective concept. *Technological Forecasting & Social Change, 20:* 275-325.

Linstone, H. A. (1984). *Multiple Perspectives for Decision Making.* New York: Elsevier Science (North Holland).

Linstone, H. A. & Turoff, M. (Eds.) (1975). *The Delphi Method.* Reading, MA: Addison Wesley.

Litterer, J. A. (1966). Conflict in organizations: A reexamination. *Academy of Management Journal, 9:* 178-186.

Lodge, G. (1975). *The New American Ideology.* New York: Alfred Knopf.

Long, L. (1989). *Management Information Systems.* Englewood Cliffs, NJ: Prentice-Hall.

Lorange, P., Scott-Morton, M.F. & Ghoshal, S. (1986). *Strategic Control.* St. Paul, MN: West.

Lorens, C. S. (1964). *Flowgraphs for the Modeling and Analysis of Linear Systems.* New York: McGraw-Hill.

Lundberg, C. C. (1984). Strategies for organizational transitioning. In J.R. Kimberly & R.E. Quinn (Eds.), *Managing Organizational Transitions* (pp. 60-82). New York: JAI Press.

Lyneis, J. M. (1980). *Corporate Planning and Policy Design: A System Dynamics Approach.* Cambridge, MA: MIT Press.

Mackenzie, K. D. (1989). The process approach to organizational design. *Human Systems Management, 8* (1): 31-43.

MacMillan, I. C. & McCaffery, M. L. (1982). How aggressive innovation can help your company. *Journal of Business Strategy, 2* (4): 213-234.

MacNulty, C.A.R. (1977). Scenario development for corporate planning. *Futures* (April).

Magnet, M. (1985). Who needs a trend-spotter? *Fortune, 112* (Dec.): 51-56.

Mandelbrot, B. B. (1963). The variation of certain speculative prices. *The Journal of Business, 36:* 394-419.

March, J. & Simon, H. A. (1958). *Organizations.* New York: Wiley.

Marris, S. (1985). *Deficits and the dollar: The world economy at risk.* Washington, DC: Institute of International Economics.

Marschak, J. & Randers, R. (1972). *Economic Theory of Teams.* New Haven, CT: Yale University Press.

Martens, B. K. & Witt, J. C. (1984). Assessment and prediction in an ecological system: Application of the general linear model to the response class concept. *Journal of Behavioral Assessment, 6:* 197-206.

Maruyama, M. (1963). The second cybernetics: Deviation-amplifying mutual causal processes. *American Scientist, 51:* 164-179 & 250-256.

Mason, R. O. (1969). A dialectical approach to strategic planning. *Management Science, 15* (8): B403-B414.

Mason, R. O. & Mitroff, I. I. (1981). *Challenging Strategic Planning Assumptions.* New York: Wiley.

Meadows, D. H., Meadows, D. L., Randers, J. & Behrens, W. W., III (1972). *The Limits to Growth.* New York: Universe Books.

Melcher, A. J., Acar, W., DuMont, P. F. & Khouja, M. (1990). Standard-maintaining and continuous-improvement systems: Experiences and comparisons. *IN-TERFACES, 20* (3): 24-40.

Merten, P. P. (1991). Loop-based strategic decision support systems. *Strategic Management Journal, 12* (5): 371-386.

Meyer, A. D. (1982). Adapting to environmental jolts. *Administrative Science Quarterly, 27:* 515-537.

Meyer, A. D., Brooks, G. R. & Goes, J. B. (1990). Environmental jolts and industry revolutions: Organizational responses to discontinuous change. *Strategic Management Journal, 11* (Summer Special Issue): 93-110.

Miles, R. E. & Cameron, K. (1982). *Coffin Nails and Corporate Strategies.* Englewood Cliffs, NJ: Prentice-Hall.

Miles, R. E. & Snow, C. C. (1978). *Organizational Strategy, Structure and Process.* New York: McGraw-Hill.

Miles, R. E., Snow, C. C. & Pfeffer, J. (1974). Organization-environment: Concepts and issues. *Industrial Relations*: 244-264.

Milgrom, P. & Roberts, J. (1992). *Economics, Organization and Management.*

Englewood Cliffs, NJ: Prentice-Hall.

Miller, D. & Friesen, P. H. (1978). Archetypes of strategy formulation. *Management Science, 24:* 921-933.

Miller, D. & Friesen, P. H. (1983). Strategy making and environment: The third link. *Strategic Management Journal, 4:* 221-235.

Miller, D. & Friesen, P. H. (1984). *Organizations: A Quantum View.* Englewood Cliffs, NJ: Prentice-Hall.

Miller, G. A. (1956). The magical number seven plus or minus two: Some limits on our capacity for processing information. *Psychological Review, 63* (2): 81-97.

Millet, S. M. & Randles, F. (1986). Scenarios for strategic business planning: A case history for aerospace and defence companies. *Interfaces, 16* (6): 64-72.

Milliken, F. J. (1987). Three types of perceived uncertainty about the environment: State, effect and response uncertainty. *Academy of Management Review, 12* (1): 133-143.

Mintzberg, H. (1973). *The Nature of Managerial Work.* New York: Harper & Row.

Mintzberg, H. (1979). *The Structuring of Organizations.* Englewood Cliffs, NJ: Prentice-Hall.

Mintzberg, H. (1987). Opening up the definition of strategy. In J.B. Quinn, H. Mintzberg, R. James (Eds.), *The strategy process: Concepts, contexts and cases,* Englewood Cliffs, NJ: Prentice-Hall.

Mintzberg, H. (1990). The design school: Reconsidering the basic premises of strategic management. *Strategic Management Journal, 11* (3): 171-195.

Mintzberg, H. (1993). *The Rise and Fall of Strategic Planning.* New York: Free Press.

Mintzberg, H. & McHugh, A. (1985). Strategy formation in an adhocracy. *Administrative Science Quarterly, 30:* 160-197.

Mintzberg, H., Raisinghani, P. & Théorêt, A. (1976). The structure of "unstructured" decision processes. *Administrative Science Quarterly, 21:* 246-275.

Mintzberg, H. & Waters, J. A. (1982). Tracking strategy in an entrepreneurial firm. *Academy of Management Journal, 25:* 465-499.

Mitroff, I. I. (1987). *Business NOT as Usual.* San Francisco, CA: Jossey-Bass.

Mitroff, I. I. & Emshoff, J.R. (1979). On strategic assumption making: A dialectical approach to policy and planning. *Academy of Management Review, 4* (1): 1-12.

Mitroff, I. I., Emshoff, J. R. & Kilmann, R. H. (1979). Assumptional analysis: A methodology for strategic problem solving. *Management Science, 25* (6): 583-593.

Mitroff, I. I. & Turoff, M. (1975). Philosophical and methodological foundations of Delphi. In H. A. Linstone & M. Turoff (Eds.), *The Delphi Method*, Reading,

MA: Addison Wesley.

Mohapatra, P.K.J. & Sharma, S. K. (1985). Synthetic design of policy decisions in system dynamics models: A modal control theoretical approach. *System Dynamics Review, 1* (1): 63-80.

Mohr, L. B. (1982). *Explaining Organizational Behavior*. San Francisco, CA: Jossey-Bass.

Morecroft, J.D.W. (1982). A critical review of diagramming tools for conceptualizing feedback system models. *Dynamica, 8* (1): 20-29.

Morecroft, J.D.W. (1983). Portraying bounded rationality. *OMEGA: The International Journal of Management Science, 11* (2): 131-142.

Morecroft, J.D.W. (1984). Strategy support models. *Strategic Management Journal, 5* (3): 215-229.

Morecroft, J.D.W. (1985a). The feedback view of business policy and strategy. *System Dynamics Review, 1* (1): 4-19.

Morecroft, J.D.W. (1985b). Rationality in the analysis of behavioral simulation models. *Management Science, 31* (7): 900-916.

Morecroft, J.D.W. (1988). System dynamics and microworlds for policymakers. *European Journal of Operational Research, 35:* 310-320.

Morecroft, J.D.W. (1990). Strategy support models. In R.G. Dyson (Ed.), *Strategic Planning: Models and Analytical Techniques*, Chichester, UK: Wiley.

Morecroft, J.D.W. (1992). Executive knowledge, models and learning. *European Journal of Operational Research, 59* (1): 9-27.

Morecroft, J.D.W. & van der Heijden, K.A.J.M. (1992). Modelling the oil producers: Capturing oil industry knowledge in a behavioral simulation model. *European Journal of Operational Research, 59* (1): 102-122.

Morris, G. K. (1982). The use of futures research in product planning. *Long Range Planning, 15* (6): 67-73.

Morrison, A. J. (1991). *Strategies in Global Industries*. Westport, CT: Greenwood.

Mosekilde, E., Aracil, J. & Allen, P. M. (1988). Instabilities and chaos in nonlinear dynamic systems. *System Dynamics Review, 4* (1-2: Special Issue on Chaos): 14-55.

Myrdal, G. (1957). *Economic Theory and Under-developed Regions*. London: Duckworth.

Nadler, D. A. (1970). *Work Design: A Systems Concept*. Homewood, IL: Irwin.

Nadler, D. A., Hackman, J. R. & Lawler, E. E., III (1979). *Making Organizational Behavior*. Boston: Little, Brown & Co.

Naisbitt, J. (1982). *Megatrends*. New York: Warner Books.

Neave, E. H. & Petersen, E. R. (1980). A comparison of optimal and adaptive decision mechanisms in an organizational setting. *Management Science, 26* (8): 810-822.

Nelson, R. G. & Winter, S. G. (1982). *An Evolutionary Theory of Economic Change*. Cambridge, MA: Harvard University Press.

Newgren, K. E., Rasher, A. A. & LaRoe, M. E. (1984). An empirical investigation of the relationship between environmental assessment and corporate performance. In *Proceedings of the 44th Annual Meeting of the Academy of Management* (12-15 Aug.), Boston: 352-356.

Nonaka, I. (1988). Toward middle-up-down management: Accelerating information creation. *Sloan Management Review, 30* (2): 9-18.

Nord, W. R. & Tucker, S. (1987). *Implementing Routine and Radical Innovations.* Lexington, MA: Lexington Books.

Offodile, O. F. & Acar, W. (1993). Comprehensive situation mapping for robot evaluation and selection. *International Journal of Operations and Production Management, 13* (1): 71-80.

Ohmae, K. (1982). *The Mind of the Strategist: The Art of Japanese Business.* New York: McGraw-Hill.

Ohmae, K. (1989). Managing in a borderless world. *Harvard Business Review, 67* (3): 152-161.

Oliwenstein, L. (1992). Evolution watch: No longer human. *Discover, 13* (12): 34-35.

Ozbekhan, H. (1977). The future of Paris: A systems study in strategic urban planning. *Philosophical Transactions of the Royal Society of London, 387:* 523-544.

Page, M. & Hopwood, A. (1986). Planning for the profession in the longer term. *Accountancy, 97* (1): 108-109.

Papert, S. (1980). *Mindstorms.* New York: Basic Books.

Parnaby, J. (1986). The design of competitive manufacturing systems. *International Journal of Technology Management, 1* (3): 385-396.

Pascale, R. T. (1984). Perspectives on strategy: The real story behind Honda's success. *California Management Review* (Spring): 47-72.

Pascale, R. T. & Athos, A. G. (1982). *The Art of Japanese Management.* London: Allen Lane, Penguin Books.

Peat Marwick Management Consultants (1990). Introvert strategies. *Financial Times* (31 Oct.).

Perrow, C. (1967). A framework for the comparative analysis of organizations. *American Sociological Review, 32:* 194-208.

Peters, T. J. & Waterman, R. H., Jr. (1982). *In Search of Excellence.* New York: Harper & Row.

Peterson, S. (1992). Software for model building and simulation: An illustration of design philosophy. *European Journal of Operational Research, 59* (1): 197-202.

Pettibone, P. (1991). Negotiating a business in the Soviet Union. *Journal of Business Strategy (The)* (January-February): 18-23.

Pfeffer, J. (1981). *Power in Organizations.* Boston: Pitman.

Pfeffer, J. & Salancik, G. R. (1974). Organizational decision making as a political process: The case of a university budget. *Administrative Science Quarterly, 19* (2): 135-151.

Piaget, J. (1973). *Main Trends in Interdisciplinary Research.* New York: Harper & Row.

Pirsig, R. M. (1974). *Zen and the Art of Motorcycle Maintenance.* New York: Bantam Books.

Poensgen, O. H. & Marx, M. (1985). Coping with or profiting from size. *European Journal of Operational Research, 22* (2): 127-147.

Pondy, L. R. & Huff, A. S. (1985). Achieving routine in organizational change. *Journal of Management, 11:* 103-116.

Porter, M. E. (1980). *Competitive Strategy.* New York: Free Press.

Porter, M. E. (1985). *Competitive Advantage.* New York: Free Press.

Porter, M. E. (1986). Competition in global industries: A conceptual framework. In M. E. Porter (Ed.), *Competition in Global Industries,* Boston: Harvard Business School Press.

Porter, M. E. (1991). Towards a dynamic theory of strategy. *Strategic Management Journal, 12* (Winter Special Issue): 95-117.

Potts, R.E.E. (1985). A strategic planning system in a Canadian gas utility. *Public Utilities Fortnightly, 116* (8): 22-30.

Prahalad, C. K. & Bettis, R. A. (1986). The dominant logic: A new linkage between diversity and performance. *Strategic Management Journal, 7* (6): 485-501.

Prahalad, C. K. & Doz, Y. (1987). *The Multinational Mission: Balancing Local Demands and Global Vision.* New York: Free Press.

Prebble, J. F. & Reichel, A. (1988). Scanning the future environment for banking. *Mid-American Journal of Business, 3* (2): 23-31.

Prebble, J. F. & Rau, P. A. (1986). Planning in higher education: A multiple scenario forecasting approach. *Planning for Higher Education, 14* (2): 1-6.

Prescott, J. E. & Grant, J. H. (1988). A manager's guide for evaluating competitive analysis techniques. *Interfaces, 18* (3): 10-22.

Pugh, A. L., III & Carrasco, P. A. (1983). *DYNAMO*© *User's Manual* (6th ed.). Cambridge, MA: MIT Press.

Quinn, J. B. (1980). *Strategies for Change: Logical Incrementalism.* Homewood, IL: Irwin.

Radford, K. J. (1980). *Strategic Planning: An Analytical Approach.* Reston, VA: Reston Publishing.

Ramaprasad, A. & Poon, E. (1985). A computerized interactive technique for mapping influence diagrams (MIND). *Strategic Management Journal, 6* (4): 377-392.

Randers, J. (1980). Guidelines for model conceptualization. In J. Randers (Ed.), *Elements of the System Dynamics Method* (pp. 117-139). Cambridge, MA: MIT Press.

Rappaport, A. (1960). *Fights, Games and Debates*. Ann Arbor, MI: University of Michigan Press.

Rappaport, A. (1968). Management misinformation systems: Another perspective. *Management Science, 15* (4): B133-B136.

Rasmussen, S., Mosekilde, E. & Sterman, J.D. (1985). Bifurcations and chaotic behavior in a simple model of the economic long wave. *System Dynamics Review, 1* (1): 92-110.

Remus, W. E. & Kottemann, J. E. (1987). Semi-structured recurring decisions: An experimental study of decision making models and some suggestions for DSS. *MIS Quarterly, 11* (2): 233-243.

Remus, W. E. & Kottemann, J. E. (1986). Toward intelligent decision support systems: An artificially intelligent statistician. *MIS Quarterly, 10* (4): 403-418.

Richardson, G. P. (1991). *Feedback Thought in Social Science and Systems Theory*. Baltimore, MD: University of Pennsylvania Press.

Richardson, G. P. & Pugh, A. L. (1981). *Introduction to System Dynamics Modeling with DYNAMO*. Cambridge, MA: MIT Press.

Richmond, B. & Peterson, S. (1992a). *Continuous Process-Improvement Module (iThink^{TM})* (2.2.1 ed.). Hanover, NH: High Performance Systems.

Richmond, B. & Peterson, S. (1992b). *STELLA$^®$ II: An Introduction to Systems Thinking* (2.2.1 ed.). Hanover, NH: High Performance Systems.

Richmond, B., Peterson, S. & Charyk, C. (1992). *Introduction to Systems Thinking and iThink™* (2.2.1 ed.). Hanover, NH: High Performance Systems.

Riggs, J. L. (1987). *Production Systems: Planning, Analysis and Control* (4th ed.). Prospect Heights, IL: Waveland Press.

Rivett, A. B. (1980). *Model Building for Decision Analysis*. Chichester, UK: Wiley.

Roberts, E. B. (1978). Strategies for effective implementation of complex corporate models. In E.B. Roberts (Ed.), *Managerial Applications of System Dynamics* (pp. 77-85). Cambridge, MA: MIT Press.

Roberts, N., Andersen, D.F., Deal, R. M., Garet, M. S. & Shaffer, W. A. (1983). *Introduction to computer simulation: A system dynamics modeling approach*. Reading, MA: Addison-Wesley.

Robey, D. (1982). *Designing Organizations: A Macro Perspective*. Homewood, IL: Irwin.

Robinson, R. D. (1988). *The International Transfer of Technology*. Cambridge, MA: Ballinger.

Robinson, S. M. (1991). Extended scenario analysis. . *Annals of Operations Research, 31* (2): 385-398.

Rockafellar, R. T. (1991). Scenarios and policy aggregation in optimization under uncertainty. *Mathematics of Operations Research, 16* (1): 119-147.

Romanelli, E. & Tushman, M. L. (1986). Inertia, environments and strategic choice: A quasi-experimental design for comparative longitudinal research. *Management Science, 32:* 608-621.

Ross, S. M. (1990). *A Course in Simulation.* New York: Macmillan.

Rumelt, R. P. (1974). *Strategy, Structure and Economic Performance.* Boston: Harvard Business School Press.

Rumelt, R. P. (1991). How much does industry matter? *Strategic Management Journal, 12* (3): 167-185.

Rumelt, R. P., Schendel, D. E. & Teece, D. J. (1991). Strategic management and economics. *Strategic Management Journal, 12* (Winter Special Issue): 5-29.

Saaty, T. L. (1987). Rank generation, preservation and reversal in the analytic hierarchy process. *Decision Sciences, 18* (2): 157-177.

Sackman, H. (1975). *Delphi Technique: Expert Opinion Forecasting and Group Process.* Lexington, MA: Lexington Books.

Sakate, K. & Toyama, T. (1989). Decision support systems based on a structured matrix. In Y. Monden & M. Sakurai (Eds.), *Japanese Management Accounting: A World Class Approach to Profit Management* (pp. 211-228). Cambridge, MA: Productivity Press.

Sarason, S. B. (1982). *The Culture of School and Problem of Change* (2nd ed.). Boston: Allyn & Bacon.

Sarin, R. K. (1978). A sequential approach to cross-impact analysis. *Futures, 10* (1): 53-62.

Schares, G. E., Templeman, J., Neff, R., Holstein, W. J. & Reed, S. (1991). Think small: The export lessons to be learned from Germany's midsize companies. *Business Week* (Nov. 4), pp. 58-65.

Schein, E. H. (1969). *Process Consultation: Its Role in Organization Development.* Reading, MA: Addison Wesley.

Schlender, B. R. (1993). Yamaha: The perils of losing focus. *Fortune* (May 17), pp. 100.

Schlesinger, L. A. & Heskett, J. L. (1991). Breaking the cycle of failure in services. *Sloan Management Review, 32* (3): 17-28.

Schnaars, S. P. (1989). *Megamistakes: Forecasting and the Myth of Rapid Techonogical Change.* New York: Free Press.

Schnaars, S. P. & Topol, M. T. (1987). Multiple scenarios in sales forecasting. *International Journal of Forecasting, 3* (3): 405-419.

Schoderbek, P. P., Schoderbek, C. G. & Kefalas, A. G. (1990). *Management Systems: Conceptual Considerations* (4th ed.). Homewood, IL: Irwin.

Schoemaker, P.J.H. (1991). When and how to use scenario planning: A heuristic approach with illustration. *Journal of Forecasting, 10:* 549-564.

Schoemaker, P.J.H. (1993). Multiple scenario development: Its conceptual and behavioral foundation. *Strategic Management Journal, 14* (3): 193-213.

Schonberger, R. J. (1986). *World Class Manufacturing: The Lessons of Simplicity Applied.* New York: Free Press.

Schön, D. (1983). Organizational learning. In G. Morgan (Ed.), *Beyond Method*, London: Sage.

Schrage, M. (1991). Spreadsheets: Bulking up on data. *San Francisco Examiner*.

Schultz, D. I. (1986). Strategic information systems planning sharpens competitive edge. *Data Management*, *24* (6): 20-24, 38.

Schwartz, P. (1991). *The Art of the Long View*. New York: Doubleday Currency.

Schwenk, C. R. (1984). Cognitive simplification processes in strategic decision-making. *Strategic Management Journal*, *5* (2): 111-128.

Scott, W. R. (1987). *Organizations: Rational, Natural and Open Systems* (2nd ed.). Englewood Cliffs, NJ: Prentice-Hall.

Senge, P. M. (1990). *The Fifth Discipline: The Art & Practice of the Learning Organization*. New York: Doubleday.

Senge, P. M. & Sterman, J. D. (1992). Systems thinking and organizational learning: Acting locally and thinking globally in the organization of the future. *European Journal of Operational Research*, *59* (1): 137-150.

Shapiro, H. J. & Chanin, M. N. (1987). Dialectical materialism inquiry system: A new approach to decision making. In J.D. Greenwood (Ed.), *The Idea of Psychology: Conceptual and Methodological Issues*, Singapore: Singapore University Press.

Sherman, S. (1984). Eight big masters of innovation. *Fortune* (16 Oct), .

Shrivastava, P. (1988). *Bhopal: Anatomy of a Crisis*. Cambridge, MA: Ballinger.

Shubik, M. (1987). What is an application and when is theory a waste of time? *Management Science*, *33* (12): 1511-1522.

Simon, H. A. (1957). Rationality and decision making. In H.A. Simon (Ed.), *Models of Man*, New York: Wiley.

Simon, H. A. (1976). *Administrative Behavior* (3rd ed.). New York: Free Press.

Simon, H. A. (1979). Rational decision making in business organizations. *American Economic Review*, *69* (4): 497-509.

Simon, H. A. (1982). *Models of Bounded Rationality* (A 2-volume ed.). Cambridge, MA: MIT Press.

Singer, A. E. (1991). Meta-rationality and strategy. *OMEGA: The International Journal of Management Science*, *19* (2): 101-110.

Singer, A. E. (1992). Strategy as rationality. *Human Systems Management*, *11* (1): 7-21.

Singer, E. A., Jr. (1959). *Experience and Reflection* (Edited by C.W. Churchman). Philadelphia, PA: University of Pennsylvania Press.

Singh, J. V., House, R. J. & Tucker, D. J. (1986). Organizational change and organizational mortality. *Administrative Science Quarterly*, *31:* 587-611.

Smothers, N. P. (1990). Patterns of Japanese strategy: Strategic combinations of strategies. *Strategic Management Journal*, *11* (7): 521-533.

Snow, C. C. & Hambrick, D. C. (1980). Measuring organizational strategies: Some theoretical and methodological problems. *Academy of Management Review*, *5:*

527-538.

Stacey, G. S. (1984). *Technological forecasting and the tech-risk array: Linking R&D and strategic business decisions* (Battelle Technical Inputs to Planning Review No. 14). Columbus, OH: Battelle Memorial Institute.

Star, S. H. (1990). Rational management in the 1990s (Editorial). *Sloan Management Review, 32* (1): 3.

Stead, D. & Hof, R. D. (1993). Math genius with lab. will work for food. *Business Week* (Jun. 14), pp. 84, 86.

Sterman, J. D. (1985). The growth of knowledge: Testing a theory of scientific revolution with a formal model. *Technological Forecasting & Social Change, 28* (2): 93-122.

Sterman, J. D. (1989). Modeling managerial behavior: Misperceptions of feedback in a dynamic decision making experiment. *Management Science, 35* (3): 321-339.

Stoner, J.A.F. (1989). *What is Intgrated Process Management?* Working paper #89-103-1, Fordham University @ Lincoln Center, New York, NY.

Stoner, J.A.F., Taylor, A. R. & Wankel, C. B. (1988). On waiting for neither Godot nor the Apocalypse: Practical first steps to move US manaders toward world class managing. In M.K. Starr (Ed.), *Global Competitiveness: Getting the US Back on Track* (pp. 185-212). New York: W.W. Norton.

Stover, J. G. & Gordon, T. J. (1978). Cross impact analysis. In J. Fowles (Ed.), *Handbook of futures research*, Westport, CT: Greenwood.

Sugiura, H. & Monden, Y. (1989). Using a structured matrix as a decision support system in materials flow and cost planning. In Y. Monden & M. Sakurai (Eds.), *Japanese Management Accounting: A World Class Approach to Profit Management* (pp. 115-139). Cambridge, MA: Productivity Press.

Suro, R. (1989). Grassroots groups show power battling pollution close to home. *New York Times* (July 2), p. L1, L18.

Teece, D. J. (1987). Profiting from technological innovation: Implications for integration, collaboration, licensing and public policy. In D.J. Teece (Ed.), *The Competitive Challenge: Strategies for Industrial Innovation and Renewal* (pp. 185-219). Cambridge, MA: Ballinger.

Thompson, J. D. (1967). *Organizations in Action.* New York: McGraw-Hill.

Tinker, A. (1976). A note on 'environmental uncertainty' and a suggestion for our editorial function. *Administrative Science Quarterly, 21:* 506-508.

Tobias, A. (1991). O.R. techniques for use in redesigning manufacturing and associated business systems. *European Journal of Operational Research, 51* (2): 168-178.

Toffler, A. (1981). *The Third Wave.* New York: Bantam Books.

Tosi, H., Aldag, R. & Storey, R. (1973). On the measurement of the environment: An assessment of the Lawrence and Lorsch environmental uncertainty questionnaire. *Administrative Science Quarterly, 18:* 27-36.

Tregoe, B. B. & Zimmerman, J. W. (1980). *Top Management Strategy*. New York: Simon & Shuster.

Turing, A. M. (1952). The chemical basis of morphogenesis. *Philosophical Transactions of the Royal Society, 237* (London, Ser. B): 37-72.

Tushman, B. W. (1981). *Practicing History*. New Yotk, NY: Knopf.

Tushman, B. W. (1984). *The March of Folly*. New York: Knopf.

Tushman, M. L. & Anderson, P. (1986). Technological discontinuities and organizational environments. *Administrative Science Quarterly, 31:* 439-465.

Tushman, M. L. & Romanelli, E. (1985). Organizational evolution: Interactions between external and emergent processes and strategic choice. In B. M. Staw & L. L. Cummings (Eds.), *Research in Organizational Behavior*, 8. Greenwich, CT: JAI Press.

Tversky, A. & Kahneman, D. (1974). Judgment under uncertainty: Heuristics and biases. *Science, 185:* 1124-1131.

Utterback, J. M. (1979). Environmental analysis and forecasting. In D. E. Schendel & C. W. Hofer (Eds.), *Strategic Management: A New View of Business Policy and Planning* (pp. 134-144). Boston: Little, Brown & Co.

Utterback, J.M. & Abernathy, W.J. (1975). A dynamic model of product and process innovation. *OMEGA: The International Journal of Management Science, 3* (6): 639-656.

Van de Ven, A. & Drazin, R. (1985). The concept of fit in contingency theory. In L. L. Cummings & B. M. Staw (Eds.), *Research in Organizational Behavior*, 7 (pp. 333- 365). Greenwich, CT: JAI Press.

van de Vilert, E. (1985). Escalative intervention in small-group conflicts. *Journal of Applied Behavioral Science, 21* (1): 19-36.

van Gigch, J. P. (1978). *Applied General Systems Theory* (2nd ed.). New York: Harper & Row.

Vanston, J. H. (1977). Alternate scenario planning. *Technological Forecasting & Social Change, 10* (2): 159-180.

Voeltz, L. M. & Evans, I. M. (1982). The assessment of behavioral interrelationships in child behavior therapy. *Behavioral Assessment, 4:* 131-165.

Wack, P. (1985a). Scenarios: Uncharted waters ahead. *Harvard Business Review, 63* (5): 73-89.

Wack, P. (1985b). Scenarios: Shooting the rapids. *Harvard Business Review, 63* (6): 139-150.

Wahler, R. G. (1975). Some structural aspects of deviant child behavior. *Journal of Applied Behavioral analysis, 8:* 27-42.

Watson, H. J. (1981). *Computer Simulation in Business*. New York: Wiley.

Weick, K. (1977). Enactment processes in organizations. In B. M. Staw & G. Salancik (Eds.), *New Directions in Organizational Behavior*, Chicago: St. Clair Press.

Weick, K. (1979). *The Social Psychology of Organizing* (2nd ed.). Reading, MA:

Addison-Wesley.

Wiener, N. (1948). *Cybernetics, or Control and Communication in the Animal and Machine*. New York: Wiley.

Williamson, O. E. (1985). *The Economic Institutions of Capitalism*. New York: Free Press.

Williamson, O. E. (1991). Strategizing, economizing and economic organization. *Strategic Management Journal, 12* (Winter Special Issue): 75-94.

Winkler, R. L. & Murphy, A. H. (1973). Experiments in the laboratory and the real world. *Organizational Behavior and Human Performance, 10:* 252-270.

Winnicott, D. W. (1980). *Playing and Reality* (3rd ed.). Harmondsworth, UK: Penguin Education.

Witt, J. C. (1986). Teachers' resistance to the use of school-based interventions. *Journal of School Psychology, 24:* 27-44.

Wolstenholme, E. F. (1992). The definition and application of a stepwise approach to model conceptualization and analysis. *European Journal of Operational Research, 59* (1): 123-136.

Woodward, J. (1965). *Industrial Organization: Theory and Practice*. London: Oxford University Press.

Wright, K. (1990). The shape of things to go. *Scientific American* (May), pp. 92-101.

Wright, P. A. & Hill, T. V. (1986). Cost estimating: Dealing with uncertainty. *AACE Transactions,:* E.5.1-E.5.8.

Yankelovich, D. (1982). *New Rules*. New York: Bantam Books.

Zeleny, M. (1982). *Multiple Criteria Decision Making*. New York: McGraw-Hill.

Zeleny, M. (1986). High technology management. *Human Systems Management, 6:* 109-120.

Zeleny, M. (1988). Parallelism, integration, autocoordination and ambiguity in human support systems. In M. M. Gupta & T. Yamakawa (Eds.), *Fuzzy logic in knowledge-based systems, decision and control* (pp. 107-122). Elsevier Science (North Holland).

Zeleny, M. (1991). Knowledge as capital: Integrated quality management. *Prometheus, 9* (1): 93-101.

Zeleny, M. (1992). In this issue (Editorial). *Human Systems Management, 11* (1): 5-6.

Zentner, R. D. (1987). Scenarios and the chemical industry. *Chemical Marketing & Management* (Spring): 21-25.

Index

About the Authors

NICHOLAS C. GEORGANTZAS is Associate Professor of Management Systems at Fordham University and a management systems consultant. Widely published on topics on model-based strategy support, decision framing, and behavioral simulation modeling, he has consulted in commercial and retail banking, computer and information systems, education, entertainment and multimedia, and other industries.

WILLIAM ACAR is Associate Professor of Business Strategy, and a management consultant, at the Graduate School of Management of Kent State University. He is the author of numerous published articles, internal reports, and conference presentations on competitive strategy, organization theory, and problem simulation.

ISBN 0-89930-825-2

9 780899 308258

HARDCOVER BAR CODE